D0794227

VIRGINIA WOOLF: THE CRITICAL HERITAGE

THE CRITICAL HERITAGE SERIES

For a list of books in the series see the back end paper

VIRGINIA WOOLF

THE CRITICAL HERITAGE

Edited by
ROBIN MAJUMDAR
Assistant Professor of English
Presidency College
University of Calcutta
and
ALLEN McLAURIN
Research Fellow
University of Birmingham

ROUTLEDGE & KEGAN PAUL: LONDON AND BOSTON

First published in 1975
by Routledge & Kegan Paul Ltd
Broadway House, 68–74 Carter Lane,
London EC4V 5EL and
9 Park Street,
Boston, Mass. 02108, USA

ISBN 0 7100 8138 3

Set in 'Monotype' Bembo
and printed in Great Britain by
W & J Mackay Limited, Chatham

General Editor's Preface

The reception given to a writer by his contemporaries and near-contemporaries is evidence of considerable value to the student of literature. On one side we learn a great deal about the state of criticism at large and in particular about the development of critical attitudes towards a single writer; at the same time, through private comments in letters, journals or marginalia, we gain an insight upon the tastes and literary thought of individual readers of the period. Evidence of this kind helps us to understand the writer's historical situation, the nature of his immediate reading-public, and his response to these pressures.

The separate volumes in the *Critical Heritage Series* present a record of this early criticism. Clearly, for many of the highly productive and lengthily reviewed nineteenth- and twentieth-century writers, there exists an enormous body of material; and in these cases the volume editors have made a selection of the most important views, significant for their intrinsic critical worth or for their representative quality—perhaps even registering incomprehension!

For earlier writers, notably pre-eighteenth century, the materials are much scarcer and the historical period has been extended, sometimes far beyond the writer's lifetime, in order to show the inception and growth of critical views which were initially slow to appear.

In each volume the documents are headed by an Introduction, discussing the material assembled and relating the early stages of the author's reception to what we have come to identify as the critical tradition. The volumes will make available much material which would otherwise be difficult of access and it is hoped that the modern reader will be thereby helped towards an informed understanding of the ways in which literature has been read and judged.

B.C.S.

Contents

CONTENTS

CONTENTS

Acknowledgments

The editor and publishers would like to thank the following for permission to reprint material within their copyright or other control:

Mr Conrad Aiken for No. 65; Edward Arnold (Publishers) Ltd for Nos 67 and 87; *Atlantic Monthly* for No. 57; Mr Michael Ayrton for No. 31; Professor Quentin Bell for No. 43; The Bodley Head Ltd and Mr Philip Henderson for No. 103c; Brandt & Brandt and Mr Conrad Aiken for No. 74, copyright © 1935, 1939, 1940, 1942, 1951, 1958 by Conrad Aiken; Cambridge University Press for Nos 97b and 116; Frank Cass & Company Ltd for No. 53; Chatto & Windus Ltd, Harcourt, Brace Jovanovich Inc. and the Editor's Literary Estates, © 1956 by Leonard Woolf and James Strachey, for Nos 11, 12, 24 and 25; Mr H. P. Collins for No. 47; Constable Publishers for No. 19; *Cornhill Magazine* for No. 105a; Mr Malcolm Cowley for No. 133, copyright 1941, renewed copyright 1969, by Malcolm Cowley; Curtis Brown Ltd and Pamela Hansford Johnson for No. 113; *Daily Telegraph and Morning Post* for Nos 3 and 30; Professor William Empson and Lawrence & Wishart Ltd, for No. 97a; London *Evening News* for No. 85; London *Evening Standard* for Nos 58, 63, 73 and 81; Faber & Faber Ltd for No. 59; Victor Gollancz Ltd for No. 103b; *Guardian* for Nos 6 and 45; the late L. P. Hartley for No. 88; David Higham Associates Ltd for No. 16; Hogarth Press Ltd for No. 52; Hope Leresche & Steele and Mr Frank Swinnerton for Nos 40 and 104; Storm Jameson for Nos 77 and 90; Mrs G. A. Wyndham Lewis for No. 102a; London Express News & Feature Services for No. 109; M. Jean-Marie Marcel for No. 95; Mr Raymond Mortimer for No. 76; Mr Gavin Muir for Nos 41, 55, 66, 94, 112 and 131; *Nation* for Nos 8, 35, 93 and 134; *New Statesman* for Nos 7, 15, 18, 22, 29, 34, 37, 38, 39, 41, 51, 55, 56, 66, 86, 111, 120, 124 and 127; *New York Times* for Nos 61, 72, 89, 114 and 132, © 1927–28–31–37 and 1941 by The New York Times Company; Mr Nigel Nicolson for Nos 80 and 84; *Nuova Antologia* for No. 99; *Observer* for Nos 2, 71, 108, 119 and 130; Oxford University Press for No. 101; A. D. Peters & Co. for No. 50; Laurence Pollinger Ltd and Mr Graham Greene for No. 121; Mr Edgell Rickword for No. 46, © Edgell Rickword 1974 and Carcanet Press Ltd, from *Essays and Opinions 1921–31* (1974); the Royal Society for the Protection of Birds, and the Society of Authors for No. 9; Rutgers University Press for Nos 98 and 115, from *William Troy: Selected Essays*, edited and introduction by S. E. Hyman, © 1967, Rutgers The State University, New Brunswick, New Jersey, USA; *San Francisco Chronicle* for No. 92; *Saturday Review*, David Higham Associates Ltd, Professor Herbert Muller for Nos 48, 91a, 91b and 105b, copyright 1925, 1931, 1937 by Saturday Review Co. First appeared in *Saturday Review* 1925, 1931, 1937; Martin Secker & Warburg Ltd for No. 103; *Sewanee Review* for No. 82, first appeared in the *Sewanee Review*, xxxix (Fall 1931), 425–44; the Society of Authors, on behalf of King's College, Cambridge for Nos 4, 14 and 54; *Spectator* for Nos 10, 62, 102b, 102c, 123 and 128; Mr Stephen Spender and the *Listener* for No. 125; *Sunday Times* for No. 70; *Time & Tide* for Nos 106 and 118; *The Times Literary Supplement* for Nos 1, 13, 17, 21, 26, 44, 49, 60, 79, 83, 107, 117 and 129; *Twentieth Century Magazine* for Nos 100 and 135; Ruth Mary Underhill for No. 20; A. P. Watt & Son and Mrs Dorothy Cheston Bennett for Nos 36 and 73b; *Yale Review* for No. 75; *Yorkshire Post* for No. 32.

It has proved difficult in certain cases to locate the proprietors of copyright material. However all possible care has been taken to trace ownership of the selections included and to make full acknowledgment for their use.

Introduction

I

Virginia Woolf's genius was proclaimed, certainly during her lifetime, and by some reviewers with the publication of her first novel. It is true that newspapers hail many writers each year as geniuses, but Virginia Woolf's writing gained not only swift, but also persistent and increasing attention and praise. It is partly a question of intelligent people recognising excellence, but there are other factors to be considered.

She was a daughter of Leslie Stephen, and most people in the literary world of the time would have known of this eminent Victorian man of letters, who was famous as a literary critic and compiler of the *Dictionary of National Biography*. (He was Vernon Whitford in Meredith's *The Egoist* before becoming Mr Ramsay in *To the Lighthouse*.) And so, even in the mid-1930s Virginia was still, to some reviewers, 'Leslie Stephen's illustrious daughter'.

After her father's death, in 1904, Virginia Woolf was at the centre of a circle of friends which came to be known as the Bloomsbury Group. She gave much to, and gained a great deal from members of this group, especially Lytton Strachey and Roger Fry, whose researches, respectively into biography and the visual arts, were paralleled by her experiments in fiction. On the periphery of the circle was E. M. Forster, who was a well-known and highly regarded novelist before Virginia Woolf published her first novel. In addition to this, some members of the group had 'their hand on all the ropes'[1]—the economist Maynard Keynes, for example. They owned, edited and contributed to various newspapers and journals, and so Virginia Woolf was assured of sympathetic private and public attention from intelligent and influential people. She herself had begun reviewing for the *Times Literary Supplement* in 1905, ten years before the publication of her first novel. Her reviews were anonymous, but when she came to publish her novels she could usually rely on a sympathetic notice there (although she frequently complained in her Diary that these reviews were never enthusiastic).

We cannot here go into the complex history of the Bloomsbury

Group, but we must take some account of it in assessing the reception of Virginia Woolf's work. She was undoubtedly helped by her friends, but this did not take the form of indiscriminating praise, as is sometimes imagined. And a negative feature of her connection with Bloomsbury was that she was often incidentally dispraised in a general attack on the Group, or on what it was believed to represent. Virginia Woolf was sometimes attacked by 'outsiders' in this way and defended, more damagingly perhaps, by her associates. There was some flattery, some exaggerated praise (natural enough among friends, but here occasionally made tedious by their ability to disseminate their opinions), but the evidence is here in this selection for the reader to judge whether Strachey, Forster, and MacCarthy, for example, surrounded Virginia Woolf with uncritical adulation.

This background did not ensure success, but it was a guarantee against failure through neglect. In considering her early career, it should not be overstressed—some reviewers of *The Voyage Out* and *Night and Day* stated explicitly that they had no knowledge of the writer, and in others this ignorance is implicit, for example in a reference to 'Miss Woolf'. Further, the attention and praise she received did not bring any commercial success for her books; it was only with her sixth novel *Orlando* (1928) that she became successful in this sense.

Virginia Woolf's writings were very varied: she wrote reviews, critical essays, 'feminist' tracts, short sketches and biography in addition to her novels. And some of her longer fictional works belong only dubiously to that genre: *Orlando* and *Flush* are 'novel-biography' and *The Waves*, as many reviewers pointed out, is near to poetry. (She disliked the term 'novel' but could not find a suitable alternative to describe her writing.) The critical response to her work reflects this diversity. Her writing was, with one or two exceptions, continuously experimental. She pared away character and plot and challenged accepted ideas of 'reality', and so with the publication of her third novel, *Jacob's Room*, she was widely regarded as a 'difficult' or 'highbrow' writer.

In a pamphlet written towards the end of her life Virginia Woolf described some of the features of twentieth-century reviewing. Modern reviews, she claimed, are produced more quickly, are shorter, and more numerous than in the preceding centuries. She concluded that they are worthless, being too quickly produced to have an eye on permanent standards, too short to be more than a summary, and so numerous that there is no 'opinion' of an author's work—'praise cancels blame, and blame praise'.[2] Leonard Woolf is perhaps fairer in his dissenting note at the end of the pamphlet. He says that the honest reviewer does at least describe a book and estimate its quality, and if he comes across a real work of art he must 'descend or ascend for a short time into the regions of true criticism'. (Incidentally, *Reviewing* was itself reviewed in the *Times Literary Supplement*, the journal to which Virginia Woolf had contributed so copiously. Naturally enough, it did not like having its *raison d'être* questioned in this way.)[3]

In view of the often intelligent and sympathetic response to her work, which is evident in this selection, her remarks on reviewing are certainly too harsh. Her work was given very high praise and rarely condemned out of hand. Even the most hostile reviewer usually found at least one work excellent or one aspect praiseworthy (Arnold Bennett on *To the Lighthouse*, for example). There was, to use Virginia Woolf's terms, some 'gutting' (précis writing) and 'stamping' (opinion mongering) in these reviews, but there were also many good pieces of work. There are admirable reviews from E. M. Forster and Edwin Muir, and Conrad Aiken's discussion of *To the Lighthouse* is an example of an intelligent reviewer, himself a novelist and poet, judging a classic with reference, if not to 'eternal standards of literature', at least with a sense of a wider literary context and tradition. Perhaps because they are dealing with works of art, and were written by creative people, many of the reviews in this collection often do contain true criticism and are not simply of historical or sociological value. But we can follow here a debate which is of undoubted historical interest, that between Arnold Bennett and Virginia Woolf: a contention which is of some importance to our understanding of the development of the twentieth-century novel.

Virginia Woolf remarked that an author now has sixty reviews where in the nineteenth century he had perhaps six.[4] She could certainly expect a great number for her later works, and the problem for the editors has been one of selection. In addition to reviews, longer critical articles and book-length studies were published about her work during her lifetime. The aim has been to give a representative cross-section of these writings, but greater emphasis has been placed on the views of those who were themselves interesting literary figures. The terminus date for the volume is 1941, the year of Virginia Woolf's death and of the posthumous publication of her last novel, *Between the Acts*.

An unusual feature in studying the response to Virginia Woolf's work is that we can read in *A Writer's Diary* her reactions to the reviews as they came out. Leonard Woolf's autobiography confirms the impression given by her Diary that she was extremely, indeed, morbidly sensitive to criticism.[5] Criticism affected her peace of mind to the point of driving her near insanity, but did the reviews affect the course of her writing? Her own self-criticism was so sharp that the opinions of others were probably much less important in the development of her art: it was Virginia Woolf herself who described a certain aspect of *Mrs Dalloway* as 'tinselly'.[6] She was tempted by the success of *Orlando* to repeat the performance, but resisted and produced an extremely innovatory novel, *The Waves*. She had a constant urge to experiment and experiment. Leonard Woolf believed that the one novel which was a response to criticism was *The Years*, her 'best-seller', but arguably her poorest novel; modern criticism has diverged sharply from the first reviews, which were generally very enthusiastic. *The Years* was written at a time when Virginia Woolf was under increasing attacks from those who wanted more 'solidity' and who believed that the appropriate response to the threatening political situation of the 1930s was writing which paid attention to the economic and social ills of society. This reversion to the matter and method of *Night and Day* (*The Years* was explicitly this) may have been a failure in nerve. In which case, perhaps the reverse effect operated in the writing of her other novels: the understanding and encouragement which she received at other points in her career gave her the courage to make it new with each succeeding work. After the popular success of *The Years*, she pushed herself and the novel to the limit, with *Between the Acts*.

II

We must distinguish between the critical acclaim which we see in the reviews and popular or commercial success. A sharp separation between them is especially noticeable in the case of Virginia Woolf's early work, as the publishing history shows.

Her first two novels were published by her half-brother Gerald Duckworth, and all her subsequent work, in Britain, by the Hogarth Press, which she and her husband set up in 1917. The Press was begun as a hobby, with Leonard and Virginia Woolf doing the printing by hand, but they began to send work to professional printers and gradually their press became a serious business. (An amusing picture of the Press, in 1928, from the office boy's point of view, is given in Richard Kennedy's

A Boy at the Hogarth Press.[7]) But for a serious account of the facts and figures relating to Virginia Woolf's work we must turn to Leonard Woolf's autobiography, which contains details of books sold and money earned. Such figures are important for the reasons he states: although they are rarely revealed, they play an important part in an artist's life. They also shed light on the literary profession in the twentieth century.

There was high praise for Virginia Woolf's first novel, but a small sale. The figures show how long it took for Virginia Woolf to reach a fairly wide public. By 1929 *The Voyage Out* (1915) had sold only 2,000 copies in Britain (USA figures not known), and *Night and Day* (1919) only 2,338 (plus 1,326 in the USA). *Jacob's Room* was the first of Virginia Woolf's novels to be published by the Hogarth Press, and this is an important factor in assessing its reception, for its unusual appearance set up a resistance prior to any consideration of its experimental content. This consideration first became evident with *Jacob's Room*, but it applies to later works as well. As Leonard Woolf points out, *Jacob's Room* was simply a typical case:[8]

> The reception of *Jacob's Room* was characteristic. It was the first book for which we had a jacket designed by Vanessa. It is, I think, a very good jacket and today no bookseller would feel his hackles or his temperature rise at sight of it. But it did not represent a desirable female or even Jacob or his room, and it was what in 1923 many people would have called reproachfully post-impressionist. It was almost universally condemned by the booksellers, and several of the buyers laughed at it.

But the Woolfs were happy with a British sale of 1,413 in its first year. (Two impressions were published in the USA in 1923, of 1,500 and 1,000.) *Mrs Dalloway*, generally regarded as a difficult work, sold 2,236 in its first year (with three impressions in the USA, one of 2,000 and two of 1,500). *To the Lighthouse* was distinctly more successful than her previous books, selling 3,873 in Britain in its first year, and having three impressions in the USA, of 4,000, 1,500 and 2,100. But the real turning point in her career as a commercially successful writer was *Orlando*, which in Britain sold more in its first month than *To the Lighthouse* in a year, reaching a total of 21,135 in six months (8,104 in Britain, 13,031 in the USA). There was a levelling out with *The Waves*, but *Flush* was very popular, especially in Britain (possibly because it is a 'doggie' book—but this is pure speculation). In six months 18,739 were sold in Britain, 14,081 in the USA. *The Years*, an outright best-seller, was her most successful novel in terms of total sales, selling 43,909 copies in its first six months (13,005 in Britain, 30,904 in the USA). In Virginia Woolf's lifetime it was far ahead of her other works, but the following statistics give an idea of how things have changed. They refer to the sales made in 1964 alone: *Mrs Dalloway* 10,791, *To the Lighthouse* 31,451, *Orlando* 509 (out of print in USA), *The Waves*, 1,336, *The Years* 470 (out of print in USA).

On a personal level what the increase in sales during her lifetime meant for Virginia Woolf was that after *Orlando* (1928), she and her husband were always well-off. For an overall interpretation of these facts and figures we cannot do better than turn to Leonard Woolf:[9]

But the statistics of Virginia's earnings as a writer of books have from another point of view still greater interest and importance. They throw a curious light on the economics of a literary profession and on the economic effect of popular taste on a serious writer. *Orlando*, *Flush*, and *The Years* were immeasurably more successful than any of Virginia's other novels. *The Years*, much the most successful of them all, was, in my opinion, the worst book she ever wrote—at any rate, it cannot compare, as a work of art, or a work of genius, with *The Waves*, *To the Lighthouse*, or *Between the Acts*. *Orlando* is a highly original and amusing book and has some beautiful things in it, but is a *jeu d'esprit*, and so is *Flush*, a work of even lighter weight; these two books again cannot seriously be compared with her major novels. The corollary of all this is strange. Up to 1928, when Virginia was 46, she had published five novels; she had in the narrow circle of people who value great works of literature a high reputation as one of the most original contemporary novelists. Thus her books were always reviewed with the greatest seriousness in all papers which treat contemporary literature seriously. But no one would have called her a popular or even a successful novelist, and she could not possibly have lived upon the earnings from her books. In 1932 Mrs Leavis, rather a hostile critic, wrote:

> The novels are in fact highbrow art. The reader who is not alive to the fact that *To the Lighthouse* is a beautifully constructed work of art will make nothing of the book. . . . *To the Lighthouse* is not a popular novel (though it has already taken its place as an important one), and it is necessary to enquire why the conditions of the age have made it inaccessible to a public whose ancestors have been competent readers of Sterne and Nashe (*Fiction and the Reading Public*, 223).

Mrs Leavis exaggerates. It is not true, as the subsequent history of *To the Lighthouse* shows, that the 'common reader' who does not bother his head about 'beautiful construction' or indeed works of art, can make nothing of the book. . . . But it is of course, true, . . . that up to 1928 Virginia, although widely recognized as an important novelist, was read by a small public. The fate of her books after 1928, however, points to a conclusion quite different from, and more interesting than, Mrs Leavis's.... Nearly all artists, from Beethoven downward, who have had something highly original to say and have been through periods in which the ordinary person has found him unintelligible or 'inaccessible' but eventually, in some cases suddenly, some gradually, he becomes intelligible and is everywhere accepted as a good or a great artist. In Virginia's case she had to write a bad book and two not very serious books before her best serious novels were widely understood and appreciated.

It must be borne in mind that many of the reviews which follow are from 'papers which treat contemporary literature seriously', and so we must not see their high praise for *To the Lighthouse* and their negligence towards *Flush* as a reflection of the taste of the reading public, which are perhaps better indicated in these facts and figures.

III

The Voyage Out

In his autobiography Leonard Woolf recalls how, after Virginia Woolf had rewritten the last chapters many times, he took the manuscript of *The Voyage Out* to her half-brother Gerald Duckworth who owned the publishing firm which bears his name.[10] The novel was accepted in April 1913, Duckworth's reader, Edward Garnett, greeting the novel as evidence of an exciting new talent.[11] Garnett championed many new writers, and although his help may not have been necessary in getting *The Voyage Out* published, his enthusiastic reception was a good start to Virginia Woolf's career as a novelist. When the novel was eventually published Garnett wrote to W. H. Hudson in praise of it, but the latter was unimpressed (see No. 9).

Anxiety about the reception of her first novel may have been a factor in precipitating Virginia Woolf's mental breakdown which culminated in her attempted suicide in September 1913—she 'thought everyone would jeer at her'.[12] It was this illness which prevented the book from coming out until two years after it had been accepted for publication.[13]

The *Times Literary Supplement* review (No. 1) was typical in being very favourable. Virginia Woolf had contributed to the 'major journal' as she and Leonard Woolf called it, since 1905, and she regarded a review here as being important because of its wide readership and influence. This review emphasised the 'feminine' aspect of her writing, an elusive quality which many subsequent critics (and Virginia Woolf herself) tried to define.

In general the reviews of *The Voyage Out* raised a number of issues which recurred in the reception of her later work. Her handling of moods, of individual perceptions, and her creation of small pictures was favourably noticed (Nos 6, 10, 11)—a talent which was, and is, recognised even by hostile critics. 'Character creation' and 'form' must figure in any serious discussion of the novel, and Virginia Woolf's innovatory approach was to make these aspects contentious issues. In this, her first novel, her character portrayal was largely approved: her people were 'brilliantly drawn' (No. 1) and 'Every one seems solid' (No. 10); the *Saturday Review* thought that 'The characters have all distinct personalities.'[14] But W. H. Hudson (No. 9) thought her men were poor and E. M. Forster (No. 4) complained that her characters were not vivid, a criticism which he was to reiterate in many of his later comments on her work. Gerald Gould's observation (No. 5) that her characters were 'sophisticated and introspective' is a comment on the limited range of Virginia Woolf's characters, a limitation frequently noted, with growing hostility, in later reviews. (No. 6) found her characters' talk 'consciously eccentric' at times, and for Gould they were quite simply 'mad'. As he points out, it is not that such people do not exist—they do, but we are still struck by their 'unreality', an appropriately paradoxical employment of this slippery term. ('Reality' and 'unreality' occur inevitably in discussions of the novel, and as Virginia Woolf questioned accepted ideas of reality, the reception of her work displays some of the confusion which often lies behind these words, especially when employed as literary critical terms.) But Gould's remark is perceptive if we compare the figure of St John Hirst with what we know of Lytton Strachey (a comparison made later by Leonard Woolf, J. K. Johnstone and Michael Holroyd). In spite of these criticisms there was comparatively widespread approval of her character-drawing which came perhaps from the fact that in this, her first novel, Virginia Woolf had not turned her back entirely on the conventional mode of creating character. But although she had not yet developed her 'lyrical novel' it is evident that she was beginning to look at people from unusual angles.

A number of reviewers thought that the form or construction of the novel was a weak point (e.g. Nos 3, 5, 9). The *New York Times* reviewer emphasised this weakness when the novel was first published in America (it did not appear there until May 1920). He found the lack of a clear story-line disappointing: 'As for the story itself, it is painfully lacking, both in coherency and narrative interest. . . . These people all talk smartly, and one rather wonders what it is all about, for it does not seem to get anywhere in particular.'[15] Like a number of English reviewers (e.g. Nos. 6, 7), he thought it overloaded with detail; a fault, according to the *Sunday Times*, often associated with a first attempt in fiction.[16] For some reviewers of the period, form was identified with plot, or quite simply with story, but Forster (No. 4) understood that Virginia Woolf was seeking unity by a path other than the usual one of 'plot'. (In fact she had decided many years before that 'plots don't matter'[17]; but in her reply to Strachey (No. 12) she admits the validity of some of these strictures on the form of the novel.)

The comedy, irony and satire in the novel were praised, although (No. 5) found much of it merely caustic. Virginia Woolf perhaps had this element in mind when she re-read the novel in 1920, and feared that she might be remembered simply as the author of cheap witticisms.[18]

Most reviewers admired Virginia Woolf's handling of Rachel's illness in those last chapters which she rewrote many times (Nos 1, 5, 6, 11). This remark in *Country Life* was typical: 'No reader will ever forget her description of a girl's bewildered falling into the depths of love or of the unbelievable approach of death.'[19] Forster's comparison of these chapters with Jules Romains' *Mort de quelqu'un* prefigured many later commentaries in which comparisons were made not only to this work of Romains but more generally to *unanimiste* ideas.[20] Even hostile reviewers (Nos 3, 7) praised the close of the novel, just as future reviewers were to praise the Septimus scenes in *Mrs Dalloway*: that is to say, those parts of the novels written with an obvious intensity and based on Virginia Woolf's disturbing psychological experiences. Perhaps because it was dangerous for her to explore these areas she turned away from these final pages of *The Voyage Out*, which we can now, with her other novels in mind call 'typical', and wrote *Night and Day*, a different *kind* of novel.

In his letter to Virginia Woolf (No. 11), written nearly a year after the publication of the novel, Lytton Strachey touched on some of the themes which we have seen in these first reviews. He followed No. 10 in seeing a Tolstoyan solidity in the novel; and the witty, ironical, 'unvictorian' element naturally appealed to the future author of *Eminent Victorians*. He would no doubt have been amused at the fact that one reviewer (No. 1) found the novel 'shocking' (though successfully so), and by another's condemnation of the 'coarseness' of its language (No. 7). These comments indicate how remote from us is the world in which Virginia Woolf set out on her journey as a novelist, a world of prudery and restraint from which she and other members of the Bloomsbury Group were trying to escape. Yet they were products of that world, and Virginia Woolf herself found 'vulgarisms' and 'crudities' in the novel when she re-read it. But it is partly because of the questioning and experiment of Bloomsbury that the modern reader would find it difficult to discover anything 'shocking' or 'coarse' in *The Voyage Out*. Strachey qualified his enthusiastic praise by noting that there was no 'dominant idea', a lack of that Jamesian 'subject' which No. 6 had mentioned. Virginia Woolf acknowledged the fairness of Strachey's criticism in her reply (No. 12) and tried to explain what she had attempted to do in the novel.

TWO EXPERIMENTAL SKETCHES: 'THE MARK ON THE WALL' (1917) AND 'KEW GARDENS' (1919)

'The Mark on the Wall' appeared with a story by Leonard Woolf in a volume entitled *Two Stories*, the first publication of the Hogarth Press, which Leonard and Virginia set up as a hobby. They did the printing and binding themselves and the book was sold by private subscription to friends and acquaintances.[21] No review copies were sent out, but the volume was well received by their friends. In a letter to Leonard Woolf, Lytton Strachey said that he considered Virginia's story a work of genius: 'The liquidity of the style fills me with envy: really some of the sentences!—How on earth does she make the English language float and float? And then the wonderful way in which the modern point of view is suggested. Tiens!'[22] Virginia Woolf wrote to her brother-in-law Clive Bell to thank him for his praise of 'The Mark on the Wall', saying that he was 'the first person who ever thought I'd write well'.[23] (The letters which form Appendix D of the first volume of Quentin Bell's biography of Virginia Woolf indicate that Clive Bell played an important part in the first stages of the writing of *The Voyage Out*.) One of the features of the reception of her work was the private and public support of her friends. For example, as early as February 1918, when she had published only *The Voyage Out* and 'The Mark on the Wall', Clive Bell in a preface to a collection of his essays was prepared to assert that Virginia Woolf, Hardy and Conrad were 'our three best novelists'.[24]

Some months later Katherine Mansfield (whose 'Prelude' was the second Hogarth publication) wrote to Virginia Woolf saying how much she liked 'The Mark on the Wall'.[25] They both admired, and were probably influenced by Chekhov, whose translated works were in vogue at this time. Katherine Mansfield approved of Virginia Woolf's Chekhov review[26] and expressed admiration for her essay 'Modern Novels'.[27] This leader article in the *Times Literary Supplement* was reprinted in *The Common Reader* with the title 'Modern Fiction'. It was referred to and quoted by many subsequent reviewers of Virginia Woolf's work, the passage about life being a luminous halo rather than a series of gig-lamps being especially popular.

Virginia Woolf's next publication was 'Kew Gardens', and this time the Hogarth Press did send a review copy to the *Times Literary Supplement*. The importance of a favourable review such as this (No. 13) can be gathered from Leonard Woolf's description of the flood of orders which they received after it appeared.[28] The sketch was also reviewed (together with 'The Mark on the Wall') by E. M. Forster (No. 14). Her work now contained sufficient number of 'experimental' aspects for Roger Fry to 'hold it up to the light', as Virginia Woolf in her biography of him said he did with all literature. He saw a new pattern—one similar to that created by contemporary visual artists (see No. 15). In December of that year Fry planned to collaborate with Charles Vildrac, the French *Unanimiste* poet on a translation of one of these sketches.[29]

Night and Day: A 'TRADITIONAL' NOVEL?

In her Diary Virginia Woolf recorded the despatch of her personal copies of the novel to her friends.[30] She waited anxiously for their comments, particularly those of Lytton Strachey and E. M. Forster. Clive Bell wrote 'No doubt a work of the highest genius'[31]—but it is clear from her Diary that Virginia Woolf did not respect his judgment. Lytton Strachey was enthusiastic but it appears from her reply to his letter, that he would have liked more sex in the novel:[32]

Ah, how delightful to be praised by you! I tell myself that of course you're always too generous about me, and one ought to discount it, but I can't bring myself to. I enjoy every word. I don't suppose there's anything in the way of praise that means more to me than yours. There are myriads of things I want to ask you; about the male characters for instance. Do they convince? Then was Rodney's change of heart sufficiently prepared for to be credible? It came into my head on the spur of the moment that he was in love with Cassandra, and afterwards it seemed a little violent. I take your point about the tupping and had meant to introduce a little in that line, but somehow it seemed out of the picture—still, I regret it. . . . I only wanted to say how happy your letter had made me,—dialogue was what I was after in this book—so I'm glad you hit on that; I mean it was one of the things—there are so many million others!—but I can't help thinking it's the problem, if one is to write novels at all, which is a moot point.

To his sister Philippa, Lytton Strachey wrote, 'I think Mrs Hilbery is a chef d'oeuvre' and in a letter to Lady Ottoline Morrell he declared that it was not a book to read, but to re-read.[33] All her friends seemed to be unanimous in their praise, but then E. M. Forster wrote 'I like it less than *The Voyage Out*', and she valued his opinion 'as much as anybody's'.[34] Then the *TLS* arrived with high praise, and intelligent too, she thought (No. 17). And so Virginia Woolf records her changing moods at the reception of her novel—now elated by praise, now cast down by adverse criticism. A few days after writing his critical letter, Forster dined with the Woolfs, and explained why he preferred *The Voyage Out*. Virginia Woolf recorded their conversation in her Diary:[35]

The doubt about Morgan and *N. and D.* is removed; I understand why he likes it less than *V. O.*; and, in understanding, see that it is not a criticism to discourage. Perhaps intelligent criticism never is. All the same, I shirk writing it out, because I write so much criticism. What he said amounted to this: *N. and D.* is a strictly formal and classical work; that being so one requires, or he requires, a far greater degree of lovability in the characters than in a book like *V. O.*, which is vague and universal. None of the characters in *N. and D.* is lovable. He did not care how they sorted themselves out. Neither did he care for the characters in *V. O.*, but there he felt no need to care for them. Otherwise, he admired practically everything; his blame does not consist in saying that *N. and D.* is less remarkable than t'other. O and beauties it has in plenty—in fact, I see no reason to be depressed on his account.

It seemed to Virginia Woolf that there was no critical consensus about the work: 'So all critics split off, and the wretched author who tries to keep control of them is torn asunder.'[36]

There was high praise for *Night and Day* but generally less enthusiasm than for *The Voyage Out*, and most subsequent criticism has followed this pattern. Looking back, three months after the publication of *Night and Day*,[37] Virginia Woolf came to understand why people preferred *The Voyage Out*, but at the time these early criticisms caused her some agitation. She was particularly upset by Katherine Mansfield's review (No. 18).

Ford Madox Ford's[38] article (No. 16) was a rare instance of an attempt to establish an agreed critical vocabulary for talking about the novel. He made an interesting distinction between 'novel' and 'romance', and used *Night and Day* to illustrate the latter category, because of its inclusiveness and lack of form. But he has chosen a singularly difficult novel for his purpose, for *Night and Day* seems to be a mixture of 'novel' and 'romance' as he defines them, and is possibly an attempt to combine the elements of 'inclusiveness' and 'design' which he isolates. Indeed, the majority of critics at the time stressed the classical or 'novel' elements in it. And so, for Forster, it was a classical novel which yet has beautiful elements, rather than a 'romance' which makes no attempt to achieve form. The *London Mercury* reviewer[39] emphasised the wealth of minute details in the novel—a romance characteristic—and yet he discerned a structure holding the novel together. It was therefore in the 'older tradition' of the novel as a work of art—precisely the opposite conclusion from that of Ford. It is clear, as well, that this reviewer saw this traditional aspect as something praiseworthy, not simply a neutral classification. For Katherine Mansfield, also, an element of evaluation is involved, but for her 'traditional' had pejorative connotations: in view of her friendship with Virginia Woolf she went as far as she dared in saying that the novel was a step backwards (No. 18).

What is clear amidst this confusion is that probably the novel did result from a somewhat confused intention—a conclusion borne out by Virginia Woolf herself when she declared many years later that she was attempting to do in *The Years* what she had not 'dared' to do in *Night and Day*.[40]

The Voyage Out was published in the USA in May 1920, and *Night and Day* four months later. Reviewing the books together the *Bookman* (New York) reviewer could see the similarities as well as the differences between the two works (No. 20).

ON THE TRACK OF REAL DISCOVERIES: *Monday or Tuesday*

Virginia Woolf collected 'A Mark on the Wall', 'Kew Gardens', 'An Unwritten Novel' and five previously unpublished sketches into a volume entitled *Monday or Tuesday*, which was published 'prematurely' on 7 April 1921.[41] This confusion in the launching of the book Virginia Woolf recorded in her Diary:[42]

My book out (prematurely) and nipped, a damp firework. Now the solid grain of fact is that Ralph sent my book out to *The Times* for review without date of publication in it. Thus a short notice is scrambled through to be in 'on Monday at latest', put in an obscure place, rather scrappy, complimentary enough, but quite unintelligent. I mean by that they don't see that I'm after something interesting.

The *Times Literary Supplement* review (No. 21) also indicates that there were some technical problems in the production of the volume. Doran, the American publishers of *Night and Day*, had refused the book, and things seemed gloomy. But she looked forward to the private criticism of her friends—the 'real test'. Public criticism by a friend, Desmond MacCarthy (No. 22), made her feel 'important'[43] and then a few days later she recorded her delight at Strachey's praise of 'String Quartet', and Roger Fry's declaration that she was 'on the track of real discoveries'.[44] A sentence in the *British Weekly* caught her eye: 'Virginia Woolf in the opinion of some good judges is the ablest of women writers in fiction.'[45] This appeared in a review of Leonard Woolf's translation of Chekhov, and so the sheer gratuitousness of the praise perhaps added piquancy. To her surprise, T. S. Eliot added his praise.[46] The book was accepted for publication in America by Harcourt Brace and appeared in November 1921. She had pleased the people whose judgment mattered to her, and so was not too upset when Leonard Woolf reported an unfavourable review of the American edition in the *Dial*, although she had hoped for praise in 'that august quarter'.[47] The *TLS* (No. 21) and *Dial* (No. 23) mark the poles of reaction to her work. Virginia Woolf was unfair to the *TLS* review, for it is a perceptive discussion of the non-representational nature of her writings, and makes an interesting comparison with parallel developments in the visual arts. The *Dial* saw her work as merely 'arty' and 'vague'.

'IMPRESSIONISM': *Jacob's Room*

This was the first large-scale work to be published by the Hogarth Press and Virginia Woolf was spared what was to her the pain of submitting her novel to Duckworth.[48] There was an auspicious beginning to the reception of the novel, as Harcourt Brace wrote in glowing terms early in October and said they would be delighted to publish it in America.[49] Pre-publication praise came from Lytton Strachey (No. 24), and she was pleased, although she thought him a little extravagant, as her reply shows (No. 25). The editor of the *TLS* rang up to ask if the publication date could be brought forward[50] and its review did appear a day before the planned publication date (No. 26). A *TLS* review was important, according to Virginia Woolf, not because it was the most intelligent, but because it was the most read (we saw earlier the dramatic effect of the *TLS* review on the sales of 'Kew Gardens'). Although she called this review 'tepid'[51], it seems intelligent and reasonably enthusiastic, stressing the adventurousness of her method. These reviews help us to recapture the sense of strangeness which many readers felt when faced with Virginia Woolf's experimental work for the first time, but not all welcomed her innovations.

The *Daily News* (No. 27) headed its piece 'Middle Aged Sensualists', and Virginia Woolf with typical and delightful exaggeration managed to make this worse, if that were possible, by transforming it in her Diary into 'elderly sensualist'.[52] She felt that the *Pall Mall Gazette* (No. 28) had dismissed her as 'negligeable'. This review was entitled 'An Impressionist' and it is this element which most reviewers point to, usually with some praise, but often with the qualification that impressionism is not enough to make a good novel. A parallel to this was the comparison with poetry. Despite its disjointed appearance, the novel was felt to have a number of local successes—vivid glimpses, snapshots or vignettes. But most reviewers regretted the lack of plot, structure and solid characters. The American edition was published in February 1923, and the *Nation* (New York) reviewer followed many of the British reviews in discussing the novel in terms of Impressionism, but for him it was a complete failure (No. 35).

There were comparisons with Joyce and Dorothy Richardson and a sense that there was a growing 'school' of stream-of-consciousness writers. Middleton Murry (No. 34) remarked on the widening gap between these *avant-garde* writers and the general public, which still wanted a story. Virginia Woolf was to worry continually in the following years about Murry's implication that *Jacob's Room* was an 'impasse'. From this time she was generally thought of as a 'difficult' or 'highbrow' writer. Even T. S. Eliot thought the novel required very careful reading, but he believed that she had successfully bridged the gap between her first novels and the experimental prose of *Monday or Tuesday*.[53] However, as Siegfried Sassoon pointed out in a letter to her, if read 'visually' the novel need not be too difficult: 'Your novel gave me an immense apprehension of your subtlety of intellect. But I was able to follow your meaning—instantly—every time, because you visualise everything you write.'[54]

Virginia Woolf's only answer to the suggestion that she had reached an 'impasse' could be, and was to be, another novel, *Mrs Dalloway*. But another criticism was to draw her out in a different way. This was Arnold Bennett's article (No. 36), and her reply, the essays in which she confronted Mr Bennett with Mrs Brown.

'Mr Bennett and Mrs Brown'

In June 1923, a few months after Bennett's article appeared, Virginia Woolf recorded in her Diary her intention to reply to his criticism that she 'can't create or didn't in *Jacob's Room*, characters that survive'.[55] This reply (No. 37), the first and less well-known version of 'Mr Bennett and Mrs Brown', was first published in America and appeared a fortnight later in the *Nation and Athenaeum*. There followed in the columns of this periodical an interesting debate about the essay, with articles by the novelist J. D. Beresford, Logan Pearsall Smith, a 'man of letters' and friend of the Woolfs, and Michael Sadleir, the novelist and writer on Victorian literature. Their comments perhaps encouraged her to expand and elaborate on certain themes and to alter the emphases in her later essay. Beresford (No. 38) stressed the 'change in human nature' which novelists had reflected—a central theme in Virginia Woolf's second version. Smith's opinion was of some importance to her[56] and his views were probably carefully noted. Perhaps his article (No. 39) incited her to extend the scope of her essay to include more foreign aspects. He emphasised the idea of cultural relativity, and, more important still, the role of convention in the creation of character. His occasionally flippant tone masks some interesting insights into the nature of fictional character. Looking at the first version of 'Mr Bennett and Mrs Brown', together with these replies and the famous final version of the essay, gives us an idea of how this latter was not a 'private manifesto'[57] but the product of a stimulating milieu.

The second version of the essay was first given as a lecture to the Cambridge Heretics on 18 May 1924. T. S. Eliot asked her for something for his *Criterion* and she suggested this paper, but warned him that it was intended for an undergraduate audience. Nevertheless it appeared in that journal in July, with the title 'Character in Fiction'. Frank Swinnerton discussed it in his 'Londoner' feature in the New York *Bookman* (No. 40). It was then published as a booklet by the Hogarth Press with the title of the early version, 'Mr Bennett and Mrs Brown', and was reviewed by Edwin Muir (No. 41) and 'Feiron Morris' (Mrs T. S. Eliot) (No. 42). But its reception is much more diffuse than this, for the essay became a key document, not only in the assessment of Virginia Woolf's work, but in relation to twentieth-century fiction generally. It played a part in the decline of Bennett's reputation, although more recently there have been attempts to see the argument from his point of view.[58]

The Common Reader (First Series)

Eight days after it was published, Virginia Woolf lamented over the critical silence which greeted the publication *The Common Reader*. Then a friend reported a review in the *Star* which mocked at Vanessa Bell's cover. The reviewer had written:[59]

> What means this flaunting of crude art, this almost reverent attempt to copy the early paint-brush effects of a child? I think it is a curiously accurate reflection on the misguided effort of the author in her criticism of contemporary writers to vindicate crude literary art against the cultivated and polished literary art.

(That is to say, rating Joyce higher than Wells, Bennett and Galsworthy.) But he praised her for discussing authors other than the 'safely dead'. The *TLS* (No. 44) gave her what she called 'sober and sensible praise', and she complained that she was never given a really enthusiastic review there. She contrasted this with the very complimentary review in the *Manchester Guardian* (No. 45). This reviewer made it clear that he had previously not greatly cared for Virginia Woolf's work, which bears out Leonard Woolf's comment that many people who did not like her novels thought her a remarkable critic of literature.[60] She was pleased to receive a letter from Mrs Hardy saying that Thomas Hardy had enjoyed the book.[61] In July, reviews appeared in the *Calendar* (No. 46) and the *Criterion* (No. 47), which made serious attempts to 'place' Virginia Woolf's criticism respectively in its social and its philosophical context.

Mrs Dalloway

Quentin Bell in his *Biography* describes the correspondence which took place between Virginia Woolf and Jacques Raverat some eight months before the publication of *Mrs Dalloway*.[62] Raverat discussed the way in which a painter can achieve the effect of 'simultaneity' and Virginia Woolf described how she wished to achieve the 'splash' effect of a painter in her use of language, rather than the strictly linear 'railway-line' type of sentence of Bennett and Galsworthy. She accorded

Raverat the rare privilege of reading the novel in manuscript and was cheered by his enthusiasm.

But the public reception of the novel began badly, with Virginia Woolf noting unfavourable reviews in the *Western Mail*[63] and the *Scotsman*.[64] Both reviewers were disturbed that the novel was not split into chapters (the *Western Mail* review was headed 'A Long, Long Chapter'). It seems that the 'common reader' in the provinces needed 'resting places'. The lack of action and the commonplace nature of the characters was criticised. For the *Western Mail* the novel was simply a 'bewildering jumble', but the *Scotsman* was more discriminating, praising the Septimus-Lucrezia scenes. But both reviews bear out Murry's earlier remark about the growing distance between writers like Virginia Woolf and the reading public.

For the first time, her work was published simultaneously in Britain and America. A review by the British novelist Richard Hughes (No. 48) was a good beginning to the reception of the novel in the United States. His comparison with Cézanne is especially interesting, when we bear in mind the 'painterly' aspect of writing which Virginia Woolf discussed with Raverat. *Mrs Dalloway* was also highly praised in the Boston *Christian Science Monitor*, which described it as 'a work of art, a thing of beauty'.[65] In Britain, the *TLS* admired her persistent experimentation (No. 49). And so a month after its publication, there had been sufficient favourable notice and a good enough sale ('More of *Dalloway* has been sold this month than of *Jacob* in a year', she noted in her Diary) for her to face with equanimity the pointed remarks of Lytton Strachey, whose criticism she always noted carefully. She reported his remarks in her Diary (No. 52) and her own comments indicate that she was a harsh critic of her own work. The *Calendar*, following its policy, attempted to place the novel in its social context (No. 53). E. M. Forster had privately praised the novel, and now published a full-scale assessment of Virginia Woolf's achievement to date (No. 54). The reviews of Muir (No. 55), Carew (No. 56) and Bennett (No. 58) revolve once again around the problem of character in fiction.

To the Lighthouse

To the Lighthouse was published in May 1927, but the central section, 'Time Passes', had already appeared in France in the previous December, translated by Charles Mauron. Roger Fry wrote to the translator's wife, in connection with this translation:[66]

Good Lord, how difficult she is to translate, but I think Charles has managed to keep the atmosphere marvellously. To tell the truth I do not think this piece is quite of her best vintage. I have noticed one peculiarity. She is so splendid as soon as a character is involved—for example the old *concierge* is superb—but when she tries to give her impression of inanimate objects, she exaggerates, she underlines, she poeticises just a little bit.

The problem of this central section was raised again in the reviews. The *TLS* (No. 60) declared that 'this transitional part of the book is not its strongest part.' Writing her Diary 'under the damp cloud' of this review, Virginia Woolf expressed her anxiety lest the Time Passes section be pronounced 'soft, shallow, insipid, sentimental.'[67] But many readers were to disagree with Fry and the *TLS*. Writing to Virginia Woolf a few days later Lady Ottoline Morrell picked out this second section for special praise,[68] and for the *New York Times* reviewer it was a 'magnificent interlude' (No. 61).

Virginia Woolf received letters of praise from Vanessa Bell[69] and Roger Fry.[70] Lytton Strachey liked the novel better than *Mrs Dalloway* but was disturbed by the lack of copulation in the book (he had criticised *Night and Day* for the same reason). The final result, he thought, was little more than an arabesque, though an exquisite one.[71]

In general the novel was very favourably received even by normally hostile critics—a pattern of response seen in much subsequent criticism. (For example, F. R. Leavis, writing in 1930, described it as a work expressing the finest consciousness of the age, fit to rank with 'The Waste Land' and *Ulysses*.)[72] The characters were thought to be more fully and firmly drawn than in her previous work and the novel's construction attracted appreciation. The fleeting impressions which had been individually admired in *Mrs Dalloway* and *Jacob's Room* were here felt to be better organised. But there was still little concession to the demand for plot or story, and some reviewers found fault with this.

To the Lighthouse received high praise from other novelists. Hugh Walpole recorded the influence which the novel had on him when he was writing his novel *Hans Frost* (published two years later, in 1929): 'This will be a simple mild book but not imbecile . . . writing, I fear, rather in Virginia Woolf's manner. How can I help it when she is such a darling and *To the Lighthouse* the best of all the works yet?', and later he declared that 'Virginia Woolf has perhaps liberated me.'[73] He it was who presented to Virginia Woolf the Femina Vie Heureuse Prize awarded for the novel in May 1928. Despite her very tart remarks in her Diary about his speech on that occasion, they became friends. He was later to write 'I think Virginia has shown me—especially in *To the Lighthouse* and *Orlando*—how to get over a little of my sententiousness and sentimentality. I think both *Hans Frost* and *Herries* show the beginning of this change and I must develop it farther without surrendering too *much* to her influence.'[74] Ford Madox Ford described *To the Lighthouse* as 'the only piece of British writing that has really excited my craftsman's mind—the only piece since the decline and death of Conrad'.[75] Even Arnold Bennett, normally an unfriendly reviewer, considered it a good novel (No. 63).

What evoked this larger enthusiasm was a more tangible quality in Virginia Woolf's presentation of life and of human beings—a greater sense of external reality. In this novel the outer and inner worlds are brought much nearer together than in her previous books. Aldous Huxley's complaint about its over-refinement and remoteness, a familiar response to her other works, was an untypical reaction to this novel:[76]

Have you read a novel called *The Man Within* by Graham Greene? I think it's most remarkable.... Much better (between ourselves, for it's frightful heresy!) than Virginia's *To the Lighthouse* which I'm now rather belatedly reading. It's the difference between something full and something empty; between a writer who has a close physical contact with reality and one who is a thousand miles away and only has a telescope to look, remotely, at the world.

Conrad Aiken's review (No. 65) raises an issue which was to dominate much critical thought in later years: the idea that Virginia Woolf deals with only a narrow area of human experience, that hers was a small and sheltered world. Aiken's perceptive discussion is one of the best written during Virginia Woolf's lifetime. He maintains that Virginia Woolf's novels shut out the fiercer experiences of life and have an 'odd and delicious air of parochialism'. But is a limited range of this kind an absolute limitation in the value of a writer? Certainly, Virginia Woolf wrote about the kind of intellectual and sophisticated people she knew best. But Aiken rightly points out that the test should be how far she succeeds in making her world and its inhabitants real to us. He emphasises Virginia Woolf's success in making possible the imaginative identification between the reader and the world she has created for her characters: 'We feel the minute texture of their lives with their own vivid senses... and ultimately we know them as well, as terribly, as we know ourselves.'

Orlando

Virginia Woolf considered *Orlando* to be something of a freak[77] and explained, 'I expect I began *Orlando* as a joke and went on with it seriously.'[78] One of the first problems the book met with was that Virginia Woolf in fun had called it a 'biography', and this caused difficulties with the booksellers. They insisted that it should go on the biography shelf rather than the novel shelf, and they ordered only small quantities because, as they explained, 'no one wants biography'. But the book was to sell very well, either in spite of—or because of—being called a biography. Indeed, in terms of sales it marks the turning-point of Virginia Woolf's career as a successful novelist.[79] One imagines that today the bookseller's attitude would be the reverse, and perhaps Virginia Woolf's 'novel-biography' marks a stage in the increasing popularity of biography. But in view of Lytton Strachey's success, it is surprising that the booksellers should have thought that 'no one wants biography'.

Another possible factor in the book's success, as Quentin Bell points out in his biography, was the sexual theme, which had been given a certain topicality by *The Well of Loneliness* case. This novel, which deals with lesbianism, was banned in spite of protests by a number of prominent people, including Virginia Woolf herself. Appropriately enough, when *Orlando* was published Virginia Woolf was out of the country on holiday with the hero-heroine of the book, Vita Sackville-West. The first review she noted on her return was that of J. C. Squire (No. 71), but his 'barking', as she called it, was soon counteracted by Hugh Walpole, and by Rebecca West, who thought *Orlando* a 'poetic masterpiece of the first rank'.[80] Walpole's review was one of the oddest she received, for he archly refused to name the author or the title of the book he was reviewing—confidently leaving that for posterity to determine.[81]

There was a sharp division in the favourable reviews between those who took it in the spirit in which it was begun, as a fantasy or *jeu d'esprit*, and those for whom it was an important step forward in Virginia Woolf's development, and even in the form of the novel.

Desmond MacCarthy's review (No. 70) is significant for a number of reasons. Although he often reviewed Virginia Woolf's work, this is his most extended piece of criticism. It shows clearly his reservations about the stream-of-consciousness novel, and although he thought *Orlando* was her best and most characteristic work, it is clear from his remarks about the place of character in the novel that he did not see her as a novelist of the first rank. Here we have a clear indication that the Bloomsbury Group was not a mutual admiration society.

For Squire (No. 71) and Bennett (No. 73a) the book was simply a 'pleasant trifle' and a 'high-brow lark'. Aldous Huxley commented in a letter to D. H. Lawrence: 'A tiresome book by Virginia Woolf—*Orlando*—which is so terribly literary and *fantaisiste* that nothing is left in it at all. It's almost the most highly exhausted vacuum I've ever known.'[82] Storm Jameson's criticism was typical (No. 77). She granted that Virginia Woolf was a fine stylist, but found something missing—there was a lack of humanity in her work.

About a month after it was published Virginia Woolf recorded her own assessment of the work:[83]

> I mean the situation is, this *Orlando* is of course a very quick brilliant book. Yes, but I did not try to explore. And must I always explore? Yes I think so still. Because my reaction is not the usual. Nor can I even after all these years run it off lightly. *Orlando* taught me how to write a direct sentence; taught me continuity and narrative and how to keep the realities at bay. But I purposely avoided of course any other difficulty. I never got down to my depths and made shapes square up, as I did in the *Lighthouse*.
>
> Well but *Orlando* was the outcome of a perfectly definite indeed overmastering, impulse. I want fun. I want fantasy. I want (and this was serious) to give things their caricature value.

But the success of *Orlando* was so great that Virginia Woolf was tempted to repeat the performance—the great temptation for a popular writer, but one which, as her next novel was to show, she successfully resisted.

A Room of One's Own

Virginia Woolf often tried to predict the reception of her books, and the day before *A Room of One's Own* was published she wrote:[84]

> I will here sum up my impressions before publishing *A Room of One's Own*. It is a little ominous that Morgan won't review it. It makes me suspect that there is a shrill feminine tone in it which my intimate friends will dislike. I forecast, then, that I shall get no criticism, except of the evasive jocular kind, from Lytton, Roger and Morgan; the press will be kind and talk of its charm and sprightliness; also I shall be attacked for a feminist and hinted at for a Sapphist; Sybil will ask me to luncheon; I shall get a good many letters from young women. I am afraid it will not be taken seriously. Mrs Woolf is so accomplished a writer that all she says makes easy reading . . . this very feminine logic . . . a book to put in the hands of girls. I doubt that I mind very much.

This was only partly fulfilled. She added a note a few months later to say that E. M. Forster 'wrote yesterday, 3 Dec. and said he very much liked it'. A week after its publication she reported that it was selling well and that she had received 'unexpected letters'.

Most reviewers, including Arnold Bennett (No. 81) noted that it was only superficially a feminist tract. It is a difficult book to categorise as there is no single line of argument: as the *TLS* put it, the essay is 'delightfully peripatetic' (No. 79). But reviewers recognised that its main theme was women and writing.

There were manifestations of the kind fearfully predicted by Virginia Woolf. For example, William Plomer wrote to Leonard Woolf: 'Virginia has a fervent admirer here, who is very excited about *A Room of One's Own*, and will I hope write and communicate her enthusiasm. Her name is Irene Hadjilazaro . . . hard-boiled and hard hitting, feminist, alpinist and amazon.'[85] But generally the reviewers were fairer to her argument than she imagined they would be. They emphasised the 'androgynous vision', the balance between the masculine and feminine points of view in the book. M. E. Kelsey related this central idea to the rest of Virginia Woolf's fiction and her article prefigures many recent studies along these lines (No. 82).

In the 1930s, however, there was a growing feeling that Virginia Woolf was remote from social reality; her idea of 'five hundred pounds a year and a room of one's own' as ideal conditions for a writer indicated to many people a grave limitation in her thinking, and symbolised the inadequacies of the class she was believed to represent.

The Waves

Virginia Woolf predicted that the reviewers would not be able to 'find anything very new to say' about *The Waves*.[86] She welcomed the long and outspoken review in the *TLS* (No. 83) but found it odd that the reviewer should praise the characters 'when she had meant to have none'.[87] There was even, for the first time, a note in *The Times* itself. In view of this and other favourable reviews, she felt that the novel had been better received than any of her books.[88]

The most immediately striking feature of the novel for readers then, as now, was its extreme stylisation. Virginia Woolf's employment of soliloquies throughout the novel was frequently disliked. It was seen as a 'trick' (No. 92) and a 'desire for novelty' (No. 93) and one reviewer declared that the 'form attracts too much attention and gives little reward'.[89] It was an embarrassment to otherwise sympathetic critics:

Storm Jameson, for example, (No. 90) thought it an undergraduate scheme, but fortunately of no importance in assessing the real value of the novel. But there were some reviewers who thought that the method had advantages as well as drawbacks. Louis Kronenberger's article (No. 89) shows understanding and judgment. He sought to understand why the form was chosen and tried to estimate its relationship to the stream-of-consciousness method. His discussion is more helpful than seeing the use of soliloquies as a trick, or, like (No. 84), as an extreme form of the internal monologue as developed by Joyce. Most reviewers believed that Virginia Woolf chose her method in order to allow scope for prose-poetry and symbolism, and most allowed that she attained local successes in this direction. But although she was generally regarded as a fine writer, a remarkable stylist, the familiar objections were raised to her remoteness from life.

Some reviewers, both favourable and unfavourable, had a feeling that the novel was nearing the void—there was a sense of emptiness lying behind it (see Nos 83, 93). This underlying desolation was also sensed by Edwin Muir (No. 94), but he believed that Virginia Woolf had achieved a tragic catharsis of this emotion, and that by means of simple monologues she had come to grips with the immediate and essential truths of experience.

There was still talk of the 'difficulty' of her writing, but it seemed that since *Mrs Dalloway* 'the provinces' had caught up, and appeared to Virginia Woolf to be unanimous in praise of *The Waves*.[90]

VIRGINIA WOOLF IN ACADEME

In 1932 two book-length studies of Virginia Woolf's work appeared, Winifred Holtby's *Virginia Woolf* and Floris Delattre's *Le Roman psychologique de Virginia Woolf*. A chapter from the latter had been published in the previous December (No. 96), outlining the central thesis of the book. Many critics had previously hinted at the similarities between Virginia Woolf's work and the philosophy of Bergson: this was the first detailed analysis.

Virginia Woolf was now an 'important' writer, on the syllabus of English literature courses. She was the subject of academic lectures in France, and in more distant parts: in December 1930 William Plomer wrote: 'A Japanese professor, once a "colleague" of mine, writes to me with the news that he is "taking up Virginia Woolf for this term at the university"—the book is *Jacob's Room* and the University is the

University of Tokyo. As they used to do a great deal of Stevenson and Barrie, the news is certainly excellent.'[91]

At this time, following the pioneering work of I. A. Richards, there was a growing tendency in academic circles to emphasise the close analysis of literary texts. This approach was to become a restricting dogma in later years, but at the time was useful antidote to belle-lettrism and vagueness in literary criticism. Nos 97a and b are examples of the new approach. These articles have the merit of isolating certain elements in Virginia Woolf's style, though we may disagree with the overall conclusions. But the value of this close critical method can be seen if we contrast these discussions with an extreme example of current reviewing which appeared at about the same time.[92] In this review 'Ernle' wrote a sentence each about the two books being reviewed (one of which was *The Waves*), and devoted the remaining twenty-five pages of his article to reminiscences of his boyhood.

ISOLATION: 1932–7

During these years Virginia Woolf published no major work. The second *Common Reader* was received well enough, but the *TLS* noted 'a shade less gaiety in this volume'[93] and a lack of the kind of comment on contemporary literature which was to be found in the first series. *Flush*, published in 1933, Virginia Woolf herself did not take seriously, nor did the reviewers, as the titles of two of the reviews suggest: 'Brown Beauty'[94] and 'A Storyteller's Holiday'.[95] It was the kind of novel that Noel Coward would, and did, admire.[96] But it was a commercial success, especially in Britain.

In general the comments in the years following the publication of *Flush* until the publication of *The Years* in 1937, were unfavourable to her work. The death of her friends Lytton Strachey (in 1932) and Roger Fry (in 1934) increased her sense of isolation. This did not come from any lack of contact with the new generation of writers, for through John Lehmann, himself a poet, who helped to run the Hogarth Press, Virginia Woolf met Isherwood, Spender, and others. However, their attitude towards each other must have been equivocal. It was not that she held right-wing views: through Leonard Woolf she had had a long association with left-wing politics, but these younger writers were uneasy with some of her ideas, as Auden and Isherwood indicated in *The Dog Beneath the Skin* (1935). The Chorus warns:[97]

Do not speak of a change of heart, meaning five hundred
a year and a room of one's own,
As if that were all that is necessary.

We can gather Virginia Woolf's uneasiness about them from her article 'The Leaning Tower' (a lecture given to the Sussex WEA in 1940).

Nevertheless, Stephen Spender was prepared to spring to her defence when she was attacked by Wyndham Lewis in *Men Without Art* (see Nos 102a, b, c). To call this an attack 'from the Right' would be to ascribe to Lewis a consistent political ideology, which he never had. Perhaps this made him a more dangerous 'enemy' (as he styled himself): his attack could not be subsumed under any anaesthetising label, as perhaps 'left-wing attacks' could be. Further, it came from a man of intelligence and polemic ability, a satirist whose power Virginia Woolf recognised. Because of the caution of Lewis's publisher, who feared libel actions, she was spared from reading his next attack, in *The Roaring Queen* (first published in 1973). There, she is lampooned in the figure of Rhoda Hyman. Shodbutt is Arnold Bennett:[98]

> Grinning into the Intense Inane, this most egregious of bogus Jane Austens sat over there anyway and ignored Shodbutt—as modestly and with a startled surprise she received the congratulations slavishly offered her for having recently awarded *herself*, out of hand, the Diploma that was in her keeping for the Year's Cleverest Literary Larceny.

Lewis worried Virginia Woolf in a way that Frank Swinnerton, for example, could not (No. 104). Swinnerton had always been a hostile reviewer but she found a category for him which rendered him harmless—he was a member of her 'underworld'—a Grub Street literary hack.

Although she was friendly with members of the intellectual left wing, and, in the instance above, defended by one of them, other socialist interpreters of literature and culture found her reliance on or exploration of 'sensibility' insufficient in the face of the growing political storm. Nos 103a, b, c, are a representative selection from this school of thought. She felt the pressure of the times sufficiently to write for the *Daily Worker* an article entitled 'Why Art To-Day Follows Politics', but it was a far from orthodox contribution.

A BEST SELLER: *The Years*

No book cost Virginia Woolf as much pain to write: a pain which she recalled when reading the early reviews, which seemed to her unbelievably favourable, as she had expected the novel to fail. *The Years* is in some ways a typical best-seller, enjoying a big sale and much critical acclaim when first published, but now neglected and very much less popular both with critics and the buying public. The early reviews might help us to understand something of this phenomenon.

Virginia Woolf welcomed the review in the *TLS* (No. 107), but felt that it emphasised too much the 'death song' aspect and the 'impressionism' in the novel; she thought de Selincourt in the *Observer* was nearer the mark. A week after publication she was able to record that the majority of reviewers had acclaimed it as a masterpiece.[99] But then came Edwin Muir's review (No. 112). He had been a consistent admirer of her previous work, but now saw *The Years* as a step backwards from her greatest achievement, *The Waves*. The novel was published in America early in April and Virginia Woolf with delight saw it rise to the top of the best-seller chart in the *New York Herald Tribune*.

As usual, most of the reviewers, whether favourable or hostile, admired the novel on a detailed level: the 'cubes of live experience' (No. 108), the clarity of the little scenes, and the sense impressions which become symbols were praised. The *relative* success of this novel in comparison with her other works is simply explained: as No. 108 pointed out, it is easier to read than *The Waves*. But why was it an absolute best-seller? The *Time and Tide* reviewer (No. 106) hints that perhaps it was written to show that the author could write a traditional novel, a family saga. This idea was supported by Leonard Woolf, who believed that this was the only novel which Virginia Woolf might have written as an answer to her critics.[100] Many reviewers mentioned the family saga or 'cavalcade' aspect of the novel, often with the qualification that *The Years* goes beyond the usual formula. But evidently there were sufficient points in common with this kind of writing to appeal to the book-buyer. The novel was enthusiastically received by two writers well qualified to assess this aspect of the work. Howard Spring (No. 109) was to become a very popular novelist, and David Garnett (No. 111) had already produced a best-seller. Their reviews help to explain the book's appeal.

But Garnett was one of the reviewers who criticised the form of the novel. He found the deliberate repetitions irritating, agreeing with the *Scrutiny* critic (No. 116) who described the repetitive pattern as 'artful'. It is this element which Muir was pointing to (No. 112) when he complained that we *feel* the pattern too much. Like the *Scrutiny* reviewer he preferred the last section of the novel, dealing with the Present Day, but he thought there was a lack of continuity in the novel as a whole.

The characters, being more traditionally portrayed than in any of her novels since *Night and Day*, were more widely admired than usual, but there were exceptions. *Scrutiny* still found her people to be 'phantoms', and the American critic J. W. Beach believed that 'they fade out of the mind as individuals, to get confused with one another. . . . This is notably true in *The Years*.'[101]

The uncertainty of the times in which the novel was first read can be seen in the need felt by Garnett (No. 111) and the *Time and Tide* reviewer (No. 106) to defend the novel against possible attacks from 'class-conscious propagandists' and the 'strict communist'. This atmosphere can be indicated by the physical context of Spring's review (No. 109)—and here one gains something from looking at the newspapers themselves, which can be only hinted at in a series of excerpts. Spring's review is sandwiched between an advertisement for spectacles designed to be worn with a gas-mask and a review which quotes Dean Inge's opinion, 'I do not believe that either Germany or Italy could finance a great war. Germany is in such a plight financially that I have grave doubts whether the Hitler regime can last out the year; and Italy is not in a much better case.' Perhaps this is the best context for Inge's comment in the next day's paper: 'Take all the best-known names in fiction and drama—Shaw, Wells, Galsworthy, Arnold Bennett, Aldous Huxley, Virginia Woolf, Forster and other writers of note. Would it be going too far to say that human nature, as depicted in their works is a drab, ignoble thing?'[102]

Three Guineas

In this atmosphere *Three Guineas* was written and published. Quentin Bell recalls his own feelings when he first read the book:[103]

> What really seemed wrong with the book—and I am speaking here of my own reactions at the time—was the attempt to involve a discussion of women's rights with the far more agonising and immediate question of what we were to do in order to meet the ever-growing menace of Fascism and war. The connection between the two questions seemed tenuous and the positive suggestions wholly inadequate.

Outside the circle of Virginia Woolf's family and friends, who kept rather silent, the book was received quite favourably. She was pleased with the big splash in the *TLS* (No. 117) and with the *Time and Tide* review (No. 118). She described the reception as 'the mildest childbirth I have ever had'—a significant metaphor which casts light on her extreme reaction to adverse criticism of her work. But in this instance even Q. D. Leavis's attack (No. 122) did not upset her too much.

In general, there was little analysis in the reviews. The *New Statesman* reviewer (No. 120) pointed out that like *A Room of One's Own* it was a difficult book to talk about. This reviewer dismissed as 'quibblers' those who might feel inclined to find fault with the details of the argument. In fact, a large proportion of most of the reviews was taken up by attempts simply to précis the argument. (Perhaps the 'plotless' nature of Virginia Woolf's novels prevented, to a surprising extent, the parallel gambit of retelling the story in the novel reviews.) But there, one could at least invoke Proust or Joyce or Sterne. Here, the reviewers had to go further back, to Aristophanes—she was the 'new Lysistrata' (see Nos 117, 120). The *Observer* reviewer (No. 119), perhaps in desperation, called up the spirit of Matthew Arnold to help him fill his two columns.

Graham Greene had a temperamental dislike of Virginia Woolf's work. He was to write a few months later that she 'skims with high-minded elegance the surface'.[104] Aldous Huxley was quite right in seeing their work as polar opposites (see above, p. 20). But Greene's attitude was ambivalent, in a manner shared by many critics of her work. In his review of *Three Guineas* (No. 121) he described her brain as being like a vulgarised sea-shell, and yet the product of that same brain is a 'clear brilliant essay'.

Q. D. Leavis's article (No. 122) states directly what the *TLS* had only hinted at—that this book was written for a special, privileged class of women. Virginia Woolf no doubt gained some emotional satisfaction by impugning Q. D. Leavis's motives, but many of the points in her article are, despite this and the *New Statesman*'s pre-emptive remarks, much more than mere 'quibbles'.

Roger Fry

Roger Fry was a close friend of Virginia Woolf and a central member of the Bloomsbury Group. His ideas had an important influence on her work: one of the constant themes of these reviews is the comparison between her writing and visual art. This cross-fertilisation owed much to her friendship with Fry. Reviews of biographies usually concentrate on the subject rather than the biographer, and this was the case here, but the interest of the reviews of *Roger Fry* in relation to Virginia

Woolf is that they cast light on a figure who was important in her life and in the development of her art, and they also show the attitudes towards Bloomsbury and its values at this time. The passing remarks on Virginia Woolf's ability as a biographer were generally favourable, but the style and method was felt to be quite untypical, being rather sober and careful.

The reviews of E. M. Forster (No. 123) and Herbert Read (No. 124) show contrasting attitudes towards the Bloomsbury Group. Read thought that its members unduly emphasised the rational side of life and neglected intuition and instinct. Forster would perhaps not disagree with the terms, but for him 'liberalism' and 'intellect', which Bloomsbury and Fry embodied, were wholly laudable values.

Forster raised the question of what such a man's work, or the ideals of Bloomsbury, or Virginia Woolf's biography could 'mean' at such a time. What could they do against the Nazis? His answer is surely correct: nothing. But his qualifying remark expresses a sentiment shared by many writers during this difficult time: these things are 'part of a larger battle'.

VIRGINIA WOOLF'S DEATH

Virginia Woolf's death brought obituary notes and reminiscences from many friends. A list of their names would give an impression of the central position which Virginia Woolf occupied in the literary life of England. There were tributes from her own and from the younger generation of writers and artists (e.g. T. S. Eliot (No. 126), V. Sackville-West, Hugh Walpole (No. 127), Duncan Grant, Stephen Spender (No. 125), David Garnett, Christopher Isherwood, and many others). E. M. Forster's Rede Lecture delivered on 29 May 1941 was a tribute to his friend and also—something which is difficult on such occasions—an attempt to assess her work objectively. Forster continued a criticism which runs throughout his review of her work: 'She could seldom so portray a character that it was remembered afterwards on its own account.'[105] He stated quite bluntly that 'she was a snob' but concluded:[106]

Virginia Woolf got through an immense amount of work, she gave acute pleasure in new ways, she pushed the light of the English language a little further against the darkness. Those are the facts. The epitaph of such an artist cannot be written by the vulgar-minded or by the lugubrious. They will try, indeed they have already tried, but their words make no sense. It is wiser, it is safer, to regard her career as a triumphant one. She triumphed over what are primly called 'difficulties', and she also triumphed in the positive sense; she brought in the spoils. And sometimes it is as a row of little silver cups that I see her work gleaming. 'These trophies', the inscription runs, 'were won by the mind from matter, its enemy and its friend.'

Despite Forster's warning, Virginia Woolf's death marked the beginning of those unfortunate reminiscences about her 'intricate face' and 'intellectual bone structure' and so on. At the time these were understandable attempts to give a sense of the person behind the writer, but many subsequent comments of this sort tended to draw attention towards trivial aspects of her life and away from her real achievement.

Between the Acts

This novel, which Virginia Woolf did not revise finally, was published a few months after her death. Reviewers naturally took the opportunity to survey her achievement, and these reviews give us a picture of the critical reception of her work shortly after her death. Both friendly and hostile reviewers found this last novel typical, in its experimental form, its poetry, and, on the negative side, in its remoteness. The threat of war is in the background of the novel and it was published at a very dark time in the war. The American critic Malcolm Cowley (No. 133) believed that this prevented a true judgment of the work, but most of the reviews testify to the determination on the part of literary people at the time to preserve at least a memory of absolute values amid the pressure of war and its pervasive propaganda.

Most reviewers saw it as an imperfect book. For David Cecil (No. 128) this was a formal deficiency—a mistaken attempt to combine two conventions which do not blend. But others saw in it a more general shortcoming: as the *TLS* put it, in an otherwise sympathetic review: 'She shrank instinctively from forms of goodness and beauty other than those she had absorbed into her private vision' (No. 129). Edwin Muir was in a minority in thinking that the flaws were of such a kind that they could have been corrected by revision (No. 131).

B. G. Brooks (No. 135) placed *Between the Acts* in a survey of Virginia Woolf's work as a whole, and his article is also an early attempt to see her work in relation to the artistic and intellectual history of her time.

VIRGINIA WOOLF IN FRANCE

The French reception of Virginia Woolf's work is important because of the number and quality of the reviews and articles dealing with her work which appeared during her lifetime. She met and corresponded with a number of French intellectuals such as J.-E. Blanche, Charles Mauron, and Jacques Raverat. Her work was admired by many more artists, writers and critics who were themselves of some importance in the French literary world. In both French and English reviews her work was compared with that of French writers, expecially Proust, Jules Romains, Giraudoux and Bergson. The parallels between her writings and the philosophy of Bergson were examined in detail in one of the first books to be devoted to her work, Floris Delattre's *Le Roman psychologique de Virginia Woolf*, which was published in 1932.

A foreign novel often has two receptions—one of the original and another of the translation. In Virginia Woolf's case, the translations were not made in chronological order (for example, her first novel was the last to be translated). A translation reaches a wider audience than the original, and those of *Mrs Dalloway* in 1929 and *The Waves* in 1937 were regarded as important literary events in France and they received many interesting reviews.

French surveys of the contemporary English novel written in the early and mid-1920s speak of Virginia Woolf as an 'impressionist' writer, a description which was to be applied, in a modified form, in many subsequent articles and reviews. Abel Chevally began this trend. He wrote of the 'infinite number of minute, precise shaded strokes' in the first two novels. *The Voyage Out* and more especially *Night and Day* were constructed in such a way 'that one might say they were made by the same methods as the pictures of our great impressionists'.[107] Another critic believed she belonged to a fairly well defined 'impressionist movement' in the English novel and spoke of the kaleidoscopic rapidity with which she registers impressions.[108] (The kaleidoscope image was favoured by many early reviewers, both English and French.) In a popular survey of contemporary English literature her method was described as the juxtaposition of slight strokes—pure impressionism.[109] This writer pointed out at the beginning of his study that many English writers have had their French 'champions': Browning and Conrad in Gide, Joyce and Samuel Butler in Valery Larbaud, and so on. In the years to follow, Virginia Woolf was to find a number of illustrious commentators, for example, the novelists Edmond Jaloux, André Maurois and Marguerite Yourcenar, the painter J.-E. Blanche, the critics Floris Delattre and J.-J. Mayoux, and many others.

While writing *Mrs Dalloway* Virginia Woolf corresponded with

Jacques Raverat, the French painter. She was interested in the 'painterly' approach to literature, and in their letters they discussed the relationship between writing and the visual arts. Her remarks about trying to achieve a 'splash' effect in her writing indicate the appropriateness of these early French comparisons with painting.[110]

T. S. Eliot's article (No. 59) was an important stage in the French reception of Virginia Woolf's work. With all his authority he placed her as one of the most important and representative contemporary English novelists. From this time, the year of *To the Lighthouse*, French notice of her work became increasingly widespread and interesting.

As we have seen, even before the publication of *To the Lighthouse* French critics were sensitive to the visual element in her novels. Shortly after its publication Virginia Woolf met the French painter and man of letters J.-E. Blanche, and his 'Interview with Virginia Woolf' (No. 68) was the first French article devoted to her. He continues this tradition of finding parallels with painting in her work, but thought that she would be displeased with the 'impressionist' label—Bloomsbury was more advanced than that, he suggested. And a few weeks later the *Revue de la Quinzaine* commented: 'She has found a new realism. Her art is close to that of certain recent painters whose interpretation of forms makes one see reality from an unexpected angle.'[111] J.-J. Mayoux's fine and unusually detailed analysis of *To the Lighthouse* prefigures later 'close analyses' of her novels. This excellent article (No. 69) helps to explain why a number of English reviewers held their French counterparts in such high esteem.

The first French translation of a complete Virginia Woolf novel appeared in 1929—*Mrs Dalloway*, translated by S. David with a preface by André Maurois. It was an event of importance in the history we are tracing, for this volume became the starting-point for many subsequent discussions of her work. More recently reprinted in an inexpensive paperback edition, it is still probably the usual introduction to Virginia Woolf for most French readers. In his Preface Maurois quoted her now famous remarks about life not being a series of giglamps but a luminous halo, a transparent envelope.[112] And so this became a reference point in many French, as well as English discussions of her work. Maurois, like the critics mentioned previously, compared her methods with those of the impressionist painters, but suggests that Virginia Woolf, like Proust, goes beyond pure impressionism.

This translation with Maurois's preface was reviewed in a number of journals. Gabriel Marcel touched upon a philosophical aspect of the novel which comes close to the 'anti-psychiatry' of recent times. In *Mrs Dalloway*, a novel apparently without any philosophical pretensions, Marcel discerned a feeling for nature which is fundamentally metaphysical—especially in the scenes in which Septimus clashes with the psychiatrist Bradshaw. He thought Virginia Woolf opposed the offensive alliance which social forces inevitably conclude with mental health. He believed that this translation 'should constitute an important event in our literary history and should contribute to a much needed renewal of novelistic technique'.[113]

In her memoir of these years Simone de Beauvoir indicates the way in which Virginia Woolf raised the important problems for writers like herself, though she felt that in *Mrs Dalloway* these problems were not solved:[114]

Sometimes I admitted that Sartre was right; but on other occasions I reflected that words have to murder reality before they can hold it captive, and that the most important aspect of reality—its here-and-now presence—always eludes them. I was led from this point to ask myself, somewhat anxiously, just what functions words could, or could not perform. This was why I felt so personally affected by Virginia Woolf's reflections on language in general and the novel in particular. Though she emphasised the gulf that yawned between literature and life, she appeared to expect that the discovery of new techniques would allow a narrowing of the gap, and I hoped she might be right. But alas, her latest book, *Mrs Dalloway*, suggested no answer to the problem that she raised. Sartre was of the opinion that there was an initial fallacy here, in the framing of the question itself. He too believed that any account of an event imposes a deceptive pattern upon the truth, an idea which he expounded in *La Nausée* (*Nausea*); even though the narrator resorts to verbal incoherence, and strives to grasp experience raw, in all its random scattered shapelessness, he can produce a mere imitation only, stamped with his own shortcomings. But Sartre thought it idle to deplore this discrepancy between things and words, between the world as it is and artistic creativity; on the contrary, he regarded it as the basic condition of literature, its main *raison d'être*. The writer's achievements are all gained within the limits of this apparent handicap, and instead of longing to abolish it, he ought rather to turn it to good advantage.

The publication of *Orlando* in 1928 was for French critics, as for their English counterparts, an occasion for surveying Virginia Woolf's work to date. With six novels published, the broad lines of her development could perhaps be discerned. One reviewer pointed out that *Orlando* was a greater popular success than her other novels, but that it was too much of a collection of 'anthology pieces' such as the Great Frost scene, excellent in themselves, but not cohering to form a good novel.[115] J.-E. Blanche, in a review which Virginia Woolf described as one of the most intelligent she received for *Orlando*, was disappointed with the novel:[116]

> Why does this rounded, piquant and controlled work leave us less moved and convinced than those that have gone before? Could it be that we do not see in it the real face of one who fills all her novels, essays and critical works with her personality? Virginia Woolf seems to hide herself in rather arty and over-pretty veils which her *aficionados*, hoping for a smile, offer her before she dances. We prefer the naked body and soul as presented in *Mrs Dalloway* rather than these lendings.

Allusions, by this time familiar, were made to Bergson and Proust. J.-J. Mayoux, for example, described the novel as a Bergsonian 'intellectual comedy', but even in this 'simple interlude' he discerned a continuing concern with experiment and renewal.[117] He followed up this review of *Orlando* with a more general survey 'The Novel of Time and Space' (No. 78a). Paul Dottin's survey published at the same time described Virginia Woolf's career to date and the French reception of her work (No. 78b).

In 1931 *Orlando* appeared in a translation by Charles Mauron, a friend of members of the Bloomsbury Group, especially E. M. Forster and Roger Fry. He had published a translation of the central section of *To the Lighthouse* in December 1926, some months before the novel appeared in England. His Preface to the translation of *Orlando* introduced French readers to the Bloomsbury background to the novel. He later translated *Flush* (1935). In 1938 when Virginia Woolf was working on her biography of Roger Fry, he sent her his poem written for Roger Fry 'Esquisses pour le tombeau d'un peintre'. She wrote to say that she admired his poetry, but claimed to understand nothing of his aesthetic theories.

One of the first book-length studies of Virginia Woolf's work appeared in France in 1932, Floris Delattre's *Le Roman psychologique de Virginia Woolf*. An extract from this was published in the previous December. This chapter (No. 96) is a study of the relationship of the writings of Virginia Woolf and those of Bergson, a comparison made previously by a number of writers, but up till that time not fully explored. Delattre continued to write many reviews and articles dealing with Virginia Woolf, and was completing a second book about her at the time of his death.

In his article on the post-war English novel in *Revue de Paris* (in

1932)[118] Desmond MacCarthy remarked that at that time there was a great deal of interest in English literature in France. If an English critic, he said, wanted to compare his personal judgment with another authoritative opinion, the chances were that he would turn to a French critic. As in his English articles and reviews, he is not very enthusiastic about Virginia Woolf's work, seeing an inability to create characters as her main fault.

We mentioned earlier Gabriel Marcel's very high praise for *Mrs Dalloway*. He admired the way in which the interior monologue was subordinated to a complex play of perspective. But he felt that in *The Waves* there was a lack of perspective and an over-employment of the stream-of-consciousness technique (see No. 95). However, when the novel was published in translation in 1937 it was much more favourably received, as we shall see.

The Years was greeted with the same kind of high praise as in England and America. Delattre believed that it marked a decisive phase in her career, and that Virginia Woolf had concentrated the best of her art into it.[119] The reviewer in *Le Mois* likewise saw it as the high point of her achievement: he described it as a lyrically tragic work.[120] But for the *Mercure de France* the overall impression the novel gave was one of melancholy disillusionment, similar to that found in T. S. Eliot's poetry.[121]

Marguerite Yourcenar, herself a novelist of some importance, published her translation of *The Waves* in 1937. This translation, a rather free one,[122] caused a good deal of interest. Both André Rousseaux and René Lalou took the opportunity of comparing it with the translation of Aldous Huxley's *Eyeless in Gaza*. This was published at about the same time with the title *Le Paix des profondeurs* (The Peace of the Depths), a phrase from the end of the novel which suggests a comparison with *The Waves* more readily than the English title. Judging by his harsh criticism of her work it is unlikely that Huxley would have welcomed this comparison (see above pp. 20, 22). Rousseaux[123] points out that both science and literature had abolished the old idea of time as a reel which unwinds—it is more like a volcanic terrain where the past might at any minute explode into the present. The very language which we speak must be changed to take this modification into account, and the interior monologue will become our inevitable mode of expression. The difference between the two novels is that Huxley's characters pose the problems of identity and relationships: those of Virginia Woolf drown in them. As in English reviews of the 1930s, the question of the novel's relationship with social problems was raised. Rousseaux ended his review like this:

> Between 'the waves' and 'the peace of the depths' extends the domain of a vertiginous psychological investigation. But the desire to mix social preoccupations with this would be dangerously futile. The social dreams in which Mrs Virginia Woolf's characters are trapped and with which Mr Huxley's characters struggle depend in the last analysis upon a *unanimisme* which is very close in all respects to that of Jules Romains, and no less adventurous.

Some weeks later René Lalou took up this paragraph in his review of the two novels.[124] He objected to Rousseaux's refusal to discuss a question which had been posed by the writers themselves. Lalou believed that the social preoccupations which Rousseaux wished to keep out of the debate are necessary to every writer who attempts to present his conception of the world. Proust's reflections on time and personality had led him to enclose himself in the circle of Sodom and of Guermantes. It was no criticism of Virginia Woolf and Aldous Huxley that their meditations on the same themes had inspired in them a more poignant sentiment of human unity.

The novelist Edmond Jaloux had greeted the French translation of *Mrs Dalloway* enthusiastically—the novel was 'one of the most moving and the most beautiful which we have had for a long time'.[125] When Clive Bell met him in 1935, the French writer asked him to convey his praise to Virginia Woolf. He regarded her as 'by far the greatest writer of our age'.[126] His obituary note, dated 20 April 1941, but not published until after the war, is a moving recognition from a fellow novelist. In *The Years*, however, he detected signs of exhaustion. The mechanism of the novel was too much in evidence and grated a little—it was too systematic. But the other novels were not only fine in themselves, they were part of a historical movement:[127]

> As if by an instinctive protest against the massive materialisation of strengths and intelligences, the anti-civilising activities of mechanical progress, the sluggishness of comfort, marvellous minds have created a real psychology of the soul, which will be the honour of an epoch otherwise grown ugly. Virginia Woolf in England; Marcel Proust and Jean Giraudoux in France; Rilke and Hugo von Hofmannsthal in Austria, Hans Carossa in Germany, leave us the only hope which we might preserve; faith in the autonomous spontaneous enchantment of our imagination.

THE LATER RECEPTION OF VIRGINIA WOOLF'S WORK

In the years following her death, volumes of Virginia Woolf's essays have been published, the latest being a collection of reviews in which she considered the work of her contemporaries.[128] But many essays and reviews remain unreprinted, as B. J. Kirkpatrick's *Bibliography* shows.[129] (*Collected Essays* is a misnomer for the four volumes published in 1968 and 1969.) In 1953 Leonard Woolf published extracts from Virginia Woolf's Diary entitled *A Writer's Diary*, which was highly praised, one critic describing it as 'a work of the first importance, one of the few works which show us genius communing with itself'.[130] Work based on Virginia Woolf's manuscripts is one of the new directions of modern research, and in recent years a previously unknown piece of writing has been found in the manuscript of *Mrs Dalloway*.[131] Some juvenilia has been published.[132]

There has been a great deal of criticism written since her death, and interest in her life and work has quickened noticeably over the last three or four years, reaching a high point with the publication of her nephew's best-selling biography of her in 1972. Apart from those scattered in various publications, the only letters published so far are those she wrote to Lytton Strachey.[133] However, an edition of her letters is now being prepared.

Virginia Woolf's novels, especially *Mrs Dalloway* and *To the Lighthouse* are now generally regarded as 'classics'. Her works have been approached from all the familiar directions and indirections—'close criticism', imagery and symbolism, psychology, feminism, and so on. We can see the seeds of most of these approaches in the reviews and articles written during her lifetime, but more recent criticism has done much to increase our detailed understanding of her work. For example, Reuben Brower's acute analysis of the technique of *Mrs Dalloway* in terms of its recurrent images and metaphors is much more perceptive than most of the earlier criticisms, sympathetic or otherwise, of Virginia Woolf's form.[134] By setting his discussion in the wider context of Western literature, Erich Auerbach has clarified our idea of Virginia Woolf's approach to representation. He shows the cultural relativity involved in the idea of 'realism', and so undercuts criticism which appeals to 'reality' as an unchanging principle.[135] Such issues as Virginia Woolf's unsatisfactory characterisation, her aesthetic aloofness, and her neglect of moral values are still grounds for censure. But of course these adverse comments have not gone unanswered. Some recent critical works have a well-defined approach, or usefully explore a limited aspect of her work, but others cannot be so easily categorised. And among these figures one of the best recent discussions of Virginia

Woolf, Harvena Richter's *The Inward Voyage*.[136]

There has been a growth of interest in the Bloomsbury Group and in the 'background' to Virginia Woolf's work. (A symptom of this interest is the newly founded *Virginia Woolf Quarterly*, which has the aim of promoting interest in Virginia Woolf and her circle.) There have been many published reminiscences by members of the group, and a number of works dealing with its members which throw incidental light on Virginia Woolf. Bloomsbury is now generally regarded as an important part of English intellectual and social history in the early twentieth century. Alan Bennett draws on this background in his play *Forty Years On*, and he neatly satirises a certain aspect of the Bloomsbury myth:[137]

And then there was Virginia herself elegant and quizzical, those great nostrils quivering and the sunlight playing over her long pale face. She never used cosmetics, except to powder her nose. But then she had her father's nose. . . . Of all the honours that fell upon Virginia's head, none, I think, pleased her more than the *Evening Standard* Award for the Tallest Woman Writer of 1927, an award she took by a neck from Elizabeth Bowen. And rightly, I think, for she was in a very real sense the tallest writer I have ever known. Which is not to say that her stories were tall. They were not, they were short. But she did stand head and shoulders above her contemporaries, and sometimes of course, much more so. Dylan Thomas for instance, a man of great literary stature, only came up to her waist. And sometimes not even to there. If I think of Virginia now it is as she was when I last saw her in the spring of 1938 outside the changing-rooms in the London Library. There she stood, all flushed and hot after a hard day's reading. Impulsively perhaps I went up to her and seized her hand. 'It's Mrs Woolf, isn't it?' 'Is it?' she said and looked at me out of those large lympid eyes 'Is it? I often wonder', and she wandered away.

This is more amusing than Wyndham Lewis's lampoon in *The Roaring Queen*, perhaps because Alan Bennett's satire comes from a love-hate relationship with the material he is dealing with, whereas Lewis's is a straightforward attack.

And here we come to an issue of central importance. A writer's works live if they still affect the hearts and minds of sensitive readers, but they live vividly if they are used, borrowed, stolen or transmuted by subsequent creative writers. By taking what they need from a previous writer they give a new direction to our reading and interpretation. For example, Nathalie Sarraute, writing in 1956, declared:[138]

When the essay 'Conversation and Sub-conversation' appeared Virginia Woolf was forgotten and neglected, Proust and Joyce misunderstood as precursors opening the way to the present novel. I wished to show how the evolution of the novel since the upheaval which these authors had made it undergo in the first quarter of this century, made necessary a revision of the contents and forms of the novel and especially of dialogue.

And in a more recent interview she elaborated on this hint:[139]

Virginia Woolf . . . has always been, with Proust and Joyce, one of the great writers who opened the way to modern literature and the present-day novel. Like Proust and Kafka she contributed to the transformation of novel subject into the modern novel, to that displacement of the centre of gravity of the novel which has passed from character and plot to the novelistic substance itself.

In France, then, Virginia Woolf is seen as part of a continuing tradition of experiment, whereas in Britain since the 1950s there has been a 'reaction against experiment', in novelists such as C. P. Snow and William Cooper, for example. Angus Wilson described the situation in this way:[140]

It is surely the belief that the 'experimental' or 'Bloomsbury' novelists had erred in departing from this sort of seriousness that has more than anything else determined the general trend of post-war English novelists towards a return to the traditional forms. No sharpening of visual image, no increased sensibility, no deeper penetration of the individual consciousness, whether by verbal experiment or by Freudian analysis, could fully atone for the frivolity of ignoring man as a social being, for treating personal relationships and subjective sensations in a social void. This is, of course, an exaggerated and false picture even of the novels of Mrs Woolf, who, because of her very real genius no doubt, has been the Aunt Sally of this criticism. Nevertheless, there is about Chad or Stephen Dedalus or Birkin or Mrs Ramsay, for all the brilliant social observation that surrounds them, a sort of intellectual and emotional separateness from responsible society at large.

His own novels are an attempt to follow the programme outlined later in his article: 'To combine depth with breadth seems to me the principal problem that must preoccupy the contemporary English novelist.' That is, to blend a Victorian solidity of social reference with the individual vision which we associate with Virginia Woolf and other 'experimental' writers. For Wilson, Virginia Woolf's influence on the English novel would hopefully be as a 'leaven' rather than, as in France, as a starting-point for more extreme experiments.

It is interesting to set the remarks of these modern writers alongside those of the creative people who wrote about Virginia Woolf's work when it first appeared, and whose comments we can read among the following extracts.

NOTES

1 A leitmotif accompanying the Wilcoxes in E. M. Forster's *Howards End* (1910).
2 *Reviewing* (1939), 11.
3 *Times Literary Supplement*, 4 November 1939, 641.
4 *Reviewing*, 11.
5 Leonard Woolf, *Downhill All the Way* (1967), 56–7.
Virginia was terribly—even morbidly—sensitive to criticism of any kind and from anyone. Her writing was to her the most serious thing in life, and, as with so many serious writers, her books were to her part of herself and felt to be part of herself somewhat in the same way as a mother often seems all her life to feel that her child remains still part of herself . . . the publication of a book meant something very like torture to her.
6 *A Writer's Diary*, 79.
7 Richard Kennedy, *A Boy at the Hogarth Press* (1972).
8 *Downhill All the Way*, 76.
9 Ibid., 145–7.
10 Leonard Woolf, *Beginning Again* (1964), 87.
11 See C. G. Heilbrun, *The Garnett Family* (1961), 106.
12 Jean Thomas, letter to Violet Dickinson, 14 September 1913, quoted in Quentin Bell, *Virginia Woolf*, II (1972), 16a.
13 *Beginning Again*, 87.
14 *Saturday Review*, 19 June 1915, Supplement iv.
15 *New York Times*, 13 June 1920, 308.
16 *Sunday Times*, 4 April 1915, 5.
17 Virginia Woolf and Lytton Strachey, *Letters*, ed. Leonard Woolf and James Strachey (1956), 20.
18 *A Writer's Diary*, 24.
19 *Country Life*, 24 April 1915, 564.
20 Desmond MacCarthy published a translation of *Mort de quelqu'un* (*The Death of a Nobody*) in 1914.
21 *Beginning Again*, 236:
I do not know how many people we circularised, but we published in July and by the end of the month we had practically sold out the edition for we had sold 124 copies. (The total number finally sold was 134.) I still have a list of the 87 people who bought the 134 copies and all but five or six of them were friends or acquaintances.
22 Lytton Strachey to Leonard Woolf, 17 July 1917, quoted in Bell, *Virginia Woolf*, II, 43n.

23 Virginia Woolf to Clive Bell, 24 July 1917, quoted in Bell, *Virginia Woolf*, I, 212.
24 Clive Bell, *Pot Boilers* (1918), 11.
25 Katherine Mansfield to Virginia Woolf, early May 1918, in *The Letters of Katherine Mansfield*, ed. J. Middleton Murry, I, 162–3.
26 Katherine Mansfield to Virginia Woolf, 29 May 1918, ibid., 183.
27 Katherine Mansfield to Virginia Woolf, April 1919, ibid., 227.
28 *Beginning Again*, 241:

In the previous week a review of *Kew Gardens* had appeared in the Literary Supplement giving it tremendous praise. When we opened the front door of Hogarth House, we found the hall covered with envelopes and post-cards containing orders from booksellers all over the country. It was impossible for us to start printing enough copies to meet these orders, so we went to a printer, Richard Madley, and got him to print a second edition of 500 copies, which cost us £8 9s 6d. It was sold out by the end of 1920 and we did not reprint.

See also *A Writer's Diary*, 15.
29 Roger Fry to Marie Mauron, 31 December 1919, in *Letters of Roger Fry*, ed. Denys Sutton (1972), II, 477.
30 *A Writer's Diary*, 19–20.
31 Ibid., 19. Virginia Woolf added: 'The people whose judgment I respect won't be so enthusiastic as he is, but they'll come out decidedly on that side, I think.'
32 Virginia Woolf to Lytton Strachey, 28 October 1919, in *Letters*, 83–4.
33 Lytton Strachey to Philippa Strachey, 13 November 1919, and to Lady Ottoline Morrell, 15 November 1919, quoted in Michael Holroyd, *Lytton Strachey*, II (1968), 373.
34 *A Writer's Diary*, 20.
35 Ibid., 20–1.
36 Ibid., 21.
37 Ibid., 24.
38 At this time Ford still called himself Ford Madox Hueffer.
39 *London Mercury*, January 1920, 339–40.
40 *A Writer's Diary*, 193: 'I can take liberties with the representational form which I could not dare when I wrote *Night and Day*—a book that taught me much, bad though it may be.'
41 Miss B. J. Kirkpatrick has kindly confirmed this date, which will appear in the new (third) edition of her *Bibliography*.
42 *A Writer's Diary*, 31.
43 Ibid., 32.
44 Ibid., 33.
45 *British Weekly*, 23 April 1921. Virginia Woolf recorded the gist of this in *A Writer's Diary*, 34.
46 'And Eliot astounded me by praising *Monday or Tuesday*! This really de-

lighted me. He picked out the String Quartet, especially the end of it. "Very good" he said, and meant it, I think. The Unwritten Novel he thought not successful; Haunted House "extremely interesting."' (From the Berg manuscript of her Diary, 7 June 1921, quoted in Bell, *Virginia Woolf*, II, 78n.)

47 *A Writer's Diary*, 44.
48 'The publisher of her first two novels was her own half-brother, Gerald Duckworth, a kindly, uncensorious man who had considerable affection for Virginia. His reader, Edward Garnett, who had a great reputation for spotting masterpieces by unknown authors, wrote an enthusiastic report on *The Voyage Out* when it was submitted to Duckworth. Yet the idea of having to send her next book to the mild Gerald and the enthusiastic Edward filled her with horror and misery.' *Downhill All the Way*, 68.
49 *A Writer's Diary*, 51.
50 Ibid., 52.
51 Ibid., 54.
52 Ibid.
53 T. S. Eliot to Virginia Woolf, 4 December 1922 (unpublished letter in Sussex University collection).
54 Siegfried Sassoon to Virginia Woolf, May ?1923 (in Sussex University collection).
55 *A Writer's Diary*, 57.
56 For example, his faint praise of *The Common Reader* greatly depressed her (*A Writer's Diary*, 77).
57 Quentin Bell's description in *Virginia Woolf*, II, 105.
58 See Irving Kreutz, 'Mr Bennett and Mrs Woolf', *Modern Fiction Studies*, VIII (Summer 1962), 103–15, and Samuel Hynes, 'The Whole Contention Between Mr Bennett and Mrs Woolf', *Novel* (Fall 1967).
59 *Star*, 4 May 1925, 4.
60 *A Writer's Diary*, Preface, viii.
61 Ibid., 78.
62 *Virginia Woolf*, II, 106–7.
63 *Western Mail* (Cardiff), 14 May 1925.
64 *Scotsman* (Edinburgh), 14 May 1925, 2.
65 *Christian Science Monitor*, 3 June 1925, 8.
66 Roger Fry to Marie Mauron, 21 December 1927, in *Letters*, 598.
67 *A Writer's Diary*, 107.
68 Ottoline Morrell to Virginia Woolf, 14 May 1927 (unpublished letter in Sussex University collection).
69 Bell, *Virginia Woolf*, II, 128.
70 Ibid., 128–9.
71 Lytton Strachey to Roger Senhouse, 11 May 1927, in M. Holroyd, *Lytton Strachey*, II, 531.
72 F. R. Leavis, *Mass Civilisation and Minority Culture* (1930), 25–6.

73 Rupert Hart-Davis, *Hugh Walpole* (1952), 279.
74 Ibid., 302–3.
75 *Bookman* (New York), December 1928, 375.
76 Aldous Huxley to Robert Nichols, 17 February 1930, in *The Letters of Aldous Huxley*, ed. Grover Smith (1969), 330.
77 *A Writer's Diary*, 126.
78 Ibid., 128.
79 *Downhill All the Way*, 143.
80 *New York Herald Tribune*, 21 October 1928, XI, 1 and 6.
81 'On a Certain New Book', *Morning Post*, 25 October 1928, 10.
82 Aldous Huxley to D. H. Lawrence, 12 December 1928, in *The Letters of Aldous Huxley*, 305.
83 *A Writer's Diary*, 136.
84 Ibid., 148.
85 William Plomer to Leonard Woolf, 1 July 1930 (unpublished letter in Sussex University collection).
86 *A Writer's Diary*, 174.
87 Ibid., 175.
88 Ibid.
89 *Saturday Review*, 10 October 1931, 462.
90 *A Writer's Diary*, 176.
91 William Plomer to Leonard Woolf, 5 December 1930 (unpublished letter in Sussex University collection).
92 *Quarterly Review*, April 1932, 216–41.
93 *Times Literary Supplement*, 20 October 1932, 755.
94 *Times Literary Supplement*, 5 October 1933, 667.
95 *Listener*, 11 October 1933, Supplement xi.
96 Noel Coward to Virginia Woolf, 7 November 1933 (unpublished letter in Sussex University collection).
97 *The Dog Beneath the Skin* (1935), 1968, 155.
98 *The Roaring Queen* (1973), 96.
99 *A Writer's Diary*, 279.
100 I think that in 1932, beginning *The Years*, at the back of her mind was the desire or determination to prove these critics wrong. Leonard Woolf, *The Journey Not the Arrival Matters* (1969), 41.
101 'Virginia Woolf', *English Journal* (New York) October 1937, 603–12.
102 *Evening Standard*, 19 March 1937, 7.
103 Bell, *Virginia Woolf*, II, 205.
104 *Spectator*, 7 October 1938, 578.
105 E. M. Forster, *Virginia Woolf* (1942), 16.
106 Ibid., 27–8.
107 Abel Chevally, *Le Roman anglais de notre temps* (1921).
108 M. Loge, 'Quelque romanciers contemporaines', *Revue Politique et Littéraire*, 21 November 1925, 753–6.

109 R. Lalou, *Panorama de la littérature anglaise contemporaine* (1926), 237–8.
110 See Bell, *Virginia Woolf*, II, 106–7.
111 *Revue de la Quinzaine*, 15 September 1927, 737.
112 From 'Modern Novels', *Times Literary Supplement*, 10 April 1919, 189–90 reprinted as 'Modern Fiction', in *The Common Reader.*
113 *Nouvelle Revue Française*, July 1929, 129–31.
114 Simone de Beauvoir, *The Prime of Life*, translated by Peter Green from *La Force de l'age* (1960), Penguin ed., 1965, 40.
115 Louis Gillet, 'L'Orlando de Mme Virginia Woolf', *Revue de Deux Mondes*, September 1929, 218–30.
116 Jacques-Émile Blanche, 'Un nouveau roman de Virginia Woolf', *Les Nouvelles Littéraires*, 19 January 1929, 9.
117 J.-J. Mayoux, 'A propos d'Orlando de Virginia Woolf', *Europe*, 15 January 1930, 117–22.
118 Desmond MacCarthy, 'Le Roman anglais d'après-guerre', *Revue de Paris*, 1932, 129–52.
119 F. Delattre, 'Le Nouveau Roman de Virginia Woolf', *Études Anglaises*, July 1937, 289–96.
120 *Mois*, July 1937, 218.
121 *Mercure de France*, 15 July 1937, 423.
122 Delattre praised the translation, but pointed out a number of loose and faulty translations in his notice in *Études Anglaises*, April–June 1938, 201–2.
123 André Rousseaux, 'Plongeurs dans le temps perdu (Virginia Woolf, Aldous Huxley)', *Le Figaro*, 28 August 1937, reprinted in *Littérature du vingtième siècle*, vol. 1 (1938).
124 R. Lalou, 'Le sentiment de l'unité chez Virginia Woolf et Aldous Huxley' *Europe*, October 1937, 266–72.
125 Edmond Jaloux, 'Mrs Dalloway' in *Au Pays du roman* (1931) 185–98.
126 Clive Bell to Virginia Woolf, unpublished letter, 12 December 1935 (in Sussex University collection).
127 Edmond Jaloux, 'Mort de Virginia Woolf' dated 20 April 1941, in *D'Eschyle à Giraudoux* (1946), 253–9.
128 *Contemporary Writers*, ed. Jean Guiguet (1965).
129 *A Bibliography of Virginia Woolf* (1957) revised edition, 1967. Miss Kirkpatrick is preparing a new edition.
130 *Twentieth Century*, December 1953, 485. Review by David Daiches.
131 *Nurse Lugton's Golden Thimble* was discovered by Wallace Hildrick in the MS. of *Mrs Dalloway*. Two other short stories, *Ancestors* and *The Introduction*, were also published for the first time in 1973 in *Mrs Dalloway's Party* (ed. Stella McNichol).
132 *A Cockney's Farming Experiences*, edited by Suzanne Henig (1972).
133 Virginia Woolf and Lytton Strachey, *Letters*, ed. Leonard Woolf and James Strachey (1956).
134 *The Fields of Light* (1951).

135 *Mimesis* (1946) trans. Willard Trask, 1953.
136 Harvena Richter, *Virginia Woolf, The Inward Voyage*, 1970.
137 Alan Bennett, *Forty Years On* (1969), 57–8.
138 Nathalie Sarraute, *L'Ère du soupçon* (1956), Preface 12.
139 Interview with Nathalie Sarraute, 'Virginia Woolf ou la visionaire du "Maintenant" ', *Les Lettres français*, 29 July–5 July 1961, 1 and 3.
140 Angus Wilson, 'Diversity and depth', *Times Literary Supplement*, 15 August 1958.

Note on the Text

Original texts have been followed apart from obvious typographical errors. Omissions are of three major kinds: lengthy quotations from Virginia Woolf's works, whenever they are not essential to the point the writer is making, have been replaced by page references (to the Uniform Edition, published by the Hogarth Press). Plot summaries, and in the case of Virginia's non-fictional writings, précis of her argument, have often been omitted. Occasionally lengthy articles have been quoted only in part. All omissions are clearly marked.

Numbered footnotes are the addition of the present editors. Original footnotes are marked by asterisks and daggers.

THE VOYAGE OUT

26 March 1915

1. Unsigned review, *Times Literary Supplement*

1 April 1915, 110

Mr. Richard Dalloway remarks in *The Voyage Out* by Virginia Woolf, that Jane Austen is 'incomparably the greatest female writer we possess,' because 'she does not attempt to write like a man. Every other woman does; on that account I don't read 'em.' Mr. Dalloway would certainly have to except this novel, were he able to read it, from that but slightly too sweeping 'every other' of his; not that the influence of his favourite is very apparent, but because—those who share his dislike of imitation men's books may be reassured—never was a book more feminine, more recklessly feminine. It may be labelled clever and shrewd, mocking, suggestive, subtle, 'modern', but these terms do not convey the spirit of it—which essentially is feminine. That quality is, of course, indescribable; but it must not, in this case, be taken to suggest a spirit shallow and weak or one fanatically strong; it must not be supposed that the book is sentimental or cynical, frivolous or hard, as individual experience or prejudice may lead one hastily to assume; it stands here for tolerance and that feminine sort of strength (or inertia) that accepts what is, whether beautiful or ugly; for cruelty, perhaps, wilfulness certainly, and a quivering eagerness about life, admirably dissembled behind an air of detachment. The wit, too, is feminine with its alert scampering from one point to another and the space between taken for granted; one smiles and grows grave and chuckles just as one would in the company of the picturesque aunt who is not the chief personage, but who somehow dominates the whole tragic comedy. And most feminine are the shocks that are plentifully administered; most of them are just contrariness and so one laughs, but some come from one or another of those modern obsessions by notions that most of us are too old-fashioned to blurt out in mixed company, and at these we duly catch our breaths—which is really to say that the shocks are successful.

The story of the late development of a young woman who has been too long sheltered from life is nearly always sentimental or brutal, but it is here candidly told. Rachel Vinrace, the daughter of a shipowner, who remains quite ignorant of the world at twenty-four, and has only her music to soothe the disquiet that such sheltering as she has had makes inevitable, goes on a voyage to South America in one of her father's ships, and in the few months that she spends in a little port where there is a queer English colony, she comes to some understanding of the practical meaning of life. The people among whom she passes are brilliantly drawn—particularly that aunt, who is so real and so baffling—the manners are so amusingly satirized, and nature, over all, is so vividly described, that one follows Rachel's career, not quite sure of the meaning of it all, but hoping confidently that some design will finally appear. Suddenly a foreboding of some tragic ending makes one fear; a catastrophe, one feels, cannot now be significant; it can be no more than an evasion of the difficulties of the girl's life. And it *is* illogical, this sudden tragedy, but it is made almost to seem like the illogic of life; it is so intense that one is desolated by a sense of the futility of life and forgets the failure of design.

2. Unsigned review, *Observer*

4 April 1915, 3

This is just the story of a voyage, and some rather unusual people, interspersed with some highly usual ones, who spent some time shut up together. Two of them agree to love each other, and one of the two died. That is all, in vaguest outline; but the filling in is done with something startlingly like genius. That is not a word to use inadvisedly, but there is something greater than talent that colours the cleverness of this book. Its perpetual effort to say the real thing and not the expected thing, its humour and its sense of irony, the occasional poignancy of its emotions, its profound originality—well, one does not wish to lose the critical faculty over any book, and its hold may be a personal and subjective matter, but among ordinary novels it is a wild swan among good grey geese to one reviewer, to whom its author's name is entirely new and unknown.

3. Unsigned review, *Morning Post*

5 April 1915, 2

This reviewer, like a number of others (e.g. Nos 1, 5, 8), criticised the fragmentary nature of *The Voyage Out*. He praised the final section (see Nos 1, 5, 6) but felt it to be 'disconnected' from the rest of the novel (see Introduction, p. 8).

The Voyage Out is a bewildering kind of book. We get confused among a mass of people, and worried by all the talk that goes on whirling around us. As regards Miss Woolf's characters, she needlessly complicates matters by first introducing them by their surnames and suddenly referring to them by their Christian names only. The book begins on board ship, where most of the people are out of their usual element, and relationships and conversation are queer and strained. They are landed at Santa Marina, and we are brought into contact with numerous people staying in the hotel. We get to know them in a disjointed sort of way, and their conversation is as unsatisfactory as the conversation of casual acquaintances meeting in that sort of way usually is. It is certainly true to life, but it is an unsatisfactory way of living, and we do not get to know enough of the people and their real selves to be interested in them. The tragedy of the girl's illness and death is vividly and artistically told, but even that incident seems disconnected and a part of a whole that is not there. There is some good writing in the book, though nothing of exceptional merit.

4. E. M. Forster, review, *Daily News and Leader*

8 April 1915, 7

E. M. Forster (1879–1970). Novelist and essayist. A friend of Virginia Woolf and peripheral member of the Bloomsbury Group. Virginia Woolf always took careful note of his criticisms.

In this review, headed 'A New Novelist', Forster made a point which was to be the keynote of his later assessments of her work: that her portrayal of moments of experience was admirable, but that her greatest weakness was her characterisation. For his later views see Nos 14, 54.

One of the men in Mrs Woolf's book complains: 'Of course, we're always writing about women—abusing them, or jeering at them or worshipping them; but it's never come from women themselves. I believe we still don't know in the least how they live, or what they feel, or what they do precisely. . . . They won't tell you. Either they're afraid, or they've got a way of treating men.' And perhaps the first comment to make on *The Voyage Out* is that it is absolutely unafraid, and that its courage springs, not from naiveté, but from education. Few women-writers are educated. A gentleman ought not to say such a thing, but it is, unfortunately, true. Our Queens of the Pen are learned, sensitive, thoughtful even, but they are uneducated, they have never admitted the brain to the heart, much less let it roam over the body. They live in pieces, and their work, when it does live, lives similarly, devoid of all unity save what is imposed by a plot. Here at last is a book which attains unity as surely as *Wuthering Heights*, though by a different path, a book which, while written by a woman and presumably from a woman's point of view, soars straight out of local questionings into the intellectual day. The curious male may pick up a few scraps, but if wise he will lift his eyes to where there is neither marrying nor giving in marriage, to the mountains and forests and sea that circumscribe the characters, and to the final darkness that blots them out. After all, he will not have learnt how women live, any more than he has learnt from Shakespeare how men perform that process; he will only have lived more intensely himself, that is to say, will have encountered literature.

Mrs Woolf's success is more remarkable since there is one serious defect in her equipment; her chief characters are not vivid. There is nothing false in them, but when she ceases to touch them they cease, they do not stroll out of their sentences, and even develop a tendency to merge shadowlike. Rachel and her aunt Helen are one example of this. Hewet and his friend Hirst another. The story opens with Helen. Helen, though an accomplished Bohemian, is discovered in tears close to Cleopatra's Needle—she is off for a holiday to South America, but does not like leaving the children. Her husband, a Pindaric scholar, beats the air with a stick until she has finished and can gain the boat, where Rachel, a pale idle girl of twenty-four, awaits them. Helen is bored at first. But at Lisbon they are joined by a kindly politician—he, like most of the minor characters, is sketched with fine foolery and malice—and he, by kissing Rachel, wakes her up. When he has disembarked, she expounds to her aunt, they become friends, and when the Voyage Out, so far as it is by water, has ended, she goes to spend the winter with Helen at Santa Marina. Below their villa in the English hotel dwell two young Cambridge intellectuals, Hewet and Hirst. The pairs become acquainted, and for a time there is a curious darkness, while one of the men—we know not which—and one of the women—we known not which—are nearing each other. When the darkness clears, Helen is definitely the confidante, Hirst the onlooker, and Hewet and Rachel have, in the recesses of a primaeval forest, become engaged to be married. The Villa acquiesces, the Hotel smirks, and, until the final note, we expect wedding bells.

Life as an Adventure

If the above criticism is correct, if Mrs Woolf does not 'do' her four main characters very vividly, and is apt to let them all become clever together, and differ only by their opinions, then on what does her success depend? Some readers—those who demand the milk of human kindness, even in its tinned form—will say that she has not succeeded; but the bigness of her achievement should impress anyone weaned from baby food. She believes in adventure—here is the main point—believes in it passionately, and knows that it can only be undertaken alone. Human relations are no substitute for adventure, because when real they are uncomfortable, and when comfortable they must be unreal. It is for a voyage into solitude that man was created, and Rachel, Helen, Hewet, Hirst, all learn this lesson, which is exquisitely reinforced by the setting of tropical scenery—the soul, like the body, voyages at her own risk. 'There must be a reason,' sighs nice old Mrs Thornbury, after the catastrophe. 'It can't only be an accident. For if it was an accident—it need never have happened.' Primaeval thunderstorms answer Mrs Thornbury. There is no reason. Why should an adventure terminate that way rather than this, since its essence is fearless motion? 'It's life that matters,' writes a novelist of a very different type; 'the process of discovering, the everlasting and perpetual process, not the discovery itself at all.' Mrs Woolf's vision may be inferior to Dostoieffsky's—but she sees as clearly as he where efficiency ends and creation begins, and even more clearly that our supreme choice lies not between body and soul, but between immobility and motion. In her pages, body v. soul—that dreary medieval tug-of-war—does not find any place. It is as if the rope has broken, leaving pagans sprawling on one side and clergymen on the other, while overhead 'long-tailed birds chattered and screamed and crossed from wood to wood, with golden eyes in their plumage.'

Life as a Jest

It is tempting to analyse the closing chapters, which have an atmosphere unknown in English literature—the atmosphere of Jules Romains' *Mort de Quelqu'un.*[1] But a word must be said about the comedy: the book is extremely amusing. The writer has a nice taste in old gentlemen, for instance. They talk like this:

[Quotes p. 10 ' "Jenkinson of Cats" ' to ' "arches on one's pigsties." ']

In the humour there is something of Peacock. When the ball at the Santa Marina Hotel turns into a bacchanal, and the aforesaid Mr Pepper executes a pointed step that he has derived from figure skating, there is

[1] Published in 1911. It was translated by Desmond MacCarthy and Sydney Waterlow with the title *The Death of a Nobody* (1914) (see Introduction p. 9).

an effect of cumulative drollery that recalls the catastrophe in *Nightmare Abbey*, when Mr Toobad fell into the moat. The writer can sweep together masses of characters for our amusement, then sweep them away; her comedy does not counteract her tragedy and at the close enhances it, for we see that the Hotel and the Villa will soon be dancing and gossiping just as before, that existence will continue the same, exactly the same, for everyone, for everyone except the reader; he, more fortunate than the actors, is established in the possession of beauty.

5. Gerald Gould, review, *New Statesman*

10 April 1915, 18–19

Gerald Gould (1885–1936). Poet and journalist. Chief among his poetical works are *Lyrics* (1906), *The Happy Tree* (1919) and *Collected Poems* (1929). His paradoxical idea of the lifelike unreality of Virginia Woolf's characters raises many problems and indicates how uncertain the notion of 'reality' can be in literary discussion (see Introduction, p. 8). Gould later reviewed *Jacob's Room* (No. 31).

The world of *The Voyage Out* is a quite extraordinary world. The people are unreal, not in the sense that such people don't exist—they do—but in the sense that they give one all the impression of unreality when one meets them in life. They are sophisticated and introspective, they are learned and witty, and they are abundantly interested in themselves. Mrs Woolf's account of them is very long and very clever—so long that even the cleverness cannot always hold the attention. We are told exactly what people look like, and what they see, and what they say—all in a series of detached assertions, many of them brilliant in themselves, but somehow none of them knit into the unity of narrative with the others. The girl who occupies, so to say, the centre of the stage has reached the age of twenty-four, and become an excellent pianist without having gathered the alphabet of the relations between the sexes. She attributes this largely to the literature on which she has been brought up, and lays special stress on Cowper's Letters. When she is, most unconvincingly, kissed by a sentimental member of Parliament, she likes it and doesn't know why. At Santa Marina, a picturesque South American resort of jaded European intellectuals, she has a love affair with a young man who writes. When she asks him, 'Are you a good writer?' he replies, 'Yes, I'm not first-rate, of course; I'm good second-rate; about as good as Thackeray, I should say.' His intellectual friend explains himself to be 'one of the three most distinguished men in England'. Nor are these jokes meant to expose the people concerned as fools, for when Mrs Woolf wants to make jokes she makes good ones. It simply is that all the characters in her book are, in a way, mad; so that when the girl at the end dies, and the characters suddenly develop reality and humanity, one feels they are sane too late. But these concluding scenes show how powerful a novel Mrs Woolf could write if she chose, and they make it all the more a pity that she should have concentrated such gifts on being, for so many pages, merely caustic. That she *can* be caustic is well illustrated by the musings of the sentimental M.P.'s wife:

> 'I often wonder,' Clarissa mused in bed, over the little white volume of Pascal which went with her everywhere, 'whether it is really good for a woman to live with a man who is morally her superior, as Richard is mine. It makes one so dependent. I suppose I feel for him what my mother and women of her generation felt for Christ. It just shows that one can't do without *something*.'

There is a great deal as good as that—any amount of observation and incisive description, of satire and wit. But the humanity which ought to pull the whole together and make an excellent book of it should surely not have been delayed till the end.

6. A. N. M., review, *Manchester Guardian*

15 April 1915, 4

The initials A.N.M. are those of Allan Monkhouse, novelist and playwright, who was associated with the *Manchester Guardian* for many years. His praise of Virginia Woolf's 'penetration into certain modes of consciousness' was significant. Like many reviewers he admired the final chapters of the novel (see Nos 1, 3, 5, 11) and his final remark epitomises the overall reception of *The Voyage Out*: 'there is not merely promise, but accomplishment.'

This is a strong and unconventional novel of a design so simple that we can imagine Mr Henry James asking, as he did of the younger novelists generally, why a subject should be lacking. Rachel Vinrace is a girl who has been hedged by conventions, is launched into a world of people who think and speak freely, and expands fearlessly among them. She loves and dies, and her brief career is half disillusion, for she has little of the easy joys of youth. Brought up in 'sheltered gardens', 'her mind was in the state of an intelligent man's in the reign of Queen Elizabeth', and we are shown something of her education under the influence of her friends with their floods of talk and recommendations of Ibsen, Gibbon, and the rest. She has the faculty, which does not belong only to youth, of finding strangeness even in the world of familiar things, and the interest and success of this book is the penetration into certain modes of consciousness. The people are not lovable, they have not a common fund of geniality, but, though the talk may sometimes seem too consciously eccentric, they are not content with facts and habits and exteriors. They do their best to give ideas their place in the world, and most of those in this inner circle are only too ready to flout manners. Even the conversation that is reported with a satirical intention is clever, and the manner in which the able politician translates Rachel's gropings into a neat formula is good comedy. But sometimes the characters talk, or think, like lotus-eaters, and sometimes they suggest a 'Dodo' of more serious intent than Mr Benson's; their recklessness does represent some effort for freedom, some attempt to get at the essences, and not just a playing with fire. The scene shifts from shipboard to Spanish America, and there is some very good description in tune with character or circumstance. It may be a sleeping hotel or a spacious landscape, but it is related; it is not guide-book work.

Perhaps some readers will not be without the sense of redundancy, of explanation that is not always penetration, and even of a certain insolence of withdrawal from a world condemned as ponderous or meaningless. But beauty and significance come with Rachel's illness and death, and these modern lovers are justified in the depth and in the exaltation of their emotions. The phases of illness and delirium are marked with delicacy and imagination, and the changes in the man's mood show insight and sympathy. 'It seemed to him as he looked back that their happiness had never been so great as his pain was now,' and again, 'He was alone with Rachel, and a faint reflection of the sense of relief that they used to feel when they were left alone possessed him'. It is good to read, too, of a 'little elderly lady . . . her eyes lighting up with zeal as she imagined herself a young man in an aeroplane'—'If I was a young fellow,' she said, 'I should certainly qualify.' And, among a thousand other things, there is St. John's jaunty manner, 'which was always irritating because it made the person he talked to appear unduly clumsy and in earnest'. A writer with such perceptions should be capable of great things. There is character in the book—Helen, Rachel's friend, is good if not, perhaps, a full success,—but it is difficult to give character in terms of conversation. And the events or definite projections of persons are so admirably done that we want more of them; nothing could be better in its way than the two doctors. If this be a first novel, as we believe it is, it is a very remarkable one; there is not merely promise, but accomplishment.

7. Unsigned review, *Athenaeum*

1 May 1915, 401

There is some good work in *The Voyage Out* not to mention erudition; the favourite reading of the ship's steward was Huxley, Herbert Spencer, and Henry George, while he turned to Emerson and Mr Hardy for relaxation. The central idea of gathering a small company into the isolated world of a passenger ship and later in a South American island and leaving them to explore each other's natures is full of possibilities. The author has sketched her characters with a few deft strokes, but the incidents are too loosely put together, and there is a great deal of superfluous material. The language is not always grammatical, and sometimes forcible to the verge of coarseness, but there is a considerable amount of shrewd observation and clever cynicism. The pathos of the heroine's death is the more poignant for the restraint with which it is treated, and such egotism as that of the young man who says of his novel-writing: 'I'm good second rate; about as good as Thackeray I should say', is delightful in its frankness.

8. Unsigned review, *Nation*

1 May 1915, 156

This review was one of the many (e.g. Nos 3, 5, 9) which criticised the form of *The Voyage Out*, but the psychological insight in the novel is emphasised and praised (see also No. 6).

Why is it that people will read about anything rather than about themselves? Is it sheer modesty, or moral cowardice, or a method of escape, or a pathetic confidence in something they believe beyond their escape, or what? If they would only realize that their own psychology is far more romantic, mysterious, unknown, exciting, and potentially emotional than the adventures, heroisms and melodramas with which they are fed! *The Voyage Out*, for instance, is an analysis and, in parts, a powerful and significant one, of the personalities of some English visitors in a South American hotel. It is hardly a work of art, partly because of its form, partly because it is too passionately intent upon vivisection. It falls, itself, into the snare of talking about characters, whose loquacious introspectiveness about their natures and emotions it is its purpose to satirize. For all that, its conscientious and acute methods of dissection are full of interest. It has the mark of a very promising first novel. If so, Mrs Woolf has every incentive to write another. But will it have many readers? That lies between Mrs Woolf's natural artistic gifts and the system which discourages them.

9. W. H. Hudson, a sharp criticism

1915

From a letter to Edward Garnett, 12 June 1915, in *Letters from W. H. Hudson to Edward Garnett* (1925), 147–8.

W. H. Hudson (1841–1922). Novelist and naturalist.

Edward Garnett, Duckworth's reader, was very enthusiastic about this first novel, and could not believe that Hudson was altogether sincere in his harsh criticism, as this warning in his Introduction indicates: 'But the reader must however guard himself from taking all Hudson's sharp criticisms *au pied de la lettre*. A number of them such as that on *The Voyage Out* were rejoinders to some encomiums of mine and were rapier thrusts at my ribs' (p. 10).

Before Mrs Woolf's book vanishes altogether from my memory I must tell you just what I think about it. . . . It has good things in it. The trouble is that the framework is so clumsily constructed. Here are a lot of people put on a ship and when it gets to its destination they find themselves mixed up with a lot more at a hotel—all English people of one class (that of the author) all thinking, talking, and acting exactly like the people one meets every day in every London drawing-room. All their talk, and God knows there's a lot of it—and all they think and do has no relation to the environment—the place they are supposed to be in which only differs from an English background in having a sky of Reckett blue. Somewhere in S. America it is supposed to be and once or twice 'natives' are mentioned. The scene might just as well have been in some hotel on the south coast of England. There are about twenty characters, men and women, but there is not one real man. She is more successful with her own sex. All types, more or less familiar especially Helen—the author's portrait of herself or what she would like to be. But Helen is in some ways a failure. Where she succeeds best is in drawing a kind of woman that interests her and that she has really observed—the woman with an eager shallow mind, intensely emotional, and with a strain of hysteria in her. There are three, Mrs Dalloway is the best, next is Evelyn Murgatroid and last, Rachel. On Rachel she has spent most care and thought and for this reason perhaps is less successful. She cannot finish the portrait, and so without rhyme or reason takes this, the youngest and healthiest of the whole crowd, and puts her to death. A rather brutal way of bringing the work to an end. I mean from an artistic point of view.

10. From an unsigned review, *Spectator*

10 July 1915, 54–5

The reviewer was 'Mr James', an unidentified regular contributor to the *Spectator* between 1912 and 1915.

Mrs Woolf's book, *The Voyage Out*, is that rarest of things a novel of serious artistic value. Some of its readers may find it irritating or even boring at moments; but none of them is likely to find it unimportant. A few will even be enthusiastic, and will almost be inclined to hail the author as a genius and the story as a classic. Before trying to show what are the merits of the book it will be well to begin by giving some idea of its character. In the first place, it is a novel of modern life: all of its characters are contemporary English people of the upper-middle classes. Next, as to the plot, if it can be so described.

[There follows a summary of the plot.]

. . . It will be gathered that it is not in any thrilling plot or in any dramatic climax of events that we must expect to find the book's value. We must look in other directions. First, it must be said that the whole story has an almost Tolstoyan appearance of reality. The psychology, though it never opens the deepest recesses of the mind, creates all the illusion of real life. Every one seems solid, every one seems to have an independent character and a collection of past experiences—to have a separate existence, in fact, outside the pages of the book. Even the final catastrophe, which from the purely artistic point of view might be held to overbalance the work emotionally, may be justified on the ground of its overwhelming reality. How often in real life does a long string of trivialities give place without a moment's warning to the most tremendous issues; and how often does an apparently intentional *crescendo* of interest collapse suddenly into pointlessness. But Mrs Woolf is by no means a mere bleak realist. One of her greatest gifts is satirical, and this side of her work makes it hard to refrain from a comparison with Jane Austen. The visitors at the hotel, each of them a distinct portrait, mockingly though sympathetically painted, form an astonishingly brilliant group. It is unfair to isolate scraps from such a picture, but this description of afternoon tea on the lawn outside the hotel will give an inkling of Mrs Woolf's gifts in this direction:

[Quotes pp. 317–18 'The tea-party included' to 'sees the sky above.']

Not only does Mrs Woolf possess a keen intellect, but she has imagination as well of a strange and individual sort. Her pages are filled with delightful and unexpected comparisons and brilliantly coloured descriptions. An instance of this aspect of her writing deserves to be set beside the other:

[Quotes p. 164 'A great encampment' to 'of the million tassels.']

Above all, perhaps, Mrs Woolf is a consummate artist in writing. The purity of her style and the certainty of her taste carry her through every difficulty, and enable her to describe with equal directness the mysterious depths of a tropical jungle and a gentleman cutting his toe-nails. She is never at a loss for a word, and she never overweights herself with too many. She can be simple, elaborate, romantic, or prosaic at her will. With such a weapon at her command, and with such an intelligence to wield it, it is small wonder that Mrs Woolf has made of *The Voyage Out* a novel which deserves to be read.

11. Lytton Strachey on the unvictorian aspect of *The Voyage Out*

1916

From a letter to Virginia Woolf, 25 February 1916, in *Letters*, ed. L. Woolf and J. Strachey (1956), 55–6.

Lytton Strachey (1879–1932). Biographer. A close friend of Virginia Woolf and central figure in Bloomsbury. His irreverent biographies were popular and widely imitated.

Two years after this letter Strachey published his satirical account of the lives of four famous Victorians, *Eminent Victorians* and so it is no surprise that he admired the satirical, unvictorian element in *The Voyage Out*. A number of critics have pointed out the similarity between Strachey and St John Hirst (see Introduction p. 8). For his comments on *Jacob's Room* see No. 24.

The Voyage Out—! You know how I adore that book. I read it with breathless pleasure, the minute it came out—a special messenger came running out with it from Bickers. I don't think I ever enjoyed the reading of a book so much. And I was surprised by it. I had naturally expected wit and exquisiteness—what people call 'brilliance', but it's a wretched word—but what amazed me was to find such a wonderful solidity as well! Something Tolstoyan, I thought—especially that last account of the illness, which really—well!—And then the people were *not* mere satirical silhouettes, but solid too, with other sides to them: Shakespeare wouldn't have been ashamed of some of them, I thought. I love, too, the feeling reigning throughout—perhaps the most important part of any book—the secular sense of it all—18th century in its absence of folly, but with colour and amusement of modern life as well. Oh, it's very, very unvictorian! The handling of the detail always seemed to me divine. My one criticism is about the conception of it as a whole—which I am doubtful about. As I read I felt that it perhaps lacked the cohesion of a dominating idea—I don't mean in the spirit—but in the action. I wonder if you at all agree about this—but it is difficult to explain in writing. There seemed such an enormous quantity of things in it that I couldn't help wanting still more. At the end I felt as if it was really only the beginning of an enormous novel, which had been—almost accidentally—cut short by the death of Rachel. But perhaps that really *was* your conception.—I won't say any more now, we must meet soon, and talk about it. But oh! the Chapel scene!—That I think is the best morçeau of all.—And the Dalloways—oh!—

12. Virginia Woolf, reply to Strachey

1916

From a letter to Lytton Strachey, 28 February 1916, in *Letters*, ed. L. Woolf and J. Strachey (1956), 57.

Your praise is far the nicest of any I've had—having as you know, an ancient reverence for your understanding of these things, so that I can hardly believe that you *do* like that book. You almost give me courage to read it, which I've not done since it was printed, and I wonder how it would strike me now. I suspect your criticism about the failure of conception is quite right. I think I had a conception, but I don't think it made itself felt. What I wanted to do was to give the feeling of a vast tumult of life, as various and disorderly as possible, which should be cut short for a moment by the death, and go on again—and the whole was to have a sort of pattern, and be somehow controlled. The difficulty was to keep any sort of coherence,—also to give enough detail to make the characters interesting—which Forster says I didn't do. I really wanted three volumes. Do you think it is impossible to get this sort of effect in a novel;—is the result bound to be too scattered to be intelligible? I expect one may learn to get more control in time. One gets too much involved in details.

'KEW GARDENS'

12 May 1919

13. Unsigned review, *Times Literary Supplement*

29 May 1919, 293

The Woolfs received a flood of orders for the volume after this favourable review. The reviewer was Harold Child who was on the staff of *The Times* and wrote fairly frequently for the *TLS*. Virginia Woolf was therefore wrong in her guess that it was written by Logan Pearsall Smith. She thought that 'as much praise was allowed me as I like to claim' (see Introduction, p. 11). The review also indicates how unfamiliar in appearance Hogarth Press books were at the time.

What in the world, one asks, on picking up this volume, can be the connexion between Kew Gardens and this odd, Fitzroy-square-looking cover? We should be prepared for Camden Town, or Whitechapel, or the Great Sahara, or the Andes—for anything that is decisively something. But Kew Gardens, surely, are neither something nor nothing; neither formal nor wild; neither old nor new; neither urban nor rural; neither popular nor choice. What are Mrs Woolf and Mrs Bell going to find in Kew Gardens worth writing about, and engraving on wood and binding in a cover that suggests the tulips in a famous Dutch-English catalogue—'blotched, spotted, streaked, speckled, and flushed'?

The answer is—not perhaps Kew Gardens, but 'Kew Gardens by Virginia Woolf'. When we have read these pages (they are not numbered, but we have counted ten of them), we are firmly convinced of the truth of 'Kew Gardens', and as firmly convinced that it does not matter a tram-fare whether there are any Kew Gardens, or, if so, whether they are in the least like 'Kew Gardens'. In other words, we have a new proof of the complete unimportance in art of the *hyle*, the subject-matter. Titian paints Bacchus and Ariadne; and Rembrandt paints a hideous old woman; and Renoir paints a lot of people huddling under umbrellas in a rain-storm. Flaubert wrote about St. Anthony, and Felicité, and Bouvard and Pécuchet. And Mrs Woolf writes about Kew Gardens and a snail and some stupid people. But here is 'Kew Gardens'—a work of art, made, 'created', as we say, finished, four-square; a thing of original and therefore strange beauty, with its own 'atmosphere', its own vital force.

Quotation cannot represent its beauty, or, as we should like to say, its being, any more than a 'thumb-nail' photograph of Ariadne's right hand could represent the Titian; because the work of art is not this passage or that, but 'Kew Gardens' in ten pages. But we should like to tempt others into 'Kew Gardens', and must take the risk.

[Quotes from '"Wherever *does* one have one's tea"' to 'its fierce soul.']

That, at any rate, is enough to give some little idea of the colour, the rhythm, the 'atmosphere', the 'observation' (as we call it, when for all we know or care it is pure creation), the suggestiveness of Mrs Woolf's prose. Perhaps the beginning might be better were it a little suppler; but the more one gloats over 'Kew Gardens' the more beauty shines out of it; and the fitter to it seems this cover that is like no other cover, and carries no associations; and the more one likes Mrs Bell's 'Kew Gardens' woodcuts.

14. E. M. Forster, 'Visions', *Daily News*

31 July 1919, 2

Early in the previous June, Forster wrote to Leonard Woolf telling him that the *Daily News* wanted a review of 'Kew Gardens'. His main aim, he said, would be to present the book and inform the public where they could obtain a copy. A few days before the review appeared he wrote again, saying that the review was merely good journalism. But Forster's approach, through the idea of 'vision', was a useful introduction to this unusual, and 'unEnglish', kind of writing. He included 'The Mark on the Wall', published two years earlier, in his review, and so this work was given a belated notice even though it was originally distributed only to subscribers (mainly friends and acquaintances), and no review copy was sent out (see Introduction, p. 10).

Some nations see, others hear or think, and the English have never been good at seeing. The very word vision (Latin video) has in our language come to mean something that perhaps ought to exist, but certainly doesn't, like a legacy or an angel. 'I have a vision of a great united people,' say politicians, when they mean that what they do see is neither united nor great, and the visionary man is one who duly cowers before the practical. Can we rescue the valuable word to its proper sense? A vision has nothing to do either with unreality or with edification. It is merely something that has been seen, and in this sense Mrs Woolf's two stories are visions.

In the first she sees a mark on her wall just above the mantelpiece. Instead of getting up, as all well-conditioned Englishwomen should, and discovering it is a —, she continues to see it, rambling away into the speculations and fantasies that it inspires, but always coming back to the mark. Sometimes she thinks it is a hole—no, it seems to project, not a hole—like a tumulus more—tumulus—she begins to get rather sleepy —antiquarians—retired colonels—leading parties of aged labourers to the top and getting into correspondence with the neighbouring clergy, which, being opened at breakfast time, gives them a feeling of importance, and the comparison of arrow-heads. And on and on the sentence goes, until she comes back to the mark with a jump, sees it again, wonders whether it may not be a nail, and rambles off again. It requires an intruder from the outside world before the mark can be actually examined and proved to be a —. What does the reader think it was? His verdict, whether right or wrong, is not of the least value. For in this queer world of Vision it is the surfaces of things, not their names or natures that matter; it has no connection with the worlds of practical or philosophic truth; it is the world of the Eye—not of supreme importance, perhaps, but, oh, how rarely revealed!

Flowers and Men

In 'The Mark on the Wall' there is, as Mrs Woolf sadly points out, a moral of a sort; she is a poor housekeeper, or the mark would not be there. But it is impossible to extract any moral from 'Kew Gardens'. It is vision unalloyed. Or, rather, there are two visions which gradually draw together (as when one adjusts field-glasses), until they grow unforgettably bright and become one. Flowers and men are the two items at which Mrs Woolf is looking, and, at first, they seem strongly contrasted. The flowers are down in their bed with a snail, the men, erect and sentient, are strolling past with their womenkind, and the possibility of tea. And the men sometimes look at the flowers, whereas the flowers never look at the men. But as the story goes on this difference becomes terribly unimportant, and at the end the flowers, if anyone, have the upper hand. They win not in any allegorical sense—Mrs Woolf is no pantheist. Their victory is over the eye: they cause us to see men also as petals or coloured blobs that loom and dissolve in the green blue atmosphere of Kew. One cannot quote from this extraordinary story, because it is constructed with such care that the fun and the beauty—and there is much of both—depend for their main effect on their position in the general scheme. But those who like it will like it very much, and those who do not like it are to be pitied.

They are to be pitied, but not to be despised. Mrs Woolf's art is of a very unusual type, and one realises that quite good critics, especially of the academic kind, may think it insignificant. It has no moral, no philosophy, nor has it what is usually understood by Form. It aims deliberately at aimlessness, at long loose sentences, that sway and meander; it is opposed to tensity and intensity, and willingly reveals the yawn and the gape. Most writers seem to be so solemn even when being funny; they are so anxious to express their devotion to their art, and they frown when we do not attend to their jokes. Mrs Woolf, though she doubtless welcomes attention, is very careful to make no bid for it. She only says, 'Oh, here is something that I have seen,' and then strays forward. Forward it is, but those who are blind to the newer developments of English prose may not think so, and may complain at the end that the authoress has left them where she found them. Which is, no doubt, exactly what she would wish to do.

The stories are not to be had through the booksellers. Those who would experiment in them should write to the Hogarth Press, Richmond.

15. Roger Fry, an 'unintentional Parody'

1919

From 'Modern French Art at the Mansard Gallery', *Athenaeum*, 8 August 1919, 723–4.

Roger Fry (1866–1934). Art critic and close friend of Virginia Woolf. His work in the visual arts paralleled her literary experiments. The significance of this article is his direct comparison at this early date between Virginia Woolf's writing and contemporary developments in painting.

Just for the fun of testing my theory of these pictures, I will translate one of them into words; however clumsy a parody it may be, it will illustrate the point:

The Town

Houses, always houses, yellow fronts and pink fronts jostle one another, push one another this way and that way, crowd into every corner and climb into the sky; but however close they get together the leaves of trees push into their interstices, and mar the drilled decorum of their ranks; hard green leaves, delicate green leaves, veined all over with black lines, touched with rust between the veins, always more and more minutely articulated, more fragile and more irresistible. But the houses do not despair, they continue to line up, precise and prim, flat and textureless; always they have windows all over them and inside, bannisters, cornices, friezes; always in their proper places; they try to deny the leaves, but the leaves are harder than the houses and more persistent. Between houses and leaves there move the shapes of men; more transient than either, they scarcely leave a mark; their shadows stain the walls for a moment; they do not even rustle the leaves.

I see, now that I have done it, that it was meant for Mrs Virginia Woolf—that Survage is almost precisely the same thing in paint that Mrs Virginia Woolf is in prose. Only I like intensely such sequences of ideas presented to me in Mrs Virginia Woolf's prose, and as yet I have a rather strong distaste for Survage's visual statements.

NIGHT AND DAY

20 October 1919

16. Ford Madox Hueffer, 'novel' and 'romance', *Piccadilly Review*

23 October 1919, 6

An extract from the first of a series of articles, entitled 'Thus to Revisit . . .', in which the novelist and publisher Hueffer (1873–1939; later known as Ford) attempted to establish an agreed critical language in order to discuss various forms of writing. His distinction between 'Novel' and 'Romance' is an interesting one but he has chosen in *Night and Day* a very debateable example to illustrate his second category (see Introduction p. 13).

In the beginning, as far as one knows, were the *Satyricon* and the *Golden Ass*; then came the Contes, Fabliaux, Nouvelles; then Cervantes, Defoe; then Fielding and Smollett; then Richardson—and so the mainstream of imaginative prose passed again across the Channel to flow from the pens of Diderot, Chateaubriand, and Stendhal, and not to return to these islands until Flaubert and Turgenev had elevated the spinning of loose and formless Romances that you 'read in', into the art of constructing novels that you must read.

I trust the reader will allow me to get so far without violently cavilling; for this series of papers is intended rather as a friendly enquiry into how literature has survived Armageddon than as any browbeating disquisition. And it would be a good thing if we could come, now, to some agreement as to the definition applied to varying forms of writing. For before 4th August, 1914, we certainly had not even the rudiments of an agreed critical language. If one had, for instance, to write about the production of novels considered as an Art, one had to use almost exclusively French words—to write of *progressions d'affet*, *mots justes*, and so on. I used, I remember, to write high-spiritedly of Novels and Nuvvles, and thus to cause offence.

Novels and Romances

I propose, now, for the purpose of these Causeries to use the words 'Romances' and 'Novels'. Let us say that amorphous, discursive tales containing digressions, moralisations and lectures are Romances, and that Novels have unity of form, culminations and shapes. In the Romance it matters little of what the tale teller discourses, so long as he can retain the interest of the reader; in the Novel every word—*every word*—must be one that carries the story forward to its appointed end. The Romances then would be the *Satyricon; Don Quixote; Tom Jones; Vanity Fair;* or the *Brothers Karamazoff* of Dostoievsky; the Novels—well, there are very few Novels. There are the *Neveu de Rameau* of Diderot; *Le Rouge et le Noir* by Stendhal, *Madame Bovary* and *Education Sentimentale* of Flaubert; practically all the imaginative writings of Turgenev, and of the late Mr James.

The disadvantage of this nomenclature is that, if we adopt it, we must include amongst Romances a great many works eminently unromantic in texture. For you could not say, however loosely constructed they may appear to be, that *Humphrey Clinker*, the *Satyricon*, or, on the face of it, the works of Dostoievsky, are inspired by what is usually called the Romantic Spirit. On the other hand the two almost perfect novels by Mr W. H. Hudson—*Green Mansions*, and the *Purple Land*, are the very embodiment of the Spirit of Romance. As, however, I do not propose to say very much about formless narratives, I am content to leave the matter there. But I should like to add that I do not wish to be taken as thinking—or as trying to induce the reader to believe—that all formless narrative is to be regarded with contempt. I am ready to aver that *The Way of All Flesh*, by Samuel Butler, is one of the four great books in the English language, and that *Humphrey Clinker* is, when one is in the mood, as 'good reading' as *Fort Comme la Mort*—when one isn't! I hope, indeed, to be allowed to return to Butler next week.

And again; it must not be forgotten that certain writers are sometimes Romanticists and sometimes Novelists; that certain books of Novelists have the aspect of Romances—and that many books which appear to be loose in texture are actually almost devilishly intent on carrying their 'story' forwards. In *Madame Bovary* or in *Education Sentimentale* you have pages and pages that appear to be nothing but digressions. You have Homais and you have the cripple—but every word devoted to either of them makes the suicide of Emma more a matter of destiny; and, if you take the greatest—present company always excepted!—writer of to-day you will find that Mr Conrad goes to almost extraordinary lengths of apparent digression in order to 'justify' the existence of a Police Sergeant who shall arrest a cornered criminal. Or again, you have the Mr George Moore—that great writer of *Esther Waters* and the *Drama in Muslin*—or the Maupassant of *Une Vie* and *Bel Ami*. These books do not appear to be tight constructed—but he would be a bold man who said, dogmatically, that they are without 'form'. I hope, therefore, that it will appear that nothing strikingly dogmatic is intended in these arguments, for no proper man can to-day be dogmatic, since all proper men for the last five years have been shaken, earthquaked, and disturbed, to the lowest depths of their beings. It is the queerest thing in the world to return to the grey regions of Covent Garden and to find that still there are 'firms' in Henrietta Street, in Bedford Street, or in King Street, and that an 'Autumn Publishing Season' is apparently in contemplation. Queer! One walks the grey streets wondering where they all are . . .

Modern Instances

So that this is an enquiry into that question which has tormented me all my life—as to where we really stand. And here are Mr Cannan, who before the war was one of *les jeunes*, and Mrs Woolf, of whom I know nothing. *Time and Eternity* and *Night and Day* are interesting examples of the two tendencies of which I have written. Speaking as it were, in shorthand, you might say that Mr Cannan's book is a Novel, Mrs Woolf's a Romance. Mr Cannan carries excision almost to extremes: in reading Mrs Woolf one seems to hear of families and unmistakable voice[s] of one's childhood. It is surely the voice of George Eliot—but it is the voice of a George Eliot who, remaining almost super-educated, has lost the divine rage to be didactic. Mrs Woolf records passionlessly the mental attitudes, the house furnishings, and the current literature of the intellectual governing class just before the war. You find it difficult to know whether she approves of them or whether—as is probably the case—she isn't mocking at them tenderly. Her characters are the descendants of great, but rather academic poets, the editors of huge monthly reviews:

The Hilberys, as the saying is, 'knew everyone,' and that arrogant claim was certainly upheld by the number of houses which, in a certain area, lit their lamps at night, opened their doors after 3 p.m., and admitted the Hilberys to their dining rooms, say, once a month. An indefinable freedom and authority of manner, shared by most of the people who lived in these houses, seemed to indicate that whether it were a question of art, music, or government, they were well within the gates, and could smile indulgently at the vast mass of humanity which is forced to wait and struggle and pay for entrance with common coin at the door.[1]

How different from us, Miss Beale and Miss Buss! Or rather, how different from the characters and the atmosphere of Mr Cannan's book. For, whereas *Night and Day* is a severe love-story, a *chassez-croisez* of engaged couples in a Parnassian and pre-war atmosphere, Mr Cannan's book is written with lurid heat and deals with murder in an atmosphere of alcoholic and rag-time Bohemia when Armageddon was at its height . . .

It is queer to find that, in these modern developments, Mrs Woolf, who is the spiritual descendant of the George Eliots, the Ruskins, the Spencers, the Pollocks, and all the other moral adornments of Victorianism, writes skilfully a moral-less but very entertaining book which is all ado about nothing; and that Mr Cannan, the literary descendant of the Maupassants, the Goncourts, and all the non-moral overseas writers, has become an almost virulent and certainly an incoherent moralist. Incoherent is not, perhaps, the exactly right word. For, just as Mrs Woolf is mistress of inclusion, so Mr Cannan is to such an extent a master of excision that you cannot quite tell what are the ideals which he violently proclaims.

I shall probably return to both these books when it comes to discussing other technical points. My space is, I imagine, at an end. But I should just like to add that if I did not think that the books of these two writers were not interesting and suggestive I should not write about them.

1 Not a quotation.

17. Unsigned review, *Times Literary Supplement*

30 October, 1919, 607

Virginia Woolf commented on this review in her *Diary*: 'Then there's a column in *The Times* this morning; high praise; and intelligent too; saying among other things that N. and D., though it has less brilliance on the surface, has more depth than the other; with which I agree' (*A Writer's Diary*, p. 20). The reviewer was Harold Child. He thought that Virginia Woolf had achieved both firm structure and suggestive allusion in the novel (see Introduction p. 12).

In Mrs Woolf's new novel the Victorian age gives place to the present, and common human wisdom is seen running through both to unite them. The story begins in a choice upper-middle-class house in Chelsea, full of the tradition and the worship of a great Victorian poet. In the end of it Highgate has come to Chelsea; raw strength to exquisite tradition. And common human wisdom, comical in one aspect, reverend in another, brings the two together.

Night and Day is only a love-story. It leaves politics, and war, and sociology and things like that, alone. But the story as a whole and every separate incident of it show an apprehension of values which is rarely found even in days like these when fiction is commonly supposed to be troubled with too much thinking. The story keeps close to the love affairs of five young people; but, as we read, we feel that here is the heart of the matter. Could we fully understand the love affairs of William Rodney and Cassandra Otway, of Mary Datchet and Katherine Hilbery and Ralph Denham—and especially of the last two—then we should understand a great deal more than we do of the age we live in, a great deal more than is commonly understood. Mrs Woolf devotes herself to trying to make us understand—and she succeeds. But we never feel that the story stops there. Round each scene and round the tale as a whole sound sympathetic notes, that are not definitely struck, but respond to those which are. We feel the dignity of a love story worthily told. We see much more than we are shown.

Ralph Denham was Highgate, strong, raw, ugly; Katherine Hilbery was Chelsea (Cheyne-walk, that is, not the King's Road or the side streets), mellow, august, exquisite. We should expect in Denham, who was discovering the world for himself, the passion for intellectual and spiritual truth and the rather heady pride which made him unable to decide whether he loved or did not love Katherine Hilbery, unable even to tell what love was. These active brains, with no refuge of inherited standards and acceptances to run to, must try everything for themselves, and will take nothing for granted. But where did Katherine Hilbery get her scepticism and uncertainty? It is in trying to answer such questions as that that we come to see in the mind's eye the long rows of volumes that might be written on the truths about society and human development which Mrs Woolf has been so careful to refrain from mentioning in the novel, built on them though it be. There, at any rate, is Katherine, rooted in the Victorian era and shooting up into the untried future; now asking William Rodney to keep her safely in the sure comfort of her origin; now dreading and daring with Ralph Denham, her true partner in the adventure of life. These two, coming together after goodness knows what of queer reluctance and fear and fantasy, are going, at least, to make their lives something that shall be true. They are going to be honestly themselves. We foresee for them a hard and glorious time. Let William and Cassandra meanwhile play delightfully together on the surface, yielding as slowly as they can and with all the pretence they can make of not noticing that they yield at all, to the pressure of the new age; while Mary Datchet, missing what she most wanted in life, works out for herself something that is as true, though not nearly so exciting as the adventure of Katherine and Ralph.

We hesitate to use the word wisdom because it suggests something pompous and dull; but *Night and Day* is a book full of wisdom. And having said that, let us hurry on to talk of its brilliance—a quality that is much less obvious than it was in *The Voyage Out*, but underlies the whole book and is here and there allowed to come to the surface. No comic scene has delighted us more of late than that in which Katherine Hilbery's father (excellent gentleman!) gets lost in the maze of these astonishing young people's inexplicable love affairs and tries to find the way out by his sturdy Victorian sense of the right thing. And the more of Mrs Hilbery the better! An old fool—a woolly-brained chatterbox? We laugh a delighted assent—and go on to remember that we are laughing at one to whom alone love and the everlasting woman-wisdom have given the power of putting things right for her bewildered tortured girl.

Next to the brilliance must come what is called the construction—the planning and proportion of the story. The book is very long. Perhaps it might have been written shorter; but we have looked in vain for anything that we should like to see left out. There are one or two little slips in it. When Mrs Woolf set Mary Datchet and her sister cutting roses in the rectory garden, she forgot that the season was Christmas and the county Lincoln. Was Mrs Sallie Seal, the suffragist, a spinster or a married woman? No flowers grow on Shakespeare's tomb; and to get laurel-boughs from it Mrs Hilbery must have robbed the church (which she would cheerfully have done, we admit). Such inaccuracies are compatible with Mrs Woolf's unmistakable mastery in firm and shapely building. Yet building is hardly the word. It suggests immobility. The reader of *Night and Day* will find that, while each scene is complete, full of life, present significance, suggestive allusion, the progression of scenes is so arranged as to draw him on to a point in the story which—'only a love-story' though this be—is so exciting that to read it is to pass through a keen emotional experience. And thence comes the gradual descent, not into a house with shut doors and windows, but to a point whence the future prospect can be seen stretching away into the blue distance.

18. Katherine Mansfield, review, *Athenaeum*

21 November 1919, 1227

Katherine Mansfield (1888–1923). Short story writer. Married to John Middleton Murry (see No. 34). She had written to Virginia Woolf eighteen months previously, expressing her admiration for 'The Mark on the Wall' (see Introduction, p. 11). But in this review, entitled 'A Ship Comes into Harbour' it is clear that she considered *Night and Day* to be a step backwards: Virginia Woolf has retreated into the harbour of traditional fiction after her daring early experiments. Katherine Mansfield's overall assessment of this novel has not been seriously questioned by subsequent critics. For a fuller discussion of the background to this review, see Introduction, p. 12.

There is at the present day no form of writing which is more eagerly, more widely discussed than the novel. What is its fate to be? We are told on excellent authority that it is dying; and on equally good authority that only now it begins to live. Reviewers might almost be divided into two camps. Present each camp with the same book, and from one there comes a shout of praise, from the other a chorus of blame, each equally loud, determined and limited. One would imagine from a reading of the press notices that never in the history of the world was there such a generous distribution of the divine fire together with such an overwhelming display of ignorance, stupidity and dreariness. But in all this division and confusion it would seem that opinion is united in declaring this to be an age of experiment. If the novel dies it will be to give way to some new form of expression; if it lives it must accept the fact of a new world.

To us who love to linger down at the harbour, as it were, watching the new ships being builded, the old ones returning, and the many putting out to sea, comes the strange sight of *Night and Day* sailing into port serene and resolute on a deliberate wind. The strangeness lies in her aloofness, her air of quiet perfection, her lack of any sign that she has made a perilous voyage—the absence of any scars. There she lies among the strange shipping—a tribute to civilization for our admiration and wonder.

It is impossible to refrain from comparing *Night and Day* with the novels of Miss Austen. There are moments, indeed, when one is almost tempted to cry it Miss Austen up-to-date. It is extremely cultivated, distinguished and brilliant, but above all—deliberate. There is not a chapter where one is unconscious of the writer, of her personality, her point of view, and her control of the situation. We feel that nothing has been imposed on her: she has chosen her world, selected her principal characters with the nicest care, and having traced a circle round them so that they exist and are free within its confines, she has proceeded, with rare appreciativeness, to register her observations. The result is a very long novel, but we do not see how it could be otherwise. This leisurely progression is essential to its manner, nor could the reader, even if he would, drink such wine at a gulp. As in the case of Miss Austen's novels we fall under a little spell; it is as though, realizing our safety, we surrender ourselves to the author, confident that whatever she has to show us, and however strange it may appear, we shall not be frightened or shocked. Her creatures are, one might say, privileged; we can rely upon her fine mind to deliver them from danger, to temper the blow (if a blow must fall), and to see their way clear for them at the very last. It is the measure of Mrs Woolf's power that her 'happy ending' could never be understood as a triumph of the heart over the mind. But whereas Miss Austen's spell is as strong upon us as ever when the novel is finished and laid by, Mrs Woolf's loses something of its potency. What is it that carries us away? With Miss Austen, it is first her feeling for life, and then her feeling for writing; but with Mrs Woolf these feelings are continually giving way the one to the other, so that the urgency of either is impaired. While we read we scarcely are aware which is uppermost; it is only afterwards, and, specially when recalling the minor characters, that we begin to doubt. Sally Seal of the Suffrage Society, Mr Clacton with his French novel, old Joan in her shabby dress, Mrs Denham peering among the cups and saucers: it is true that these characters are not in any high degree important—but how much life have they? We have the queer sensation that once the author's pen is removed from them they have neither speech nor motion, and are not to be revived again until she adds another stroke or two or writes another sentence underneath. Were they shadowy or vague this would be less apparent, but they are held within the circle of steady light in which the author bathes her world, and in their case the light seems to shine at them, but not through them.

Night and Day tells of Katherine Hilbery's attempt to reconcile the world of reality with what, for want of a better name, we call the dream world. She belongs to one of the most distinguished families in England. Her mother's father was that 'fairest flower that any family can boast'—a great poet. Katherine's father is an eminent man of letters, and she herself as an only child 'had some superior rank among all the cousins and connections'. Grave, beautiful, with a reputation for being eminently practical and sensible beyond her years, she keeps house for her parents in Chelsea, but this activity does not exhaust Katherine. She has her lonely life remote from the drawing-room in Cheyne Walk, and it is divided between dreams 'such as the taming of wild ponies on the American prairies, or the conduct of a vast ship in a hurricane round a promontory of rock', and the study of mathematics. This last is her half-unconscious but profound protest against the family tradition, against the making of phrases and (what Mrs Woolf rather curiously calls) 'the confusion, agitation and vagueness of the finest prose'.

But it is only after she has contracted an engagement which is in every way highly suitable with William Rodney, a scholar whose knowledge of Shakespeare, of Latin and Greek, is not to be disputed or denied, that she realizes in so doing she has in some mysterious way betrayed her dream world—the lover on the great horse riding by the seashore and the leaf-hung forests. Must life be for ever this lesser thing, this world as we know it, shapely, polished and secure? Katherine had no impulse to write poetry, yet it was the poet in her that made her see in Ralph Denham the man for whom she could feel that strange great passion which is like a fire lighting up the two worlds with the one exultant flame. . . .

It would be interesting to know how far Mrs Woolf has intended to keep this dream world of Katherine's and of Ralph's a deep secret from her readers. We are told that it is there, and we believe it; yet would not our knowledge of these two be wonderfully increased if there were something more than these suggestions that are like delicate veils hiding the truth? . . .

As for the real world, the world of Mr and Mrs Hilbery, William Rodney, Cassandra Otway—there we appreciate to the full the author's exquisite generosity. It is so far away, so shut and sealed from us to-day. What could be more remote than the house at Cheyne Walk, standing up in the night, with its three long windows gilded with light, its drawn velvet curtains, and the knowledge that within a young creature is playing Mozart, Mrs Hilbery is wishing there were more young men like Hamlet, and Katherine and Rodney are faced by the incredible sight of Denham, outside in the dark, walking up and down. . . .

We had thought that this world was vanished for ever, that it was impossible to find on the great ocean of literature a ship that was unaware of what has been happening. Yet here is *Night and Day*, fresh, new and exquisite, a novel in the tradition of the English novel. In the midst of our admiration it makes us feel old and chill: we had never thought to look upon its like again!

19. W. L. George, from 'A Painter's Literature', *English Review*

March 1920, 223–34

W. L. George. English novelist, whose first novel *A Bed of Roses* (1911) made him popular.

The five 'Neo-Georgians' here compared with Virginia Woolf were Joyce, Wyndham Lewis, Romer Wilson, Dorothy Richardson, and May Sinclair.

The Neo-Georgians, with exceptions, can be described as painters rather than as writers. It is thus permissible to say that *the modern novel is becoming a painter's literature*. There are practical reasons for this: whereas the novelist of an older generation mixed very little with painters and musicians, the new generation tends to form composite cliques, where literature and dancing, sculpture and music, convince each other that they are expressing the same thing through a variety of media. Which is true and not true. Whereas one may compare a passage in Dante with a fear motif in Wagner, one must recognise that the impressions received by the brain through the eye are tainted by the eye, and that the brain will not record the result in the same way as if it came through the ear. Professor Rimington's colour organ is, I am sure, an ingenious instrument, but none save a wilful man will proclaim that when he sees a pale blue tint he hears the *vox celeste*.

The result is notable. For the last ten or twelve years British painting has been in a volcanic state. It discovered the ideas of Cézanne, Matisse, Gauguin, Rousseau, Kandinski, etc. Instead of depicting, it began to interpret. Then it attacked the intellectual side, and strove to express ideas; to do this it threw off conventional form, and set up distortion to liberate what one might call ideal form. I must not dilate upon this, but the reader will realise that in the mixed groups where the painters were so revolutionary, so eloquent, so vital, while the novelists were still Victorian, the painters must prevail. The painters have imposed themselves upon the novelists, have made them believe that intellectual influence is a smudge upon art . . . unless the intellectual process is devoted to painting, which alone can express intellect. In other words: *thou shalt have none other gods but paint*. . . .

Without stressing the pictorial comparison, one can say that the five are the slaves of impression. Their work seems to rest on that alone, and to amount to impression without conception. They make pictures of states of mind, and, by giving all the details of these states of mind, they end by imparting to all impressions the same value. (They will say that this is their object, because the eye, unlike the brain, is not a judge; thus they define their divorce from pure literature.)

This leaves only Mrs Virginia Woolf, who has no link with the five, but has entered their period, as have also Mr Alec Waugh, Miss Clemence Dane, and Miss V. Sackville-West. Mrs Woolf is a complete writer, for she combines the intellectual outlook with the pictorial sense. In her book, *Night and Day*, we find amazing sensitiveness in the evocation of persons and places:

> At the same time it seemed to Mr Denham as if a thousand softly padded doors had closed between him and the street outside. A fine mist, the etherealised essence of the fog, hung visibly in the wide and rather empty space of the drawing-room, all silver where the candles were grouped on the tea-table, and ruddy again in the firelight. . . . His deep, oval-shaped eyes were fixed upon the flames, but behind the superficial glaze seemed to brood an observant and whimsical spirit, which kept the brown of the eye still unusually vivid. But a look of indolence, the result of scepticism or of a taste too fastidious to be satisfied by the prizes and conclusions so easily within his grasp, lent him an expression almost melancholy.

This is not flung down as pearls among the curds and whey of self-consciousness. It is linked, nobly coherent. Character develops; event follows on this development. Here is perfect aloofness, entire distinction; Mrs Virginia Woolf outstrips all novelists of her period, for she possesses two qualifications for high literature: pity, and fine disdain.

Only, and that is perhaps why Mrs Virginia Woolf finds strange bed-fellows in the Sacred Grove, her interest is so far confined to love in cultured society. Only the tip of her wing touches social impulses and intellectual movements in the masses of mankind. Here again, excessive prominence is given to minor emotions, while no space at all is accorded to social stirrings. There, presumably, is the burden of my present discontent. In regard to all this writing, however sincere, however distinguished, the same thing can be said: we are in the midst of a social rebirth, the prey of world movements, where Labour, Religion, Sex, Kingship, must be dealt with because they cannot be left out. Well, there so far arises in the Sacred Grove no one inclined to handle broad questions; the individual and the nature of art alone are interesting. But even if the Sacred Grove cared, a picture of the social revolution 'written through the consciousness', or wholly seen from the terrace of a *café* in the Quartier Latin, would compare ill with the product of a cinema camera man. We cannot here enter into the obvious objection: mental revolutions do not concern literature. One can dismiss that with the reply that everything is the business of literature, and that the function of the novel is to hold up a mirror to the writer's period. The present moderns cannot do it, and do not want to. Thus they abandon illumination, and prove themselves unfit to fulfil the high function of the novel, which it took up a hundred years ago: to dispel error by exhibiting the period in which it flourishes, to use the battleaxe of understanding upon the thickets of prejudice and folly, to cut a trail through the foolish forests of the present, along which to drive the chariot of the future.

20. R. M. Underhill, review, *Bookman* (New York)

August 1920, 685–6

Ruth Murray Underhill (b. 1884). American anthropologist.

The Voyage Out was published in America in the previous June, and *Night and Day* in the following September. The reviewer was able to see similarities between the two novels, as well as differences. (The latter tended to be emphasised in British reviews.)

The term *realism* has gathered a depressing sense. Unjustly our minds connect it with accuracy about the less welcome facts of life, pictures of dullness or brutality. Yet we admit reality to be miraculous. To eyes not so jaded as ours, the spectacle of human beings against their background of aeons and planets would be absorbing, entry into the mind of one such being, even at his dullest moment, a stupendous adventure.

Such eyes Virginia Woolf has, toward such an adventure she leads us in her two novels *The Voyage Out* and *Night and Day* (the latter forthcoming). These are stories of pleasant people, who move quietly through a quiet environment. Yet they are to be read breathlessly. The curious fabric of minute-by-minute daily life, compound of emotion, sensation, thoughts half seized, actions half intended, becomes in these pages almost tangible. The half uttered sentence, the impulse poignant and inexplicable, go to the very roots of our remembrance and produce a thrill of revelation. This is true.

The plot of each story is simple, for it is not outward events that, to Mrs Woolf, make history. In *The Voyage Out* a young girl makes her entry into the world outside the secluded home of her maiden aunts. But she is not plunged straight into a treasure mystery nor into the chase of a criminal. She sails on her father's ship, with some clever and well-bred people, to South America and, very slowly, through their agency and that of the others she meets at Santa Marina, she reaches some understanding of the nature of human beings and of love.

Night and Day has an even simpler motive. A nice girl tries to find her way, among a group of pleasant and cultured people, containing two young men, toward the reality of love.

The very young heroine is, at present, regnant in fiction. She may be seen every month, directing a whole staff of detectives or rescuing the business of her father or lover from ruin, always with perfect self-possession and knowledge of what she wants. Mrs Woolf's girls are not of that breed: they are people, in all the ignorance and fallibility that the term implies. They do not know what they want, but they go out to look for it.

To the reviewer, the opportunity to read about people who are real, but intelligent, is an unusual delight. These people employ self-control and common sense, even as you and I, and the plot proceeds without misunderstanding or murder. It is no psychological disquisition; it is profoundly moving. But, given Mrs Woolf's perspective, it is not the conventionally emotional scenes by which one is stirred,—it is rather those reminiscent and elusive moments when both heroine and reader palpitate at the approach to truth.

The aura of magnificence about the adventure is perhaps greater in *The Voyage Out* than in *Night and Day*. The splendour of the ocean and of the clear-cut southern scenery lends a perspective to the faltering human action which London cannot supply. The half expressed thought, the interrupted sentences by which the action of *Night and Day* proceeds, are baffling. Carry this sort of thing a few steps further and you have Maeterlinck. Yet even this intent study of a fragmentary and delicate thing strikes one as in the spirit of Tennyson's 'flower in the crannied wall' whose complete comprehension means comprehension of what God and man is.

MONDAY OR TUESDAY

7 April 1921

21. Unsigned review, *Times Literary Supplement*

7 April 1921, 227

Harold Child was the reviewer (as for 'Kew Gardens' and *Night and Day* (Nos 13, 17)). He makes an interesting parallel between Virginia Woolf's writing and non-representational painting. His criticism at the end of the review indicates that the Hogarth Press was having some production difficulties. In fact three of the sketches had been previously published, not two as he states in his first sentence ('An Unwritten Novel' had appeared in the *London Mercury* in July 1920).

Two of the stories in Virginia Woolf's new book, *Monday or Tuesday* have been published before. 'Kew Gardens' and 'The Mark on the Wall' are already on the shelves of those who collect Hogarth Press books, and in the memories of those who follow Mrs Woolf's writings. The piece which gives its title to the new volume, *Monday or Tuesday*, is an example of the 'unrepresentational' art which is creeping across from painting to see what it can make of words. It sounds beautiful; it suggests beautiful, or at least life-full things—the heron flying, the busy street, the fire-lit room, and others. The trouble with it is that even this sort of art cannot empty itself altogether of intellectual content. One sentence seems to 'mean'—that is, to represent—something; the intrusion of this representation makes the next sentence, or the other portions of the same sentence, 'mean' nothing. We complain of *Monday or Tuesday*, not that it means too little that is intelligible to the plain mind, but that it cannot help meaning too much for its purpose. Prose may 'aspire to the condition of music'; it cannot reach it.

Some measure of this objection applies to 'Blue and Green', though there the aim is different; and Mrs Woolf does perfectly in a few lines what J. A. Symonds once did imperfectly (and spread thin) over many pages. But the plain mind must be very plain if it does not find itself almost at once 'inside' the strange beauty of 'A Haunted House' (which would be very sentimental were it not exquisitely strange). 'The String Quartet' musicians will decry, because it shows that while Mrs Woolf listens to music she is thinking, not in terms of music, but of life—she is making music 'represent'; but it is excellently done. 'An Unwritten Novel', besides being a comically worked instance of a 'sell' for the imaginative reader of character, teems with the touches of detail which set suggestions of states of life and of mind swarming in the reader's head—all so trivial, all so significant. And while the whole book is either humorous or witty, there is a thread of hearty, 'masculine' fun woven in with the shrewd and wicked wit of that very feminine (almost feminist) tale, 'A Society', which brings one to outright laughter. We wish George Meredith could have read this story, the work of a woman. But we long to ask one indiscreet question. Was that really the end of the tale of a certain famous hoax? And we want also to make one slight complaint. The Hogarth Press has done better printing than this. In the copy before us the inking is often faulty; and Mrs Bell's delightful woodcuts (the one with the fiddles is peculiarly exciting and suggestive) have left ghosts of themselves on the pages opposite; and also they show through the paper, so that the backs are difficult to read.

22. 'Affable Hawk', review, *New Statesman*

9 April 1921, 18

'Affable Hawk' was the pseudonym of Desmond MacCarthy (1877–1952), one of the central members of the Bloomsbury Group, a literary critic who never fulfilled his friends' hope that he would write a good novel. A number of critics have pointed out that there is something of MacCarthy in Bernard, the phrase-maker in *The Waves*. After reading the review, Virginia Woolf noted: 'There was an Affable Hawk on me in the *New Statesman* which at any rate made me feel important (and it's that that one wants)' (*A Writer's Diary*, p. 32).

The Hogarth Press is a small, out-of-the-way tree which grows at Richmond and bears from time to time peculiar fruit. On the occasions it does so, one pictures on the face of the public the slow considering look of a child who has put its teeth into the fruit of an unknown flavour, and is about either to nod emphatically, swallow and bite again, or to grimace and fling the fragment into the bushes. 'Wait!' the critic cries, 'Pause and taste again.' The last fruits from this tree are a slim volume of short stories by Leonard Woolf, called *Stories of the East*, and a collection of sketches, rhapsodies and meditations—there is no general name for them—by Virginia Woolf, labelled *Monday or Tuesday*. They are accompanied, rather than illustrated, by wood-cuts of a rough, blottesque, pleasantly vigorous kind by Vanessa Bell.

Mrs Woolf has published two novels, *The Voyage Out* and *Night and Day*. The first is remarkable, indeed unique, the second cousin to all respectworthy psychological love stories of the moment. The peculiarity of *The Voyage Out* was its sensitive presentment of the criss-cross of tragedy and commonplace, sweetness and drabness, ecstasy and *ennui*, rationality and nonsense of which the texture of experience is woven. In tragedy and romance obviously the author was at home, but the commonplace was ever strange and queer to her. Take a dull half-hour in any dull person's mental life, or for that matter in any interesting one's; it seems a limpid drop of tasteless water. (An old lady is knitting, or a young man cutting his toe-nails.) But place that drop under the lens of a divining imaginative attention and, behold! it is swarming with the lashings and splashings of the queerest animalculae, a flurry of life as irrelevant to the intentions of that person as the bustle of bacilli in his or her veins. Most of the time, perhaps, our actions are those of automatons, and our minds only a swarm of images, reflections and emotions, ever twisting and hovering, rising and falling, ever tying and untying knots, like flies above the head of a sleeper—emblem, he, of our temporarily suspended, moral and rational being. This aspect of life is never far away from the author's consciousness. She uses it perpetually for artistic purposes; to produce effects of humour—the chirp of a somewhat acidulated Ariel overhead—and effects of a beauty which shall blend the apparently unassimilable commonplace with the ethereally fantastic, thus affording opportunity for the exercise of a style which is at once delicate and dry, impulsive and deliberate, extreme, quick and flashing. The rhythm of some passages in *Monday or Tuesday* is very remarkable.

In naming her new book *Monday or Tuesday*, Mrs Woolf seems to suggest that this is the stuff, unlikely as it might appear, of which the mental life of any ordinary day is made. You may remember how in *The Voyage Out* the author was not satisfied with telling us what, at a given moment, her principal characters were doing, but took us from bedroom to bedroom of the large hotel in which they were staying, and described rapidly but with extreme precision how the occupants were simultaneously engaged. The effect of this was to impress us with the oddity and irrelevance of the setting which life provides for the adventures of the individual soul. We are used to a love story or a tragedy being set against the background of the irrelevant activities and indifference of nature, but a background made up of other human beings, each like a little clock keeping its own time and striking independently, had a curious effect. Anatole France sometimes uses this device lightly in the service of irony. In one of the best pieces in *Monday or Tuesday* it is used to produce a disconcerting poetic effect. The scene is an oval flower bed in Kew Gardens on a sunny afternoon. The author follows the thoughts not only of the different people who pass by, but of the snail that crawls tentatively along under the plants. First a man and his wife pass: he is thinking of a courtship, which years ago came to nothing, in Kew Gardens; she answers her memories of a kiss, a kiss given her as a child by an old grey-haired woman. Then we become aware of the snail.

[Quotes 'Kew Gardens': 'In the oval flower bed' to 'other human beings.']

Now a madman and his keeper pass, and though the elderly man is mad, he hardly lives more completely isolated in the bubble of his own imaginings than the others. His bubble is a bubble of more arbitrary fancies, but is is hardly less unreal. He is followed by two elderly women talking of sugar and household worries, and they by two lovers who are attempting to blend their bubbles. Once more under the unifying blaze of the afternoon sky we watch the tentative purposeful movements of the snail.

It is these iridescent, quickly-pricked, quickly-blown-again bubbles, made of private thoughts and dreams, which the author is an adept at describing. In neo-Buddhistic books we sometimes come across pictures of little human figures, like the nuclei in the many coloured albumen of their eggs, and we are told that these are people's auras. Auras, in the sense of temporary and shifting integuments of dreams and thoughts we all carry about with us while pursuing practical aims, are her subject-matter. 'The Mark on the Wall' and 'The String Quartet' are prose lyrical effusions which trace every streak and change in them. The first is a wonderful description of wool-gathering beside a fire; the second of such fancies as are woven like a cocoon round the mind while listening to music.

[Quotes 'The String Quartet': 'The meaning is plain' to ' "I go that." ']

In the piece called 'An Unwritten Novel' she guesses at the inner life of a woman opposite her in a railway carriage—only to find she was entirely wrong. The contrast between the diversity and arbitrariness of the inner life and the uniformity and conventionality of the life without fills her alternately with laughter and amazement—and sometimes with contempt; for of the two the inner life seems to her incomparably the more vivid and real. But the inner life of dreams and straying thoughts has not authority to impeach the other, and when, as in 'A Society', she writes from contempt, her work is not her best.

23. Unsigned review, *Dial* (New York)

February 1922, vol. lxxii, no. 2

Virginia Woolf joins with Katherine Mansfield, Dorothy Richardson, and T. S. Eliot to mark the four compass points of ultra-modern tea, she and Mr Eliot, perhaps, bringing it all closest to metaphysics. In her present volume of sketches Mrs Woolf becomes much more arty than in her novels, although she never surpasses the technical superbness of *The Voyage Out*. The most alluring feature here is to be found in the exciting knack she has mastered of starting anywhere and arriving anywhere. But when form is vague, one has a right to ask for more frequent minor illuminations, whereas these stories too often give the effect of William Carlos Williams' *Improvisations* with the sudden flashes left out. Perhaps no brief quotation could give a better idea of the attack than this gem of cosmic dialogue: 'Good night, good night. You go this way? . . . Alas, I go that.'

JACOB'S ROOM

27 October 1922

24. Lytton Strachey on the romantic element in *Jacob's Room*

1922

From a letter to Virginia Woolf, 9 October 1922, in *Letters*, ed. L. Woolf and J. Strachey (1956), 103–4.

Thoby Stephen, whom Strachey refers to in this letter, was Virginia Woolf's elder brother who died in 1906 at the age of twenty-six.

I finished Jacob last night—a most wonderful achievement—more like poetry, it seems to me, than anything else, and as such I prophesy immortal. The technique of the narrative is astonishing—how you manage to leave out everything that's dreary, and yet retain enough string for your pearls I can hardly understand. I occasionally almost screamed with joy at the writing. Of course you're very romantic—which alarms me slightly—I am such a Bonamy. Once or twice I thought you were in danger of becoming George-Meredithian in style—or was that a delusion? Something of the sort certainly seems to me *the* danger for your genre. But so far you're safe. You're a romantic in Sirius, I fancy—which after all is a good way off from Box Hill. The impression left on one as a whole is glorious. And then, as one remembers detail after detail—the pier at Scarborough, the rooks and the dinner-bell, the clergyman's wife on the moors, St Paul's, the British Museum at night, the Parthenon—one's head whirls round and round. Jacob himself I think is very successful—in a most remarkable and original way. Of course I see something of Thoby in him, as I suppose was intended.

25. Virginia Woolf, reply to Lytton Strachey

9(10?) October 1922

In *Letters*, ed. L. Woolf and J. Strachey (1956), 104–5.

Virginia Woolf's Diary indicates that she was quite sincere in thinking Strachey's praise extravagant: a few days after writing this letter she recorded her feelings as publication day drew near:

> My sensations? they remain calm. Yet how could Lytton have praised me more highly? prophesies immortality for it as poetry; is afraid of my romance; but the beauty of the writing etc. Lytton praises me too highly for it to give me exquisite pleasure; or perhaps that nerve grows dulled. I want to be through the splash and swimming in calm water again. I want to be writing unobserved (*A Writer's Diary*, 52).

I breathe more freely now that I have your letter, though I think your praise is extravagant—I can't believe you really like a work so utterly devoid of so many virtues; but it gives me immense pleasure to dream that you do. Of course you put your infallible finger upon the spot—romanticism. How do I catch it? Not from my father. I think it must have been my Great Aunts. But some of it, I think, comes from the effort of breaking with complete representation. One flies into the air. Next time, I mean to stick closer to the facts. There are millions of things I want to get your opinion on—This is merely to heave a sigh of relief that you don't cast me off, for nobody else's praise ever gives me quite as much pleasure as yours.

26. Unsigned review, *Times Literary Supplement*

26 October 1922, 683

The editor of the *TLS* had earlier written to Virginia Woolf to ask if the publication date of *Jacob's Room* could be put forward so that it could be reviewed on the first day of publication. Presumably Virginia Woolf agreed, as this review appeared a day before the date given in Kirkpatrick's *Bibliography*.

The review was entitled 'The Enchantment of a Mirror' but the reviewer (A. S. McDowall) hinted that, so far as the characters were concerned, it was a surface enchantment: 'But it might be questioned whether her beings, while they intersect, really act upon each other, or whether her method does not condemn them to be external.' Virginia Woolf noted this criticism: 'There was *The Times* review on Thursday—long, a little tepid, I think—saying that one can't make characters in this way; flattering enough' (*A Writer's Diary*, 54).

One might describe Mrs Woolf's new novel as the opposite of *Night and Day*, her last; or one might say that it is rather like the method of *Monday or Tuesday* applied to a continuous story. But this novel is limpid and definite. It would be truer to say that it is different from any other—Mrs Woolf's or anyone else's—though the remark sounds both vague and sweeping. At first you may be drawn by resemblances. This bright and endless race of things and thoughts, small acts, incongruous sensations, impressions so brief and yet pervasive that you hardly separate the mental from the external, what is it but the new vision of life as practised by So-and-so or So-and-so? The vision may be as old, indeed, as Heracleitus; but could he, or Pater even, have guessed how far artists would carry the process of weaving and unweaving? Mrs Woolf, you will say, is in this movement. Possibly; but her fabric is woven with threads so entirely of her own that it becomes quite different.

First, however, for its unlikeness to the normal. Jacob Flanders, absorbed with the half-savage, half-winning absorption of youth, and lovable since his friends and several women love him, is in the brief career which we follow by glimpses the mutest of all heroes. He is a 'silent young man'; Mrs Woolf's method increases his silence. But there is his room, his behaviour, his impressions; there are the scenes, the numerous people who float into the story for a moment or eddy round its centre. There is Mrs Jarvis, for example:

[Quotes pp. 25–6 'Short, dark, with kindling eyes' to 'give it her.']

Is Mrs Jarvis, then, a vivid little excrescence? When we ask what she and others are doing to the story, and find possible but not very obvious, answers, we are getting nearer to the real interest of Mrs Woolf's novel. It is not Jacob's history simply, nor anyone else's, but the queer simultaneousness of life, with all those incongruous threads which now run parallel, now intersect, and then part as unaccountably. Jacob is in the middle like a waif or a little marching soldier. And these odd conjunctions and sequences of life, which are much too delicate to be called slices, have been brought to a focus in Mrs Woolf's mirror.

It is an amusingly clear and yet enchanted glass which she holds up to things; that is her quality. This stream of incidents, persons, and their momentary thoughts and feelings, which would be intolerable if it were just allowed to flow, is arrested and decanted, as it were, into little phials of crystal vividness. Mrs Woolf has the art of dividing the continuous and yet making one feel that the stream flows remorselessly. The definite Mrs Durrant, the romantic little light-of-love Florinda, shy and charming Clara, the people in the streets, the moors and the sea, London and Athens—they all rise into delicious moments of reality and light before they melt back into the shadow. And each of those moments has caught a gleam of wit from the surface of the mirror, or a musing thought from the reflective depths in it. Ought we to complain, then, because Mrs Woolf can make beauty and significance out of what we generally find insignificant, or because her own musings tinge those of her personages sometimes? We know the stream of life at first-hand already; what this novel adds, with the lightest strokes, and all the coolness of restraint, is a knowledge of the vision of the author.

And it is much to be taken as far as we are here into that subtle, slyly mocking, and yet poignant vision; for Mrs Woolf has seldom expressed it more beguilingly than she does in this novel. It will even make us forget to treat the novel as a story. If, however, we come back to that, we should have to say that it does not create persons and characters as we secretly desire to know them. We do not know Jacob as an individual, though we promptly seize his type; perhaps we do not know anyone in the book otherwise than as a really intuitive person knows his acquaintances, filling in the blanks, if he is imaginative, by his imagination. And that, Mrs Woolf might say, is all we can know in life, or need to know in a book, if we forgo the psychology which she spares us. But it might still be questioned whether her beings, while they intersect, really act upon each other, or whether her method does not condemn them to be external. It is an ungrateful suspicion to have about a book which has embodied their passing thoughts so vividly. But what she has undoubtedly done is to give a quickened sense of the promise and pity in a single destiny, seen against those wilful, intersecting lines of chance and nature. And, with the pity of it, there is the delicious humour which infects every page, the charm of writing that seems as simple as talking but is always exquisite. It is a great deal to have brought back from an adventure; yet, after all, what we relish as much as anything in Mrs. Woolf's method is its adventurousness.

27. Lewis Bettany, review, *Daily News*

27 October 1922, 7

From a review headed 'Middle Aged Sensualists'. Arnold Bennett's *Lilian* was one of the books reviewed in the same article (see Introduction, p. 15).

In many of his stories of the 'Five Towns', Mr Bennett used to bore his greatest admirers by his tiresome trick of presenting a girl's naive interest in boarding a bus or taking a railway journey as a passion for romance. This sense of wonder, a wonder very different from that expressed by Browne and Traherne, is an irritating feature of Mrs Woolf's new story, which is so full of parentheses and suppressions, so tedious in its rediscoveries of the obvious, and so marred by its occasional lapses into indelicacy, that I found great difficulty in discovering what it was all about. Those who care to read about the adolescent ardours of a half-baked young Cambridge man in literature, love and travel, will find what they like in *Jacob's Room*. I thought most of the book very pretentious and very cheap; but some of the observations and impressions seemed to me quite happy.

28. Unsigned review, *Pall Mall Gazette*

27 October 1922, 6

The impressionist element in *Jacob's Room* was emphasised by many reviewers, and this typical review was headed quite simply 'An Impressionist' (see Introduction, p. 15).

Mrs Woolf is a very clever writer, whose originality expends itself in ways that are only doubtfully worth while. She attempts in prose what so many have attempted in verse—the achievement of art while evading the problems of form—and we can see little sign of the product becoming of more than technical interest. Most deftly does she catch and convey the impression of a scene, an incident, a passing figure, or a relationship, but no true novel can be built out of a mere accumulation of these notebook entries. In *Jacob's Room* there is not only no story, but there is no perceptible development of any kind. We get an outline of the kind of young man that Jacob was and of the kind of woman that his mother was, and very subtly and admirably are some of the features touched in.

29. Rebecca West, review, *New Statesman*

4 November 1922, 142

Rebecca West (b. 1893). Novelist and critic. Like many reviewers, she saw Virginia Woolf's books as something other than novels, and once again the comparison is with the pictorial arts: we should read *Jacob's Room* 'not as a novel but as a portfolio'.

There is an expression, one of those unused phrases that nest in the tall tree-top of the idiom book, 'I would rather have his room than his company.' One learned its French equivalent, which was not less excluded from common speech (strange and beautiful it is, like one of Swinburne's nature poems, this mating of unuttered phrases with their alien fellow-outcast over frontier seas and mountains, through the kind ponderous idiom-book), and it was forgotten, till it should be recalled by Mrs Woolf's last book. Very strongly has Mrs Woolf preferred Jacob's room to his company. Jacob lives, but that is hearsay. Jacob dies; there could be nothing more negative than the death of one who never (that we could learn for certain) lived, reported by a mouth that makes every human event she speaks of seem as if it had not happened. But his room we know. 'The eighteenth century has its distinction. These houses were built, say, a hundred and fifty years ago. The rooms are shapely, the ceilings high; over the doorways a rose or a ram's skull is carved in wood. Even the panels, painted in raspberry-coloured paint, have their distinction.' We know so much about it; how his mother's letter, in its pale blue envelope, lay waiting for him by the biscuit-box; how the *Globe* looked pinkish under the lamplight and was stared at, but not read, one cold night; how the room heard, at hours when the elderly lie abed, young men disputing on whether this or that line came in Virgil or Lucretius; and how, Jacob dead in the war, it felt his absence. 'Listless is the air in an empty room, just swelling the curtain; the flowers in the jar shift. One fibre in the wicker arm-chair creaks, though no one sits there . . .'

Mrs Woolf has again provided us with a demonstration that she is at once a negligible novelist and a supremely important writer. The novel may be exactly what it likes. It may be fifteen thousand words, or five hundred thousand; it may be written as simply as a melody in one part or as elaborately as a symphony. But it must, surely, submit to one limitation. It must primarily concern itself with humanity. Only the long drive of the human will can be fitly commemorated in the long drive of the novel form. Now from that point of view *Jacob's Room* is a failure. The fault of it is not that it is about commonplace people—that, indeed, is never a fault—but that it is not about individuals at all but about types as seen through the refractions of commonplace observers' eyes. Jacob's mother, Betty Flanders, is based on the conventional exclamations that such a figure of bluff maternity would evoke from a commonplace observer; so, too, Florinda the whore, so, too, Mother Stuart, her *entrepreneuse*; so, too, Clara Durrant, the nice girl; and Sandra Wentworth Williams, humorous but wholly a reported thing, dredged up from the talk of some cosmopolitan tea-party.

But take the book not as a novel but as a portfolio, and it is indubitably precious. A portfolio is indeed an appropriate image, for not only are Mrs Woolf's contributions to her age loose leaves, but they are also connected closely with the pictorial arts. Though she may have read Jane Austen and the Russians and James Joyce with more than common delight and intelligence, it is nothing in literature that has made her. She can write supremely well only of what can be painted; best of all, perhaps, of what has been painted. Take, for example, one of the rare occasions when the people in the book evoke emotion, the short and subtle and extremely funny conversation between Miss Edwards and Mr Calthorp at the Durrants' party. The temptation is to ascribe it (since it plainly hardly came of itself) to the influence of Jane Austen. But if that had been the source the conversation would have had some high lights of verbal amusingness on it instead of being simply a success in suggestion, in the evocation of a prim social atmosphere. The derivation is surely a drawing in *Punch*, a pre-Du Maurier drawing of discreet ladies in spread skirts and young men with peg-top trousers and curling beards, sitting at parties glorious with the innocent pretentiousness of hired pineapples and *ad hoc* waiters from the pastrycook's.

There is dull stuff near the beginning about the Scilly Isles; none of the old people whose hints Mrs Woolf can take, painted those parts. There is a good outing with the foxhounds in Essex, to which Morland and the old hunting prints have given their jollity. But best of all are

Mrs Woolf's London series. There was a gentleman who lived in the prime of the nineteenth century, when it was at once prim and fresh and artificial like a newly-plucked gardenia, named Mr Boys, who made many lithographs of London. It was all as lovely then as Nash's Quadrant when we were young. Exquisitely did the industrious Mr Boys capture its beauty, looking through an eye clear and bright as a dewdrop, wielding a neat hand as neatly as any old maid at her embroidery, to record the near-classicism of those stately streets, the pediments which were usually mitigated in their Latinity by emblems of Britannia and sculptural allusions to the Royal Family, the proud pillars that were painted the colour of pale soup and marbled, as likely as not, with pink veinings. Taste was his absolutely. He was, one remembers, not so good with his people, save with such oddities as sweeps and hurdy-gurdy men. Yet it was not all masonry. He knew God as well as Nash. Above his streets there were limitless skies (by them alone you may know whether your copy is coloured by his hand or a hireling's) full of light, full of real sailing clouds.

His talent was blood-brother to that of Mrs Woolf. Always and whimsically enough, since her tale is of this day, she suggests that young virgin-spirited London of his time. Her eye, too, is clear and bright as a dewdrop, her industry immense and humble, her taste as final. She can tell how dawn comes to London,

[Quotes pp. 162–3 'The Bank of England emerges' to 'chairs standing askew.']

She tells how Rotten Row looks on a sweet afternoon; how the leather curtain flaps at the door of St Paul's; how the morning army looks pouring over Waterloo Bridge. She is less successful with her considered characters than with her odd vignettes, less successful with Jacob than with Mrs Grandage. Yet this is no brick-counting, no extension of the careful cataloguing 'Nature Notes' method to the phenomena of town. It is authentic poetry, cognisant of the soul.

30. W. L. Courtney, review, *Daily Telegraph*

10 November 1922, 4

W. L. Courtney (1850–1928), English philosopher and journalist, taught for some time at New College, Oxford. In his long journalistic career, Courtney worked for the *Fortnightly Review*, the *Edinburgh Review* and the *Daily Telegraph*, of which he became the chief dramatic and literary editor.

In estimating the tendencies of a particular era in literature it is well to take extreme cases. We recognise that there are certain distinctive peculiarities about modern novels. But in order to make sure of the fact we need only take up a book like *Jacob's Room*, by Mrs Virginia Woolf. Even so, we shall be a little perplexed, for sometimes—perhaps oftener than not—we do not quite understand what the authoress is driving at, nor are we in a position to feel certain that she achieves the results at which she aims. One thing is clear. Instead of a straightforward narrative dealing with certain characters, with the interactions of those characters on one another, and with the destiny which carries them to their appointed end, we have a perfectly different art form. There is no particular story to tell, unless, indeed, you can gather some kind of story out of the piecemeal references to personages and things. But what does emerge is the constant activity, the perpetual reaction of a sensitive mind upon the impressions which come through the senses—so that an event or a character is not viewed as it is, but only as steeped in the consciousness of the author. That is the great and decisive difference between an older art-method and a later, and sometimes the contrast is a little embarrassing. The old craving for a plot still remains in our unregenerate breasts, and when all that we receive in compensation for what we have lost is the attitude of Mrs Virginia Woolf towards her creations—or rather, perhaps, a theory of life as interpreted by a clever observer—there must inevitably be some confusion and a mixture of mere narration with the intrusions and philosophisings of a superior mind. Anything like an objective creation becomes impossible. By an objective creation I mean the portrayal of a particular thing, person, or incident as it exists in itself. Flaubert thought that that was the only right way of writing a novel, and hence his theory—driven hard by a man who consciously lived his life apart from others—was the absolute exclusion of the author's personality from the written page. Mrs Woolf confidently chatters as though she were seated in an armchair playing with her puppets. It is she who gives them life. It is she who imparts to them such character as they are allowed to possess. They talk well because the author of their being talks well. They say clever things, not as from their own mouths, but as prompted by their creator. And if their creator appears to be a clever and original woman, her creations have the stamp of real life. But does she really care for them? Is she enamoured of her puppets? I wonder.

We begin merrily enough with something that looks as if it might be interesting narrative. Here is Mrs Flanders, anxious about her children, of whom Jacob is the prominent one, and Archer and John are allowed to fall into the background. Jacob is obviously to be the hero. He has his own definite views, young as he is. He is not made for obedience. He clearly determines to live his life in his own way. And he is very handsome. Most women admire him, though they concede that he is very shy and awkward, a youth who often prefers silence to speech. Mrs Flanders has her own little romance to think of, but that does not interfere with her duty towards her children. And so, somehow or other, money is got together to send Jacob to college, and to enable him to make his big plunge into life. Then, of course, the usual incidents happen. We pass through a number of scenes of revelry and boredom, and such names are tossed up on the surface of the story as Florinda—who is not much better than she should be—Clara Durrant, Sandra, and others. His male friends also flit hither and thither—Timothy Durrant, Clara's brother, and Bonamy, and Mr Benson. But the way in which these personages are treated is, of course, the chief point in *Jacob's Room*. Although Mrs Woolf abjures realism, yet she is realistic enough when it comes to the treatment of ordinary episodes. No one is more happily inspired than she when it comes to dialogue and conversation. She will give us the impression of a conversation by making several people talk, as it were, at once, each with his or her own particular interest, so that you get voices coming from left and right, voices up by the window or by the fireplace, voices bidding farewell or saying good-day—all the mixture of different interests which a crowded drawing room can contain. The result to an old-fashioned reader is sufficiently curious. For example, thus:

[Quotes pp. 56–7 'Did you quarrel' to 'one coin on to the table.']

In similar fashion Mrs Woolf achieves her backgrounds with a great deal of skill. Whether we find ourselves at Cambridge or on Hampstead Heath, in the suburbs of London or on board a yacht, or in Athens, we find the same graphic and picturesque touch, and the picture is drawn, arresting, vivid, intriguing, just as this point or that point in the mise en scène is brought out for a moment in high light. She gets atmosphere in her own fashion without aiming at any special exercise of cleverness; she uses similes and strange locutions, often bizarre, but undoubtedly adding to the effect. Take, for example, the following picture, very suggestive of Mrs Woolf's style:

[Quotes p. 54 'The rooks settled' to 'white as china.']

Yes, the author knows how to give us atmosphere, and perhaps that is a sufficient justification of her method. She is very unlike other writers, except that now and again she reminds us of Dorothy Richardson. But in her instinct for the nuances of character, in the keen discernment of those small, unessential things which go to the making of life, she scores again and again. Her theory of art ought, I suppose, to be called 'impressionist'. She does not describe; she merely indicates; throughout there is always the pervasive character and spirit of Virginia Woolf. It is she who makes the vital difference. Without her names are merely names, and do not represent anything alive. For some readers it is a drawback, though others will perhaps consider it a fortunate circumstance, that there is so little sense of unity, so striking a want of connection and harmony between the different stages of her history. To be impressionist is often to be incoherent, inconsequent, lacking all design and construction. But if you want to know what a modern novel is like, you have only to read *Jacob's Room*, by Virginia Woolf. In its tense, syncopated movements, its staccato impulsiveness, do you not discern the influence of Jazz?

31. Gerald Gould, review, *Saturday Review*

11 November 1922, 726

Gould's comparison in the first sentence of this extract is with Evelyn Scott's *Bewilderment* which he reviewed in the same article.

Mrs Woolf's *Jacob's Room* is a very different matter: for, though the technique is similar, and the theme not much more satisfying, a far finer and bigger intelligence is at work on them. Mrs Woolf can give us beauty. She has lyrical passages—one, in particular, about crossing Waterloo Bridge in a wind: she can make us feel what she calls 'the ecstasy and hubbub of the soul'. But still, the dot-and-dash method leaves much to be desired. One wonders that so clever a writer should attach so much importance to cleverness. Almost everybody is clever: but to stress one's own cleverness by a sort of humorous indulgence towards one's creations, and to leave the simple-minded reader guessing at connexions which might just as well be made clear for him, is a positive injury to art. It distracts from the solid object of the imagination. It destroys concentration. And it throws into violent contrast the lapses from the entirely unnecessary 'intellectual' standard—such, for instance, as the crude caricature of the feminist in the British Museum, 'wetting her pen in bitterness, and leaving her shoe laces untied'.

Jacob is loved by an inarticulate girl, and drifts away from her. He has some rather sordid sexual experiences of the transitory kind. He goes to Greece and falls in love with an unpleasant married woman. He is killed in the war. That is all, but out of that Mrs Woolf has made something wholly interesting and partly beautiful. It is at once irritating and encouraging to reflect how much better she would do if her art were less self-conscious.

32. Unsigned review, 'Dissolving Views', *Yorkshire Post*

29 November 1922, 4

Those who, like the present writer, thought, after reading *Night and Day*, that Mrs Woolf's next novel would be something of an event, must be prepared to find that *Jacob's Room* bears hardly any resemblance to its predecessor. Mrs Woolf has, indeed, discovered a somewhat new way of writing a novel—a way that is just a little like that developed by Mr James Joyce, but far more detached and far more selective. The method, briefly, is snapshot photography, with a highly sensitive, perfected camera handled by an artist. The result is a crowded album of little pictures—of Jacob as a boy; of Jacob's mother and home at Scarborough; of Jacob at Cambridge (an admirable one, this, full of compressed but very significant and satisfying detail); of Jacob in London, and the women who fall in love with him there; of Jacob travelling in Greece, half in love himself now with the vaguely emotional Mrs Sandra Wentworth Williams; of Jacob's room, empty, being tidied by his friend Bonamy, after Jacob (we gather) has been killed in the war.

No one could question Mrs Woolf's great abilities as a writer. There are passages in this book, such as that describing Jacob and a Cambridge friend approaching the Scilly Isles in a little sailing yacht, which contain nothing resembling a 'purple patch', and yet achieve a remarkably pure, lyrical beauty; there are many passages in which some impression—of London in summer, of a drawing-room conversation, of a character or a landscape—is seized and presented with admirable economy and truth. But all this seems to us no more than the material for a novel, and Mrs Woolf has done hardly anything to put it together. *Jacob's Room* has no narrative, no design, above all, no perspective: its dissolving views come before us one by one, each taking the full light for a moment, then vanishing completely. One remembers with regret the strong, harmonious structure of *Night and Day*; beside that *Jacob's Room*, beautiful as much of it is, seems flickering, impermanent. Nevertheless, if, as we think probable, Mrs Woolf has experienced a strong impulse to adopt this form, and no other, for her new novel, she is certainly doing right to obey: for she is, unlike most of her contemporaries, a genuine artist.

33. Unsigned review, *New Age*

21 December 1922, 123

When Browning's Pippa passed and sung her song she effected, unknown to herself, profound changes in the lives of others. Mrs Woolf's attempts at a new technique have puzzled us for some time; but this lengthy series reveals the method. She is Pippa, not singing, but eavesdropping; not effecting changes, but snapshotting things with and without meaning. The result is that we never know what she is talking about, except that life presents itself to her as a phantasmagoria. 'There is but one art—to omit!' cried Stevenson, but Mrs Woolf has not learned it. Where these people come from, who they are, what they do or suffer, what they think or feel, we cannot learn from Mrs Woolf; she transcribes faithfully the fragments she overhears in tube, tram, or train, in the Express Dairy restaurant and the Reading Room of the British Museum, anywhere where people are saying things that have no meaning for anyone else. The little flurries of prose poetry do not make art of this rag-bag of impressions.

34. Middleton Murry on the impasse of prose fiction

1923

John Middleton Murry (1889–1957). Man of letters, editor, literary critic. Married to Katherine Mansfield (see No. 18).

From 'Romance', *Nation and Athenaeum*, 10 March 1923, 882.

This aside, in a review, not of Virginia Woolf, but of L. H. Myers's *The Orissers* and Michael Sadleir's *Desolate Splendour*, was to worry Virginia Woolf: perhaps her experiments were leading to a dead end (see Introduction, p. 15).

The most original minds among those of the younger generation who have chosen prose-fiction for their medium have seemed to care less and less for plot. Not even a desultory story attracts them. Character, atmosphere, an attitude to life, a quality of perception—these things have interested a D. H. Lawrence, a Katherine Mansfield, a Virginia Woolf; but the old mechanism of story not at all. They represent a logical and necessary development of the realism of twenty years ago. Not one of them has solved the problem of the *novel*; neither did Marcel Proust, nor has Mr Joyce or Miss Richardson solved it. None of them has really any use for a story. It is a kind of nursery-game for them—at the best a trick; and they have more important things to do than waste time playing tricks or learning how to play them.

The consequence is that the novel has reached a kind of *impasse*. The artists have, to a very large extent, outrun their audience. Perhaps they have outrun themselves a little, too. At any rate, it seems to be true that they have as yet achieved creative perfection only in the short story. 'Prelude', 'Wintry Peacock', 'The Daughters of the Late Colonel', are things which will pass to immortality entire; of the novels, probably no more than scraps. They lack constructive solidity, they are fluid and fragmentary, brilliant and incoherent. And the public still likes a story.

35. Maxwell Bodenheim, 'Underneath the Paint in Jacob's Room', *Nation* (New York)

28 March 1923, 368–9

Maxwell Bodenheim (1893–1954), American poet and novelist. He reviewed *Paint* by Thomas Craven in the same article.

The art of painting, on the whole, seems to be animated by a swifter boldness than that of literature, and is less inclined to consolidate its victories and to remain timidly within the conquered realm of blended content and expression. The impressionists, headed by Monet, flourished in painting many decades ago, but the impressionists in English literature have only arrived during the past four or five years. The recent revolts in literature—the Dadaists and expressionists—have attained more intensity and publicity than numbers and influence, and have, after all, dominated only one-hundredth of the output in contemporary literature, while the rebellions in painting have gained a larger and more commanding position. In addition, the work of cubist painters has been far more important than that of the literary Dadaists and has attained a greater precision and sureness. On the whole, the art of painting has been sturdier and less uncertain than its rival, the belated impressionist school in literature.

Ironically enough, the founder of this method, Dorothy Richardson, has been practically ignored, while her lesser imitators are reveling in the praise of myopic critics, and among these imitators Virginia Woolf flourishes. Her novel, *Jacob's Room*, is a rambling, redundant affair, in which the commonplace details and motives of ordinary people are divided and subdivided until they form a series of atoms, and the author's speculations upon these atoms have the volubility of conversation in a drawing-room. Mrs Woolf does not seem to believe that anything should be omitted, and lingers over the little, everyday motives and waking impulses of her undistinguished people, and the significance held by the hosts of inanimate objects which these people touch and see. The result is frequently an endless parade of details that grow more and more uninteresting, proceeding in an impulsive fashion and darting here and there with indefatigable minuteness. The following passage is an apt illustration:

[Quotes p. 91 'Let us consider letters' to 'or the scowl.']

So far the analysis has been diverting, although the author might have realized that I would be well acquainted with the customary times of arrival and the color of the stamps, but, alas, the subject has only commenced! For another eight hundred words or more I am to read all about letters and every possible shade of meaning attached to them. 'This is just like life', as one critic wrote in praise of *Jacob's Room*, but I do not approach the novel for a verbatim account of life and I am more intrigued by a condensation that displays only the salient items. There are too many moderately subtle stenographers in literature at present. *Jacob's Room* revolves jerkily around the figure of Jacob Flanders, from his boyhood to his death in the late World War, while still a young man. His groping for thoughts, emotions, and prejudices, and his occasional affairs with blithely shallow women, reveal him as an average young man, half pathetic and half ludicrous, but he is advanced with such a microscopical effusiveness and with so many irrelevant details that one is tempted to mutter: 'I see and meet at least fifty Jacob Flanders every month of my life, and if the introduction must be repeated it should hold a brevity and suggestiveness which these actual men do not possess.'

[There follows a discussion of Thomas Craven's *Paint*, and the review ends]:

This novel is crudely written in parts, and hastily molded in others, but it holds a vicious strength and concentration that is far removed from the deftly garrulous, thinly sad descriptions and meditations of *Jacob's Room*. Those who like *Jacob's Room* will not be overresponsive to Mr Craven's novel, and the reason is that few people care to see life struck by an accurate and unpitying sledgehammer. The result is somewhat injurious to their various complacencies.

36. Arnold Bennett, 'Is the Novel Decaying?', *Cassell's Weekly*

28 March 1923, 47

Arnold Bennett (1867–1931). Novelist.

Virginia Woolf's reply to this article is the next item (No. 37). For the background to the debate between Arnold Bennett and Virginia Woolf, see Introduction, p. 16.

If I have heard it once, I have heard fifty times during the past year the complaint that no young novelists with promise of first-rate importance are rising up to take the place of the important middle-aged. Upon this matter I have two lines of thought.

What makes a novel important enough to impress itself upon both the discriminating few and the less discriminating many? (For first-class prestige is not obtained unless both sorts of readers are in the end impressed.) The first thing is that the novel should seem to be true. It cannot seem true if the characters do not seem to be real. Style counts; plot counts; invention counts; originality of outlook counts; wide information counts; wide sympathy counts. But none of these counts anything like so much as the convincingness of the characters. If the characters are real the novel will have a chance; if they are not oblivion will be its portion.

The Sherlock Holmes stories have still a certain slight prestige. Because of the ingenuity of the plots? No. Because of the convincingness of the principal character? No. The man is a conventional figure. The reason is in the convincingness of the ass Watson. Watson has real life. His authenticity convinces everyone, and the books in which he appears survive by reason of him. Why are *The Three Musketeers* and *Twenty Years After* the most celebrated of Dumas's thousand volumes? Many other novels of Dumas have very marvellous and brilliant plots. For instance, *Monte Cristo*. But the *Musketeer* volumes outshine them easily because of the superior convincingness of the characters. Why is Sinclair Lewis's *Babbitt* a better book than his *Main Street*? Because in the latter the chief character (heroine) is a sentimental stick, while in the former the chief character (Babbitt himself) is a genuine individual that all can recognise for reality.

To render secure the importance of a novel it is necessary, further, that the characters should clash one with another so as to produce strong emotion, first in the author himself and second in the reader. This strong emotion cannot be produced unless the characters are *kept* true throughout. You cannot get strength out of falsity. The moment the still small voice whispers to the reader about a character, 'He wouldn't have acted like that,' the book is imperilled. The reader may say: 'This is charming. This is amusing. This is original. This is clever. This is exciting.' But if he also has to say, 'It's not true', the success of the book cannot be permanent.

The foundation of good fiction is character creating, and nothing else. The characters must be so fully true that they possess even their own creator. Every deviation from truth, every omission of truth, necessarily impairs the emotional power and therefore weakens the interest.

I think that we have to-day a number of young novelists who display all manner of good qualities—originality of view, ingenuity of presentment, sound common sense, and even style. But they appear to me to be interested more in details than in the full creation of their individual characters. They are so busy with states of society as to half forget that any society consists of individuals, and they attach too much weight to cleverness, which is perhaps the lowest of all artistic qualities.

I have seldom read a cleverer book than Virginia Woolf's *Jacob's Room*, a novel which has made a great stir in a small world. It is packed and bursting with originality, and it is exquisitely written. But the characters do not vitally survive in the mind because the author has been obsessed by details of originality and cleverness. I regard this book as characteristic of the new novelists who have recently gained the attention of the alert and the curious, and I admit that for myself I cannot yet descry any coming big novelists.

But nevertheless—and here is my second line of thought—I am fairly sure that big novelists are sprouting up. Only we do not know where to look for them. Or we cannot recognize them when we see them. It is almost certain that the majority of the great names of 1950 are writing to-day without any general appreciation. They have not been spotted as winners by the sporting prophets, and publicity paragraphs are not published about them. Few or none recognized the spring of greatness in the early Hardy, or in the early Butler, or in the early George Moore, or in the early Meredith. And there is scarcely a permanently great name in the whole history of fiction who was not when he first wrote overshadowed in the popular and even in the semi-expert esteem by much inferior novelists. The great did not at first abound in glitter and cleverness. As a rule they began by being rather clumsy, poor dears! Hence I am not pessimistic about the future of the novel.

'MR BENNETT and MRS BROWN' (First Version)

1923

37. Virginia Woolf, 'Mr Bennett and Mrs Brown' (First Version), *Nation and Athenaeum*

1 December 1923, 342–3

This was written in answer to the previous article by Arnold Bennett (No. 36). It is the first version of the later more famous essay. For the background to the debate between Virginia Woolf and Arnold Bennett see Introduction, p. 16.

This article also appeared in *New York Evening Post*, 17 November 1923.

The other day Mr Arnold Bennett, himself one of the most famous of the Edwardians, surveyed the younger generation and said: 'I admit that for myself I cannot yet descry any coming big novelist.' And that, let us say in passing, is all to the good—a symptom of the respectful hostility which is the only healthy relation between old and young. But then he went on to give his reasons for this lamentable fact, and his reasons, which lie deep, deserve much more consideration than his impatience, which lies on the surface. The Georgians fail as novelists, he said, because 'they are interested more in details than in the full creation of their individual characters. . . . The foundation of good fiction is character-creating, and nothing else. To render secure the importance of a novel it is necessary, further, that the characters should clash with one another,' or, of course, they will excite no emotion in the breast of the author or anybody else. None of this is new; all of it is true; yet here we have one of those simple statements which are no sooner taken into the mind than they burst their envelopes and flood us with suggestions of every kind.

The novel is a very remarkable machine for the creation of human character, we are all agreed. Directly it ceases to create character, its defects alone are visible. And it is because this essence, this character-making power, has evaporated that novels are for the most part the soulless bodies we know, cumbering our tables and clogging our minds. That, too, may pass. Few reviewers at least are likely to dispute it. But if we go on to ask when this change began, and what were the reasons behind it, then agreement is much more difficult to come by. Mr Bennett blames the Georgians. Our minds fly straight to King Edward. Surely that was the fatal age, the age which is just breaking off from our own, the age when character disappeared or was mysteriously engulfed, and the culprits, happily still alive, active, and unrepentant, are Mr Wells, Mr Galsworthy, and Mr Bennett himself.

But in lodging such a charge against so formidable a library we must do as painters do when they wish to reduce the innumerable details of a crowded landscape to simplicity—step back, half shut the eyes, gesticulate a little vaguely with the fingers, and reduce Edwardian fiction to a view. Thus treated, one strange fact is immediately apparent. Every sort of town is represented, and innumerable institutions; we see factories, prisons, workhouses, law courts, Houses of Parliament; a general clamour, the voice of aspiration, indignation, effort and industry, rises from the whole; but in all this vast conglomeration of printed pages, in all this congeries of streets and houses, there is not a single man or woman whom we know. Figures like Kipps or the sisters (already nameless) in the *Old Wives' Tale* attempt to contradict this assertion, but with how feeble a voice and flimsy a body is apparent directly they are stood beside some character from that other great tract of fiction which lies immediately behind them in the Victorian age. For there, if we follow the same process, but recall one novel, and that—*Pendennis*—not one of the most famous, at once start out, clear, vigorous, alive from the curl of their eyelashes to the soles of their boots, half-a-dozen characters whose names are no sooner spoken than we think of scene after scene in which they play their parts. We see the Major sitting in his club window, fresh from the hands of Morgan; Helen nursing her son in the Temple and suspecting poor Fanny; Warrington grilling chops in his dressing-gown; Captain Shandon scribbling leaders for the *Pall Mall Gazette*—Laura, Blanche Amory,

Foker; the procession is endless and alive. And so it goes on from character to character all through the splendid opulence of the Victorian age. They love, they joke, they hunt, they marry; they lead us from hall to cottage, from field to slum. The whole country, the whole society, is revealed to us, and revealed always in the same way, through the astonishing vividness and reality of the characters.

And it was perhaps on that very account that the Edwardians changed their tactics. Such triumphs could scarcely be rivalled; and, moreover, triumphs once achieved seem to the next generation always a little uninteresting. There was, too (if we think ourselves into the mind of a writer contemplating fiction about the year 1900), something plausible, superficial, unreal in all this abundance. No sooner had the Victorians departed than Samuel Butler, who had lived below-stairs, came out, like an observant bootboy, with the family secrets in *The Way of All Flesh.* It appeared that the basement was really in an appalling state. Though the saloons were splendid and the dining-rooms portentous, the drains were of the most primitive description. The social state was a mass of corruption. A sensitive man like Mr Galsworthy could scarcely step out of doors without barking his shins upon some social iniquity. A generous mind which knew the conditions in which the Kippses and the Lewishams were born and bred must try at least to fashion the world afresh. So the young novelist became a reformer, and thought with pardonable contempt of those vast Victorian family parties, where the funny man was always funny, the good woman always good, and nobody seemed aware, as they pursued their own tiny lives, that society was rotten and Christianity itself at stake. But there was another force which made much more subtly against the creation of character, and that was Mrs Garnett and her translations from Dostoevsky. After reading *Crime and Punishment* and *The Idiot*, how could any young novelist believe in 'characters' as the Victorians had painted them? For the undeniable vividness of so many of them is the result of their crudity. The character is rubbed into us indelibly because its features are so few and so prominent. We are given the keyword (Mr Dick has King Charles's head; Mr Brooke, 'I went into that a great deal at one time'; Mrs Micawber, 'I will never desert Mr Micawber'), and then, since the choice of the keyword is astonishingly apt, our imaginations swiftly supply the rest. But what keyword could be applied to Raskolnikov, Mishkin, Stavrogin, or Alyosha? These are characters without any features at all. We go down into them as we descend into some enormous cavern. Lights swing about; we hear the boom of the sea; it is all dark, terrible, and uncharted. So we need not be surprised if the Edwardian novelist scarcely attempted to deal with character except in its more generalized aspects. The Victorian version was discredited; it was his duty to destroy all those institutions in the shelter of which character thrives and thickens; and the Russians had shown him—everything or nothing, it was impossible as yet to say which. The Edwardian novelists therefore give us a vast sense of things in general; but a very vague one of things in particular. Mr Galsworthy gives us a sense of compassion; Mr Wells fills us with generous enthusiasm; Mr Bennett (in his early work) gave us a sense of time. But their books are already a little chill, and must steadily grow more distant, for 'the foundation of good fiction is character-creating, and nothing else', as Mr Bennett says; and in none of them are we given a man or woman whom we know.

The Georgians had, therefore, a difficult task before them, and if they have failed, as Mr Bennett asserts, there is nothing to surprise us in that. To bring back character from the shapelessness into which it has lapsed, to sharpen its edges, deepen its compass, and so make possible those conflicts between human being which alone rouse our strongest emotions—such was their problem. It was the consciousness of this problem, and not the accession of King George, which produced, as it always produces, the break between one generation and the next. Here, however, the break is particularly sharp, for here the dispute is fundamental. In real life there is nothing that interests us more than character, that stirs us to the same extremes of love and anger, or that leads us to such incessant and laborious speculations about the values, the reasons, and the meaning of existence itself. To disagree about character is to differ in the depths of the being. It is to take different sides, to drift apart, to accept a purely formal intercourse for ever. That is so in real life. But the novelist has to go much further and to be much more uncompromising than the friend. When he finds himself hopelessly at variance with Mr Wells, Mr Galsworthy, and Mr Bennett about the character—shall we say?—of Mrs Brown, it is useless to defer to their superior genius. It is useless to mumble the polite agreements of the drawing-room. He must set about to remake the woman after his own idea. And that, in the circumstances, is a very perilous pursuit.

For what, after all, is character—the way that Mrs Brown, for instance, reacts to her surroundings—when we cease to believe what we are told about her, and begin to search out her real meaning for ourselves? In the first place, her solidity disappears; her features crumble;

the house in which she has lived so long (and a very substantial house it was) topples to the ground. She becomes a will-o'-the-wisp, a dancing light, an illumination gliding up the wall and out of the window, lighting now in freakish malice upon the nose of an archbishop, now in sudden splendour upon the mahogany of the wardrobe. The most solemn sights she turns to ridicule; the most ordinary she invests with beauty. She changes the shape, shifts the accent, of every scene in which she plays her part. And it is from the ruins and splinters of this tumbled mansion that the Georgian writer must somehow reconstruct a habitable dwelling-place; it is from the gleams and flashes of this flying spirit that he must create solid, living, flesh-and-blood Mrs Brown. Sadly he must allow that the lady still escapes him. Dismally he must admit bruises received in the pursuit. But it is because the Georgians, poets and novelists, biographers and dramatists, are so hotly engaged each in the pursuit of his own Mrs Brown that theirs is at once the least successful, and most interesting, hundred years. Moreover, let us prophesy: Mrs Brown will not always escape. One of these days Mrs Brown will be caught. The capture of Mrs Brown is the title of the next chapter in the history of literature; and, let us prophesy again, that chapter will be one of the most important, the most illustrious, the most epoch-making of them all.

38. J. D. Beresford, 'The Successors of Charles Dickens', *Nation and Athenaeum*

29 December 1923, 487–8

J. D. Beresford (1873–1947). Publishers' reader, reviewer, and prolific novelist.

Virginia Woolf reviewed Beresford's novel *An Imperfect Mother* in an anonymous article entitled 'Freudian Fiction' (*TLS*, 25 March 1920, 199). In this article Beresford emphasises the 'change in human nature' which Virginia Woolf only hints at in the first 'Mr Bennett and Mrs Brown', but which was an important part of the second version.

In a recent article, Mrs Woolf suggested, pertinently and convincingly, that the chief failing of those three important novelists, Wells, Galsworthy, and Bennett, has been their inability to create character in the manner of, say, Dickens and Thackeray; and she quotes Bennett himself to uphold her criticism, in the statement: 'The foundation of good fiction is character-creating and nothing else.'

This suggestion is of peculiar interest inasmuch as it does not seem possible to confute it in the sense—a perfectly justifiable one—intended. But before we condemn our selected trio by this single criterion, it may be worth while to extend our examination and consider whether or not there may be a valid psychological explanation for this apparent weakness. Can we not, for example, find some reason why the figures of Edward Ponderevo, Arthur Kipps, Soames or Jolyon Forsyte, Edwin Clayhanger or Constance Povey do not leave quite the same definite impression on the mind as the more outstanding portraits drawn by Dickens and Thackeray?

The first and most obvious explanation is that which Mrs Woolf lightly sports with at the end of her article. When we had turned the century with Hardy, Meredith, and Kipling as our three leading writers of fiction, we witnessed a quite definite movement in the development of actualism. Whether or not Wells, Galsworthy, and Bennett consciously tried to approach their art from a new angle, is a question that we need not consider for our present purposes. What is of importance is that we find in their novels a presentation of human beings that satisfies our sense of probability; inasmuch as they are, like ourselves, composite, full of irresolutions, often self-conscious, and apt to change their minds; whereas in the novels of Dickens we find a single salient characteristic which is often given to us as portraying the complete man or woman.

What would Dickens, for instance, have done with Sophia Baines? In her youth she is shown, more or less determinedly, as reckless, flighty even, of a not too exemplary honesty. Can we doubt that having thus shaped her, Dickens would have maintained the mould? The last state of Sophia, as a result of the steady confirmation and deepening of these salient and instantly recognizable characteristics, would have been far worse than the first. But Mr Bennett—*pace* all you worshippers of Victorian greatness—was aware of many things of which Dickens was blandly ignorant. Mr Bennett was aware, in the first place, of heredity. He knew his Baineses; and he recognized those inherited qualities in Sophia which, in the circumstances, would presently override the impulses of youth and leave her a successful, if not an altogether satisfied, woman. Hers is, in short, an absolutely convincing portrait. We know for certain—as soon as Mr Bennett has told us—that she could have acted only as she is shown to have acted. Furthermore, she represents a type in the same sense that so many characters in Dickens represent types. Yet the average mind will forget a Sophia Baines and remember a Mrs Nickleby or a Betsey Trotwood.

Further examples are hardly necessary, but to point the application of the one cited to our other two novelists, it may be as well to add Edward Ponderevo and Soames Forsyte to the list. Both, according to the rigid classification of the Dickensian methods, are 'bad' men; and in the case of the former we know what Dickens would have done from the sad instance of Montague Tigg. Soames Forsyte, with his business capacity and his one act of brutality to his wife Irene, might possibly have become in Dickens's hand a kind of Dombey. And we know quite well what Dickens would have done with Irene.

Now, at first sight, the difference of treatment seems to be due solely to a change of attitude and of method. The older attitude with its resultant method evidences the fading influence of classicism, with its fundamental assumptions of a strict division into categories and the inescapable vigilance of a presiding and deeply interested Fate. Our three Edwardians had all pitched Fate out onto the rubbish-heap at the bottom of the garden—where it fell and failed to sprout. They were empiricists, a-posteriorists, and so far under the influence of the scientific method that they passionately desired to get as near the truth as a mere novelist may. They wanted before all things to present men and women as they themselves had seen them, not as Dickens did in a startling cartoon, but in three dimensions—at least three. After Fate had landed on the rubbish-heap, all sorts of queer things had gone after it, such things as predestination, the chronology of Bishop Usher, the theory of the divine origin of mankind, no end of funny-looking stuff; and our three novelists sat down in their clean and rather bare houses to write of themselves and us in the light of observation and reason.

But when we have justified their attitude, when we have admitted that they could not and should not have written in any other way about the men and women of their own time, we are still confronted with that difficult question as to whether the effect of their art on the public mind is as stimulating as that of Dickens. Just as, in the case of young children, Pip, Squeak, and Wilfred leave a clearer impression than Lewis Carroll's White Rabbit or his Red Queen; so, in the parallel case of our hypothetical average of public intelligence, the cartoonist will succeed where the chiaroscurist will fail. Your average reader of novels loves hard outlines, not subtleties and vague distances; certainties (or the appearance of them) rather than suggestions. But if we really care about our influence on him (Dickens, remember, was distinctly educative), ought we not to use the medium that reaches him more directly?

The answer to that question necessitates an inquiry into the further consideration that was hinted at when we began this development with a conditional 'at first sight'. For we have reached a stage at which we may boldly ask whether the change of attitude in the novelist does not foreshadow a parallel change, as yet far from complete, in the reader. Is it perhaps true, for instance, that in the eighteen-forties there were more queer, one-ideaed, less complicated, less self-conscious people about in England than there are in the nineteen-twenties? Has that marked change in the tendency of philosophic thought that became comparatively wide-spread in the last quarter of the nineteenth century—opening so many doors on to unguessed-at vistas which retreat, and lose themselves in infinite distances, where once was the calm assurance of such definite labels as Heaven, Purgatory, and Hell to dissuade the adventurer from opening the door for himself—has that change of thought had its influence on the public mind, or, alternatively, is it an indication of a rapidly developing change of consciousness?

Personally—for, lacking the witness of the Galtonian Institute in this matter, I am driven back to expressing a personal opinion—I favour the latter solution. I believe that, taking the average English man or woman, we shall find them more aware of their own diversity, more introspective, and hence more complicated, than would be the corresponding specimens picked out from a sample of early Victorians. I remember my mother's stories (she was born in 1837) of the friends who came to her father's house in her youth, and many of these friends, with their stock tricks of speech and their stock reactions to religion, politics, and society, could have gone straight into a Dickens novel. And the characterization of them would have been adequate. I even remember similar specimens in my own boyhood. Now, among my contemporaries, I search for them in vain. The world of to-day, as I see it, is filled with people who are too aware of themselves to be peculiar by conviction. The great divergencies of what we call 'types'—which means the abstraction of a preponderating characteristic—tend to converge by assimilation. For when we become more aware of ourselves, we inevitably become more aware of other people.

Even in politics, the process is displayed for us. Our parties witness to no passionate certitudes. Our leaders are no longer willing to die for their convictions, in the manner of a Burke, a Lincoln, or a Gladstone. They are conscientiously aware that there are two sides to every question; and only in the squalid emergencies of a general election should we now taunt a man with having changed his mind in regard to the advantages of, say, a fiscal policy.

And if we admit this growing change due to the evolution of consciousness, shall we say that the art of Wells, Galsworthy, or Bennett is of a lower order of achievement than that of Dickens or Thackeray, because our selected trio have presented us with a characterization that is truer to our own day than the depicting of the older 'type'? Has not, for example, Mr Bennett fully justified his dictum in his own work? Are his character-creating powers less than those of Dickens because they are more subtle? And, finally, is not the failure, such as it is, with those of us who are still in that condition in which we prefer Pip, Squeak, and Wilfred to the Red Queen?

I await the verdict.

39. Logan Pearsall Smith, 'First Catch Your Hare', *Nation and Athenaeum*

2 February 1924, 629–30

Smith (1865–1946) American literary man associated with Bloomsbury, especially Roger Fry, who was a close friend. The Woolfs published his *Stories from the Old Testament* in 1920. Leonard Woolf gives a picture of him about the time of this article:

> I did occasionally go to Logan's tea-parties where one drank Earl Grey's china tea amid china, furniture, pictures, books, and human beings, not easily distinguishable from one another or from the tea with its delicate taste and aroma, for they were all made, fabricated, collected in accordance with society's standards of sophisticated culture and good taste. Earl Grey has never been my cup of tea, nor was Logan (*Downhill All the Way*, pp. 99–100).

This portrait accords with the precious style of the following essay, which is, nevertheless an interesting discussion of character in fiction. Perhaps his remarks encouraged Virginia Woolf to widen the scope of the second version of 'Mr Bennett and Mrs Brown' (see Introduction, p. 16).

Mrs Woolf, in her recent answer to Mr Arnold Bennett in these columns, and Mr Beresford, with his reply to Mrs Woolf, have started a hare, and inaugurated a hunt of such fascination that even the most grizzly and retired of critical greyhounds must be irresistibly tempted to leap from his kennel and join the exhilarating chase.

The essence of fiction, the *sine qua non* of novel-writing, is the game they are after: that [it] is the creation of character, they agree with Mr Bennett; but where, in what covert the elusive animal is hidden, is among them a matter of lively dispute. I should like to suggest (if I may join them) that the field to which they confine themselves is rather too narrow. It isn't a question merely of English fiction; or, in English fiction, of the Victorians, the Edwardians, and our contemporary novelists. Indeed, to make sure that one has left no covert unexplored one should include, I think, not only foreign novels, but the drama, and even the epic; for these portray character as well as novels; they are also, if I may permit myself the pun, 'forms' in which our essential hare may be found lurking.

If, then, we wish to arrive at some definite idea of what we mean by character-creation in fiction, and, taking the word in its widest meaning, we summon up before our memories all the vast populations which people these worlds of the imagination, we shall see, I think, that those personages divide themselves pretty definitely into two groups. By far the great majority of them are stock figures, devoid of any independent existence. Personifications of the passions, idealizations of abstract qualities, embodiments of simple forces, or types of various professions, these heroes and lovers and heroines and villians and lords and misers and millionaires and clergymen and lawyers have all their names, their places in the social fabric; they all are endowed, and sometimes over-endowed, with the characteristics of their sex; they are upholstered in different kinds of clothes; they are often described and analysed and dissected at enormous length—and yet they almost all remain puppets: we see the strings that pull them; and when the play or novel in which they figure is over, their life ceases, they are laid aside, and we think of them no more.

But in the works of certain great writers some of the figures (though by no means all) present a very different appearance. They seem to be framed in a different manner and composed of other materials, to be real human beings, discoveries and not invention; they are no sooner brought into existence than they seem to have always existed: and when the novel is closed, or the curtain falls upon the drama, they go on living in our imaginations, and are as familiar to us as our relations and our best-acquainted friends. These are the figures which we call 'characters'; and the power of evoking them is what we call 'character-creation'. It is a power possessed in the highest degree by Shakespeare; we find it also in Scott, in Jane Austen, in Thackeray; and Dickens possessed it almost to madness. It is commonly regarded as the greatest gift of these novelists, and the very essence of their art. And yet, curiously enough, none of our critics, with, as far as I know, only one exception, have attempted an analysis of this creative power, or at least any real discrimination between stock figures and 'created' characters.

This exception is that obscure, almost forgotten diplomatist and politician of the eighteenth century, Maurice Morgann, who published in 1777 one small masterpiece of criticism, an *Essay* on the character of Falstaff, in which he deals with this question in a profoundly interesting way. What is the essential difference, he asks, between Shakespeare's characters and the stock figures of the other playwrights? The answer he gives—and I think it is essentially a true answer—can be paraphrased in our modern vocabulary as follows. No personage can be put whole into a work of art; the writer can only present the qualities and aspects which he needs for his purpose; and in other playwrights the parts which are not seen do not in fact exist; their makers have told us all they know about them; there is nothing more in these figures, as they conceive them, than what we see, and their hidden interiors are, as we may put it, filled, like dolls, with sawdust.

But Shakespeare's characters are created as vital wholes; they possess independence as well as relation; they are living organisms, in which each part depends upon, and implies, the complete person. Although we see them in part only, yet from these glimpses we unconsciously infer the parts we do not see; and when Shakespeare makes them act and speak, as he sometimes does, from their unportrayed but inferred aspects, he produces an astonishing effect of unforseen, yet inevitable truth.

Morgann does not discuss the means by which Shakespeare presents these characters to us, so as to make them seem real and living in our eyes. We have only, however, to look at one of his plays to perceive his method. He does not, of course, describe them—that as a dramatist he could hardly do—but he makes them, as it were, talk themselves into existence. The impression of individual character is produced by an individual way of speech; each personage possesses an idiom, a diction, a rhythm, a sort of sing-song of his own, so distinctive that, without reading their names, we can recognise each speaker by his voice. And when we look into it, we see that all our great character-creating novelists have adopted this Shakespearean method; we find it in Scott, in Jane Austen, in Thackeray, and above all in Dickens, who created hundreds of living beings, endowing each with his own inner song, his excited or drowsy twitter, his personal 'note', as distinctive as the note of a wren or chaffinch. Dickens and the other Victorians no doubt abused this enchantment, this way of making their characters sing themselves into existence; they reiterated their little tunes and catchphrases so monotonously that their successors became disgusted with this method, and adopted the method of description and analysis instead. Is this, perhaps, the cause of that loss of character-creating power which Mrs Woolf notes in them—the reason why our novelists no longer people our imaginations with living forms? Human nature nowadays, Mr Beresford suggests, is too complex, too self-conscious, too irresolute, to be moulded into salient and definite characters like those of our older writers. But does human nature change so rapidly? Are many of us more complex, more self-conscious, more irresolute than Hamlet? And yet has not Shakespeare created in Hamlet a most unmistakable and distinct and living being? And, let us note, Hamlet is made real to us very largely by his speech-rhythms and intonations—there is, for instance, as Mr Bradley has finely noted, nothing in the play more intensely characteristic, and more unmistakably individual, than Hamlet's trick of verbal repetitions. 'Words, words, words'—'very like, very like'—'thrift, thrift, Horatio'—'except my life, except my life, except my life'—is not the very essence of Hamlet embodied in these little phrases? Could any number of pages of analysis and description have made him more living to us?

If, then, this power of conceiving, and creating, and presenting character is found in the greatest of our playwrights and novelists, and in them alone (for no really second-rate writer possesses it); if, moreover, we find it present in proportion to their greatness, and if its presence always gives enduring value to their works, is it not possible that we have found in this creative power the *sine qua non*, the quintessential quality of fiction? Is our hunt over, our hare captured, and ready to be jugged and served up at last?

I do not think so; the doctrine, which is now so fashionable, of the single essential ingredient, has always seemed to me too great a simplification of esthetic problems. Even suppose we do find a *sine qua non* in art, a quality in the absence of which esthetic value is always absent, how can we say that other qualities, non-esthetic in themselves, do not acquire an intrinsic art-value when they combine with the essential quality in, as it were, a kind of chemical combination?

But however that may be, once we think of foreign literature, we shall see that character-creation is not really even a *sine qua non* in fiction—that it is hardly more an essential element in it than portraiture is an essential ingredient in the art of painting. To make hare-soup, one must, of course, first catch one's hare; but there are many other excellent kinds of soup brewed in the world's kitchens. How many of these living and self-subsistent beings, like Hamlet or Falstaff or Pickwick or

Mr Micawber, do we find outside of English literature? Hardly as many, I feel inclined to say, as in one play of Shakespeare, or one novel of Dickens or Jane Austen.

It would be pleasant to sit down and read through the whole of European fiction to find if this is really so; but not having leisure now for that perusal, I can only look into the phantasmagoria of memory to see what personages of foreign literature start to life at the evocation of their names. The Achilles and Agamemnon of Homer appear and speak with their individual voices; and Nausicaa is clad with an exquisite immortality. In my memory of the Greek drama I find ideal types and noble beings, but no really independent self-subsisting characters. Nor do I find them in Racine, nor in French fiction—in Stendhal or in Balzac. The truth is, I think, that this kind of creation is a special characteristic of English literature. We may find its roots perhaps in Chaucer, but it was in Shakespeare that it burst into exuberant and amazing blossom; and it is from Shakespeare that our great novelists derived their conception of it, and their method of portrayal.

Continental writers, whose ideal has on the whole been the classical one of turning events into ideas, and making them into food for the mind, have on the whole found typical personages, rather than 'characters', better and more transparent vehicles for their criticism of life—for their study of human relations and passions and circumstances. There are exceptions no doubt—there is Cervantes, who created Don Quixote; and there are the Russians, who have imitated English fiction. In our own day also there is Proust, who, as I should like to suggest to my fellow-huntsmen, has succeeded in moulding into living characters, with their own idiosyncrasies of speech, the most subtle complexities of our modern and self-conscious human nature. Nevertheless, character-creation, as we find it in English literature, is not, on the whole, an essential element in Continental fiction.

If we should attempt to take, from a classical and Continental standpoint, a general view of our English novels, might they not appear, in spite of—and even, perhaps, on account of—their swarming abundance of living characters, somewhat trivial and superficial as analyses of life? Are not our immense miscellaneous English novels rather like immense picnics and meaningless outings, in which a lot of odd people meet together in irrelevant horseplay, and then separate or pair off for no especial reason? Are not their different episodes of more importance than the whole impression they create? And have the individual characters in them much more than a casual relation with the novel in which they happen to appear? Could not the great characters of Dickens have figured just as well in almost any other of his novels? And hasn't the power of creating independent beings in some ways embarrassed even our greatest writers? Didn't that monster of exuberance, Falstaff, pull down, like Samson, the structure of the plays in which he figured, and didn't the most consummate of English artists endanger the scheme of his great epic by making his Devil so much more alive, and so much more interesting, than his God?

'By all means,' a Continental spectator of our coursing might address us, 'by all means hunt your hare, and when you catch it and serve it up, we hope that we shall be invited to the feast. The brown hare of your meadows is a creature which, though it sometimes goes mad in March, possesses admirable and even magical properties. And certainly its antics are a source of inexhaustible amusement. But it is indigenous to England, and is scarcely to be found abroad, save in Russia, whither its breed has been imported from your shores. The game we are after, our *lièvre*, is the mountain hare; to us it seems a creature of a rarer, more quintessential and almost divine quality; and its native home is on those ranges of thought, upon those high, Muse-haunted mountains where the ancient Greeks, not unaccompanied by the Immortals, were wont to pursue the chase.'

'CHARACTER IN FICTION'

1924

40. 'Simon Pure', from a review, *Bookman* (New York)

October 1924, 193–5

'Simon Pure' was the novelist, Frank Swinnerton (b. 1884). He is reviewing Virginia Woolf's essay 'Character in Fiction' which appeared in the *Criterion* in the previous July, and which was published in the following December in the Hogarth Essay series, with the title 'Mr Bennett and Mrs Brown': not to be confused with the first essay of that name (see Introduction, p. 16).

Mrs Woolf also tells us a little story about two people in a railway carriage, at the same time disclaiming any attempt to illustrate her own cleverness in telling the story. Mrs Woolf does herself injustice. Her story is very clever. So are her satiric accounts of Mr Wells and Mr Bennett and Mr Galsworthy. But just as the story is principally amusing as a revelation of Mrs Woolf's cleverness, so are the satiric accounts of Mr Wells and Mr Bennett and Mr Galsworthy amusing for the same reason. That is, Mrs Woolf strikes at familiar foibles of all three writers, but she does not create convincingly the characters of Mr Wells and Mr Bennett and Mr Galsworthy. If she had been a real Georgian novelist, she would have cast aside all her details about Mr Bennett and Mr Wells and Mr Galsworthy, and would have made these three men live before us. We should have been reminded of the very character of their work. We are only so reminded because we find that Mrs Woolf's descriptions are inadequate. Mr Wells is *not*—in his stories of emotional excess—always picturing an oversanitary world. Mr Galsworthy's emotional novels are generally free from social propaganda. Mr Bennett, depicting a form of society alien from Mrs Woolf's world of aesthetic cliques, may use cumbrous machinery to establish that world in the reader's eye, but at least when he gets to business, he does stimulate the reader's imagination, which Mrs Woolf never does. Would it not be open to me to take the long—the excessively long—page of *Night and Day* and make fun of them? Somehow I believe it would. But there is no need to make fun of *Night and Day*. Mr Massingham once attempted to count the number of times the people in *Night and Day* had tea; but when he had passed two hundred he gave up the computation. He let the characters go on having their tea. But he did not remember anything about the characters themselves. I doubt if anybody could now tell us anything about the characters in *Night and Day*. The one thing about them that I now recall is that one of them once looked out of a window. I think this is significant. Mrs Woolf does not, if I may say so, think in terms of character at all. She thinks in terms of intuitions. Her story of the old lady called Mrs Brown is an instance of this. She does not allow me to realize a Mrs Brown, but she does remind me of my own attitude to people in railway carriages. That is, she indicates the vague, rambling currents of intuition which pass through the consciousness in face of railway carriage companions more than of any other class of people. She is occupied in receiving intuitions. But the creation of character is something quite different from this. It is not something picked up in railway carriages, but something generated in the imagination of the writer. Of this imagination Mrs Woolf gives no sign, either in her critical writings or in her novels. Given a person, one can speculate about his or her character—that is easy. It is the novelist's off-time job. To create character that is subsequently memorable is a different thing. One does not remember the characters in Mrs Woolf's books, because Mrs Woolf's method is the vague and speculative method of an inactive dreamer. One does remember characters in Mr Bennett's books or Mr Wells's books, or Mr Galsworthy's books, because these characters have been created, and not dreamed about. One remembers them as one remembers real people, whom one has known actively, not as casually encountered strangers about whom one has idly speculated. Do I make myself clear? Mrs Woolf, like other expositors, is again making qualities of her own defects.

There is another point. Mrs Woolf comes to the conclusion that human nature changed about 1910. She bases this information upon the character of her own cook. Strange how expert our women writers have become upon cooks and household helps. We had Rebecca West the other month being very authoritative about servants, and now it is Mrs Woolf's turn. Her cook, apparently, comes in and out of the drawing room to borrow the *Daily Herald* and to discuss a new hat. This Mrs Woolf regards as sufficient proof that human nature changed in or about 1910. If Mrs Woolf will read again the plays of Shakespeare or the novels of Fielding or Dickens, she will find that servants were quite alive in the Elizabethan era, the eighteenth century, and the nineteenth century. It may be true that the servants she remembers as a child were subdued in face of their masters and mistresses, but those perhaps were servants in large establishments, where segregation was practicable. In smaller households, such as the smaller establishments of the present day make inevitable, the servants have always been upon more friendly terms with their mistresses. Let Mrs Woolf read that great book, *Little Women*, and decipher the character of Hannah. Let her read any domestic chronicle of a family which supports only one or two servants. In each one of these she will find that servants were human beings before 1910. It is not human nature that has changed. It is Mrs Woolf who has become self conscious. She should mix with the world a little more, and learn from the lives of her comrades in the field. It is much better training for the novelist than the introspectiveness which has spun a short yarn about hypothetical Mrs Brown. As for Mrs Woolf's list, apart from Mr Lawrence, all the members of it are intellectually capable, but creatively sterile. It is not a revolutionary impulse, as she seems to think, which makes these writers so very refined and pernickety. Their trouble is that they can none of them think what the devil to write about.

'MR BENNETT and MRS BROWN'
(Second Version)

30 October 1924

---

41. Edwin Muir, from a review, *Nation and Athenaeum*

6 December 1924, 370

Edwin Muir (1887–1959). Poet and literary critic. Leonard Woolf, who became literary editor of the *Nation* in 1923, printed one of Muir's poems, and they met and became friends. Woolf gave him some reviewing for the magazine and the Hogarth Press published his *First Poems* in 1925. A précis of the argument of 'Mr Bennett and Mrs Brown' has been omitted from the beginning of the review.

The case is admirably stated, and it is irrefutable. But surely Mrs Woolf magnifies the strength of the Edwardian convention. It cannot be such an appalling obstacle as she makes out. Certainly, the Georgians she mentions—Mr Joyce, Mr Eliot, Mr Strachey, Mr Lawrence, and Mr Forster—are writing against the current, and that is always immensely difficult. Still, part of their difficulty—I except Mr Strachey and Mr Forster from this generalisation—is caused by the fact that they do not clearly know how they want to do what they want to do. The temporary strength of the Edwardians consisted in the fact that they knew that. This enabled them to run up their convention expeditiously. Indeed they scarcely had to run it up at all; they ordered its parts from France and from the Fabian Society, and fitted them together. The result is that, after working successfully, these have very quickly fallen asunder. The formulae were wrong: the difficulty at present is that there are no formulae which everybody will accept. And all the signs point to the probability that these will only be discovered by experiment, wasteful as that method is to the artist. Thus, the artist has to do not only his own work for the time being, but that of the critics as well, for criticism has for more than a decade been obviously of little use.

42. 'Feiron Morris', review, *Criterion*

January 1925, 326–9

The reviewer was Mrs T. S. Eliot.

'I believe,' says Mrs Woolf, in her brilliant essay—already known to readers of the *Criterion*—an essay which should arouse all the elder novelists to spring to the defence of their threatened territories—'that all novels begin with an old lady in the corner opposite.' Mrs Woolf proceeds to describe her encounter with the old lady in the third-class carriage, the old lady whom she labels 'Mrs Brown', and introduces us to some of 'the myriads of irrelevant and incongruous ideas' which crowded into her head as she observed Mrs Brown. Mrs Woolf makes a bold, direct challenge to controversy.

It is difficult to confute a writer of Mrs Woolf's powers of style and persuasion, especially when these powers are backed by Mrs Woolf's prestige in the art of English prose; and all the more difficult because her contrast is partly between Mr Bennett and Tolstoi, and partly between Mr Bennett and Mr Forster, Mr Lytton Strachey, Mr Joyce, and Mr Eliot. What she says about Tolstoi is so obviously true and worth saying, what she says about the other writers mentioned is such brilliant criticism, that the simple reviewer is bewildered as to what, in her remarks, is relevant to 'the art of the novel'. So we are thrown back to the point: who and what is Mrs Brown?

Mrs Woolf's Mrs Brown is a romantic creature—the romance of the humble to the humble's betters. She is 'tragic, heroic, yet with a dash of the flighty and fantastic'. This sounds like Don Quixote. But no: Don Quixote was not picked up in a railway carriage. The first comment that comes to one's mind when one has digested Mrs Woolf's summary of Mrs Brown is that 'there ain't no sich person.' That there *was* such a person, we know. Mrs Brown survived, panting a little at the last, until somewhere about 1913—when, and not in 1910, we believe a change occurred. Indeed, a great deal of minor Victorian fiction is based on Faith in Mrs Brown. Since 1913 it may be conceded that the shade of Mrs Brown has been seen or felt by various persons practising the art of fiction; but it cannot be disputed that Mrs Brown is no longer flesh and blood and apprehensive. She belongs to the Age of Heroes, or Myth-making Age. Not the youngest—least of all, perhaps, the youngest—of shingled heads on male or female shoulders, concerns itself now with 'incongruous or irrelevant ideas' about fellow travellers in railway trains, or sees the denizens of a bus as 'tragic, heroic, or with a dash of the flighty or fantastic'. Modern young intellectuals—and here I distinguish between the minority of really modern young intellectuals and the semi-modern majority who still think that Katherine Mansfield's stories are 'simply too marvellous for words'—refuse any longer to be filled with romantic interest in the doings and sayings of some patchwork Petroushka, pieced together out of a few possibly inaccurate and probably biased observations on which are imposed some 'fantastic or flighty' situations born of romantic day-dreams. Mrs Brown may puzzle the young people—but only as to why she was concocted. For them she is a mystery of Udolpho.

The sort of flight of imagination, the fictive Mrs Brown, in which Mrs Woolf indulges is very pleasant to make; but what, we ask, has it to do with the creation of character? And in what respect is the Mrs Brown of Mrs Woolf more 'real' than the Mrs Brown of Mr Bennett, whose reality is said to consist of a vast number of accurate 'external' facts? Mrs Woolf distinguishes sharply between the period of the novel before 1910, when Mr Bennett was still a modern novelist and servants lived in the basement, and the period of the novel since 1910, when Mr Bennett is old-fashioned and servants borrow the *Daily Herald* from their mistresses, and live all over the house. Is it unfair to ask whether the incursion of irrelevant and incongruous ideas, as well as of the *Daily Herald*, is a symptom of the period since 1910?

Is it indeed true that the genesis of a novel—which Mrs Woolf believes to be, for all novelists, including herself, the *creation of a character*—begins with the 'old lady'—that is, with some person observed externally, about whom we form 'irrelevant and incongruous ideas'? If so, it is only fresh evidence that the age of 'the novel' is ended. Is it true that Mr James Joyce—for Mrs Woolf cites him—arrived at Bloom by observations in a Dublin tram? and did Mr Eliot—for Mrs Woolf cites him also—deduce Sweeney from observations in a New York bar-room?

Now, Mrs Woolf's analysis of the method of Mr Wells, Mr Galsworthy, and Mr Bennett is not only very witty, but, we think, very sound. According to this method, if you observe accurately a vast number of the facts surrounding a character—if you observe *enough* of the facts—you reach the character itself. And this we believe to be true. We agree that this was not the method of *War and Peace*. Nevertheless, Mr Polly and Hilda Lessways are real, although not eternal, as Prince André is. But Prince André is a symbol: of the eternal reality of Death. We believe that one of the motives of the modern age is its desire to find reality—even, and especially, the most barren, elementary, stripped reality. And the age finds it through the symbolic figure. But—to modern eyes—Mrs Brown, the creature of fancy, would evaporate into thin air long before the Richmond train reached Waterloo.

In an age of machinery, an age of horrid young people who won't fall in love, and who talk in harsh staccato tones, with no nonsense about it, an ominous demon has slipped into old Mrs Brown's corner. We will call him, if he must be named, Mr Leopold Bloom; or we may call him Mr Zagreus; or we may call him Sweeney. Here are three unpleasant travelling companions in a third-class carriage, who are neither 'tragic, heroic, nor with a dash of the flighty or fantastic' in the ordinary sense; yet our young people seem to be at ease with them, and handle them with the same terrible efficiency as they do their motor-cars and their dancing. They watch with calm understanding the activities of the machine-like insect, which is man, in the form of Mr Bloom, held steadily for their inspection under the microscope of Mr Joyce's intellect.

Mr Bloom is real: he might almost be called, by friends of Mrs Brown, 'photographic'—a dreadful word. But what can one hang on one's walls now? What is there, unless one keeps a lodging-house, except the photographic and the abstract? And has not modern literature solved its problem by finding the symbolic in the photograph—as Mr Bloom is both a photograph and a symbol?

But are we to accept these three nightmare figures, James Joyce, T. S. Eliot, and Wyndham Lewis as the only representatives of modern literature? Such an idea is ludicrous. What about Proust, for instance? Proust is by no means a negligible figure to the young 'intellectuals'. They like Proust—and if they cannot read him in French they are properly grateful to Mr Scott Moncrieff. But did Proust impose upon his readers a Mrs Brown? The most interesting, real, photographic character in the whole of that immense chronicle and document of scientific and aesthetic research is Proust himself. And Proust himself cunningly leads them into every by-way of sensibility, showing them philosophies and theories of life, and above all, cultivating their self-consciousness.

Mrs Woolf has written a very able argument upon a thesis which we believe to be wrong. The argument is so clever that it is difficult to disprove the thesis: we can only wait in the hope that Mrs Woolf will disprove it herself.

43. Clive Bell on Virginia Woolf's painterly vision, *Dial*

December 1924, 451–65

Clive Bell (1881–1964). Art critic and journalist, who married Virginia Woolf's sister, Vanessa, in 1906. A central member of the Bloomsbury Group, his *Art* (1914) and *Civilization* (1928) are often read as embodiments of Bloomsbury thinking on art and culture. (A notion which implies a greater cohesiveness in the Group than was the case.) *Civilization* was dedicated to Virginia Woolf, but it is evident from *A Writer's Diary* that she took his judgments on her work with more than a pinch of salt.

For most of those even who had followed her career from the time when she first found editors not unwilling to give a chance to a girl who happened to be the daughter of Leslie Stephen, most, I say, felt that, till the publication of *Jacob's Room*, she had never publicly proved what they had never doubted—that she possessed genius of a high order. For you must not forget that her earliest work—reviews, generally long ones, written for the *Times Literary Supplement*, at that time perhaps the best critical weekly in the world—was anonymous. Simultaneously she was writing, and confiding in manuscript to a few friends, purely imaginative work, stories and sketches; and it is significant that to her friends these appeared less interesting and characteristic than her reviews. I think I can see why. In reviews, as in her purely imaginative writings, she depended on that familiar impressionist method of hers: she read the book, saw it whole from her peculiar yet widely out-looking corner, and then created a form to match her impression. Thus, her critical essays have the quality, the individuality, and some of the intensity of works of art; and it will be a thousand pities if they are not soon collected into a volume, since such a volume would give a great deal of pleasure to people who are worth pleasing.

But, besides her creative gift, Mrs Woolf possesses a delicate intellect, and already in these early days possessed what one may call 'inherited culture'. Now in her purely imaginative pieces she could make but sparing use, at that time, of this intellectual equipment; whereas, in reviews, she was not obliged to fly off into space trusting solely to the thread of imagination, but, whenever she chose, could catch hold of and rest upon the recognised props of criticism. She had a right to chop ideas and toy with history; and she did. And it was in these moments of rest from the painful business of self-expression that she gave us our first taste of that delicious wit which I would like at once to distinguish from those flights of humorous fancy which continually enchant us in the novels . . .

Her first novel, *The Voyage Out*, does no more than adumbrate a reply. In my opinion it was a remarkable failure: a failure partly because, like a sauce that has over-simmered, it had been writing too long and had grown stiff; partly because one felt some discrepancy between the comic and tragic parts. Yet both were parts of the same vision; and it was of that vision the author was trying to express her sense. Here was her problem. What made the book remarkable, apart from the extraordinary beauty of the prose, was that the vision was her own. Neither did Mrs Woolf accept the ready cooked, hot and strong, cinematographic world beloved of modern novelists, nor yet that amalgam of nicely tested instances and inferences which for the ordinary cultivated person—for Mr Galsworthy to take a modern example or Thackeray to take a more ancient—does duty for a picture of life; she had her peculiar vision. What is more, I do not recall, fatiguing though it must be to remain for ever perched on that minute pinnacle which is a personal point of view, a single occasion—even in this first novel—on which she observes her characters through one of those street-corner telescopes up which we can all have a squint for tuppence.

In 1917 Virginia Woolf published at the Hogarth Press 'The Mark on the Wall'. This is perfect in its kind; and, till the publication of *Jacob's Room* remained for me her masterpiece. It is the expression of one continuous state of mind—a day-dream. And the realized impression of a subtle and various consciousness floating on deep and slightly ruffled waters with no hand at the rudder is so close, that at first reading one is tempted to exclaim, 'This is no sculpted form, but a life-mask.' One would be wrong, however. This is no realistic study, no miracle of observation. I have no notion what a psychologist would say about it, nor I fancy could an intelligent psychologist feel that any professional comment would be in place; for what we have before us is not the description of a reverie, but the equivalent of a reverie—a work of art that is to say. Only we cannot help noticing the peculiar beauty of the mind that dreams, the unexpected though fundamentally rational transition from mood to mood, while we are moved by the shapes in which the moods clothe themselves.

To show how very little control of our possessions we have—what an accidental affair this living is after all our civilization—let me just count over a few of the things lost in one lifetime, beginning, for that seems always the most mysterious of all losses—what cat would gnaw, what rat would nibble—[with] three pale blue canisters of book-binding tools? Then there were the bird cages, the iron hoops, the steel skates, the Queen Anne coal-scuttle, the bagatelle board, the hand organ—all gone, and jewels too. Opals and emeralds, they lie about the roots of turnips. What a scraping paring affair it is to be sure! The wonder is that I've any clothes on my back, that I sit surrounded by solid furniture at this moment. Why, if one wants to compare life to anything, one must liken it to being blown through the Tube at fifty miles an hour—landing at the other end without a single hair pin in one's hair! Shot out at the feet of God entirely naked! Tumbling head over heels in the asphodel meadows like brown paper parcels pitched down a shoot in the post office!

Here, it seems to me, whatever our aesthetic theories, we cannot be indifferent to the mind of the writer. It is the sense of a mind at once concrete and imaginative that we are given, a mind logical in its most lively flights and intensely sensitive to the essential absurdity of every situation in which human beings play a part.

Night and Day is, I think, her most definite failure. She chose a perfectly conventional, a Victorian, theme, the *premiers amours* of five young people: it is all about a pair of engagements. Naturally this shocked the novelists of the red-flower-of-passion school, most of whom write reviews also—a convenient habit in many ways. She should have written about the *quatre-vingt-dixième* to make her work strong and passionate and *real* (the grand *desideratum*); she should have written about Life. Intelligent people know, of course, that there is no sort of reason why an artist should not choose a conventional theme if it happens to suit him: many of the greatest artists have. Before taking exception to the subject, our young tigers and yours, Mr Editor of the *Dial*, should have meditated Jane Austen more profoundly. A conventional theme is as good in itself as another; for art consists not in theme, but in expression, a truism which to the student of contemporary fiction may well come as a surprise. The only question about subject to be asked is—has the artist chosen one the matching of which with his aesthetic experience will call forth all his powers and gallop the last ounce out of them? I thought we had agreed years ago, when we used to wrangle about painting, that, *qua* subject, a pot of flowers is as good as the crucifixion. From which it follows that a conventional theme may be as good as an unconventional, and an unconventional as a conventional. Only, when an artist relies on the nature of his theme for producing what passes for an aesthetic effect, as Gautier and Poe, Mr Masefield and Dostoevsky, Greuze and Blake seem to do, there is some reason for suspecting him of artistic feebleness. That way melodrama lies. To feel a need for violent and surprising subjects does seem to imply inferiority in the artist, and a coarse palate in the critic: to feel the need I say, not to feel that, in a particular case, such a subject affords the only appropriate medium of expression. Mrs Woolf, at any rate, has no need to stun us with her subject, since she can move us to the limit of our sensibility by her art.

Yet the theme of *Night and Day* was ill-chosen: it was ill-chosen because it cramped and choked the natural deflagration of the artist's mind. She chose the time-honoured complication: A thinks he is in love with B, who, thinking this is as much as can be expected of life, accepts him; C appears on the scene and is at once recognized as the right man for B, but in despair almost marries D for whom he feels rather what B feels for A; arrives, to save the situation, E who turns out to be just the girl for A. Here is a subject for Jane Austen, into which she could have fitted all her curious knowledge of the upper-middle-class heart. But Mrs Woolf is not a born story-teller, wherefore, so much of her energy had to go into manipulating the stiff little levers of her machine, so considerable an effort was required to keep in hand all the straining weights and compensations of her narrative, that, though she often contrives to let her fancy roam, rarely does she find space and energy to drive it to the limit of its endurance. She is cramped by her subject. Given the theme, the story has to develop along lines of strict probability, off which on one occasion—the scene where Katharine is discovered in an alcove and the grand manner—it rather alarmingly jumps. To bring all her chickens home to roost is a job too exacting to allow of many pranks by the way. We seek—not in vain—but seek we must those exquisite digressions which, if I may be allowed what at first looks like a paradox, are an integral part of *Jacob's Room*, of which —to go a little further in perversity—'The Mark on the Wall' is an example standing alone, a digression from nowhere. All which notwithstanding, in this as in the first novel, you will find scene after scene of exquisite beauty and surprising depth, and one—that between Rodney and Katharine on the road to Lampsher—hardly to be matched in contemporary literature.

Follow several short stories and sketches, brought together and published in 1921, under the title of *Monday or Tuesday*. This is Virginia Woolf practising. Apparently, she herself was dissatisfied with *Night and Day* and felt the need of discovering an appropriate form. Hence, I presume, these experiments: of which one, 'A Society', is quite beneath her genius; and another, 'A Haunted House', in style at any rate, seems to me unfortunately redolent of contemporary influences: by the way, in this volume is reprinted 'The Mark on the Wall'. She is in search of a form in which to express a vision—a vision of which she is now perfectly sure. That is the problem of which *Jacob's Room* is the brilliantly successful solution; but before attempting to analyse the solution I had better try to formulate, what so far I seem only to have fumbled, my notion, that is, of the vision to be expressed.

What makes Virginia Woolf's books read queerly is that they have at once the air of high fantasticality and blazing realism. And the explanation of this is, unless I mistake, that, though she is externalizing a vision and not making a map of life, the vision is anything but visionary in the vulgar sense of the word. Her world is not a dream world; she sees, and sees acutely, what the reviewer in a hurry calls 'the real world'—the world of Jane Austen and George Eliot, of *Madame Bovary* and *War and Peace* if you want to be agreeable, of Mr Wells and Mr Bennett if you want to be comprehensive. Emphatically the world of her vision is not the romantic world of Balzac, Meredith, or Hardy, nor the melodramatic of Dickens or Dostoevsky. It is a perfectly comprehensible world in which no one has the least difficulty in believing; only she sees it through coloured, or I had rather say oddly cut, glasses. Or is it we who see it through stained glass—glass stained with our ruling passions? That is a question I shall not attempt to decide. Only let me give one example of the difference between her vision and ours. When we—most of us I should say—see a pair of lovers sitting on a seat we feel—if we feel anything worth writing about—not purely the romance of the scene, or of the situation even: to some extent we share the feelings of the lovers. Our emotion, I mean, is not purely aesthetic; it is sympathetic in the strictest sense of the term. And it is because we to some extent share the excitement of the actors that, more often than not, we miss the full aesthetic import of the drama. We fail to feel some things because we feel others too much. Now Mrs Woolf sees more purely or, if you will, less passionately. At all events her emotion is not in the least self-regarding. She watches life, as it were through a cool sheet of glass: let those who dare, call the glass distorting. She knows what the lovers are saying; she knows (not feels) what they are feeling; she misses not one subtle, betraying, gesture. Assuredly, she feels the romance of the situation, but she does not share the romantic feelings of the actors.

No one could be more conscious of the romance of life. Open a book of hers almost anywhere and catch her expressing a vision of the country or, better still, of the town: not Flaubert, in that famous scene in *L'Education Sentimentale*, gives a stronger sense of the romance and excitingness of a great city than Mrs Woolf has given in half a dozen descriptions of London. But when Jacob and Florinda are together in the bedroom, and when Jacob walks out 'in his dressing-gown, amiable, authoritative, beautifully healthy, like a baby after an airing,' and Florinda follows 'lazily stretching, yawning a little, arranging her hair in the looking-glass,' we have not had the thrill we couldn't help expecting: we have not been given a love scene as we understand it. Nothing of much consequence, we feel, has been going on behind that door; or rather, something of consequence only in relation to Mrs Flanders' letter which is lying on the table. Nor is this surprising when we reflect that it was not the love affair, but the effect of the love affair, which really interested Mrs Woolf. What was going on in the bedroom caught her imagination not as an end, but as a means. And though it is a particular Jacob and a particular Florinda that she sees, acutely, beautifully, through her wall of glass, it is in relation to a comic, poignant, familiar little tragedy, which beginning in Scarborough spreads round the world, that she sees them.

Take two other love-scenes from *Jacob's Room*—one happy, the other pathetic: Clara Durrant picking grapes and dimly realizing that she is in love with Jacob; Clara Durrant walking in the park with kind Mr Bowley and realizing that Jacob is not in love with her. Each is all over in a page or so—large print too: in the first there is more lyricism than a nineteenth century poet would have got into a hundred stanzas; and an eighteenth century novelist would have allowed himself half a volume at least to give a less devastating picture of a broken heart. Both are scenes of affecting beauty—I use these two grave words as seriously as it is possible for a notoriously frivolous person to use them:

neither is passionate. Both are seen with unsurpassable precision; both are rendered by means of touch and elimination attainable only by an artist of genius; both give a vision—I use the word again and advisedly —of someone feeling intensely; but the feeling which the artist has observed and expressed she has not shared. Also, if I understand her art aright, she does not intend us to share it: she intends us to appreciate, to admire. Her emotion comes from her sense of the scene, and ours from reacting to that sense. This pure, this almost painterlike vision is Virginia Woolf's peculiarity: it is what distinguishes her from all her contemporaries.

Of course a first-rate literary artist can never really be like a painter; for it is out of words that literary artists have to create the forms that are to clothe their visions, and words carry a significance altogether different from the significance of lines and colours. Certainly Mrs Woolf's vision, and superficially her style, may remind any one, as they reminded that sound critic. M. Abel Chevalley, of the French impressionists—of their passion for the beauty of life, loved for its own sake, their abhorrence of symbolism, their reputed inhumanity, technically of their little touches and divisions of tones. To our joy we are all familiar with the way in which Renoir and Claude Monet express their sense of a garden blazing in the sun. It is something which comes to them through shapes and colours, and in shapes and colours must be rendered. Now see how an artist in words deals with a similar experience.

How hot it was! So hot that even the thrush chose to hop, like a mechanical bird, in the shadow of the flowers, with long pauses between one movement and the next; instead of rambling vaguely the white butterflies danced one above another, making with their white shifting flakes the outline of a shattered marble column above the tallest flowers; the glass roofs of the palm house shone as if a whole market full of shiny green umbrellas had opened in the sun; and in the drone of the aeroplane the voice of the summer sky murmured its fierce soul. Yellow and black, pink and snow white, shapes of all these colours, men, women, and children were spotted for a second upon the horizon, and then, seeing the breadth of yellow that lay upon the grass, they wavered and sought shade beneath the trees, dissolving like drops of water in the yellow and green atmosphere, staining it faintly with red and blue. It seemed as if all gross and heavy bodies had sunk down in the heat motionless and lay huddled upon the ground, but their voices went wavering from them as if they were flames lolling from the thick waxen bodies of candles. Voices. Yes, voices. Wordless voices, breaking the silence suddenly with such depth of contentment such passion of desire, or, in the voices of children, such freshness of surprise;

breaking the silence? But there was no silence; all the time the motor omnibuses were turning their wheels and changing their gear; like a vast nest of Chinese boxes, all of wrought steel turning ceaselessly one within another the city murmured; on the top of which the voices cried aloud and the petals of myriads of flowers flashed their colours into the air.

No one, I suppose, will deny the beauty of this. No one—no one who counts at all I mean—ever has denied that Mrs Woolf chooses and uses words beautifully. But her style is sometimes accused, injuriously, of being 'cultivated and intellectual', especially by people who themselves are not particularly well off for either culture or intellect. Cultivated it is, in the sense that it reveals a finely educated mind on terms of easy acquaintance with the finest minds of other ages—a privilege reserved for those who have been at pains to learn Greek. And, perhaps, it is cultivated also in the sense that to enjoy it thoroughly a reader must himself have been well educated. It makes, no doubt, unobtrusive references to and recalls associations with things of which the unlettered dream not. Intellectual? Yes, it is intellectual, too; that is to say, words are used to affect the understanding rather than the senses. It is nearer to the last act of *Figaro* (though colder far—a love-scene by Virginia Woolf never put any one into the mood for a love-affair)—to the last act of *Figaro* which gives you an ethereal sense of a summer night's romance than to the second act of *Tristan* which gives you . . . Well, an over-sexed person will never appreciate the art of Virginia Woolf; nor will a fundamentally stupid. But, of course, her style is never intellectual in the sense that the style of what are called philosophic writers is: not for ideas, but for visions does she find equivalents. And, as a vision is neither an idea nor a sensation, her prose can be at once cool and coloured: no need for those deep drum notes which endear the style of Mr D. H. Lawrence to the half-educated and protect him, for all his sham science, from the charge of intellectuality. Also, her prose, though it is sometimes witty besides being fantastically humorous, is never, or rarely, pointed. In *Monday or Tuesday* it strikes me, as I have said, sometimes as being needlessly unfamiliar in arrangement; but, generally speaking, one may say that any difficulty which a moderately intelligent person may find in following the movements of her mind comes, not of eccentricity of expression, but of the complexity of what is being expressed. Those who call her style 'bizarre' or 'outrageous' are—unless merely thick-witted—making the mistake that was made by the more enlightened opponents of impressionism. They are puzzled by a technique which juxtaposes active tones, and omits those transitions which have no other function than to provide what the impressionists and Mrs Woolf and many other modern writers hold to be unnecessary bridges. For my part, I shall not deny that I am a little old for jumping, and that in literature I love a bridge, be it merely a plank. My infirmities, however, are unimportant. The important thing is that Mrs Woolf's tones are chosen deliberately, with exquisite tact, and that they form a whole which perfectly envelops her vision: that, though some come from the imagination and others from the intellect, none flies from the object merely to the shell of her mind and thence ricochets onto the page: in a word, that her prose is not violent, but vibrant.

It is not quite true to say that the form Mrs Woolf discovered for herself and employed in *Jacob's Room* was a development of 'The Mark on the Wall'. That form contained admirably well a single vision, complete in itself; what she now needed was a form to match that series of visions, glimpses and glances, stunning crashes and faint echoes, fainter perfumes and pungent stinks, which we, God forgive us, are pleased to call life. . . . 'Who saw life steadily, and saw it whole.'

Well, Mrs Woolf is not Sophocles, nor Matthew Arnold either; so she wanted something to hold together in a unity her series of fragmentary revelations, glimpses, glances, and scraps of glances: she wanted a thread that could be cut and knotted at both ends. Obviously, the only principle of unity in her kaleidoscopic experience was her own personality, and no great wizardry is needed to see that an equivalent for this in a work of imagination would be an imagined personality—a hero in fact. The question was, how to establish an equivalence between the various and disinterested aesthetic experience of a contemplative artist and the early life and adventures of a kinetic, not to say strapping, young gentleman. Her solution is charming and ingenious. The hero is gradually to be built up out of other people's reactions to him: other people's reactions and, I must be allowed to add the reactions—if reactions are what they have—of places. We are gradually to infer the character of the cause from the nature of its effects on persons, places, and things. Here is impressionism with a vengeance: if the technique consisted in 'little touches', the composition is a matter of 'frank oppositions' and the whole will dawn on us only when the last harmony is established.

Jacob's character, Jacob's temperament, Jacob's way, Jacob's personal appearance, Jacob in fact, must always be present to hold together the bright fragments which are the author's sense of life—

not of Jacob's life, but of the life in which Jacob moves. We shall find him first an active ingredient in his mother's world, then conditioning a scene or two at Cambridge, a source of feeling and speculation in a country house, in what the Sunday papers call 'Bohemia', in the hearts of men and women, in London, Paris, and Athens. And all the while Jacob is not merely affecting, he is being affected: reverse the engines, the principle of unity works just as well. Jacob is growing up, Jacob is being revealed: the men and women who love or are loved play their parts; Cambridge, Cornwall, London, Paris, and Athens play theirs; the trains, the taxicabs, the omnibuses, the changes of season, St Paul's Cathedral, jute-merchants, charwomen, the crowds crossing Waterloo Bridge, all add their quota to that vision of the young man who for one second stands revealed before he vanishes in the war for ever. Down he goes; leaving a pair of shoes to wring the hearts of a man and woman as they rummage in the characteristic disorder of Jacob's room.

The form which Mrs Woolf evolved in *Jacob's Room* gave her a freedom she had not enjoyed in either of her preceding novels. The coherence of the work is assured by the fact that the author cannot leave go of the thread without losing interest in her theme. Jacob is the sole theme; and since Jacob is to be built up gradually and so revealed, however discursive she may be in giving her sense of his surroundings she dare not cease to be for ever looking to the beginning and the end. And the reader too feels that he must keep tight hold; for in the pieces given he knows that he must see the whole, and the pieces will not be given twice. Yet, for the author, compared with the difficulties of such a novel as *Night and Day* (the difficulty of keeping each thread on a separate finger and weaving all together at the appointed moment) the difficulty of grasping this one thread firmly is child's play. For there is but one thread; and since she has no fear of losing it, she can venture to explore every corner of her vision. Anywhere, on anything, Jacob can leave his mark and so relate it to the whole. Best of all, so pervasive is the hero's temperament, so wide the sphere of his influence, and so easily can he be kept moving towards his goal—which is our enlightenment—that Mrs Woolf cannot only fly to the ends of her vision and back again, but, without stepping outside the charmed circle of an artistic unity, can, from time to time, hush the instruments of her orchestra to make, in her own voice, her own cool, humorous comment. She has found a form in which to be completely herself.

THE COMMON READER (First Series)

23 April 1925

44. From an unsigned review, *Times Literary Supplement*

7 May 1925, 313

Virginia Woolf remarked in her Diary, 'As for *The Common Reader*, the Lit. Sup. had close on two columns sober and sensible praise—neither one thing nor the other—my fate in *The Times*', and she went on to complain that 'I never get an enthusiastic review in the Lit. Sup' (*A Writer's Diary*, p. 76). Inevitably with a work of this kind much of the review was simply expository, and so this item has a number of clearly marked excisions.

But the transfusion of a reader's impressions into these bright shapes is the work of an artist. The Pastons live again here, adroitly juxtaposed with Chaucer. It is as critic and artist in one that Mrs Woolf lets the Pastons and the poet illuminate each other; and all, it would seem, because the thriftless Sir John sat reading Chaucer by the fire instead of attending to business like his relatives.

A lively zest for human beings runs through this volume. Montaigne observed, even in his day, that most books were written about other books; Mrs Woolf also writes of books, yet leaves us feeling that books are about persons. All that side of an author's individuality which shapes his work is significant, so is the frame in which characters are moulded; 'the drawbacks of being Jane Eyre', for instance—'always to be a governess and always to be in love'. . . .

The wit and the charm in these presentations are very seductive, but they must not run away with us. We have to see how Mrs Woolf, reading for her pleasure and with an artist's interest, has read also as a critic. It might be enough to say that a writer can scarcely help doing that; but what, then, is the art of writing? It is, as Mrs Woolf remarks in one place, 'on the back of an idea, something believed in with conviction or seen with precision and thus compelling words to its shape', that writers are borne to their achievement. 'Seeing with precision' would be no bad definition of her criticism, as of her style. In one way or another she tests the degree in which books have the transforming strength of new reality. With whatever modern refinements, this is the classic standard, and it is employed here with a sense of what creation means and, as one might fancy, with an inherited love of truth. . . .

But Mrs Woolf varies her approaches. In the case of Montaigne it is the method of statement, couched as an interrogatory that follows him through the recoils of his thought and the contradictions of his moods: a method not unlike Pater's in two well-known chapters, but pressing closer to an issue, even if the pillow of doubt stifles the last question. With the lesser Elizabethan dramatists she builds up impressions, and we enjoy their brilliance; but from the contrast of Elizabethan realities with ours, of our novels and their poetry, down to the final confession of a mood there is always, implicit or explicit, a criticism. Only in this case and one other does Mrs Woolf deal with poets, each time with something of a side glance. But on novelists and the novel there is a compact nucleus of papers. Here, from time to time, there is a judgment which is final and refreshing, as that we read Charlotte Bronte's novels for their poetry, and *Wuthering Heights* for the same reason, but with a difference, because Emily faces a vaster task without personal limitations:

[Quotes '*Jane Eyre* and *Wuthering Heights*', 'It is as if she could tear' to 'wind blow and the thunder roar.']

In one or two papers, on modern fiction or contemporary literature in general, Mrs Woolf glances freely at its present discontents and dilemmas. They are useful for that very reason, and they attest the worth of the critic by showing that a lively sympathy with the age she lives in does not prevent her from seeing its maladies. Despite her relish for new work she lays bare the flaw in it; which is, to speak summarily, a want of conviction. Our contemporaries are sincere but unpersuasive. They transcribe impressions, but they lack the conviction, the confidence that their impressions will hold good for others, which enabled Scott or Jane Austen to neglect opportunities, to slumber and yet write great books. What should be the remedy? Here we might wish Mrs Woolf to go on, but when one convention has been broken another can hardly be prescribed in advance. It may be an error, as a rule, to shift the failings of literature on to life; but literature certainly appears to be suffering less for its own sins than from the divisions of the age. From Mrs Woolf, at any rate, we get that valuable thing, a true perspective. It implies the sanity of criticism which is common sense enlightened.

It draws us back again to the common reader. After all, perhaps, the main truth which this book suggests, however unconsciously, is that readers, critics, and writers are not secluded in water-tight compartments. On their sensibility they all depend; the depth and direction of it will settle what comes out; but the most high-ranging critic is only drawing on his combined impressions. It was not Mrs Woolf's ambition to evoke principles, and it can hardly be said that she does, although she lets fall sentences which illuminate a great deal. But we find a standard which we never distrust, and this is possibly something rarer. It has the breadth which only a real possession of the past can give, and the vitality of a fresh imaginativeness.

45. H. I'A. Fausset, initialled review, 'The Art of Virginia Woolf', *Manchester Guardian*

14 May 1925

Hugh I'Anson Fausset (b. 1895). Critic and literary biographer. He reviewed for the *TLS* and *Listener* in addition to the *Manchester Guardian*.

Virginia Woolf commented 'I was really pleased to open the *Manchester Guardian* this morning and read Mr Fausset on the Art of V.W.; brilliance combined with integrity; profound as well as eccentric.' She was still grumbling about the *TLS* review (No. 44): 'Now if only *The Times* would speak out thus, but *The Times* mumbles and murmurs like a man sucking pebbles. Did I say that I had nearly two mumbling columns on me there?' (*A Writer's Diary*, p. 76).

'Journalism,' writes Virginia Woolf, 'embalmed in a book is unreadable.' No one has more right to proclaim the fact than she, who has discovered how to write for the newspapers without ceasing to be an artist and how to exalt criticism into a creative adventure which, though intensely personal and provocative, is yet preserved by the finest sense of values from the quixotry of Impressionism. Certainly we have seldom read a volume of essays which, by their sufficiency and freshness, insight and accomplishment, so captivate and satisfy the mind. It is the combination of brilliance and integrity which is so rare, and we will confess that until we read this volume we credited Virginia Woolf with more charm and vivacity than vision, delighted in her style for its supple simplification of complexity, but with a suspicion that her victory was more often over words than ideas. Such a misjudgment was made easier because her ideas are seldom explicit: she is so fine an artist because her thought, concentrated and effective as it is, is not starkly separated from the fluid elements of experience, from her immediate human response to the life that literature and writings too humble to rank as literature embody. It is thus that she succeeds in combining keen analysis with a synthesising humanity and can disentangle the ideas which animated an individual or a people in the very process of picturing, with a selective fidelity to detail, the objective circumstances of their lives. And being thus both exact and imaginative, her intercourse with her subjects is really that of a contemporary, and not that kind of ironic intimacy which, however stealthily, betrays a detached egotism by its tendency to exploit.

This illusion of complete critical identity with her subject Virginia Woolf achieves in almost all her studies, particularly in her vivid picture of the lives of the Pastons, of Montaigne, Evelyn, Addison, and of those 'stranded ghosts' whom she delivers from the obscurity of an 'obsolete library'. It is nowhere more shiningly displayed than in her reconception of the Greek drama and the hard, sharply outlined Greek world that was its stage and dictated its emphasis, brevity, and elemental force. For here, as in her studies of Charlotte and Emily Brontë and of the Russian novelists, a writer whom we had supposed to be somewhat of the self-centred and self-limited order, rather mistress of the incisive phrase than a diver in deep waters, reveals, too, an expansiveness and profundity of understanding which is so seldom served by transparency, a sense of the primitive and elemental as remarkable as her knowledge of the mannered and the eccentric.

46. Edgell Rickword, initialled review, *Calendar*

July 1925, I, V, 320–2

Edgell Rickword (b. 1898). Poet and critic. Editor of *Calendar of Modern Letters* (at this time simply called the *Calendar*), which had as its aim the relating of literature to society. Rickword therefore emphasises in his discussion of *The Common Reader* the theme of 'the influence on a writer of the society in which he lives.'

There is no explicit link between the literary essays which make up this volume and to be just to Mrs Woolf it would be necessary to criticise each of them separately, the longer ones at any rate, for it is a great virtue in these pieces to stimulate a sort of private discussion in the reader's consciousness. If however the reader is of the sort that finds discussion harsh and unprofitable, the picturesque is sufficiently in evidence to enable him to ignore very comfortably the deeper implications of Mrs Woolf's criticism. The essay called 'The Pastons and Chaucer' is to our mind the most substantial in the book and it shows as clearly as any what is constantly the subject of her inquiry, the influence on a writer of the society in which he lives—the relation of artist and audience.

Analysing the freedom with which Chaucer absorbs into his verse every kind of experience, ignorant of our uncomfortable distinction between the poetic and the unpoetic subject, Mrs Woolf says 'He could sound every note in the language instead of finding a great many of the best gone dumb from disuse, and thus, when struck by daring fingers, giving off a loud discordant jangle out of keeping with the rest.' And of course, this freedom from any necessity of verbal compromise is simply the reflection of an unprejudiced relationship to experience, of an 'unconscious ease . . . which is only to be found where the poet has made up his mind about the world they (his women) live in, its end, its nature, and his own craft and technique, so that his mind is free to apply its force fully to its object.'

This happy state has been, in some considerable degree, the lot of the writers of any age remarkable for its literature, the Elizabethan, the Augustan, and the Victorian. In spite of internal dissension, the writers of these periods had a solid stratum to which finally they could refer to give value to their emotional utterances. For the Elizabethans it was the passionate life, for the Augustans the social life, the 'honnête homme' of polite scepticism replacing the chivalrous knight of the literature of religious idealism. The Victorians, of course, lack the serenity of their predecessors; the protestations of Carlyle and Browning are symptoms of the insidious ravages of the will to believe which replaces in-bred conviction. Still, they took advantage of the lull before the storm and produced the last examples of the literature which retains its expressive value along the whole scale of group-sensibilities. Since then, the reading-public has split. We have the small body of educated sharp-witted readers from whom a small spark of intelligence sometimes flickers, but being passionate, if at all, only about values and not experience, ultimately uncreative; and themselves so frequently practitioners as to be unsatisfactory even as audience. Beyond lies the vast reading-public which is led by the nose by the high-class literary-journalist-poet type and its tail tweaked by the paragraphist with pretentions not rising above personal gossip. Mrs Woolf sketches this gloomy scene with a restraint and delicacy which we cannot emulate. But her essay 'How it strikes a contemporary', coming as it does at the end of a volume which begins with Chaucer, flings the contrast of then and now into unmitigated light and shade. Mrs Woolf concludes that as all the signs point to this as an off-season, the best the critic can do to fill in the time is 'to scan the horizon; see the past in relation to the future; and so prepare the way for masterpieces to come'.

This is advice which the middle-aged will perhaps welcome; but we doubt if these studious evangelists are of much use as path-straighteners for the Messiah. If the past is any guide, he will come with none of the signs of grace and perhaps attempt to borrow five pounds from the ladies and gentlemen scanning the horizon. For what, in fact, does all the present fuss about literature amount to? It is the disease of an age which has no proper outlet for a great deal of its energy and so directs the surplus into forms which retain a certain amount of prestige from the time when they were the ornaments of the life of educated aristocrats. It should be clearly understood that creative literature has nothing whatever to do with the mass of material which in books and periodicals is produced as literary criticism. The public has never been so confused and debased in its tastes as during the fifty years in which the discussion of literary questions has become general. The only useful criticism must be technical, but the stuff the public swallows now is, like the pap the mother-monkey provides for its young, a masticated product easy of digestion; only the parent monkey does not extract all the nourishment.

If the discussion of literature is of little help towards the production of masterpieces, in itself not an inspiring aim, the admission of boredom from the public might lead to better results. In its present tendencies literature is far too destructive, too anti-social, or at least enquiring, to be appreciated by those whose appetites are sufficiently keen, or gross, to enable them to approve the contemporary spectacle. Modern work appeals necessarily to a restricted audience, of no particular class but with a common sensibility, and there is no object in trying to expand this audience artificially. It is certainly to the advantage of literature, now, to fall below commercial standards of value. If the common reader could really be identified with the author of these essays we should not have been able to make them the excuse for a tirade. Unfortunately the sensitiveness which is common to them is a quality with which we rarely meet in contemporary criticism. Perhaps we may hope it is a property of the inarticulate, who silent and unnamed, form the real modern audience. Whether or not Mrs Woolf's title be an appeal from the self-styled *illuminati* to the anonymous throng, at any rate she may claim the attribute which is the most valuable of those in Johnson's definition of the common reader, one whose sense is 'uncorrupted by literary prejudices'.

47. H. P. Collins, from a review, *Criterion*

July 1925, 586–8

H. P. Collins (b. 1901). Literary critic. At this time, literary editor of the *Adelphi*. Author of *Modern Poetry* (1925).

The rich individuality of Mrs Woolf's mind may be taken for granted: to stress it is not the best way to approach an estimate of her critical position. She might have been a queen among the 'impressionists'; her sensibility is more profound, her discursiveness more entertaining, her wingéd words more wingéd than theirs. That is a fate which she has escaped; and one has only to note her remarks on Pater or on the Essay to see how consciously she has done so. Mrs Woolf is in no danger of confounding a higher with a lower form of literary intelligence; or of confusing the essayist's craft with the critical art. An historical sense and the instinct for synthesis she found, if one may put it so, in her cradle; and this alone would give significance to her views. The spirit of inquiry, of intellectual curiosity, is rarely *explicit* in her essays: she avoids both the most penetrating kind of analysis and the *philosophical* synthesis; she inclines rather to a semi-creative interest in men and women which makes the final impression of her criticism less pure, less inevitable, than it might be. But this imaginative element is modulated, firmly controlled so that it never lets us doubt Mrs Woolf's awareness of the aim in view. The importance of a writer's life in the study of his work is still an open ground of debate, and Mrs Woolf seems to come in on the opposite side from that of Signor Croce (which we happen to think the sounder); but her method of using biography is different from that of, for instance, Mr Middleton Murry or Mr Fausset. She sketches in an author's own life, and that of his characters, to capture the *atmosphere* of his period; and thence makes one feel, by subtle suggestions, its intellectual and emotional quality. That is an historical act; and it enables us to go on to determine how far the individual writer's mind partook of this quality, how far differed from and ultimately altered it;

which is a critical act. A more valuable act, we suggest, than expounding a writer's whole work purely as the expression of a personality (a personality necessarily changing, maturing or dwindling); though Mrs Woolf would probably not wholly agree. But it may be well to insist that only a very small part of a man's experience—and that not always the most 'original' part—affects his work at all; and only a small part of his work is *expressive* of the quality in him that can take on significance when set in a wider critical and philosophical synthesis.

In Mrs Woolf's closing words on Montaigne she shows, half-unconsciously, her own position: 'Is the beauty of this world enough, or is there, elsewhere, some explanation of the mystery? To this what answer can there be? There is none. There is only one more question: "Que sçais-je?"' If we substitute 'literature' for 'this world' we see exactly the reason for Mrs Woolf's middle position in critical theory. She is sceptical of explanations. She interprets art in terms of men and women. She never willingly accepts any impersonal standards of aesthetic value. None the less, we believe that to Mrs Woolf—to anybody—definite comparison or judgment would be impossible had she not, willy-nilly, absorbed something of the courage of others' convictions—dogmas, if you must.

[A discussion of the essay 'On Not Knowing Greek' is omitted.]

Though Mrs Woolf's words are rarely very explicit, she can measure Shakespeare against the Attic dramatists; Greene, Peele, and Chapman against Tolstoi, and leave a surprisingly balanced and satisfying impression. She has glimpsed, though she will not avow it, that what matters most to literature in human psychology is not the variation but the norm, the essence, what is unchanging. Her impatience with our prominent novelists to-day is plainly traceable to a half-articulate rebellion against the immediacy, the accidentality, of their 'psychological' perception.

The end of literature, says Longinus, 'is not persuasion, but rapture'. But a degree of persuasion is needed first, and the rapture itself is a kind of further persuasion. Mrs Woolf seems to have this always at the back of her mind: and that it is which probably urged her to the quaintly diffident and unexpected preface in which she compares herself with the Common Reader, he with whom Dr Johnson 'rejoiced to concur'!

MRS DALLOWAY

14 May 1925

48. Richard Hughes, 'A Day in London Life', *Saturday Review of Literature* (New York)

16 May 1925, 755

Richard Hughes (b. 1900). British novelist.

Hughes makes an interesting comparison with Cézanne (see Introduction, p. 18).

To the poet the visible world exists: it shines with an intense brilliance, not only to the eye but to the touch, ear, smell, inward vision. (To the man-of-the-world, the visible world is unreal: his reality is a spiritual one: the only things which exist for him are his desires, and—in a lesser degree—his beliefs.) In Mrs Woolf's new novel, *Mrs Dalloway*, the visible world exists with a brilliance, a luminous clarity. In particular, it is London: to the reader, London is made, for the first time (this will probably surprise him) to exist. It emerges, shining like crystal, out of the fog in which all the merely material universe is ordinarily enveloped in his mind: it emerges, and stays. The present writer has 'known' London all his life: but Mrs Woolf's evocation of it is of a very different quality from his own memories: a quality which answers the farmer's question, when he was puzzled as to why folk should pay five hundred guineas for a painting of his farm, when they could have the house itself for two hundred. To Mrs Woolf London exists, and to Mrs Woolf's readers anywhere and at any time London will exist with a reality it can never have for those who merely live there.

Vividness alone, of course, is not art: it is only the material of art. But Mrs Woolf has, I think, a finer sense of form than any but the oldest living English novelist. As well as the power of brilliant evocation she has that creative faculty of form which differs from what is ordinarily called construction in the same way that life differs from mechanism: the same quality as Cézanne. In the case of the painter, of course, this 'form' is purely visual; the synthesis—relation—rhythm—whatever you call it, is created on this side of the eye; while in the case of the poet the pattern is a mental one, created behind the eye of the reader, composed directly of mental processes, ideas, sensory evocation—not of external agents (not of the words used, I mean). So, in the case of Mrs Woolf, and of the present novel, it is not by its vividness that her writing ultimately stays in the mind, but by the coherent and processional form which is composed of, and transcends, that vividness.

Philosophy as much as smell of violets is grist to the artist's mill: in actual practice it is generally more so. Here, Mrs Woolf touches all the time the verge of the problem of reality: not directly, like Pirandello, but by implication. (She is not so prone to emphasis as Pirandello.) In contrast to the solidity of her visible world there rises throughout the book in a delicate crescendo *fear*. The most notable feature of contemporary thought is the wide recognition by the human mind of its own limitation; i.e., that it is itself not a microcosm (as men used to think) but the macrocosm: that it cannot 'find out' anything about the universe because the terms both of question and answer are terms purely relative to itself: that even the key-words, *being* and *not-being*, bear no relation to anything except the mind which formulates them. (This is at least as old as Tao Tse, but until now has seldom been recognised by ordinary man.) In short, that logical and associative thinking do not differ in ultimate value—or even perhaps in kind. So, in this book each of the very different characters—Clarissa Dalloway herself, the slightly more speculative Peter, the Blakeian 'lunatic', Septimus Warren Smith, each with their own more or less formulated hypothesis of the meaning of life—together are an unanswerable illustration of that bottomlessness on which all spiritual values are based. This is what I mean by fear.

To come to the matter of chronicle, this novel is an account of a single day in London life; its sole principal event is the return from India of Mrs Dalloway's rejected suitor; the other characters are in many cases not even acquainted with the principals—sometimes simply people they pass in the street, or even people who merely see the same aeroplane in the sky. Towards the end, one of these strangers flings himself from a window; and Mrs Dalloway, after spending most of the morning wandering about Bond Street, gives a party in the evening. But then, Chronicle is an ass; this is an unusually coherent, lucid, and enthralling book, whatever he may suggest to the contrary.

49. Unsigned review, 'A Novelist's Experiment', *Times Literary Supplement*

21 May 1925

All Mrs Woolf's fiction shows such an instinct for experiment that we may have to show cause why this new book should be called peculiarly experimental. *Jacob's Room*, too, was an adventure. But there is one obvious difference between that novel and *Mrs Dalloway*. While the other, however innovating in its method, observed the usual time-span of a novel, this one describes the passage of a single day. The idea, though new enough to be called an experiment, may not be unique in modern fiction. There was a precedent in *Ulysses*. But Mrs Woolf's vision escapes disaster and produces something of her own. People and events here have a peculiar, almost ethereal transparency, as though bathed in a medium where one thing permeates another. Undoubtedly our world is less solid than it was, and our novels may have to shake themselves a little free of matter. Here, Mrs Woolf seems to say, is the stream of life, but reflected always in a mental vision.

Life itself, with the first cool radiance of a June morning in London, is wafted to Clarissa Dalloway as she goes out to buy flowers for her party in the evening—the same Clarissa who made a brief irruption into *The Voyage Out*, so exquisite there and brightly, almost excessively, interested; and now, at fifty-one, a little wiser, more pensive, but adoring life. An hour or two later, and Peter Walsh, whimsically sympathetic, who had been Clarissa's suitor years ago and has just returned from India, is falling asleep on a bench in Regent's Park to dream of memories, and will awake to think them out. Near him is a young couple who seem to be having a grim quarrel; but the man is a war victim who has gone out of his mind, and we shall read the last page of his tragedy before dusk falls. We shall be also at luncheon with Lady Bruton, at tea in the Army and Navy Stores, where Miss Kilman is making her last tense effort to snatch Clarissa's lovely daughter from her mother. But how often these lives and doings seem to distil themselves in something as immaterial as the passing of sunlight or the sound of a clock striking the hour. Distances gleam in the liquid clearness of that drop or bubble. For Mrs Woolf's sensitiveness can retain those wayward flashes as well as the whole chain of mixed images and feelings that unwinds from some tiny coil of memory. If in *Jacob's Room* she suggested the simultaneousness of life, here she paints not only this but its stream-like continuity.

Outwardly, however, the book is a cross-section of life. It does not simplify and concentrate as a play would do, nor does it thread everything on a single mind's experience. On the contrary, Mrs Woolf expands her view with the fullest freedom of a novelist, although she has the briefest limit as regards time; and the fusion of these opposing tendencies into one is a thrilling and hazardous enterprise. Only through sheer vision can it have form and life; and here the finely imaginative substance into which Mrs Woolf has woven it all is certainly reassuring. Moreover, while delineating processes she does not efface persons; on them all the threads depend, and theirs are the values. Theirs too, that final riddle of separateness, of otherness in the midst of the continuous, thinks Clarissa, watching an old lady in the house opposite:

> The supreme mystery which Kilman might say she had solved, or Peter might say he had solved, but Clarissa didn't believe either of them had the ghost of an idea of solving, was simply this: here was one room; there another. Did religion solve that, or love?

Watching Mrs Woolf's experiment, certainly one of the hardest and very subtly planned, one reckons up its cost. To get the whole value of the present you must enhance it, perhaps, with the past. And with her two chief figures, Clarissa and Peter, meeting after a long severance, Mrs Woolf has a full scope for the use of memories. They are amusing and they illuminate; yet either because of the rest of the design, or one's sense of the probable, or both, one fancies that sometimes these remembrances stretch almost too far. And the tragedy of poor Septimus, the war victim, although poignant in contrast, makes a block in the tideway now and then.

Although there is a surprising characterization in the process, characters must necessarily be shown with the tantalising fluidness of life itself. Lesser figures like Richard Dalloway or Lady Bruton or Miss Kilman, that grimly pathetic vampire, do well enough in outline; but as soon as we are shown more of a character, like Clarissa's or Peter's, we want more still, craving a further dimension that we cannot get. Also the cinema-like speed of the picture robs us of a great deal of the delight in Mrs Woolf's style. It has to be a little clipped, a little breathless; and the reading of her book is not so easy as it seems. Her wit is irresistible when it can escape a little way, as in the vision of those rival goddesses, Proportion and Conversion. In the end no one will complain of her for using all the freedom that she can. All her technical suppleness is needed to cope with the new form. It remains experimental in so far as we are uncertain what more can be done with it, and whether it can give the author's rare gifts full play. But something real has been achieved; for, having the courage of her theme and setting free her vision, Mrs Woolf steeps it in an emotion and irony and delicate imagination which enhance the consciousness and the zest of living.

50. Gerald Bullett, from a review, *Saturday Review*

30 May 1925, 558

Gerald Bullett (1893–1958), English poet and novelist, reviewed Edith Wharton's *The Mother Recompense* in the same article.

These two novels, each good in its own way, offer an interesting study in contrast. Mrs Woolf is a brilliant experimentalist, while Mrs Wharton, having emerged from her Henry James period, is now content to practise the craft of fiction without attempting to enlarge its technical scope.

Mrs Dalloway resembles *Jacob's Room* in essentials, its chief obvious difference from that remarkable book being that it records the life of a single day.

[Plot summary omitted]

The searchlight of Mrs Woolf's suggestive art passes zigzag over the minds of men and women, illuminating those dark interiors with the light of an extraordinarily subtle vision. It rests, this penetrating ray, longest upon Peter Walsh himself, who is just returned from long exile in India.

Peter calls on Clarissa in the morning; he attends her party at night. With this second meeting the book closes. In the interval we have watched minutely the quivering activity of his cerebrum. And not his alone, but Clarissa's and Septimus Smith's and Miss Kilman's and Elizabeth's, to name but a few others. It is to be noted that we watch these intimate experiences rather than share them, that the emotions which we know, by inference, must accompany this cerebral activity do not always communicate themselves to us; we remain a little more than usually detached. We are moved, when we are moved at all, less by the particular emotions of these people than by the poetry of thought and phrase (seldom of rhythm), and by that curious sensation which is the book's continuous effect: the sensation of seeing and feeling the very stream of life, the undeviating tide of time, flowing luminously by, with all the material phenomena, streets and stars, bicycles and human bodies, floating like straws upon its surface. Whether to communicate this sense of the incessant flux was part of Mrs Woolf's intention I cannot undertake to say: I can only record my own reaction to her book. To add that there are very definite limitations to the scope of this curious technique is hardly necessary, for there is no form of writing to which the same remark would not in some degree apply. Highly impressionistic work such as this lacks external drama, for its intellectual and technical bias provides that the most startling action—a young man's throwing himself out of the window, for example—shall seem trivial compared with the bright ferment of consciousness. Mrs Woolf's is an inversion of the ordinary method of narration, the method of which Mrs Wharton offers us a very respectable example. The fact that the life of the mind is more significant than the movement of the body is reflected in the very texture of the narrative, action being treated as a mere parenthesis:

[Quotes pp. 12–13 'How much she wanted' to 'could have looked even differently!']

And even when the action is not apparently subordinate it is actually so. One part of this method's general effect on the reader is to make him feel that he is observing, from a great height, a world of disembodied spirits. It is not so much that the picture lacks definition as that it lacks stability; its outlines are incessantly flowing into new, bright patterns. Nothing for a moment stands still; the flying landscape daubs across our vision a myriad bright streaks of changing colour; shapes are perpetually disintegrating and resolving into new shapes. To those who desire a static universe, in which they can examine things at their leisure, this speed, this insubstantiality, this exhilarating deluge of impressions, will be perhaps unpleasing.

51. P. C. Kennedy, from a review, *New Statesman*

6 June 1925, 229

Mrs Dalloway is in many ways beautiful; but I think it sets out to be, and continues until the end to pretend to be, what it is not. I think it quite sincerely claims to employ a new method, and I think it employs an old one. Personally, I see no reason for trying to escape the old one, which I believe will still answer all purposes of subtlety and excitement; but, if one sets out to escape, one should succeed in escaping. People will tell you, with a face of praise, that the whole action of *Mrs Dalloway* passes in one day. But it doesn't pass in one day. In order to create that impression, Mrs Woolf makes her characters move about London, and, when two of them come into purely fortuitous and external contact, she gives you the history of each backwards. She might just as well—better—have given it forwards. The novelty in not a novelty. It is a device that is used constantly, especially on the 'pictures', where the hero closes his eyes, a blur crawls across the screen, and the heroine is seen in short skirts and ringlets, as he knew her in the old home-village before she was betrayed. Seven years elapse between Parts I and II; and the hero is still dreaming; but no one would say that the action of the film passes in one day. Mrs Woolf has really imposed on several quite different stories a purely artificial unity. But, it may be said, the threads are knit at the close. They are indeed —the more's the pity. Peter Walsh, home from India, has all his life loved Clarissa, who has married Richard Dalloway and borne a daughter, Elizabeth. Clarissa goes for a walk, and sees a motor-car containing a Personage. A crowd gathers outside Buckingham Palace; it sees an aeroplane writing on the sky; the same portent is seen by Lucrezia Warren Smith, sitting with her husband in Regent's Park. First connection. A slender one, you will admit; those smoky tendrils might bind anything to anything; an eye sufficiently remote could see everything at once. Peter calls upon Clarissa. They are still, after all these years, uncomfortable. They are middle-aged, reminiscent, critical, resentful; they part. Peter goes for a walk; he is still reminiscent;

he hears an old woman singing opposite Regent's Park Tube Station; the same old woman is heard by the Warren Smiths; connection number two. Smith is a 'shell-shocked' soldier; he has moments of vision, of certainty, of the kind that is called illusion; he goes to a specialist; he kills himself; the specialist attends Clarissa Dalloway's party in the evening and talks about the death. Connection number three! One sees the significance of it. Clarissa's apprehension of the tragedy is to interpret Clarissa's character:

> Somehow it was her disaster—her disgrace. It was her punishment to see sink and disappear here a man, there a woman, in this profound darkness, and she forced to stand here in her evening dress. She had schemed; she had pilfered. She was never wholly admirable.

But any tragedy would have served for that contrast; the artificial link is purely redundant, purely improbable, purely pointless. It is the sort of coincidence which mars the conventional novel; but it is less distracting there, because there it at any rate serves a purpose.

Mrs Woolf, too, has—or so it seems to me—a purpose: and a genuinely splendid one. The whole trouble is the incongruity between the apparent purpose and the distracting method. I take it (and, though there is always a certain impertinence in attempting to say, or even to see, what anybody else means, the critic cannot avoid it)—I take it that Mrs Woolf means to show us the kaleidoscope of life shaken into a momentary plan; the vagueness, the casualness, the chaos, suffering the compulsion which gives orders and makes order. And that, I repeat, is splendid. All art aims, consciously or unconsciously, at that. But all the novelty of Mrs Woolf's technique simply distracts from it. And if, as I suspect, she has the subsidiary but still vital purpose of stressing the incoherence, of catching the bubble, the spark, the half-dream, the inexplicable memory, the doubt, the snare, the joke, the dread, the come-and-go of the moment on the wing—then again the needless links, the coincidences, distract.

Mrs Woolf has extraordinary gifts; the only doubt is whether they are the specific gifts of the novelists. She excels in description of mood or sudden scene; but the mood might always be anybody's; anybody might occupy the scene. In all this brilliant novel (and the brilliance is at times quite dazzling) there are no people. It is like that ghostly world of Mr Bertrand Russell's philosophy, in which there are lots of sensations but no one to have them. If Mrs Woolf had created a single character, I cannot conceive that she would have *wanted* to deviate from the ordinary manner of the novelist; who, after all, could want a better or a bigger job than to tell us about a real person, about what happened to him or her? But Mrs Woolf's masterly and masterful intellect is critical (I don't use the word in opposition to 'creative'—there is, of course, creation in criticism, in page after page of Mrs Woolf's delicately hurrying prose). She understands a mood; she analyses it; she presents it; she catches its finer implications; but she never moves me with it, because she never makes me feel that the person credited with it is other than an object of the keenest and most skilful study. She uses the words 'terror', 'ecstasy', 'excitement', with perfect justice; but it isn't justice they want. I hope I have made it clear that my admiration for what Mrs Woolf has achieved outweighs my dislike of the fetters she has put on her achievement. Call *Mrs Dalloway* an intellectual triumph, and I agree. I could quote scores of fine and profound things from it—here is a typical one: 'Conversion, fastidious Goddess, loves blood better than brick, and feasts most subtly on the human will.' But I want to weep with Peter Walsh and leap to death with poor Septimus Warren Smith; and my trouble is that I can't.

52. Lytton Strachey, 'You have not yet mastered your method'

18 June 1925

Virginia Woolf was very sensitive to criticism, but this extract indicates that she was receptive when it came from a source which she respected. Her comments at the end give us a glimpse of her own self-criticism in the course of composing the novel.

Strachey's comments were recorded by Virginia Woolf in *A Writer's Diary*, pp. 78–9.

No, Lytton does not like *Mrs Dalloway*, and, what is odd, I like him all the better for saying so, and don't much mind. What he says is that there is a discordancy between the ornament (extremely beautiful) and what happens (rather ordinary—or unimportant). This is caused, he thinks, by some discrepancy in Clarissa herself: he thinks she is disagreeable and limited, but that I alternately laugh at her and cover her, very remarkably, with myself. So that I think as a whole, the book does not ring solid; yet, he says, it is a whole; and he says sometimes the writing is of extreme beauty. What can one call it but genius? he said! Coming when, one never can tell. Fuller of genius, he said, than anything I had done. Perhaps, he said, you have not yet mastered your method. You should take something wilder and more fantastic, a framework that admits of anything, like *Tristram Shandy*. But then I should lose touch with emotions, I said. Yes, he agreed, there must be reality for you to start from. Heaven knows how you're to do it. But he thought me at the beginning, not at the end. And he said the *C.R.* was divine, a classic, *Mrs D.* being, I fear, a flawed stone. This is very personal, he said, and old fashioned perhaps; yet I think there is some truth in it, for I remember the night at Rodmell when I decided to give it up, because I found Clarissa in some way tinselly. Then I invented her memories. But I think some distaste for her persisted. Yet, again, that was true to my feeling for Kitty and one must dislike people in art without its mattering, unless indeed it is true that certain characters detract from the importance of what happens to them. None of this hurts me, or depresses me. It's odd that when Clive and others (several of them) say it is a masterpiece, I am not much exalted; when Lytton picks holes, I get back into my working fighting mood, which is natural to me. I don't see myself a success. I like the sense of effort better. The sales collapsed completely for three days; now a little dribble begins again. I shall be more than pleased if we sell 1500. It's now 1250.

53. J. F. Holms, review, *Calendar of Modern Letters*

July 1925, 404–5

The *Calendar* published some excellent criticism during its short life (1925–7). It had a 'conviction about literature as a field worthy of close exegetical study and yet open to larger issues about its social background and its moral content'. The *Calendar* had praised *The Common Reader* (No. 46) but this review was more critical.

Mrs Woolf has culture and intelligence; she writes from a strong and genuine productive impulse; her sensibility, when she does not force it, is fresh, individual and admirable in its kind; for its expression she has developed a fastidious and accomplished technique; and finally, in *Mrs Dalloway* it is clear that what she intended to do, she has done, in the sense in which this statement holds truth. These are uncommon merits, they have gained Mrs Woolf the reputation of what is called a distinguished writer, and their possession entitles her to criticism on her own standards.

Mrs Dalloway is considerably the best book she has written; in it her gifts achieve their full effect, and her capacity to say what she wants to is almost complete. How then, one asks, as the tide rises through her pages, can such talent co-exist with a sentimentality that would be remarkable in a stockbroker, and inconceivable among educated people? Sentimentality is an interesting term, more liable to misconstruction than most; and it is perhaps clearer to say of this novel that it is impossible to believe that if its author were asked directly whether the thoughts that pass during an hour through the head of any man of fifty bear any resemblance whatever to the soliloquies of Peter Walsh and other characters that fill her pages, her answer could differ from our own. This, however, is what we have to believe, with the result that in spite of, or on account of Mrs Woolf's talent, her writing conveys an effect of automatism that is curious, and aesthetically corrupt. *Mrs Dalloway* has the design, apparent intensity, and immediate aspect of a work of art, and it is an interesting problem of aesthetic psychology to explain so self-subsistent a mirage entirely unconnected with reality. This is not to say that falsity is inherent throughout Mrs Woolf's writing. Her natural and unvitiated talent springs immediately from sensation, and her sensibility of this kind is rare and valuable. When she resists the virtuoso's temptation to expanded bravura pieces, her transcriptions of immediate sensation have the freshness, delicacy and vitality of direct perception, a quality that is not relative, and is sufficient in itself to distinguish her work from intelligent novel-writing. But here Mrs Woolf's talent stops, in more senses than one. For this quality of direct sensational perception is precisely that of a child's, undisturbed by thought, feeling and other functions to be acquired in the course of its development as a social organism. And Mrs Woolf is by no means entirely a child; she is thoroughly involved in human relationships, which form moreover her subject matter as a novelist. But her essential reactions to them are a child's automatic reactions, who believes what he reads in a book, who believes life is what he is told it is, that some people are good and others bad—though bad ones are not to be found among persons he knows—who believes, in short, in the absoluteness of his first social impressions as a group member. Together with this more essential Mrs Woolf exists an intelligent, experienced and sensitive adult, whose business it is to justify her to the world. But these are unhallowed partnerships whose offspring, as I have said, are sentimentality and aesthetic corruption. When she leaves immediate impressions of experience, Mrs Woolf's treatment of character and human relations is almost ludicrously devoid of psychological and aesthetic truth; as soon as she touches them she is as false as her rendering of impressions is true. The motives, thoughts and emotions she attributes to her characters have precisely as much and as little relation to the truth of life as the motives, thoughts and emotions postulated of the ideal person who forms its public by the daily paper. There are one or two exceptions to this, in particular the character of Septimus Warren Smith, where Mrs Woolf rather shakily approaches imaginative truths; but most of the book, despite its pure and brilliant impressionism, is sentimental in conception and texture, and is accordingly aesthetically worthless. Such judgements, as is evident in this review, cannot be expressed in terms of purely literary criticism, which, indeed, is an instrument not applicable to the valuation of contemporary literature, as should be clear from experience and history.

54. E. M. Forster, a survey of Virginia Woolf's work

1926

From 'The Novels of Virginia Woolf', *New Criterion*, April 1926, 277–86.

It is profoundly characteristic of the art of Virginia Woolf that when I decided to write about it and had planned a suitable opening paragraph, my fountain pen should disappear. Tiresome creature! It slipped through a pocket into a seam. I could pinch it, chivy it about, make holes in the coat lining, but a layer of tailor's stuffing prevented recovery. So near, and yet so far! Which is what one feels about her art. The pen is extricated in time, but during the struggle the opening paragraph has escaped; the words are here but the birds have flown; 'opals and emeralds, they lie about the roots of turnips.' It is far more difficult to catch her than it is for her to catch what she calls life—'life; London; this moment in June'. Again and again she eludes, until the pen, getting restive, sets to work on its own and grinds out something like this, something totally false such as: 'Mrs Woolf is a talented but impressionistic writer, with little feeling for form and none for actuality.' Rubbish. She has, among other achievements, made a definite contribution to the novelist's art. But how is this contribution to be stated? And how does she handle the ingredients of fiction—human beings, time, and space? Let us glance at her novels in the order of their composition.

The Voyage Out, was published in 1915. It is a strange, tragic, inspired book whose scene is a South America not found on any map and reached by a boat which would not float on any sea, an America whose spiritual boundaries touch Xanadu and Atlantis. Hither, to a hotel, various English tourists repair, and the sketches of them are so lively and 'life-like' that we expect a comedy of manners to result. Gradually a current sets in, a deep unrest. What are all these people doing—talking, eating, kissing, reading, being kind or unkind? What do they understand of each other or of themselves? What relations are possible between them? Two young men, bleak and honest intellectuals from Cambridge, ask the question; Rachel, an undeveloped girl, answers it. The uneasiness of society and its occasional panics take hold of her, and nothing can exorcise them, because it is her own desire to face the truth; nothing, not even love.

> They stood together in front of the looking-glass, and with a brush tried to make themselves look as if they had been feeling nothing all the morning, neither pain nor happiness. But it chilled them to see themselves in the glass, for instead of being vast and indivisible they were really very small and separate, the size of the glass leaving a large space for the reflection of other things.

Wedded bliss is promised her, but the voyage continues, the current deepens, carrying her between green banks of the jungle into disease and death. The closing chapters of the book are as poignant as anything in modern fiction, yet they arise naturally out of what has gone before. They are not an interruption but a fulfilment. Rachel has lost everything—for there is no hint of compensation beyond the grave—but she has not swerved from the course honesty marked out, she has not jabbered or pretended that human relationships are satisfactory. It is a noble book, so noble that a word of warning must be added: like all Virginia Woolf's work, it is not romantic, not mystic, not explanatory of the universe. By using a wrong tone of voice—over-stressing 'South America' for instance—the critic might easily make it appear to be all these things, and perhaps waft it towards popular success. His honesty must equal the writers; he is offered no ultimate good, but 'life; London; this moment in June'; and it is his job to find out what the promise entails.

Will *Night and Day* help him? It is the simplest novel she has written, and to my mind the least successful. Very long, very careful, it condescends to many of the devices she so gaily derides in her essay on 'Mr Bennett and Mrs Brown'. The two principal characters are equipped with houses and relatives which document their reality, they are screwed into Chelsea and Highgate as the case may be, and move from their bases to meet in the rooms and streets of a topographical metropolis. After misunderstandings, they marry, they are promised happiness. In view of what preceded it and of what is to follow, *Night and Day* seems to me a deliberate exercise in classicism. It contains all that has characterised English fiction for good or evil during the last hundred and fifty years—faith in personal relations, recourse to humorous side shows, insistence on petty social differences. Even the style has been normalised, and though the machinery is modern, the resultant form is as traditional as *Emma*. Surely the writer is using tools that don't belong to her. At all events she has never touched them again.

For, contemporary with this full length book, she made a very different experiment, published two little—stories, sketches, what is one to call them?—which show the direction in which her genius has since moved.[1] At last her sensitiveness finds full play, and she is able to describe what she sees in her own words. In 'The Mark on the Wall' she sees a mark on the wall, wonders what it is . . . and that is the entire story. In 'Kew Gardens' she sees men, sometimes looking at flowers, and flowers never looking at men. And, in either case, she reports her vision impartially; she strays forward, murmuring, wandering, falling asleep. Her style trails after her, catching up grass and dust in its folds, and instead of the precision of the earlier writing we have something more elusive than has yet been achieved in English. If a drowsy and desultory person could also be a great artist he would talk like this:

[1] Republished in *Monday or Tuesday*, 1921.

[Quotes the end of 'Kew Gardens' from 'Yellow and black' to 'colours into the air.']

The objection (or apparent objection) to this sort of writing is that it cannot say much or be sure of saying anything. It is an inspired breathlessness, a beautiful droning or gasping which trusts to luck, and can never express human relationships or the structure of society. So at least one would suppose, and that is why the novel of *Jacob's Room* (1922) comes as a tremendous surprise. The impossible has occurred. The style closely resembles that of 'Kew Gardens'. The blobs of colour continue to drift past; but in their midst, interrupting their course like a closely sealed jar, rises the solid figure of a young man. In what sense Jacob is alive—in what sense any of Virginia Woolf's characters live—we have yet to determine. But that he exists, that he stands as does a monument is certain, and wherever he stands we recognise him for the same and are touched by his outline. The coherence of the book is even more amazing than its beauty. In the stream of glittering similes, unfinished sentences, hectic catalogues, unanchored proper names, we seem to be going nowhere. Yet the goal comes, the method and the matter prove to have been one, and looking back from the pathos of the closing scene we see for a moment the airy drifting atoms piled into a colonnade. The break with *Night and Day* and even with *The Voyage Out* is complete. A new type of fiction has swum into view, and it is none the less new because it has had a few predecessors—laborious, well meaning, still-born books by up-to-date authors, which worked the gasp and the drone for all they were worth, and are unreadable.

Three years after *Jacob's Room* comes another novel in the same style, or slight modification of the style: *Mrs Dalloway*. It is perhaps her masterpiece, but difficult, and I am not altogether sure about every detail, except when my fountain pen is in my hand. Here is London at all events—so much is certain, London chorussing with all its clocks and shops and sunlit parks, and writing texts with an aeroplane across God's heaven. Here is Clarissa Dalloway, elderly, kind, graceful, rather hard and superficial, and a terrible snob. How she loves London! And there is Septimus Warren Smith—she never meets him—a case of shell shock—very sad—who hears behind the chorus the voices of the dead singing, and sees his own apotheosis or damnation in the sky. That dreadful war! Sir William Bradshaw of Harley Street, himself in perfect health, very properly arranges for Septimus Warren Smith to go to a lunatic asylum. Septimus is ungrateful and throws himself out of the window. 'Coward' cries the doctor, but is too late. News of which comes to Clarissa as she is giving an evening party. Does she likewise commit suicide? I thought she did the first time I read the book; not at my second reading, nor is the physical act important, for she is certainly left with the full knowledge—inside knowledge—of what suicide is. The societified lady and the obscure maniac are in a sense the same person. His foot has slipped through the gay surface on which she still stands—that is all the difference between them. She returns (it would seem) to her party and to the man she loves, and a hint of her new knowledge comes through to him as the London clocks strike three. Such apparently is the outline of this exquisite and superbly constructed book, and having made the outline one must rub it out at once. For emphasis is fatal to the understanding of this author's work. If we dared not overstress 'South America' in *The Voyage Out*, still lighter must fall our touch on London here, still more disastrous would be the application to its shimmering fabric of mysticism, unity beneath multiplicity, twin souls . . .

> Why creeds and prayers and mackintoshes? when, thought Clarissa, that's the miracle, that's the mystery; that old lady, she meant, whom she could see going from chest of drawers to dressing table. She could still see her. And the supreme mystery which Kilman might say she had solved, or Peter might say he had solved, but Clarissa didn't believe either of them had the ghost of an idea of solving was simply this: here is one room: there another. Did religion solve that, or love?

As far as her work has a message, it seems to be contained in the above paragraph. Here is one room, there another. Required like most writers to choose between the surface and the depths as a basis of her operations, she chooses the surface and then burrows in as far as she can.

After this glance we can better understand her equipment, and realise that visual sensitiveness—in itself a slight tool for a novelist—becomes in her case a productive force. How beautifully she sees! Look at 'those churches, like shapes of grey paper, breasting the stream of the Strand', for instance. Or at 'The flames were struggling through the wood and roaring up when, goodness knows where from, pails flung water in beautiful hollow shapes as of polished tortoiseshell; flung again and again; until the hiss was like a swarm of bees; and all the faces went out.' How beautiful! Yet vision is only the frontier of her kingdom. Behind it lie other treasures; in particular the mind.

Her remarkable intellectual powers have nothing to do with common sense—masses of roses can be gathered at Christmas for instance, and the characters in one book need bear no resemblance to their namesakes in another. Nor is she much occupied in presenting clever men and women. What thrills her—for it starts as a thrill—is the actual working of the brain, especially the youthful brain, and there are passages in *Jacob's Room* where the process becomes as physical as the raising of a hand. Moreover she reverences learning; it gives her disinterested pleasure, increases the natural nobility of her work.

[Quotes from *Jacob's Room* pp. 108–9 'Stone lies solid over the British Museum' to 'by the pillar box, arguing.']

It is easy for a novelist to describe what a character thinks of; look at Mrs Humphry Ward. But to convey the actual process of thinking is a creative feat, and I know of no one except Virginia Woolf who has accomplished it. Here at last thought, and the learning that is the result of thought, take their own high place upon the dais, exposed no longer to the patronage of the hostess or the jeers of the buffoon. Here Cambridge, with all its dons, is raised into the upper air and becomes a light for ships at sea, and Rachel, playing Bach upon a hotel piano, builds a momentary palace for the human mind.

But what of the subject that she regards as of the highest importance: human beings as a whole and as wholes? She tells us (in her essays) that human beings are the permanent material of fiction, that it is only the method of presenting them which changes and ought to change, that to capture their inner life presents a different problem to each generation of novelists; the great Victorians solved it in their way; the Edwardians shelved it by looking outwards at relatives and houses; the Georgians must solve it anew, and if they succeed a new age of fiction will begin. Has she herself succeeded? Do her own characters live?

I feel that they do live, but not continuously, whereas the characters of Tolstoy (let us say) live continuously. With her, the reader is in a state of constant approval. 'Yes that is right,' he says, each time she implies something more about Jacob or Peter: 'yes that would be so: yes.' Whereas in the case of Tolstoy approval is absent. We sink into André, into Nicolay Rostoff during the moments they come forth, and no more endorse the correctness of their functioning than we endorse our own. And the problem before her—the problem that she has set herself, and that certainly would inaugurate a new literature if solved—is to retain her own wonderful new method and form, and yet allow her readers to inhabit each character with Victorian thoroughness. Think how difficult this is. If you work in a storm of atoms and seconds, if your highest joy is 'life; London; this moment in June' and your deepest mystery 'here is one room; there another', then how can you construct your human beings so that each shall be not a movable monument but an abiding home, how can you build between them any permanent roads of love and hate? There was continuous life in the little hotel people of *The Voyage Out* because there was no innovation in the method. But Jacob in *Jacob's Room* is discontinuous, demanding—and obtaining—separate approval for everything he feels or does. And *Mrs Dalloway*? There seems a slight change here, an approach towards character construction in the Tolstoyan sense: Sir William Bradshaw, for instance, is uninterruptedly and embracingly evil. Any approach is significant, for it suggests that in future books she may solve the problem as a whole. She herself believes it can be done, and, with the exception of Joyce, she is the only writer of genius who is trying. All the other so-called innovators are (if not pretentious bunglers), merely innovators in subject matter and the praise we give them is of the kind we should accord to scientists. Their novels admit aeroplanes or bigamy, or give some fresh interpretation of the spirit of Norfolk or Persia, or at the most reveal some slight discovery about human nature. They do good work, because everything is subject matter for the novel, nothing ought to be ruled out on the ground that it is remote or indecent. But they do not advance the novelist's art. Virginia Woolf has already done that a little, and if she succeeds in her problem of rendering character, she will advance it enormously.

For English fiction, despite the variety of its content, has made little innovation in form between the days of Fielding and those of Arnold Bennett. It might be compared to a picture gallery, lit by windows placed at suitable intervals between the pictures. First come some portraits, then a window with a view say of Norfolk, then some more portraits and perhaps a still life, followed by a window with a view of Persia, then more portraits and perhaps a fancy piece, followed by a view of the universe. The pictures and the windows are infinite in number, so that every variety of experience seems assured, and yet there is one factor that never varies: namely, the gallery itself; the gallery is always the same, and the reader always has the feeling that he is pacing along it, under the conditions of time and space that regulate his daily life. Virginia Woolf would do away with the sense of pacing. The pictures and windows may remain if they can—indeed the portraits must remain—but she wants to destroy the gallery in which they are embedded and in its place build—build what? Something more rhythmical. *Jacob's Room* suggests a spiral whirling down to a point, *Mrs Dalloway* a cathedral.

55. Edwin Muir, 'Virginia Woolf', *Nation and Athenaeum*

17 April 1926, 70–2

Muir gives unusually high praise to *Night and Day*, a book which was not enthusiastically received when it came out, and was largely neglected afterwards.

The historian writing fifty years hence of the literature of today will find in it a certain note of inhumanity. He will speak of our hostility to mankind, and he will remark how different Mr. James Joyce's attitude to his characters is from that of Scott, for example, or Jane Austen. A thorough dislike of their creations characterizes, indeed, the majority of modern novelists. Mr. Joyce hates and scorns his characters; Mr. Huxley's inspire him with disgust or with ill-natured laughter; Mr. Lawrence hews his down right and left in the name of his 'dark god'; Mr. Stephen Hudson submits his, most severe test of all, to a scrupulous intellectual scrutiny. These writers do not accept the character as an end in himself; he is always a means to them; he is always on a different plane from the mind which evoked him. The contemporary novelist does not walk through his crowds, on easy terms with them, good and bad, as Fielding and Thackeray walked through theirs. He is not among the works of his hands, but detached from them; he watches their movements as a scientist might watch the progress of an experiment. Jane Austen, we feel, is always at the excursions and tea parties she describes; she is one of the characters, the least observed and most observing of all. But this can scarcely be said of Mr. Joyce or Mr. Huxley, or Mr. Hudson, even when they are portraying figures clearly autobiographical. There is always detachment in their spirit, a certain hostile watchfulness, a barrier of conscious or unconscious irony. They do not meet their characters on the same level as we should, if we were given the chance.

It may be said of Mrs. Woolf that she does meet her characters on this level. She accepts them as ends; she accepts them, that is to say, as people of the same status and existing in the same dimension as herself. She might walk into her novels and be at home in them. She stands in the same relation to her characters as almost all the chief English novelists have stood to theirs. Her attitude, like theirs, is eminently practical, tolerant, appreciative, intelligent; it has the good sense and sagacity of the English prose tradition.

The point is important, for an easy coming and going between the mind of the novelist and the world he creates has characterized the bulk of great fiction. It characterizes all the Russian fiction we know; it characterizes French fiction to the time of Flaubert; it has characterized English fiction up to Mr. Joyce and Mr. Lawrence. The advantage it gives to the novelist is clear. It endows his imaginary world with an everyday actuality, a toughness which will stand wear and tear. It insensibly inclines us to the useful illusion that all we are reading about is actual; and when we once believe that, the background of the world will fill in readily behind it, as it fills in behind the happenings we hear of in actual life. But for the artist himself the pragmatic attitude has deeper virtues. If it does not make his imagination more profound, it makes it, at any rate, more dependable, sets it working more thoroughly. His relation to his characters being horizontal, being, that is to say, on the same plane if in one important respect not the same, as the relations of the characters among themselves, he will understand their reactions to each other more naturally and feel them more concretely than he could if he were surveying them from a height, if he were sinking his mind into them instead of sharing it with them. For this practical, everyday, distinctively prose way of approaching the theme perhaps the best term is intelligence. It is not a purely intellectual quality; it consists rather in the use of the intellect and the imagination in a comprehensive but common-sense way, as if, exercised on imaginary situations, they were being exercised on the actual problems of life.

The quality of intelligence Mrs Woolf has in a high degree. It is to be seen equally and is of the same quality in her novels, and in her volume of essays, *The Common Reader*; for intelligence works by the same means, whatever theme may confront it. All the notable English novelists of the past have possessed it; the only contemporary novelist, besides Mrs. Woolf, who has it in a striking degree is Mr. E. M. Forster. Mr. Joyce lacks it completely. He has a powerful, erratic intellect, but it is the differentiated intellect of the artist; it is hardly concerned at all with what is normal, expedient, practicable, but simply with what is, whether it be humanly possible or impossible. Mr. Joyce has objectified magnificently his personal world, but it is not a world in which we could live, and to him that is, indeed, a matter of no concern. Yet it is a matter of the first importance in the actual world, and an imaginative work which ignores it ignores something essential; that work may have truth, but it will not be an approximate image of the truth. Mrs. Woolf's novels are an approximate image of the truth. The world she shows us is not of such vast dimensions as Mr. Joyce's, but it is on a perfect scale; there are all the elements in it that there are in any of the worlds we actually live in, and there is, moreover, a perpetual reference to the world itself, the modern world which looms behind and makes possible our smaller, personal worlds.

Width and justice of comprehension are chiefly necessary in the writer who tries to grasp all these implications and strives to make the picture complete. They were shown in Mrs. Woolf's first novel, *The Voyage Out*; they were shown still more remarkably in *Night and Day*. Nothing was more striking in these first two books than the undeviating sobriety of treatment, the absence of facility, the resolve to take all the factors into account and to be just to them all. The convention of the novel is accepted. The author, we feel, has resolved to take the novel as it is, and to make it do all that up to now it has done. In *The Voyage Out* she uses among other methods that of Chekhov. That book is still a little tentative, but *Night and Day*, which followed it, remains in some ways the finest of Mrs. Woolf's novels. In depth, in meaning behind meaning, some of the scenes in it are superior to anything else written in our time. The meeting between Denham and Rodney on the Embankment, the description of Katherine's aimless wanderings through London on the evening that she broke her appointment with Denham; the Hilbery household, the delightful but pathetic irrelevancies of Mrs. Hilbery: these, brought intimately together in the book, as they would be in life, give us that sense of the rich variety of existence which only Mrs. Woolf's predecessors in the English novel can give. Certain complex effects which were once characteristic of the English novel, effects in which comedy and tragedy jostle, have been almost entirely lost in our time. Sterne was perhaps the first great prose master of them; Scott is full of them; by Dickens they are exploited freely but crudely. The conversation between Bartoline Saddletree and Davie Deans about the trial of Effie is a perfect example of this style; but we find it again and again in Scott; it is an element in almost all his great scenes. Nothing perhaps can give us a stronger sense of the reality of the situation we are reading about than this juxtaposition of the comic and the tragic. We feel that the writer has seen all its aspects, even the most unexpected; that his imagination has not been canalized by the theme, but is free and can move as it wills. Intelligence once more, the taking of all the factors into account, produces these imaginative juxtapositions; and in *Night and Day* it is Mrs Woolf's intelligence that recreates them. There are dull passages in the book; the various threads of the story are not gathered up, do not become dramatic, until we are a quarter of the way through, but once gathered up, they are never released until the end; the growth and development of the complex of situations is steady. One character after another is caught into the action; and it leaves none of them what they were before. The easy course, the short cut, is never taken; everything is worked out anew. For comprehensiveness of understanding the author has never surpassed *Night and Day*. Yet we feel, regarding Mrs Woolf's later works, that there is something lacking in it: the satisfaction of the artist working within conditions shaped for herself. The given conditions, it is true, are scrupulously observed; but we feel them as a compulsion on the writer; they are too impersonal; they have not been resolved into a completely individual means of expression. *Night and Day* is a book which a writer might execute, submitting to the form rather than finding complete expression through it.

In the small volume of short stories, *Monday or Tuesday*, the experimentation with form began which later gave us *Jacob's Room* and *Mrs Dalloway*. It is tentative, but lighter, more buoyant, than anything Mrs Woolf had written before. *Jacob's Room* was a great advance; its plan was admirable; the recreation of a figure through memories and associations was a suggestive and perfectly valid device. The book contains several beautiful scenes, but it is not sure, like Mrs Woolf's earlier and like her later work; it has a good deal of the sentimentality which so often comes out of the mind along with a first attempt to express something in it which has not been expressed before. When the artist tries to liberate his essential emotion toward experience, at first he is likely to liberate a great deal more along with it, until in this new kind of expression he learns to distinguish what is essential from what appears so.

Jacob's Room has a more living quality than Mrs Woolf's earlier work, but it is less critical. *Mrs Dalloway* is the most characteristic work Mrs Woolf has written. It is so unlike *Night and Day* that they can hardly be compared. It has not the earlier book's finely dramatic development, nor its intensity; but it is more organic and, in a more living sense, it is infinitely subtle in its means, and it has on all its pages, as *Night and Day* had not, the glow of an indisputable artistic triumph. As a piece of expressive writing there is nothing in contemporary English fiction to rival it. Shades of an evanescence which one might have thought uncapturable, visual effects so fine that the eye does not take them in, that only in the memory are guessed at from the impression they leave in passing, exquisitely graded qualities of sound, of emotion, of reverie, are in Mrs Woolf's prose not merely dissected but imaginatively reconstructed. All that in the earlier novels was analysed is resolved in *Mrs Dalloway* into evocative images. There is nothing left of the stubborn explanatory machinery of the analytical novel; the material upon which the author works is the same as before, but it has all been sublimated, and, although the psychology is subtle and exact, no trace remains of the psychologist:

> And Clarissa had leant forward, taken his hand, drawn him to her, kissed him,—actually had felt his face on hers before she could down the brandishing of silver-flashing plumes like pampas grass in a tropic gale in her breast, which, subsiding, left her holding his hand, patting his knee, and feeling as she sat back extraordinarily at her ease with him and light-hearted, all in a clap it came over her, If I had married him, this gaiety would have been mine all day!

How much more exact that is than analysis could be! It is more exact, for the ebb and flow of the imagery, the rhythm of the sentence, follow the course of the emotion. First we have Clarissa's effusion of uncontrolled, blind emotion evoking the image, 'the brandishing of silver-flashing plumes'; then the emergence from it to a recognition of diurnal reality, reported rather than described, 'leaving her holding his hand, patting his knee'; and finally in the accelerating pace with which the sentence ends, the sudden thought that if she had married him! It is exquisitely done.

Then there is the passage, too long to quote, in which the sound of the bells of St Margaret's, which 'glides into the recesses of the heart, buries itself in ring after ring of sound, like something alive which wants to confide itself, to disperse itself, to be, with a tremor of delight at rest', is wedded in Peter Walsh's mind with the image of Clarissa in her house, so that when 'the sudden loudness of the final stroke' comes, it seems to be tolling 'for death that surprised in the midst of life, Clarissa falling where she stood in her drawing-room. No! No! he cried. She is not dead!' The mood that Mrs Woolf catches here is quite beyond the reach of the psychological, analytical method; yet how perfectly it is conveyed. But more striking perhaps than either of these is the description of Clarissa sewing her green dress:

Quiet descended on her, calm, content, as her needle, drawing the silk smoothly to its gentle pause, collected the green folds together and attached them, very lightly, to the belt. So on a summer's day waves collect, overbalance, and fall; collect and fall; and the whole world seems to be saying 'that is all' more and more ponderously, until even the heart in the body which lies in the sun on the beach says too, That is all. Fear no more, says the heart. Fear no more, says the heart, committing its burden to some sea, which sighs collectively for all sorrows, and renews, begins, collects, lets fall. And the body alone listens to the passing bee; the wave breaking; the dog barking, far away barking and barking.

The transition here is daring, but wonderfully successful. While Mrs Woolf is describing the falling of the waves, we never forget Clarissa sewing. The greater rhythm as it were accompanies the less, and it brings into the room where Clarissa is sitting its serenity and spaciousness. There is something in the ritual of sewing, a memory of another rhythm buried deep within it, which an image such as this, so unexpected, so remote, reveals to us. The rhythm of the prose is exquisitely graded; it has profited, one feels, as prose may, whether poetry may or not, from the experiments which have been made in *vers libre*: in the daring and fulness of the metaphors it has a remote indebtedness to Homer. There is no English prose at present, except Mr Joyce's, which in subtlety and resource can be compared with it.

In a novel like *Mrs Dalloway*, where the sensory impressions are so concretely evoked and are so much more immediate than they were before, a sort of rearrangement of the elements of experience insensibly takes place. In the traditional novel we have on the one hand the characters and on the other the background, each existing in a separate dimension, and the one generally more solid than the other. Sometimes the environment reacts strikingly on the characters, as, for instance in *Wuthering Heights* and in Mr Hardy's Wessex novels, but the reaction is not complex and continuous. It is indicated rather than treated, and the character and the background retain their peculiar values. But in *Mrs Dalloway* they are more intimately connected; the one merges into the other; the character is suffused with the emanations of the things he sees, hears, feels; and almost inevitably what is presented is a complex of life of which character and background are elements and are both animate, rather than the living character stalking among inanimate things. The characters in *Mrs Dalloway* are real; they have their drama; but the day and the properties of the day move with them, have their drama too; and we do not know which is the more real where all is real—whether the characters are bathed in the emanations of the day, or the day coloured by the minds of the characters. The result is less akin to anything else attempted in the novel than to certain kinds of poetry, to poetry such as Wordsworth's, which records not so much a general judgment on life as a moment of serene illumination, a state of soul. What nature is in *The Excursion*, London is in *Mrs Dalloway*, a living presence, a source of deep pleasure. The mood in which this presence is felt is perhaps the farthest removed from the dramatic, realistic mood. In *Night and Day* the chief thing is the action of the characters upon one another; in *Mrs Dalloway* it is their intimate daily life with all the things which make it up and have reference only to themselves, but which are nevertheless more certainly their being than their actions are. Mrs Woolf is not concerned in *Mrs Dalloway* with the character, which is shown in action, in crises (and novels are consequently full of crises), but with the state of being. To give it its value she catches it at a particularly fortunate moment, at a moment of realization; but the means are justified and are, indeed, the normal means of art. To reveal character the novelist concentrates on crises, comic or tragic, leaving untouched the vast, inert mass of experience: in concentrating on the daily existence when it is most significant Mrs Woolf is in a different way obeying the same principle, the principle, indeed, of all imaginative art.

The Common Reader, in which Mrs Woolf's mind deals with figures familiar to us all, shows it perhaps at its best. Her themes range from Chaucer to Conrad, from George Eliot to the Duchess of Newcastle, and in them all she shows abundantly the intelligence and practicality of temper of the critic. She has the informed enthusiasm which criticism should never lack, but which is tending to disappear from it; her judgments have admirable breadth. The one important quality of the critic which she lacks is the power of wide and illuminating generalization. She holds the scales even, as she does between her characters in *Night and Day*; she uses her sensibility as she uses it in *Jacob's Room* and *Mrs Dalloway*. It is the same mind, and we never doubt its competence to deal with anything which it fixes upon.

56. Dudley Carew on Virginia Woolf's characterisation, *London Mercury*

May 1926, 40–9

After all, the most dangerous, as well as the most difficult, task of criticism lies precisely in the discovery of motives, of seeing, that is, into the mind of the writer, knowing what it is that he intends to do and delivering judgment in strict accordance. The danger is, of course, in misrepresenting, in misreading the mind of the author, and, with novelists who use the bewildering, subjective method of writing, this danger is very real indeed. With Mrs Woolf, however, it is not too great. Even her titles, *Jacob's Room*, *Mrs Dalloway*, are significant; her main purpose, and here again her own 'Mr Bennett and Mrs Brown' can be quoted in evidence, is to create character, to use those vivid perfectly-phrased descriptions of outside events, of people pouring out of the Underground, of the London streets, of tourists at the Acropolis, of which she is fortunately so prodigal, for one end only—to illustrate character:

> I believe that all novels begin with an old lady in the corner opposite. I believe that all novels, that is to say, deal with character, and that it is to express character—not to preach doctrines, sing songs, or celebrate the glories of the British Empire, that the form of the novel, so clumsy, verbose, and undramatic, so rich, elastic, and alive, has been evolved.

That is to say the sight of those people pouring out of the Underground is important only for the light it throws on the mentality of Jacob. Her characters, in other words, are not meant to be the curious, closed-in little vehicles they so much resemble, through which a never-ending reel of impressions can flow and flow, but people, distinct and upstanding, without whom those impressions would be without value, would be non-existent.

But it is in that that Mrs Woolf has been so unfair to herself, for she has made her great gift, that of imaginative description, play second fiddle to an inferior one, that of creating character. Indeed, the richness of that gift, the keenness of that sense of restless, abundant, exhilarating life, has completely ruined whatever success she might have gained in the work she most values, for her characters, far from moving about in worlds half-realised, move, half-realised themselves, in worlds of bright, hard outlines and curious chequered colours, where it is impossible to tell whether their next step will bring them into a dark place of shadows or into a direct blaze of sunshine. The world is there and the people in it:

[Quotes *Mrs Dalloway*, p. 30 'Both seemed queer' to 'she knew'.]

Immediately we know Maisie Johnson, immediately we recognise Regent's Park, but what of the people around whom her books are built? Instead of being the live, vivid actors in front of this carefully painted but relatively unimportant background which Mrs Woolf would like us to believe, they are really far more dangling puppets which seem designed to show off the skill of the painting on the back cloth to its greatest effect.

57. E. W. Hawkins, 'The Stream of Consciousness Novel', *Atlantic Monthly*

September 1926, 357–60

The writer saw Virginia Woolf's fiction as part of a literary movement, to which Katherine Mansfield and Dorothy Richardson also belonged. Each had developed, in her individual way, this 'Continentally born, Continentally nurtured method, half analytical, half lyrical'. (No doubt a reference to the work of Marcel Proust.) The following discussion of *Mrs Dalloway* is a short extract from the article.

Mrs Dalloway, the history of one day in the life of a woman, is a stream of consciousness undiluted, and pure pattern. Through it run a primary and a secondary figure, sometimes drawing near, never intersecting, sometimes swerving apart, always held in relation, as by a woven strip of gold, by the striking of Big Ben through the hours of the day. The primary figure is the heart of Clarissa Dalloway, who loves life with passion, whose only creed is that 'one must pay back from the secret deposit of exquisite moments'; the secondary figure is the heart of poor Septimus Smith, victim of deferred effects of shell shock, to whom life has become an intolerable horror. The pattern that results is a curiously living thing. As in *Jacob's Room*, sunlight seems poured across the pages; and, more than in *Jacob's Room*, the reader is made aware of a background of innumerable lives. More subtly than either of the other novels, this shows the play of one personality upon another. The method is like the flick of a wing in flight; the revelation is complete. Clarissa's loathing of her own hatred for the fanatical Miss Kilman, who would do anything for the Russians, starved herself for the Austrians, but in private inflicted positive torture, so insensitive was she; the panic and despair of poor Septimus under the robust authoritativeness of the great neurologist; the comfort felt by old Mrs Hilbery, at Clarissa's party, in the jolly laughter of Sir Harry, 'which, as she heard it across the room, seemed to reassure her on a point which sometimes bothered her if she woke early in the morning and did not like to call her maid for a cup of tea; how it is certain we must die'—countless sharp impressions such as these strike up from the smooth flow of the stream. Smooth, for—though in this novel, too, the point of view constantly shifts—the transitions are made with suavity. The impersonal voice of Big Ben, falling upon different ears, is not the only device used. Clarissa in her exultant morning mood and Septimus in his agony of apprehensiveness are stopped by the same traffic block; the golden sunlight that lifts up the heart of young Elizabeth Dalloway as she rides on the top of a London bus makes patterns on the wall of Septimus's sitting-room, and gives his tormented mind one last moment of vague pleasure; and the bell of the ambulance that is carrying his shattered, unconscious body to the hospital clangs pleasantly to Peter Walsh, speaking to him of the efficiency of London. This novel throws light, as by a prism, not upon a score of lives, but upon life as felt by a score of people; its pursuit of Clarissa Dalloway through one day in London leaves an impression of a real woman, but a stronger impression of a woven fabric of life, gay and tragic and dipped in mystery.

To one reader the highly developed manner of such a novel as *Mrs Dalloway* seems intolerably artificial; to another it seems an excellent vehicle for wit, for acute sympathy, for the sense of beauty, above all for the sense of life as a thing 'absorbing, mysterious, of infinite richness'. Probably the most vehement apostle of stream of consciousness fiction no more wishes that all novels now and hereafter should be cast in that form than he deplores that *Tom Jones* is not written in the manner of *Fräulein Else*. But he must wonder passionately—and surely it is no fanaticism to wonder—how long so potent a movement in the art of literature will continue to be regarded by a large part of the reading public as an eccentric fad.

58. Arnold Bennett, from 'Another Criticism of the New School', *Evening Standard*

2 December 1926, 5

Another round in the Woolf–Bennett argument. A year earlier, Bennett had written, in a letter to Harriet Cohen 'My child, I reck little of V. Woolf. This is putting it mildly. I have had trouble with Dorothy over this authoress. But Swinnerton and I *know* we are right about her.' (13 December 1925, in *Letters of Arnold Bennett*, ed. J. Hepburn, vol. 3, 256.)

My remarks last week about the younger novelists have aroused some complaint, and it has been said to be odd that I, for years the champion of the young, should turn and rend them. I will therefore proceed further. What I have already written is nothing compared to what I will now write.

The real champion of the younger school is Mrs Virginia Woolf. She is almost a senior; but she was the inventor, years ago, of a half-new technique, and she alone, so far as I know, came forward and attacked the old. She has written a small book about me, which through a culpable neglect I have not read. I do, however, remember an article of hers in which she asserted that I and my kind could not create character. This was in answer to an article of mine in which I said that the sound drawing of character was the foundation of good fiction, and in which incidentally I gave my opinion that Mrs Woolf and her kind could not create character.

I have read two and a half of Mrs Woolf's books. First, *The Common Reader*, which is an agreeable collection of elegant essays on literary subjects. Second, *Jacob's Room*, which I achieved with great difficulty. Third, *Mrs Dalloway*, which beat me. I could not finish it, because I could not discover what it was really about, what was its direction, and what Mrs Woolf intended to demonstrate by it.

To express myself differently, I failed to discern what was its moral basis. As regards character-drawing, Mrs Woolf (in my opinion) told us ten thousand things about Mrs Dalloway, but did not show us Mrs Dalloway. I got from the novel no coherent picture of Mrs Dalloway. Nor could I see much trace of construction, or ordered movement towards a climax, in either *Jacob's Room* or *Mrs Dalloway*. Further, I thought that both books seriously lacked vitality.

These three defects, I maintain, are the characteristic defects of the new school of which Mrs Woolf is the leader. The people in them do not sufficiently live, and hence they cannot claim our sympathy or even our hatred: they leave us indifferent. Logical construction is absent; concentration on the theme (if any) is absent; the interest is dissipated; material is wantonly or clumsily wasted, instead of being employed economically as in the great masterpieces. Problems are neither clearly stated nor clearly solved.

The new practitioners have simply returned to the facile go-as-you-please methods of the eighteenth century, ignoring the important discoveries and innovations of Balzac and later novelists. How different is the new school of fiction from the new school of painting, with its intense regard for logical design!

Lastly, there is absence of vital inspiration. Some novelists appear to have no zest; they loll through their work as though the were taking a stroll in the Park. I admit that I may be wrong on the second count; I may be blind to evidences of a design which is too subtle for my perception. But I do not think that I can be wrong on the first and third counts.

And I admit that some of the younger school write very well. In the novels of Mrs Woolf some brief passages are so exquisitely done that nothing could be done better. But to be fine for a few minutes is not enough. The chief proof of first-rateness is sustained power.

59. T. S. Eliot, 'places' Virginia Woolf for French readers

1927

From 'Le Roman Anglais Contemporain', *Nouvelle Revue Française*, May 1927, vol. 28, 672–4.

Eliot met the Woolfs in 1918 and the Hogarth Press published his *Poems* in 1919 and *The Waste Land* in 1923. There are a number of points of contact between his work and that of Virginia Woolf. In this essay Eliot speaks of the necessity of rediscovering, as something new, a 'moral interest': one cannot simply 'restore' it, for example, through the image of the Strong Man. A striking line from 'Ash Wednesday', which began to appear at about this time, crystallises the theme of the paradoxical co-existence of power and inadequacy: 'The infirm glory of the positive hour', which perhaps had its origin in this passage from Virginia Woolf's *Night and Day*:

> In times gone by, Mrs Hilbery had known all the poets, all the novelists, all the beautiful women and distinguished men of her time. These being now either dead or secluded in their infirm glory, she made her house a meeting-place for her own relations, to whom she would lament the passing of the great days of the nineteenth century, when every department of letters and art was represented in England by two or three illustrious names (pp. 31–2).

Some critics have seen a similarity between Eliot and Louis in *The Waves*.

Mrs Woolf is very different from Mr Lawrence. Not only is she civilized, but she prefers civilization to barbarity; she writes with great care, exceptionally well, while following at least one of the great traditions of English prose, and her style is sometimes of astonishing beauty. She possesses as well a remarkable gift for description (witness the two short pieces 'Kew Gardens' and 'The Mark on the Wall'), and this gift she controls vigorously. She does not let herself go into ecstasies over a momentary perception as Mr Lawrence does. Her observation, which operates in a continuous way, implies a vast and sustained work of organisation. She does not illumine with sudden bright flashes but diffuses a soft and placid light. Instead of looking for the primitive, she looks rather for the civilized, the highly civilized, where nevertheless something is found to be *left out*. And this something is deliberately left out, by what could be called a moral effort of the will. And, being left out, this something is, in a sense, in a melancholy sense, present. Of all contemporary authors Mrs Woolf is the one who reminds me most of Joseph Conrad. For if you remove from Conrad's books the Strong Man, the lonely man warring against the forces of nature or of the jungle—and this lonely European of Conrad's stories is a residual survival of the moral purpose, of the 'deeper psychology' of Shakespeare or of Racine—then you will have the equivalent of the novels of Virginia Woolf. If the loss of the strong man is not a great loss, then Mrs Woolf should be praised for having accomplished at Kew and on English beaches what Conrad has accomplished in the Tropics and the South Seas.

But if Mrs Woolf does not construct life, like Mr Lawrence, with isolated sentiments, she does it with sentiments connected with each other: and that is, in a sense, a construction, though it may not be a structure. And so, being a psychologist, she also has been restricted to strata which lie near the surface. This judgment obviously implies a whole theory; for it would be incorrect to say that her work is 'superficial' in the usual sense of the word. You can maintain that her work is deeper, but in that case you must possess your own theory.

The work of Mrs Woolf is what Mr Lawrence's could never be—the perfection of a type. It faithfully represents the contemporary novel, even though one may find nothing in the latter which is quite like her writing. Her work is perhaps more *representative* than that of Joyce. To follow a new line, the novelist should possess not only great talents but great independence as well. One cannot simply 'restore' the 'moral interest': the strong man of Conrad, now fallen, is already no more than a sentimental relic. One must rediscover this moral interest as something new.

TO THE LIGHTHOUSE

5 May 1927

---

60. From an unsigned review, *Times Literary Supplement*

5 May 1927, 315

Each of Mrs Woolf's novels has inspired a lively curiosity as to the next. One wondered what would follow *Mrs Dalloway*; and its successor, with certain points of likeness, is yet a different thing. It is still more different from most other stories. A case like Mrs. Woolf's makes one feel the difficulty of getting a common measure to estimate fiction; for her work, so adventurous and intellectually imaginative, really invites a higher test than is applied to most novels.

In form *To the Lighthouse* is as elastic as a novel can be. It has no plot, though it has a scheme and a motive; it shows characters in outline rather than in the round; and while it depends almost entirely on the passing of time, it expands or contracts the time-sense very freely. The first and longest part of the book is almost stationary, and describes a party of people gathered in the summer at a house on the Scottish coast:

[Plot summary omitted]

Such are the bare bones of the framework; but one feels they are no more like the whole story than the skeleton carved in a mediaeval tomb is to the robed and comely effigy above it. For the book has its own motion: a soft stir and light of perceptions, meeting or crossing, of the gestures and attitudes, the feelings and thoughts of people: of instants in which these are radiant or absurd, have the burden of sadness or of the inexplicable. It is a reflective book, with an ironical or wistful questioning of life and reality. Somehow this steals into the pages, whether there is a sunny peace in the garden, or Mr Ramsay is interrupted in a fairy-tale, or a couple is late for dinner, so that one is inclined to say that this question of the meaning of things, however masked, is not only the essence but the real protagonist in the story. One is hardly surprised when it emerges openly now and again towards the end:

[Quotes p. 277 'What was it then?' to 'The tears ran down her face.']

Perhaps this is one reason why you are less conscious of Mrs Woolf's characters than they are of each other. They have an acute consciousness which reminds you of the people in Henry James, but with a difference. The characters of Henry James are so absorbed in each other that they have no problem beyond the truth, or otherwise, of their relations; and they are so intensely seen as persons that they are real. But the people in Mrs Woolf's book seem to be looking through each other at some farther question; and, although they interact vividly, they are not completely real. No doubt, as Lily Briscoe the painter thinks in the novel, to know people in outline is one way of knowing them. And they are seen here in the way they are meant to be seen. But the result is that, while you know quite well the kind of people represented in the story, they lack something as individuals. Mr Ramsay, certainly—masterful and helpless, egotist and hero—does leave a deep mark by the end. His wife, with her calm beauty, her sympathy and swift decided actions, is more of a type, though her personality is subtly pervasive even when she has ceased to live. But there is a significant curtness in the parenthesis which . . . announces her death: 'Mr Ramsay stumbling along a passage stretched his arms out one dark morning, but Mrs Ramsay having died rather suddenly the night before, he stretched his arms out in vain. They remained empty.' Here Mrs Woolf's detachment seems a little strained, and, in fact, this transitional part of the book is not its strongest part.

One comes back, however, to the charm and pleasure of her design. It is carried through with a rare subtlety. Every little thread in it—Mr Ramsay writing a book, Lily Briscoe struggling with her picture, the lights in the bay, the pathos and the absurdity—is woven in one texture, which has piquancy and poetry by turns. A sad book in the main, with all its entertainment, it is one to return to; for it has that power of leaving a vision which is less often found, perhaps, in novels than in a short story. This springs from a real emotion, best described in words of Mrs Woolf's own: 'There might be lovers whose gift it was to choose out the elements of things and place them together and so, giving them a wholeness not theirs in life, make of some scene, or meeting of people (all now gone and separate), one of those globed compacted things over which thought lingers and love plays.'

61. Louis Kronenberger, from a review, *New York Times*

8 May 1927, 2

Louis Kronenberger (b. 1904). American novelist and critic. This was more favourable than his later reviews of *The Waves* (No. 89) and *Between the Acts* (No. 134).

It was with *Mrs Dalloway* that Virginia Woolf achieved a novel of first-rate importance rather than of great promise and talent, and as a method in fiction *Mrs Dalloway* has begun already to make its influence keenly felt. Two novels of the present season seem to pay it the tribute of imitation: it is written all over Nathalie S. Colby's highly successful *Green Forest* and just a faint flavour of it creeps into Babette Deutsch's much less successful *In Such a Night*. The method of *Mrs Dalloway* is substantially retained by Mrs Woolf in this new novel, *To the Lighthouse*, but though one encounters again her strikingly individual mingling of inward thought with outward action—in which the 'stream of consciousness' style is liberated from its usual chaos and, by means of selection and sense of order, made formally compact—one finds the method applied to somewhat different aims.

Mrs Dalloway, of course, is Clarissa Dalloway from cover to cover, and for that reason it has a magnificently concentrated clarity. It is Clarissa in relation to herself, her family, her friends, her servants, her milieu; it is her servants, her family, her friends, in relation to her.

To the Lighthouse, on the other hand, is a book of interrelationships among people, and though there are major and minor characters the major ones are not, as Clarissa Dalloway was, the alpha and omega of the story, but more truly the means for giving to the story its harmony and unity, its focal points. Those who reject *To the Lighthouse* as inferior to *Mrs Dalloway* because it offers no one with half the memorable lucidity of Clarissa Dalloway must fail to perceive its larger and, artistically, more difficult aims. They must fail to notice the richer qualities of mind and imagination and emotion which Mrs Woolf, perhaps not wanting them, omitted from *Mrs Dalloway*. They must fail to appreciate that as an author develops he will always break down the perfection he has achieved in an earlier stage of his writing in order to reach new objectives . . .

[A few expository paragraphs omitted here]

It is the final portion of the book which is most perplexing. It seems to sound in the minor what the long first portion sounded in the major, to persist as an ironical mood, to re-establish a scene with the sorry changes time has wrought, to reduce a symbolical achievement when it is finally made to the level of negation. The long opening portion seems to be carrying you ahead toward something which will be magnificently expressive, and then this final portion becomes obscure, a matter of arcs, of fractions, of uncoordinated notes. By comparison with the rest this final portion seems pale and weak. Perhaps there is a reason for this: perhaps Mrs Woolf meant to show that with Mrs Ramsay's death things fall apart, get beyond correlation. Mr Ramsay is no longer interesting—can it be because he is no longer counterpoised against his wife? Life seems drifting, as the Ramsays drift over the bay in their boat, and all their physical vigor and all their reaching of the lighthouse at last conveys no significance.

The truth is that this final portion of the book strikes a minor note, not an intentional minor note which might still in the artistic sense be major, but a meaningless minor note which conveys the feeling that one has not quite arrived somewhere, that the story which opens brilliantly and carries on through a magnificent interlude ends with too little force and expressiveness.

At any rate the rest of the book has its excellencies. Like *Mrs Dalloway* it is underlaid with Mrs Woolf's ironic feeling toward life, though here character is not pitted against manners, but against other character. Once again Mrs Woolf makes use of her remarkable method of characterization, a method not based on observation or personal experience, but purely synthetic, purely creational. Clarissa Dalloway is a marvelous synthesis, and it is just for that reason that *Mrs Dalloway* which has been identified because of its modernity with the *Ulysses* school, differs from it in character fundamentals, for it is as objective as *Ulysses* is autobiographical and observational. There is nothing 'photographic' about Mrs Woolf's characters, here or in *Mrs Dalloway*. Neither Clarissa nor Mrs Ramsay has anything autobiographical about her; both are complete creations and both, for all their charm and graces, must suffer a little beneath the searchlight of Mrs Woolf's independently used mind and sense of irony.

In *To the Lighthouse* there is nobody who even approaches Clarissa Dalloway in completeness and memorability, but on a smaller and perhaps more persuasive scale Mrs Ramsay achieves powerful reality. The other characters are not fully alive because they are not whole enough. Most of them are one-dimensional fragments that have been created with great insight but insufficient vitality. They have minds, moods, emotions—but they get all three through creative intellect. For passion Mrs Woolf has no gift—her people never invade the field of elementary emotions: they are hardly animal at all.

It is, I think, in the superb interlude called 'Time Passes' that Mrs Woolf reaches the most impressive height of the book, and there one can find a new note in her work, something beyond the ironic sophistication and civilized human values of *Mrs Dalloway*. In this description of the unused house in the Hebrides, entered for ten years only by old and forlorn women caretakers and the wind and the sea air and the light of the lighthouse lamp, she has told the story of all life passing on, of change and destruction and solitude and waste—the story which more than a little embodies the plot action of the rest of the book, but above all the story which has for man the profoundest human values of all, though for ten years the house itself never received a human guest. The great beauty of these eighteen pages of prose carries in it an emotional and ironical undertone that is superior to anything else that the first-class technician, the expert stylist, the deft student of human life in Mrs Woolf ever has done. Here is prose of extraordinary distinction in our time: here is poetry:

[Quotes p. 198 'But what after all is one night' to 'plates of brightness.']

To the Lighthouse has not the formal perfection, the cohesiveness, the intense vividness of characterization that belong to *Mrs Dalloway*. It has particles of failure in it. It is inferior to *Mrs Dalloway* in the degree to which its aims are achieved; it is superior in the magnitude of the aims themselves. For in its portrayal of life that is less orderly, more complex and so much doomed to frustration, it strikes a more important note, and it gives us an interlude of vision that must stand at the head of all Virginia Woolf's work.

62. Rachel A. Taylor, review, *Spectator*

14 May 1927, 871

Rachel A. Taylor (1876–1960). Scottish poetess.

'The dark light, the bright shadow' was what Leonardo sought, he said, through all the sciences and all the arts. The bright shadow, the dark light, seem to shift and flicker and fuse in strange pavane to make the fascinating chiaroscuro of the novels of Mrs Woolf. The woven paces of dark and bright on the lovely superficies of any book of hers offer an aesthetic pleasure so deep that at moments you almost forget the dreaming figures beneath, whose vibrating hearts actually create that enigmatic pattern.

Enigmatic, darkly bright, flowing into the secret recesses of the consciousness, floating out its rose-pale shells, its wavering shapes, its blood-red coral, moulding people that combine a modern irony with a mystic reverie, the genius of Virginia Woolf is at once more difficult and more original than that of any other woman novelist to-day. *Mrs Dalloway* is a thing perfect in its kind, a gleaming super-subtle piece of fine filaments of impression and emotion gathered into the pattern of the Rose, a complete crystal eddy of the River of Life. *To the Lighthouse* is not so flawless in its aesthetic effect. The Unities agree with this novelist's power; and here the Unity of Time is rather violently broken, while the parts of the book seem disproportionate. But it is even more wistfully human, perhaps. Nothing happens, and everything happens. To the lighthouse the child James desires to go; and, sitting by his mother's feet, is tauntingly denied by his despotic, myriad-mooded father. To the lighthouse, long years after, he does go, dragged there reluctant by that despotic myriad-minded father, and is suddenly, mysteriously reconciled with him in his heart. Between these incidents people are born and marry and die, but all these matters are incidental to the souls that cross and intercross in the web of an everlasting reverie.

In this book there are secret flames in flowers and inanimate things, waking in response to the fixed gaze of the unconscious symbolists who are weaving them into the tapestry of their dreams. Subtle sensations are caught here that are elusive as a fragrance or a flavour. Psychical processes are laid bare by burning piercing images. Cadences are heard that never violate the rhythm of prose, yet chime aerial and strange as the rhythm of verse. In the ghostly second part, where the perishing life of the house sighs away, the lamenting style, with its lilted-in refrains, and its bitter tragic parentheses, in some passages chants heavily and dreamily like the prose litanies of Mallarmé. 'Frisson d'Hiver', for example.

Indeed more beauty and penetrative characterization than can here be described resides within this book. The Ramsays, husband and wife, move at the centre of attention, along the red torch-plants in the twilight garden. The husband is a remarkably observed figure; but I prefer to linger a moment on his wife, who has the deathless grace, regality, and sweetness of legendary women. She is whimsical, extravagant in speech, absurd a little, versed in all tender ways of loving. She bewitches you. Even the crude Tansley thinks of cyclamen and violets when he sees her as if 'stepping though fields of flowers, taking to her breast buds that had broken and lambs that had fallen'. Yet she is lost in an endless sad reverie: she feels remote and lonely like the white beam of the lighthouse laid on the darkness. She is sorrowful for something lost out of Time—something that, found, would illuminate eternity. So her spirit goes veiled and dreamy like the carved Greek women mourning on the side of a Sidonian sarcophagus.

Under the modern talk all the folk around her go sunken also in their peculiar meditation. But why, when this account of the interaction of 'naked thinking hearts' needs merely a setting of a house and a terrace, some rocks, a bay and a lighthouse, must the house be placed in the Hebrides? Mrs Woolf creates her own atmosphere wherever she takes her people; but to anybody who has been subdued by the magic of the Hebridean atmosphere, there is a disturbance of impression, a collision of spiritual values. Her pattern should never be superimposed.

63. Arnold Bennett, review, *Evening Standard*

23 June 1927, 5

Like many hostile reviewers (and subsequent unfavourable critics) Bennett spared *To the Lighthouse* from his usual condemnation.

I have read a bunch of novels. I must say, despite my notorious grave reservations concerning Virginia Woolf, that the most original of the bunch is *To the Lighthouse*. It is the best book of hers that I know. Her character drawing has improved. Mrs Ramsay almost amounts to a complete person. Unfortunately she goes and dies, and her decease cuts the book in two. Also there are some pleasing records of interesting sensations outside the range of the ordinary novelist. The scheme of the story is rather wilful—designed seemingly, but perhaps not really, to exhibit virtuosity. A group of people plan to sail in a small boat to a lighthouse. At the end some of them reach the lighthouse in a small boat. That is the externality of the plot.

The middle part, entitled 'Time Passes', shows a novel device to give the reader the impression of the passing of time—a sort of cataloguing of intermediate events. In my opinion it does not succeed. It is a short cut, but a short cut that does not get you anywhere. To convey the idea of the passage of a considerable length of time is an extremely difficult business, and I doubt if it can be accomplished by means of a device, except the device of simply saying 'Time passes', and leaving the effort of imagination to the reader. Apart from this honest shirking of the difficulty, there is no alternative but to convey the impression very gradually, without any direct insistence—in the manner of life itself.

I have heard a good deal about the wonders of Mrs Woolf's style. She sometimes discovers a truly brilliant simile. She often chooses her adjectives and adverbs with beautiful felicity. But there is more in style than this. The form of her sentences is rather tryingly monotonous, and the distance between her nominatives and her verbs is steadily increasing. Still, *To the Lighthouse* has stuff in it strong enough to withstand quite a lot of adverse criticism.

64. Orlo Williams, review, *Monthly Criterion*

July 1927, 74–8

Mrs Woolf is not an inventive writer: but then—what time or need has she for inventing, when she cannot overtake all that she sees and feels and observes that other people see and feel? Miss Lily Briscoe, in this last novel, as she is painting in the garden at Skye where, ten years before, Mrs Ramsay, her dead friend, made part of the picture, sitting in the window with her youngest boy upon her knee, becomes the vehicle of a reverie upon which all Mrs Woolf's novels are simply variations.

[Quotes pp. 249–50 'She must rest for a moment' to 'Mrs Ramsay said.']

And, in the last lines of the book, 'Yes, she thought, laying down her brush in extreme fatigue, I have had my vision.'

These passages—one could find many others akin to them—supply a perfect text for a survey, more exhaustive than space here allows me, of all Mrs Woolf's novels. They reveal, in a way that makes commentary superfluous, the nature of her inspiration, and they explain the recurrence of certain preoccupations, even of certain typical characters and details, in her work. It you read the five novels consecutively, this recurrence is very striking. *The Voyage Out* is nothing but a tentative piecing together of the riddles of life, in which, through inexperience, Mrs Woolf used far too many pieces. The large company at Santa Marina, given overmuch to argumentative dialogue, a little overpower the mind with their partial contributions to the stating and solving of the riddles: yet the essential focuses of the great mysteries—as they appear to Mrs Woolf—are there. Mr and Mrs Ambrose, the elderly, egotistical scholar and his wife, besides Mr and Mrs Dalloway, focus that supreme riddle of human relations which is marriage; Rachel focuses the mystery of a child growing up; Hewet and she, Susan and Arthur, the mystery of falling in love; and Rachel again, dying in a glow of this mystery, focuses that other mystery, the deepest, of death. *Night and Day*, this author's second and last essay in the traditional novel-style—of all her novels the most *serré*, the most careful, and, in the sense of achieving its purpose, the most striking—is concerned with nothing else but the riddle of young people of different temperaments in love and at cross purposes. The contrast drawn between those who find marriage easy, and those who find it difficult, to envisage is most subtly drawn, and with notable humour. If the situation between Katherine Hilbery and Ralph Denham is drawn out in too tenuous an intricacy, these characters are nobly seen. Katherine and Ralph are finer natures whose high visions, even of one another, can only be momentary, and yet seem to degrade the grosser realities of every day. Does Katherine love the everyday Ralph, or Ralph the everyday Katherine? They torture themselves in this debate till dear, inconsequent Mrs Hilbery solves the question by saying 'We have to have faith in our vision'—the motto, in a larger sense, of all Mrs Woolf's art.

Jacob's Room, her first long excursion in the fragmentary style, is nothing more than a picture of a young man's life: Cambridge, London, Paris, Greece, flashes from numberless facets, gay, serious, fleshly, trivial, now the inconsequent mind, now the body, now one vision, now another; and it puts the riddle in another way. If such a life is ended by a fragment of shell—what does it mean? Where is, where was, its reality? *Mrs Dalloway*, again, is an attempt to see how much of the riddle can be got into twenty-four hours.—'Life, heaven only knows why one loves it so?', love (Peter Walsh), marriage (the Dalloways), death and madness or visions pushed to excess (Septimus Smith), the change wrought by years, the intricacies and inconsistencies of character, not to be summed up by arithmetic, the old lady next door seen daily but unknown, 'the supreme mystery . . . was simply this: here was one room; there another. Did religion solve that, or love?' And now in this last novel, who should appear again but Mr and Mrs Ambrose (of *The Voyage Out*), under the name of Ramsay, with their problem more poetically stated and their characters drawn with a far greater beauty? Who but the dry Mr Pepper of that same novel—vast knowledge, a dry heart, no aptitude for family life, and views on the cooking of vegetables—under the name of Bankes? The unsuccessful don called Jenkinson, casually mentioned by Mr Ambrose, here takes flesh as Augustus Carmichael, a poet, with a moustache stained yellow by opium and an unwisely married wife in the background. And the riddle of life is re-compounded in the Ramsays' summer house on the island of Skye, of these things—that Mr Ramsay was an egotistic, tyrannical man, conscious of partial failure though distinguished, and needing oh so much sympathy, praise and reassurance from Mrs Ramsay; that, at the same time, he had certain elements of fineness not possessed by Bankes, who had greatness but no inner fire; that Mrs Ramsay wore herself out giving, and giving, to her husband, yet she knew his faults, and she worshipped him as her moral superior, but still she had to hide from him domestic worries, and she could not tell him that she loved him (as Richard Dalloway could not tell Mrs Dalloway), but he understood it; yet that his children, especially James, did not love him, because he crushed the life out of their mother by his demands upon her emotions; and Mrs Ramsay, though extremely beautiful and impressive, was a little imperious and masterful to other people, who often resented it; that Mrs Ramsay suddenly died; and that Lily Briscoe, painting on the same spot ten years later, while Mr Ramsay had carried off two secretly rebellious children to the Lighthouse—James, ten years before having desired to kill his father for disappointing his hopes of this very expedition—tries to make out what really Mrs Ramsay stood for, in relation to Mr Ramsay, to other people, to the world in general and to eternity. The upshot, the only possible upshot, is that she stands as a lovely vision, as unsubstantial, as vivid, as fleeting, as eternal, as past, as immortal, as are all the visions of those who truly see. One can only say, Life stand still; and life stands still, long enough for the seeing, wondering mind, not long enough for the brush or the pen. To have had the vision—to have lived—is the thing: if one has little to show for it, never mind.

Having enjoyed, through the five novels, all the rich variety of impressions which illustrate the main themes, the humour that is never studied or artificial, the brilliant subsidiary sketches of human character (such as Mrs Hilbery in *Night and Day*, Miss Kilman and Peter Walsh in *Mrs Dalloway*), the swift and suggestive mixture of detail and reflection, the sharp physical imagery of the passages where to the observing mind there comes what the Germans would call a *Steigerung*, the sudden loomings up of ordinary people or things, like Mr and Mrs Ramsay playing ball with their children, as symbols of tremendous import and stature, the sensitiveness of feminine observation abnormally acute, the skilfully used anger and pathos, one sees all the better how the passage quoted at the beginning of this article sums up the whole. It is not astonishing, therefore, that the society observed in Mrs Woolf's novels is more or less the same throughout—that of the cultivated intellectual, or governing, class, with its wide connections up and down, its chance contacts, its conversational trend towards Plato, Shakespeare, poetry or politics, its standards of success and failure and its typical joys and disasters—because the visions, in the last resort, are all the author's and relate, one is certain, to the visions that in the course of years have impressed themselves on her mortal eyes and brain. It is not that she puts herself into all the characters—though she puts herself into many, and deals freely with her own intimacies in certain others—but that, even when she is ostensibly portraying another mind, say that of Mr Ramsay ruminating on his failure, of Peter Walsh stalking a pretty girl, of greedy spiteful Miss Kilman, or of Septimus Warren Smith engulfed in his hallucinations, it is her mind observing the other mind of which we are conscious.

Mrs Woolf's art, in other words, is intensely personal in its stamp, especially now that she has abandoned the solidly constructive method of narration for her uniquely reflective impressionism. This is simply a statement, not a critical judgment, but it leads to the question whether she will ever succeed in embodying her personal vision so as, even faintly, to correspond to her intentions, which are those of a serious artist whose work, vivid, exciting, sympathetic, rightly excites a profound admiration.

'Making of the moment something permanent'—this is the work of the poet, the painter, the musician, not of the dramatist nor, as I believe with Mr Wyndham Lewis, essentially of the novelist. For imaginative prose of this kind there ought to be another name, since it is a thing different from the novel, verging at its most exalted moments on poetry. The average novel-reader, mainly interested in 'story' and characterization, will probably judge the first section of *To the Lighthouse*, where Mrs Ramsay is alive, the most successful. After her death the book becomes more lyrical in intonation; the second section, in particular, is a rhapsody where ten years pass away in a kind of incantation, broken by rather abrupt snapping of threads in parenthesis. Yet the whole, with its greater emotional concentration, its sharper focusing, the fuller stature of its characters, and the completer resolution of its material into a meditation in images, or symbols—compare the section describing the dinner here with Mrs Dalloway's party—shows the mark at which, with ever increasing power and sureness, Mrs Woolf is aiming. Her mastery increases with each book, but, I fear, it will always fall short of her vision. Poetry alone could give us that: in prose we shall have to be content with the 'matches struck unexpectedly in the dark'. On this score she may possibly suffer with posterity, who may desire another brand of match: but in her own day she lights a purer and more searching flame than most, by which we recognise that, whatever science applied to existence may achieve, only imagination illumines life.

65. Conrad Aiken, 'The Novel as Work of Art', *Dial* (Chicago)

July 1927, vol. 83, 41–4

Conrad Aiken (1889–1973). American novelist and poet.

A perceptive review by a poet and novelist whose own fictional experiments are of some importance in the development of the 'psychological' novel.

Among contemporary writers of fiction, Mrs Woolf is a curious and anomalous figure. In some respects, she is as 'modern', as radical, as Mr Joyce or Miss Richardson or M. Jules Romains; she is a highly self-conscious examiner of consciousness, a bold and original experimenter with the technique of novel-writing; but she is also, and just as strikingly, in other respects 'old-fashioned'. This anomaly does not defy analysis. The aroma of 'old-fashionedness' that rises from these highly original and modern novels—from the pages of *Jacob's Room*, *Mrs Dalloway*, and now again from those of *To the Lighthouse*—is a quality of attitude; a quality, to use a word which is itself nowadays old-fashioned, but none the less fragrant, of spirit. For in this regard, Mrs Woolf is no more modern than Jane Austen: she breathes the same air of gentility, of sequestration, of tradition; of life and people and things all brought, by the slow polish of centuries of tradition and use, to a pervasive refinement in which discrimination, on every conceivable plane, has become as instinctive and easy as the beat of the wing. Her people are 'gentle' people; her houses are the houses of gentlefolk; and the consciousness that informs both is a consciousness of well-being and culture, of the richness and lustre and dignity of tradition; a disciplined consciousness, in which emotions and feelings find their appropriate attitudes as easily and naturally—as *habitually*, one is tempted to say—as a skilled writer finds words.

It is this tightly circumscribed choice of scene—to use 'scene' in a social sense—that gives to Mrs Woolf's novels, despite her modernity of technique and insight, their odd and delicious air of parochialism, as of some small village-world, as bright and vivid and perfect in its tininess as a miniature: a small complete world which time has somehow missed. Going into these houses, one would almost expect to find antimacassars on the chair-backs and daguerreotype albums on the tables. For these people—these Clarissa Dalloways and Mrs Ramsays and Lily Briscoes—are all vibrantly and saturatedly conscious of background. And they all have the curious innocence that accompanies that sort of awareness. They are the creatures of seclusion, the creatures of shelter; they are exquisite beings, so perfectly and elaborately adapted to their environment that they have taken on something of the roundness and perfection of works of art. Their life, in a sense, is a sea-pool life: unruffled and secret: almost, if we can share the cool illusion of the sea-pool's occupants, inviolable. They hear rumours of the sea itself, that vast and terrifying force that lies somewhere beyond them, or around them, but they cherish a sublime faith that it will not disturb them; and if it does, at last, break in upon them with a cataclysmic force, a chaos of disorder and undisciplined violence, they can find no language for the disaster: they are simply bewildered.

But if, choosing such people, and such a *mise en scène*, for her material, Mrs Woolf inevitably makes her readers think of *Pride and*

Prejudice and *Mansfield Park*, she compels us just as sharply, by her method of evoking them, to think of *Pilgrimage* and *Ulysses* and *The Death of a Nobody*. Mrs Woolf is an excellent critic, an extremely conscious and brilliant craftsman in prose; she is intensely interested in the technique of fiction; and one has at times wondered, so vividly from her prose has arisen a kind of *self-consciousness* of adroitness, whether she might not lose her way and give us a mere series of virtuosities or *tours de force*. It is easy to understand why Katherine Mansfield distrusted 'Mr Bennett and Mrs Brown'. She felt a kind of sterility in this dexterous holding of the raw stuff of life at arm's length, this playing with it as if it were a toy. Why not be more immediate—why not surrender to it? And one did indeed feel a rather baffling aloofness in this attitude: it was as if Mrs Woolf were a little afraid to come to grips with anything so coarse, preferred to see it through a safe thickness of plate-glass. It was as if she could not be quite at ease with life until she had stilled it, reduced it to the mobile immobility of art—reduced it, even, to such comfortable proportions and orderliness as would not disturb the drawing-room. In *Jacob's Room*, however, and *Mrs Dalloway*, Mrs Woolf began to make it clear that this tendency to sterile dexterity, though pronounced, might not be fatal; and now, in her new novel, *To the Lighthouse*, she relieves one's doubts, on this score, almost entirely.

For, if one still feels, during the first part of this novel almost depressingly, and intermittently thereafter, Mrs Woolf's irritating air as of carrying an enormous technical burden: her air of saying 'See how easily I do this!' or 'This is incomparably complex and difficult, but I have the brains for it': nevertheless, one's irritation is soon lost in the growing sense that Mrs Woolf has at last found a complexity and force of theme which is commensurate with the elaborateness and self-consciousness of her technical 'pattern'. By degrees, one forgets the manner in the matter. One resists the manner, petulantly objects to it, in vain: the moment comes when at last one ceases to be aware of something persistently artificial in this highly feminine style, and finds oneself simply immersed in the vividness and actuality of this world of Mrs Woolf's—believing in it, in fact, with the utmost intensity, and feeling it with that completeness of surrender with which one feels the most moving of poetry. It is not easy to say whether this abdication of 'distance' on the reader's part indicates that Mrs Woolf has now achieved a depth of poetic understanding, a vitality, which was somehow just lacking in the earlier novels, or whether it merely indicates a final triumph of technique. Can one profitably try to make a distinction between work that is manufactured, bitterly and strenuously, by sheer *will* to imagination, and work that is born of imagination all complete—assuming that the former is, in the upshot, just as convincing as the latter? Certainly one feels everywhere in Mrs Woolf's work this will to imagine, this canvassing of possibilities by a restless and searching and brilliant mind: one feels this mind at work, matching and selecting, rejecting this colour and accepting that, saying, 'It is this that the heroine would say, it is this that she would think'; and nevertheless Mrs Woolf's step is so sure, her choice is so nearly invariably right, and her imagination, even if deliberately willed, is so imaginative, that in the end she makes a beautiful success of it. She makes her Mrs Ramsay—by giving us her stream of consciousness—amazingly alive; and she supplements this just sufficiently, from *outside*, as it were, by giving us also, intermittently, the streams of consciousness of her husband, of her friend Lily Briscoe, of her children: so that we are documented, as to Mrs Ramsay, from every quarter and arrive at a solid vision of her by a process of triangulation. The richness and copiousness and ease, with which this is done, are a delight. These people are astoundingly real: they belong to a special 'class', as Mrs Woolf's characters nearly always do, and exhale a Jane-Austenish aroma of smallness and lostness and incompleteness: but they are magnificently real. We live in that delicious house with them—we feel the minute textures of their lives with their own vivid senses—we imagine with their extraordinary imaginations, are self-conscious with their self-consciousness—and ultimately we know them as well, as terribly, as we know ourselves.

Thus, curiously, Mrs Woolf has rounded the circle. Apparently, at the outset of her work, avoiding any attempt to present life 'immediately', as Chekhov and Katherine Mansfield preferred to do; and choosing instead a medium more sophisticated and conscious, as if she never for a moment wished us to forget the *frame* of the picture, and the fact that the picture *was* a picture; she has finally brought this method to such perfection, or so perfectly allowed it to flower of itself, that the artificial has become natural, the mediate has become immediate. The technical brilliance glows, melts, falls away; and there remains a poetic apprehension of life of extraordinary loveliness. Nothing happens, in this houseful of odd nice people, and yet all of life happens. The tragic futility, the absurdity, the pathetic beauty, of life—we experience all of this in our sharing of seven hours of Mrs Ramsay's wasted or not wasted existence. We have seen, through her, the world.

66. Edwin Muir, review, *Nation and Athenaeum*

2 July 1927, 450

The book referred to in the second sentence was *The Magic Mountain* by Thomas Mann, one of the novels Muir was reviewing at the same time.

To the Lighthouse is a novel difficult to judge. Like the last volume on this list, it stands at the summit of the development of a remarkable writer. Its aim is high and serious, its technique brilliant; there are more beautiful pages in it than Mrs Woolf has written before; a unique intuition and intelligence are at work in it almost continuously, and at high pressure. The difficulties which the author surmounts in it are such as few contemporary novelists would even attempt. Its positive merits are thus very high. Yet as a whole, though showing an advance on many sides, it produces a less congruous and powerful effect than *Mrs Dalloway*. The novel consists of three parts. In the first we have a picture of Mrs Ramsay's summer household in the Hebrides before the war; in the second an imaginative evocation of time passing over the house, deserted now for several years; in the last Mr Ramsay's return as a widower with two of his family and two old friends, the remnant of the large circle which has been reduced in the meantime by death and other causes. In the first book James, a young boy, had been promised that he would be taken to the lighthouse, but it rains, and he cannot go. In the last book—he is a youth now—he goes with his father and his sister, and everything is different. The symbolism is plain enough; but in the novel, so entangled is it with other matters, interesting enough in themselves, that it becomes obscured. Actually it is obscured most by the device which should make it most clear: the intermediary book called 'Time Passes', which, to add to the difficulty, is the best of the lot, and could only have been written by a writer of profound imagination. For this section, composed in a different key, concerned with entities more universal than the human, entities which do not need human life, but, affecting everything, affect human life, too, inexorably and yet as if heedlessly, is not a real transition from the first section to the last, both conceived in human terms, but something outside them. The time which passes in this interval passes not for the characters in the story, but for everything; it is a natural, an astronomical, a cosmical transition, and not a human one except incidentally; and the result is that when Mrs Woolf returns to the human plane the sequence seems doubly abrupt. We are not only transported from James's childhood to his youth, we are switched from one dimension of time to another. That this was not the right means to mark the flight of time in this place is shown, I think, by the effect of the third section; for that effect is not intensified, it is, if anything, lessened by what has gone immediately before. Yet one cannot regret that Mrs Woolf wrote the second section in this book. For imagination and beauty of writing it is probably not surpassed in contemporary prose. But how this kind of imagination can be applied, as one feels sure it can, to the business of the novelist, the shadowing forth of human life, is still a problem to be solved.

67. E. M. Forster on Virginia Woolf and Sterne

1927

From *Aspects of the Novel* (1927) (Penguin edition, pp. 26–7).

[Forster compared a passage from 'The Mark on the Wall' (from 'But for that mark' to 'at fifty miles an hour') with chapter XXI, volume 2, of *Tristram Shandy*. He continued:]

The passage last quoted is, of course, out of *Tristram Shandy*. The other passage was from Virginia Woolf. She and Sterne are both fantasists. They start with a little object, take a flutter from it, and settle on it again. They combine a humorous appreciation of the muddle of life with a keen sense of its beauty. There is even the same tone in their voices—a rather deliberate bewilderment, an announcement to all and sundry that they do not know where they are going. No doubt their scales of value are not the same. Sterne is a sentimentalist, Virginia Woolf (except perhaps in her lastest work, *To the Lighthouse*) is extremely aloof. Nor are their achievements on the same scale. But their medium is similar, the same odd effects are obtained by it, the parlour door is never mended, the mark on the wall turns out to be a snail, life is such a muddle, oh dear, the will is so weak, the sensations fidgety . . . philosophy . . . God . . . oh dear, look at the mark . . . listen to the door—existence . . . is really too . . . what were we saying?

68. J.-E. Blanche, from 'An Interview with Virginia Woolf', *Les Nouvelles Littéraires*

13 August 1927, 1–2

Jacques-Émile Blanche (1861–1942), French painter and writer. He first met Virginia Woolf in Normandy in July 1927 and gave an account of his meeting in this article. A translation of 'Kew Gardens' appeared in the same issue. He corresponded regularly with Virginia Woolf and recommended *Mrs Dalloway* for translation to the publisher Stock. He later reviewed *Orlando* (see Introduction).

For an account of their relationship see G.-P. Collet, 'Jacques-Émile Blanche and Virginia Woolf' in *Comparative Literature*, vol. 17, 1965.

This poet, this painter who is attentive to the 'sad quotidian' is the most amusing talker, full of scintillating humour and fun, just like Laforgue. Anyone would love the opportunity of obtaining an audience with this magnetic personality, but it is rarely accorded. The small circle of the Bloomsbury Intelligentsia protects the delicate health of its captive from a public curiosity which fashion increases from year to year, in America as well as in England. One would like to discuss her work with her, but she asks about Marcel Proust and talks about French literature; she enjoys nothing more than reading our authors and incidentally creates a very flattering picture of our country.

'What was Proust like in his youth? Tell me, tell me. How did he make an entry into high society? Society must have understood little of what he wrote?' . . .

We proceeded to the bottom of the garden to rest in the shadow of the great Normandy trees, the twilight was descending upon Auppegard, the blue sky was paling; it was a time so often described by Mrs Woolf's pen.

The first part of *To the Lighthouse* ends with a scene of intense emotion between Mr and Mrs Ramsay:

[Quotes pp. 189–91 ' "No," she said' to 'she had triumphed again.']

What happens between this first part and the second? Nine short pieces make up this second part, entitled Time Passes. These pieces remind one of Joyce. Less difficult, but just as disconcerting if you are not accustomed to Mrs Woolf's way of thinking.

[Quotes p. 195 ' "Well we must wait" ' to 'longer than the rest.']

Dear Mrs Woolf, do you wish to create an atmosphere? Is there a hidden meaning there? Don't laugh at me! Then the moon disappears and a fine rain drums on the roof. Are Mr and Mrs Ramsay in the house? The second part does not tell us. They seem to have disappeared like the moon. A chance sentence, and we learn that Mrs Ramsay is dead. We did not even know that the beautiful Mrs Ramsay had been ill. She is eclipsed. But all your characters go away like this after having entered upon the scene unannounced. You assume that your readers are as intelligent as you and as accustomed to seeing into the obscurity and resolving mysteries. Your characters rarely talk amongst themselves. Instead, you give us their internal monologues. Your revolution in the art of narration does not involve the suppression of the conventional role of the author, who is the omniscient, all-seeing God. There remains the novelty and originality of the 'tempo' as Charles du Bos would say, and the fact that you are a painter; that is something I'll take this opportunity of discussing with you. The touches of colour here and there are of a lightness, but also of such incredible precision and density, that they construct the picture, delineate it within an invisible contour. The Impressionist painters proceeded in just this manner. But you would purse your lips, Madame, if I described you as *Impressionist.* One is more up-to-date than that in Bloomsbury. It is only by chance, perhaps, that you are a writer. . . . *Jacob's Room* and *Mrs Dalloway* are the work of a painter and 'synchronism' and 'futurism' are only labels which people have arbitrarily applied to your style. In *Mrs Dalloway*, a book in which the action begins in the morning and ends in the evening of the same day, you ask us to witness innumerable concomitant episodes, whose only relation to each other exists in your mind. Is it true that at the end, unknown to us, your heroine commits suicide, whilst the madman, after consulting the pompous psychiatrist in the afternoon—what a portrait!—puts an end to his frightful anguish? We predicted Mrs Dalloway's suicide. You never confirm it.

The eight little pieces given over to the abandoned house near the Lighthouse are very revealing, as is the interior monologue of Lily Briscoe, the artist, on her return.

She is before her canvas, the easel planted at the place she reoccupies after years of absence. The same refound motif inspires in her the same reflection on aesthetic problems which trouble her: composition; how to distribute the elements of the painting in the space of her canvas? Lily Briscoe is undoubtedly Virginia Woolf herself. I see Berthe Morisot once more, with her meditative face, her silences, her gestures of impatience. The ecstasies and despairs of working from Nature. The questioning of the purpose of it all.

[Quotes pp. 244–5 'and so, lightly and swiftly' to 'Why then did she do it'.]

. . . There remained many questions that I wished to ask Mrs Woolf about her writing methods. But she pressed me to tell her more about Marcel Proust, about French matters. Night chased us from the garden, Mrs Woolf had to pack her case, she was leaving on the following day for England.

69. Jean-Jacques Mayoux, from a review, *Revue Anglo-Americaine* (Paris)

June 1928, 424–38

It is unfortunately only to the 'happy few' that Virginia Woolf has just given a definitive work which contains all her vision of the world, in which all the delicate beauty of her art is to be found. It is a work so full and so luminous that one is tempted to appreciate it for itself and to explain it by means of itself. Virginia Woolf reminds one of Joyce and

Proust, of Giraudoux and Duhamel. Her fictional method is in some ways close to all the recent techniques, but it is dominated by her sensibility and grace, which are unique.

To the Lighthouse is essentially a lyrical novel; it reflects the contacts of a group of people; contacts between themselves, with things, and with life; and parallel with this it traces in these beings the continuous rhythm of their emotive life. There are no crises in the book; there is no exterior action, nor any interior drama, no conflicts or suppressions, none of those black and hooded figures who prowl watchfully in the penumbra of the unconscious—all that melodramatic paraphernalia of the ultra-modern psychological novel. There are no analyses or depth analyses of obscure motifs; there aren't any motifs at all. *To the Lighthouse* is a long contemplation, a harmonious unwinding of images and emotions, of sentiments and thoughts in an interior world as sweetly luminous as a painting by Vermeer.

Virginia Woolf preserves as much as possible the internal rhythm of the insistent promptings of action and desire; but that does not mean to say—indeed the contrary is true—that she closes the windows and shutters of consciousness, and presents us with a long procession of reveries. Nothing is more real, nothing less arbitrary than this interior movement of characters who are not fabricated in order to pose or demonstrate psychological problems, or in order to enable us to view their personalities at leisure. Neither are these characters simple lyrical themes: without acting, they find a way of living an intense life.

One is at first surprised to see peripheral sensations noted gratuitously, as it were, that is to say without cause or consequence, throughout this movement of thoughts, emotions and images. These sensations are usually not even realised, our consciousness automatically incorporates them into itself, occasionally taking note of them. Virginia Woolf uses these sensations cleverly in order to make a sort of synthesis of the two worlds. In the middle of a sentence which forms an inseparable unity in the unfolding of interior images, she places, she intercalates, a very brief notation of sensation, an object impression around which the two fragments come together—but are found to be tinged with this sensation; in such a way that for a moment we have an impression of adherence to, and diversion from the rhythm, as when a drop of water running along a window pane meets a speck of dust. But the interior life follows its own course according to its own rhythms and fluidity until it meets again the world of objects. As quickly as these contacts are repeated, our memory joins them together in a sort of continuity and in this way, by very simple means, Virginia Woolf makes us feel the parallel permanence of the outer and inner worlds, their quite separate continuities—so separate that they cannot truly be mixed. In this way she never allows our attention to be detached from the one or the other, or from their contact.

... Virginia Woolf uses to some extent, and only to some extent, the technique of 'telling from the inside'. Nothing is purely objective, altogether outside the characters. Our contacts with the things which constitute their frame, are theirs, taken from the very tissue of their lives. Nevertheless, by a characteristic modification of a rather heavy and graceless technique, we are never 'inside' either. Dialogue, reflections, reveries, everything is almost entirely in the indirect style. And this indirect style spreads its half-tones over the entire book; on the one hand it almost inevitably annexes the short passages of simple narration; but, on the other hand, it holds us at a distance from those interior lives which it allows us to see only across a transparency; instead of, as in James Joyce's *Ulysses*, for example, our being thrown into the very centre of a consciousness which we see teeming around us, monstrously.

Virginia Woolf's characters are not like those sections made in order to 'show the workings'; they are closed, and do not look at us from the corner of their eye when they speak or when they think. They live an astonishingly normal life for themselves, and not for our benefit, and do not even have hidden turpitudes to reveal to us. They discourage dubious familiarities or indiscreet intimacies. The womanly figure who dominates the book with the radiance of her charm and sympathy remains Mrs Ramsay, fine, smiling and serious, a little distant: we do not know her Christian name.

But if Virginia Woolf so places her characters in relation to us in a delicately rectified perspective, it is not to create some new illusionism, it is above all in order that we might have a truer picture of their relationships with each other. And this is one of the essential points of view in the book. It is a characteristic of the vision—perhaps of the *feminine* vision of the author—she would not repudiate the adjective—that she sees human beings not separated, but in a group; and also characteristic is her inclination to be concerned less with their internal construction than with the reciprocal contacts between human beings, and their ability to create such *rapports*.

... Such they are, reunited by evening around the Ramsays' table—assembled solitudes. They are men, and for Virginia Woolf this retrenchment into the self is an especially masculine characteristic. This is revealed perfectly in their relations with things: they do not liberate enough of themselves in order to embrace things entirely: they transform the immense richness of concrete objects into useful tokens which are easy to handle. They have lost the faculty of direct and complete emotive contact with the world: what they handle, in their theories, their opinions, their vision of life, is a universal algebra.

. . . The dinner at last becomes all rhythmic movement and collective emotion.

And when William Bankes and Carmichael and Ramsay and even Tansley, released from their individuality, from their peculiarities, make a kind of unity together, it is then that they truly defend against the worst danger, an ever-menacing decomposition, that which is most precious, their common humanity. This is the profound meaning of Mrs Ramsay's effort, it is in this way that this supremely harmonious moment is not only beauty, but also wisdom. They will pass, but the order, the harmony which exists between them at this moment, is permanent, eternal, placed outside of time and change, like all perfect communion, all order, all harmony.

Mrs Ramsay goes up to the children's room, and again is found dispensing her grace, calming their nerves, cradling them with the music of words and images; and the final task accomplished, she suddenly feels weary; and then begins one of the characteristic alternations in the rhythm of the book: a return, a descent.

. . . 'This would remain' thought Mrs Ramsay, of that moment full of humanity. And thereupon time passes; and it is like the complete reversal of the plan of the book, a new test of values. There are small and great convulsions: the death of Mrs Ramsay, and that of her daughter, and the war, in which her son is killed. The renewal is of an order which is therefore made precarious by the chaos in the Ramsay house and in the world, and everything passes just like sand trickling between one's fingers. Except for a few pages of rather conventional lyricism on the progress of the disorder in the house—one cannot help thinking of the 'Sensitive Plant'—everything takes place between brackets, with a sentence for each happening. The change, the decomposition seem so negative that even afterwards one does not know what is more unreal, that which used to be or this dissolution which has seized it. And Lily Briscoe who painted the house and the garden ten years ago, with Mrs Ramsay and the child James at the window of the sitting-room—it must have been a very different composition when she was sitting there with James: it must have cast a shadow—Lily finds herself one morning in the reopened house. By a new reversal, the design of this part becomes parallel again to that of the first (the second being, as it were, perpendicular to them). We fall again into the relative immobility of things, into a completely interior movement. Lily's thought dominates this second moment as that of Mrs Ramsay had the first.

She is at first struck, at that hour when things have not yet any vibration or colour and the spirit has not re-formed its habits, by the unreality of the things which surround her. 'The house, the place, the morning all seemed strangers to her.'

Finding herself thus without links with the present, not finding there the imprint of her actions or emotions, failing to see it disposed according to the order to which her former habits had accustomed her, Lily does not recognise the present. She discovers that she is lost and at the same time feels, in this place with which all the past was associated and which now seems scarcely to contain its dust, how perfectly the past is dead both there and in herself.

Lost between the present and the past, doubly deprived of order and solidity, doubly adrift, Lily will force herself to a two-fold reconstruction in order to return in possession of the two worlds. There is a welcome consequence to all this: by subtle modifications, a gradual evolution, this spiritual condition gives birth to its contrary. This condition is first of all a disarray mingling with an impression of the chaotic incoherence of things; without the cause—the absence of a common term between subject and object—being conscious: a single being is lost to us and all the world is unpeopled. But it is also a state of appeal, an inspiration infinitely richer than the ordinary moments when the interior life passes by in transit.

Lily paints and remembers—a rich and symbolic alternation which moves across all this part of the book. She thinks of Charles Tansley, of his harsh words, of his gauche and graceless egoism. She calls up the caricatural simplification which she has made of him; and here, all of a sudden, instead of a caricature, she has refound a living being. But at the same time she finds Mrs Ramsay again, whom she had not been looking for. Or is it that Lily did not look for her obscurely, and precisely in the way she should be looked for, not in herself, but in those who surrounded her and whom she irradiated with her grace?

[Quotes pp. 247–50 'And then, she reflected' to 'Life stand still here, Mrs Ramsay said.']

I have quoted at length the passage which seems to me to express, better than any other, the central message of the book.

. . . 'Like a work of art' thinks Lily, and here is formulated the assimilation prefigured and prepared for throughout that meditation by the constant symbolic interlacing of memory and the effort of plastic creation. There are two ways of making something permanent of the moment. But how different, even antagonistic, the concrete and direct emotive unity, which Mrs Ramsay creates in living, and the plastic and architectural unity, abstract and austere, towards which Lily strives. This involves the complete transformation, the pitiless sacrifice of even the dearest emotional values: she cannot, as she had already explained to William Bankes, make of Mrs Ramsay anything but a violet shadow. And Virginia Woolf expresses the transmutation by one of her delightful foreshortenings: during the dinner, Lily, thinking of her painting, decides to modify her composition, to move a tree towards the right, and symbolically, moves a salt cellar on the tablecloth. Now, ten years after, thinking of Mrs Ramsay's efforts to throw her into the current of life, she remembers: 'She had been looking at the table-cloth, and it had flashed upon her that she would move the tree to the middle, and need never marry anybody, and she had felt an enormous exultation.'

The evocation of the past follows the very movement of the past and with a subtle symmetry, refinds what I have called the curve of Mrs Ramsay: there is the same creation of a common identity and the same return to silence. Lily thinks, moreover, how the present is an ironic negation of the past, forbidding its resuscitation, since it is no longer active. The present puts the past in its place and situates it as something immobile, powerless, fixed and frozen:

> But the dead, thought Lily, encountering some obstacle in her design which made her pause and ponder, stepping back a foot or so, Oh the dead! she murmured, one pitied them, one brushed them aside, one had even a little contempt for them. They are at our mercy. Mrs Ramsay has faded and gone. . . . Mockingly she seemed to see her there at the end of the corridor of years saying, of all incongruous things, 'Marry, marry!'. . . . And one would have to say to her, It has all gone against your wishes. They're happy like that; I'm happy like this. Life has changed completely. At that all her being, even her beauty, became for a moment, dusty and out of date.

Lily quickly finds her vision again; but it is really this oscillation rather than the still point of her joy which is the pivot of the moment: she can find Mrs Ramsay again, rediscover her grace like a gift of eternity, and yet that grace, formerly sovereign, is for ever powerless.

And when the vision pales and passes, it seems to Lily's distant gaze that Mrs Ramsay is distanced on the sea. But at that place there is only a boat in which Ramsay, his son James, and his daughter Cam move away towards the Lighthouse.

Lily sees them going away, and here a new alternation begins within her, between her vision which journeys into the past and they who pass away into the distance. All this part is dominated by the assimilation of time and death, in their effects on human sentiments, into distance: it is a question of perspective.

And in subtle antiphony, Lily's thought on the shore corresponds with Cam's thought in the boat, in such a way that we are constantly transported from one to the other.

Lily looks at the boat fading, becoming unreal. Cam thinks 'how all those paths and the lawn, thick and knotted with the lives they have lived there, were gone: were rubbed out; were past; were unreal, and now this was real; the boat and the sail with its patch . . .'

And on the shore: 'So much depends then,' thought Lily Briscoe, looking at the sea which had scarcely a stain on it . . . 'so much depends', she thought, 'upon distance: whether people are near us or far from us; for her feeling for Mr Ramsay changed as he sailed further and further across the bay. It seemed to be elongated, stretched out; he seemed to become more and more remote.'

And this insistence on perspective, this assimilation of death and distance, would certainly not have anything really original about it independently of the grace and freshness of Virginia Woolf's vision, without, precisely, this ironic antiphony. This impression of unreality, being reciprocal, a passing which takes place in two senses at the same time, becomes absurdly illusory. And the more we feel it to be illusory, the more we feel it tyrannically inevitable, mistress of all our human relations.

This work which has no apparent articulations, we have found to be totally coherent, a combination of equilibrium and subtle correspondences.

It makes one think at first of Classical music, with its perfect balance of emotion and of form, it subtle but perfectly clear interweaving of themes, and its motifs which return, sometimes at very long intervals, but which one recognises with a delicate pleasure.

It has, moreover, something more solid than any music and it has adopted a different symbolism. When Lily Briscoe seeks to reconstruct her vision from a wedge of space, balances her lines and her masses one against the other—a light here needs a shadow there—one realises that this is also what Virginia Woolf is doing; I have compared her with Vermeer; but Vermeer is too straightforward; it is rather of Cézanne that she should remind us, Cézanne taking his forms from Nature, and imposing his form upon them, making them enter into a purely personal composition. She follows the movements, the rhythms of life; she transcribes them with an intense reality; but she integrates them into the movement and the rhythm of her thoughts and thus assigns new values to them beyond their original value, and makes symbols of them. She is Lily Briscoe making a work of art with the substance of Mrs Ramsay.

ORLANDO

2 October 1928

70. Desmond MacCarthy, review, *Sunday Times*

14 October 1928, 10

The review was headed 'Phantasmagoria'. For a discussion of this article see Introduction, p. 21.

It is a pleasure to be among the first to hail a book which is beautiful and original, of a beauty and originality too, which is not only certain to be at once recognised—for *Orlando* is a work of contemporary youthful sensibility—but will continue, in my opinion, to seem beautiful and original to readers of the future. I have been myself a backward and almost a reluctant admirer of Mrs Woolf's fiction, though *To the Lighthouse* impressed me. Perhaps if I analyse that reluctance I shall be of service to others who approach her new book in much the same spirit as I did. To do so will, at any rate, explain why in *Orlando*, which is pure fantasy, she appears to have found herself more completely than ever before.

The peculiarity of her first novel, *The Voyage Out*, was its sensitive presentment of the criss-crossing of tragedy and commonplace, sweetness and drabness, ecstasy and ennui, rationality and nonsense, which is indeed the texture of common experience. Her treatment of tragedy and romance, however, was not different from that of other novelists, while the commonplace was strangely interesting to her. Take a dull half-hour in any dull person's mental life, or for that matter of an interesting person: it seems a limpid drop of tasteless water. (An old lady is, say, knitting, or a young man cutting his toe-nails.) But place that drop under the lens of a divining attention and, behold! it is swarming with the lashings and splashings of the queerest animalculae, a flurry of life as irrelevant to the intentions of that person as the bustle of bacilli in his or her veins. Most of the day our actions are those of automatons. Nevertheless our minds contain a swarm of images and reflections; twisting and hovering, rising and falling, ever tying and untying knots, like flies above the head of a sleeper—emblem, that sleeper, of our temporarily suspended, moral and rational being.

Bubbles and Auras

This aspect of life is always present to Mrs Woolf. She has used it in all her subsequent novels, *Jacob's Room*, *Mrs Dalloway*, *To the Lighthouse*; sometimes to produce effects of humour, when we heard the chirp of a somewhat acid Ariel overhead, and sometimes as an excuse for writing pages of prose-poetry; always blending the commonplace with the ethereally fantastic, and seizing opportunities for the exercise of a style at once delicate and dry, impulsive and deliberate, quick, flashing and extreme. The rhythm of her prose is often remarkably beautiful.

Readers of *The Voyage Out* will remember that the author not only told us what, at a given moment, her principal characters were doing, but took us from bedroom to bedroom of the large hotel in which they were staying, and described with rapid precision how the occupants were engaged. The effect was to impress us with the oddity and irrelevance of the setting which life provides for the adventures of the individual soul. We are used to a love-story or tragedy being set against the background of the activities of society or the indifference of nature; but this background, made up of other human beings, each like a little clock keeping its own time and striking independently, had a curious effect. (Anatole France sometimes used this device lightly in the service of irony.)

In her subsequent novels such figures were not in separate rooms, but her vision of life isolated them as completely. In *Mrs Dalloway* each character moves in a bubble of his or her own. Contact between them is hardly possible; they exist simultaneously, that is all, and at moments fain would blend their bubbles. It is these iridescent, quickly pricked and blown-again bubbles, made up of private thoughts and dreams, which Mrs Woolf is so adept at describing. In neo-Buddhistic books we sometimes come across pictures of little human figures, like the nuclei in the albumen of their eggs, and we are told that these are people's *auras*. *Auras*, in the sense of temporary and shifting dreams and thoughts which we all carry about with us while pursuing practical aims, have been her subject matter.

Mrs Brown

Now the novel is notoriously the most elastic literary form, a kind of hold-all into which poetry, sermons, disputations can be crammed. It is, in short, peptonised experience, and the novelist's experience may be either predominantly intellectual, emotional, photographic, or fanciful —anything you like. Good novels may be made indifferently out of dreams or realities, and even (though this is dangerous) out of theories of good and evil. But when we remember the novels which have meant most to us we see they are those which contain characters who have become as familiar to us, and even more comprehensible, than people we have known ourselves. Creation of character is the triumph of the novelist, the achievement through which his work lives, though what 'character' precisely means is a question of some obscurity. Mrs Woolf herself discussed it in a well-known essay which she called 'Mrs Brown': the novelist's business was the capture of Mrs Brown. Contemporary novelists, she argued, had allowed 'character' to be lost in the description of circumstance, yet the Victorian novelist's conception of 'character' did not satisfy her either. Such methods as those of Dickens and of Thackeray did not capture the essential 'Mrs Brown'. Her own approach to the problem is to trace in each case the stream of consciousness, to follow in each person his or her inner monologue.

The Creation of Character

The danger of this method is that one stream of consciousness is apt to be indistinguishable from another. Character is, after all, a surface pattern; penetrate below it and it is lost; moreover, this deeper psychology is really just as much a literary convention as character-drawing. It was in the creation of memorable and individual characters that her work as a novelist seemed weakest. She was more interested in the strange emotional content of each moment, and in the wandering reflections of her people than in the people themselves. Facts, ordinary facts, seemed to her dull until they could be removed into the world of subjective experience where outlines melt and vary, and everything can be given—more easily and arbitrarily—the hues of poetry and romance.

It would take too long to explain the causes of the discontent of the critically alert with the modern novel, and therefore why this defect did not stand in the way of their admiration of her work. To the artist the raw stuff of life often seems heavy and unimportant, and yet the handling of it is obligatory upon the novelist. Mrs Woolf's method was a way of escape from the heaviness of actuality. But it follows that where she has least to escape from, when, that is to say, she is least tethered to external realities by her subject, it is then her lyric fantasy and power of soaring or ironic description is likely to reach its greatest perfection. This is the case in *Orlando*.

Pure Romance

To tell the story of *Orlando* would be absurd. There is no story. It would not be a theme made to her hand if it had one. It is sufficient to say that Orlando was born to vast possessions in the reign of Elizabeth, and that he never died, but changed his sex in the reign of Queen Anne, and that 'she' passes at last, alas! from our view in modern times. It is a wonderful phantasmagoria, in which imagination has it all its own way and all matter-of-factness is exorcised from the start; in which, not without frequent flashes of laughter at her own extravagance, the writer combines images and historic facts, possibilities and impossibilities, reflections upon history and manners with scenes from a dream-world.

From Orlando's great house of many corridors and towers, soft with green parks, can be seen at once the snow-mountains of Wales and the smoke of London. Time and space mean nothing to us as we read. Imagination exaggerates and recombines all the elements which it has garnered from past epochs, and the chariot of romance is driven full tilt from beginning to end, heedless of being dashed to pieces rounding the corners of nonsense. In the world of pure imagination there are no corners. But we must be rapt away into that world first. Thanks to the author's command of words and skill in *crescendo* we are rapt. There is a softly glittering splendour in the descriptions, a definiteness mingled cunningly with imprecision which secures that result. Moreover, a Sterne-like faculty for impish divagation frequently relieves the tension of this orgy of romance. It matters little which one of many pages is chosen as an illustration of the descriptive passages.

Orlando

Let me take one describing Orlando's first introduction to Elizabeth. It is late, and the boy has been dreaming of writing poetry in the park under the oak tree, which recurs as a *leit-motif* during Orlando's life down the ages.

[Quotes p. 21 'After an hour or so' to 'The Queen had come.']

He is late: he rushes back to his room; thrusts on his crimson breeches, waistcoat of taffeta, and shoes with rosettes on them as big as dahlias, in less than ten minutes. Terribly excited he enters her presence:

[Quotes pp. 23–4 'Such was his shyness' to 'or only a hand.']

Society

Orlando's impression (now a woman's) of London society in the reign of Queen Anne will serve to illustrate that element of commentary which, running through the book, relieves and delights the reader.

[Quotes p. 174 'To give a truthful account' to 'is in itself insipid.']

Critics are suspect when they praise contemporary work enthusiastically, but ruling out the judgment of the unduly literal, I have no fear in this case that praise will not be corroborated.

71. J. C. Squire, 'Prose-de-Société', *Observer*

21 October 1928, 6

J. C. Squire (1884–1958). Georgian poet, parodist, editor of *London Mercury* and at this time chief reviewer for the *Observer*. An outspoken writer, whom Virginia Woolf described in a letter to Lytton Strachey as 'more repulsive than words can express, and malignant into the bargain'. (26 May 1919). She described this review as 'barking' (see Introduction, p. 21).

This book is easier to read than to describe. It is, indeed, very easy to read and very difficult to describe. Mrs Woolf, who has not previously inclined to fairy tale and phantasy, has suddenly produced a book which has something in common with *Serena Blandish*, *The Venetian Glass Lady*, and the tales of Mr David Garnett, but which is written on a larger scale, and is of so odd and original a conception that a summary of its theme is almost impossible, and no two summaries would greatly resemble each other.

The old chroniclers, when describing the sack of cities, commonly said that the brutal victors 'respected neither age nor sex'. In this sole respect the author of *Orlando* resembles the pikemen of Alva and the musketeers of Tilly. The reader never knows when he is going to be whisked forward for a century, and in the middle of the story the hero calmly changes from a man into a woman. 'Memory,' observes Mrs Woolf in another connection,

[Quotes p. 74 'is the seamstress' to 'gale of wind.']

The spectacle of Orlando's progress is not quite so inconsequent as the sequence of verbal, visual, and conceptual associations which flow by when the mind surrenders itself completely; for anything like that one must go to the intolerable gibberings of Miss Gertrude Stein. Mrs Woolf is even on the hither side of Sterne, who said that his method was to set down one sentence and (being a clergyman) to trust to God for the next, but whose most jerky inconsequences have often a great deliberation about them. Mrs Woolf's general outline is planned and controlled; within that outline she seems to allow her narrative, which has the tenour of a day-dream, to go where it will.

Orlando, though he never goes so far as to be more than one person at one time, is a successive selection from the ancestors of a lady of our own day, for whose portrait Miss V. Sackville-West, to whom the book is dedicated, has posed. He begins as an Elizabethan nobleman-poet, a type whose features are sketched in a very characteristic page of Mrs Woolf's prose:

[Quotes pp. 69–70 'The taste for books' to 'a naked man.']

This passage may serve as an illustration of the charming manner which Mrs Woolf has ironically fabricated for the occasion, a manner with touches of all the styles, here a paragraph in the narrative mode of the eighteenth century, here a series of little clauses with the imagery and the cadence of Euphuism.

Orlando has adventures with Love and with the Muses. Disappointments with both are the more easily overcome owing to a sudden lapse of years and his appointment by Charles II as Ambassador to the Sublime Porte. Trouble with the Turks is followed by a convenient change of success and escape into the England of Queen Anne, Pope and Addison. In Lord Palmerston's day she fell in love with a sailor and in October, 1928, the sailor, after long absence, flew to her arms (so to speak) in an aeroplane. No human novelist could quite sustain a character through such vicissitudes, that it must be admitted that Orlando is never a person. Mrs Woolf says of her:

[Quotes pp. 213–14 'She had been a gloomy boy' to 'country and the seasons.']

That much is true of individuals and of families: Mrs Woolf seems also to have the story of English literature and the English people in mind. The book, however, will no more be read for any allegorical significance it may have than for its study of a character which does not exist.

Its attractions are twofold. In the first place, Mrs Woolf's scheme allows her, at will, to give us sidelights on manners and pictures of bygone social scenes—the Thames frozen in Jacobean days, Constantinople in Caroline days, the drawing-rooms and countrysides of several generations When Orlando is a poet we are presented with a very amusing satirical picture of literary life; when he is an ambassador we have a glimpse of St James's and Nell Gwynn. Orlando is a thread on which many bright beads are strung—beads both bright and well-turned. Secondly, Mrs Woolf's English is always elegant, and her selection of significant details is usually sure. On occasion she is not merely interesting but amusing:

[Quotes p. 64 'the doctors were hardly' to 'asleep for a week.']

Unfortunately the amusing passages are not very frequent; there is a wan, pervasive smile, and no more; humour can hardly be drawn out of the persons, for they change too often. I mentioned Sterne just now: to Sterne we often return, and he frequently makes us laugh aloud. To Mrs Woolf's book, I, at least, shall not return: having discovered the outline I should enjoy it less and less at each perusal: it did not make me laugh aloud at the first. Neither did it (though there are a few beautiful phrases) give me any shock of aesthetic delight, though it never for a moment bored me. There is a sort of fatigued grace, an exquisite nebulosity, about the book. It gives the impression that the author had no gusto in the writing of it, hardly a moment of ecstasy, of devotion, of self-forgetfulness of any kind, even of mere high spirits. Did we know no more about her than this book, we might suppose that her dominant feeling was a tepid amusement at the petty futility of life—'disillusionment' is hardly the word, as we have no sense that any illusions have been lost. I have no desire to break a butterfly upon a wheel, or even to impale it upon a pin: this book is a very pleasant trifle, and will entertain the drawing-rooms for an hour: a suitable companion for the jade carving and the painted snuff-boxes. But I think that even of its kind it is not in the first order. Even a trifle, to be excellent, must have enthusiasm behind it. This book, one feels, was conceived frivolously and chancily, and carried through with too painstaking a spontaneity and too little affection or respect for the reader, the intelligence in it being immeasurably in excess of the mirth, the response to beauty, the emotional interest in history, morals, character or anything else. Possibly it is the work of a mind which, at bottom, is purely critical.

72. Cleveland B. Chase, from a review, *New York Times*

21 October 1928, 7

Those who open *Orlando* expecting another novel in the vein of *Mrs Dalloway* and *To the Lighthouse* will discover, to their joy or sorrow, that once more Mrs Woolf has broken with tradition and convention and has set out to explore still another fourth dimension of writing. Not that she has abandoned the 'stream of consciousness' method which she used with such conspicuous success in her previous novels, but with it she has combined what, for lack of a better term, we might describe as an application to writing of the Einstein theory of relativity. In this new work she is largely preoccupied with the 'time' element in character and human relationships, and with a statement of the exact complexion of that intangible moment, a combination of past and future of objective reality and subjective consciousness, which we refer to as the present.

[Quotes p. 91 'An hour, once it lodges' to 'one second.' and pp. 274–5 'The most successful' to 'they call themselves.']

Mrs Woolf's hero-heroine is hundreds of years old. At the beginning of the book Orlando is a boy of 16, melancholy, indolent, loving solitude and given to writing poetry; the age is the Elizabethan; the book ends on the 11th of October, 1928, and Orlando is a thoroughly modern matron of 36, who has published a successful book of poems and has evolved a hard-earned philosophy of life. Thus, to express her very modern fourth-dimensional concepts, Mrs Woolf has fallen back upon one of the most ancient of literary forms, the allegory. In doing so she has left the book perhaps more confused than was strictly necessary.

[Plot summary omitted]

The rest of the novel may be divided into two parts; the first deals somewhat whimsically with Orlando's attempts to adjust herself to the conventions of nineteenth-century England. The second, and by far the most stimulating section of the book, describes Orlando at the present moment, and traces with breath-taking delicacy the influence of her past upon her present. It is in these last thirty-odd pages that the book springs startlingly to life. Up to this point is had seemed a pleasant narrative made notable by a number of passages of great beauty and by occasional bits of vivid description, but marred by a rather self-conscious facetiousness on the part of the author, an addiction to parenthetical whimsicalities that are not particularly effective.

In the closing pages of the novel Mrs Woolf welds into a compact whole what had seemed to be a series of loosely connected episodes. In them she seems to reach down through the whole superstructure of life and to lay bare a new, or at least a hitherto unperceived, arrangement of those ephemeral flashes of memory or perception that go to make up consciousness. Throughout the ages people have remarked that time, under certain circumstances, seems much longer than under certain other circumstances. Mrs Woolf presents concrete proof that this is not merely an impression, but a fact, by showing of what time, not as a mechanical but as a human element, consists. She has carried the 'stream of consciousness' technique a step further; she has not been satisfied to present a succession of thoughts and sensations passing through the mind; she shows what is behind those thoughts and sensations, whence they spring, and how great their relative value.

In attempting to describe such subtle and illusive qualities—or should they be called quantities?—Mrs Woolf has faced squarely one of the most puzzling technical and esthetic problems that confront contemporary novelists. The mere fact that she has stated the problem as succinctly as she does in the course of this book is immensely stimulating, whether or not one feels that she has achieved a final solution of it. It is something of a question whether the tendency of contemporary novelists to become more and more introspective can profitably be carried much further. If it is to continue, however, Mrs Woolf has pointed out the direction in which it must develop.

73. Arnold Bennett on Virginia Woolf

1928, 1929

(a) From 'A Woman's High-Brow Lark', *Evening Standard*, 8 November 1928, 7.

Virginia Woolf had written to the heroine of *Orlando*, Vita Sackville-West: '... Jack Squire annoyed you, but ... Arnold Bennett will be far worse, so be prepared' (Victoria Sackville-West, 'Virginia Woolf and *Orlando*', *Listener*, 27 January 1955, 157–8).

You cannot keep your end up at a London dinner-party in these weeks unless you have read Mrs Virginia Woolf's *Orlando*. For about a fortnight I succeeded in not reading it—partly from obstinacy and partly from a natural desire for altercation at table about what ought and ought not to be read. Then I saw that Hugh Walpole had described it as 'another masterpiece', and that Desmond MacCarthy had given it very high praise.

I have a great opinion of the literary opinions of these two critics. So I bought the book and read it. I now know exactly what I think of it, and I can predict the most formidable rumpuses at future parties.

It is a very odd volume. It has a preface, in which Mrs Woolf names the names of 53 people who have helped her with it. It has, too, an index. I admit some justification for the preface, but none for the index.

Further, the novel, which is a play of fancy, a wild fantasia, a romance, a high-brow lark, is illustrated with ordinary realistic photographs, including several of Vita Sackville-West (a Hawthornden prize-winner), to whom the book is dedicated. The portraits of Miss Sackville-West are labelled 'Orlando'.

This is the oddest of all the book's oddities....

Orlando at the end of the book has achieved an age of some four centuries. Which reminds one of the Wandering Jew and the Flying

Dutchman. Half-way through the story he changes into a woman—and 'stays put'. Which reminds one of '*Seraphita*', the dullest book that Balzac ever wrote.

I surmise that Orlando is intended to be the incarnation of something or other—say, the mustang spirit of the joy of life, but this is not quite clear to me.

The first chapter is goodish. It contains vivacious descriptions of spectacular matters—such as a big frost, royal courts, and the love-making of Orlando and a Muscovite girl in furs and in the open air amid the fiercest frost since the ice-age. Mrs Woolf almost convinces us of the possibility of this surely very difficult dalliance.

The second chapter shows a startling decline and fall-off. Fanciful embroidery, wordy, and naught else!

The succeeding chapters are still more tedious in their romp of fancy. Mrs Woolf does not seem to have understood that fancy must have something to play *on*. She has left out the basic substance. For example, Orlando, both as man and as woman, is said to have had many lovers, but details are given of only one love.

I shall no doubt be told that I have missed the magic of the work. The magic is precisely what I indeed have missed.

The writing is good at the beginning, but it goes to pieces; it even skids into bad grammar (e.g. on p. 262). Mrs Woolf has accomplished some of the most beautiful writing of the modern age, including paragraphs that Nathaniel Hawthorne himself might have signed. *Orlando*, however, has nothing anywhere near as good as her best.

The theme is a great one. But it is a theme for a Victor Hugo, not for Mrs Woolf, who, while sometimes excelling in fancy and in delicate realistic observation, has never yet shown the mighty imaginative power which the theme clearly demands. Her best novel, *To the Lighthouse* raised my hopes of her. *Orlando* has dashed them and they lie in iridescent fragments at my feet.

Mrs Woolf's publishing firm, the Hogarth Press, has just issued a critical work, *The Structure of the Novel*, by Edwin Muir. In dealing with the later developments of English fiction, Mr Muir names James Joyce, Mrs Woolf and (to a less extent) Aldous Huxley as the only important innovating novelists.

I would concede him the first and the last, but I have horrid doubts about the middle term. In particular I have failed to perceive any genuine originality in the method of *Mrs Dalloway*. If originality there is, it fails in its object of presenting character.

(b) 'An unco-ordinated mass of interesting details', *Realist*, Vol. 1 No. 1, April 1929, 3–11.

An extract from a survey entitled 'The Progress of the Novel'. Bennett was considering the innovations of Proust, Lawrence, Mottram, Joyce, and Virginia Woolf.

Virginia Woolf has passionate praisers, who maintain that she is a discoverer in psychology and in form. Disagreeing, I regard her alleged form as the absence of form, and her psychology as an unco-ordinated mass of interesting details, none of which is truly original. All that I can urge in her favour is that she is authentically feminine, and that her style is admirable. Both these qualities are beside my point. Of the above mentioned five, only Joyce is of the dynasty of precursors and sure of a place in the history of the development of the novel.

74. Conrad Aiken, review, *Dial* (Chicago)

February 1929, 147–9

That Mrs Woolf is a highly ingenious writer has been made glitteringly obvious for us in *Mrs Dalloway* and *To the Lighthouse*: which is not in the least to minimize the fact that those two novels also contained a great deal of beauty. That she is, and has perhaps always been, in danger of carrying ingenuity too far, is suggested, among other things, by her new novel, or 'biography', *Orlando*. What ever else one thinks about this book, one is bound to admit that it is exceedingly, not to say disconcertingly, clever. In England as well as in America it has set the critics by the ears. They have not known quite how to take it—whether to regard it as a biography, or a satire on biography; as a history, or a satire on history; as a novel, or as an allegory. And it is at once clear, when one reads *Orlando*, why this confusion should have arisen; for the tone of the book, from the very first pages, is a tone of mockery. Mrs Woolf has expanded a *jeu d'esprit* to the length of a novel. One might almost say, in fact—when one notes in the index that there are precisely seven references to 'The Oak' (a poem which plays an important part in the story—and which in a sense is almost its ghostly protagonist) and when one recalls that Knole, a famous English house, is at Sevenoaks, (clearly the house described in the novel) that *Orlando* is a kind of colossal pun. More exactly, one might compare it with *Alice in Wonderland*; for if the latter is an inspired dream, organized with a logic almost insanely unswerving, so the former is a kind of inspired joke, a joke charged with meanings, in which the logic, if not quite so meticulous, is at any rate pressing.

There is thus an important element of 'spoof' in *Orlando*: Mrs Woolf apparently wants us to know that she does not herself take the thing with the least seriousness—that she is pulling legs, keeping her tongue in her cheek, and winking, now and then, a quite shameless and enormous wink. With all this, which she accomplishes with a skill positively equestrian, she is obliged, perforce, to fall into a style which one cannot help feeling is a little unfortunate. It is a style which makes fun of a style: it is glibly rhetorical, glibly sententious, glibly poetic, glibly analytical, glibly austere, by turns—deliberately so; and while this might be, and is, extraordinarily diverting for a chapter or two, or for something like the length of a short story, one finds it a little fatiguing in a full-length book. Of course, Mrs Woolf's theme, with its smug annihilation of time, may be said to have demanded, if the whole question of credibility was to be begged, a tone quite frankly and elaborately artificial. Just the same, it is perhaps questionable whether she has not been *too* icily and wreathedly elaborate in this, and taken her Orlando in consequence a shade too far towards an arid and ingenious convention. Granted that what she wanted to tell us was a fable, or allegory: that she wanted to trace the aesthetic evolution of a family (and by implication that of a country) over a period of three hundred years: and that she had hit upon the really first-rate idea of embodying this racial evolution in one undying person: need she quite so much have presumed on our incredulity? One suspects that in such a situation an ounce of ingenuousness might be worth ten times its weight in ingenuity; and that a little more of the direct and deep sincerity of the last few pages, which are really beautiful and really moving, might have made *Orlando* a minor masterpiece.

As it is, it is an extremely amusing and brilliant *tour de force*. It is as packed with reference, almost, as 'The Waste Land'. Some of the references, it is true, are too esoteric—for one not in the enchanted circle—to be universally valid; and this may or may not be thought a mistake. One's private jokes and innuendoes are pretty apt to become meaningless, with the passage of time and the disappearance of the *milieu* which gave them point. This, again, is of a piece with Mrs Woolf's general air of high spirits; of having a lark; of going, as it were, on an intellectual spree; and that there is far too little of this spirit in contemporary literature we can cheerfully admit. But here too one feels inclined to enter a protest. For the idea, as has been said, is first-rate, an idea from which a poet might have evoked a profusion of beauty as easily as the djinn was released from his bottle. Mrs Woolf does indeed give us a profusion of beauty and wisdom: but it is beauty and wisdom of a very special sort. Her roses are cloth roses, her scenes are scenes from a tapestry, her 'wisdom' (that is, her shrewd and very feminine comments on men and things) has about it an air of florid and cynical frigidity, a weariness wrought into form; as if—to change the image—she were stringing for her own entertainment a necklace of beautifully polished platitudes. If only—one thinks—she could have brought an Elizabethan freshness to this admirable theme—if she could have worked her mine a little deeper, a little more honestly, a little less for diversion's sake, and a little more for poetry's; and if, finally, she were not quite so civilized, in the Kensington Gardens sense of the word, or so burdened with sophistication, or could admit now and then, if for only a moment, a glimpse into the sheer horror of things, the chaos that yawns under Bloomsbury—but then this book would not have been the charming *jeu d'esprit* that it is; it would have been something else.

75. Helen MacAfee, initialled review, *Yale Review*

1929, vol. 18, xvi

Helen MacAfee (1884–1956). American literary critic and managing editor of the *Yale Review*.

It is the right and the nature of the artist to renew the forms of expression inherited from great predecessors by impressing upon them his own intense being. Mrs Woolf, who has chosen fiction as her chief literary medium, has from the first shown herself impatient of the old categories, and now in her latest novel she declares her independence openly in the subtitle, 'a biography'. This extraordinary work, bearing as it does the clear stamp of her mind in its maturity, might in a sense have been called an autobiography. Readers who are interested in such matters may find in it a whole philosophy of creative literature, a subtle speculation upon personality and recorded time.

Orlando is a boldly conceived and finely executed dramatization of the civilized current of three centuries, imagined as flowing through the veins of a person who existed in the flesh as a man—a very young Englishman—during the spacious days of Elizabeth, was mysteriously transformed into a woman about the time of Queen Anne, and is under George V (and will always remain) in the prime of the years that consummate youth. In each of her novels Mrs Woolf has done with a sure hand the thing she set out to do—most often it has been to refine with the utmost resourcefulness upon a theme not in bare outline of great magnitude. *Orlando* may be taken as an answer to those who have questioned whether she could handle with equal success a larger scheme and implications of greater scope. It is a book rich in humanity, a spirited prose epic of intellectual adventure.

76. Raymond Mortimer, from 'Virginia Woolf and Lytton Strachey', *Bookman* (New York)

February 1929, 625–9

Raymond Mortimer (b. 1895). English literary critic and journalist. A friend of Virginia Woolf and closely associated with Bloomsbury in the 1920s. In the forty-five years since he wrote this review, he has changed his view on one point. He now believes that *Eminent Victorians*, far more conspicuously than Strachey's later books, was a propagandist work attacking religion and militarism, and that its author should not have been described as aloof.

Certainly *Elizabeth and Essex* and *Orlando* were the two most remarkable English books of the autumn season, and the magnificently generous reception thay they have had in the United States tempts me to put down a few notes on the background of each, the soil from which they have flowered. Both Mrs Woolf and Mr Strachey are firebrands: she has revolutionized fiction and he, biography. That is to say, the Galsworthy type of novel now looks as quaint and old-fashioned as a Victorian problem-picture, while the 'Life and Letters' biography written by lamenting widows or hypocritical disciples, excites only our amusement. The old biographers left out too much, the novelists put in too much. Mrs Woolf and Mr Strachey have each set a new norm. Certainly, their influence will continue for a long time: neither the novel nor the biography will ever be the same again. Yet so individual are their talents that any literal imitation of them can only be disastrous. Already we are being snowed under by biographies whose authors attempt to compensate for their lack of scholarship by cheap sneers, undergraduate epigrams and picturesque inventions. And soon some young lady is sure to caricature Mrs Woolf's methods just as

Mr Guedalla has caricatured Mr Strachey's. The techniques of both *Mrs Dalloway* and *Eminent Victorians* demand consummate tact. Like most successful makers of revolution, Mrs Woolf and Mr Strachey are unlikely to found a dynasty.

Furthermore, unlike a Cromwell or a Napoleon, they certainly have no wish to do so, since they are revolutionaries by chance. They are artists; that is to say individualists. Essentially, each is the culminating product of a long tradition. Like Aldous Huxley and unlike D. H. Lawrence, they spring from the centre of Nineteenth Century English culture. Mrs Woolf is a daughter of the late Sir Leslie Stephen, editor of the *Dictionary of National Biography* and the author of a number of scholarly and toughly reasoned books. Her father's first wife was a daughter of Thackeray. Mr Strachey's family has administered tracts of India for generations. Mrs Woolf and Mr Strachey are related to half the most scholarly families in England, Darwins and Maitlands and Symondses; they are even related to each other. The weapons they have turned on the Victorians were forged in Victorian homes. The integrity which made Leslie Stephen give up his living as a parson on intellectual grounds is repeated in another form in his daughter's novels. The mastery of a mass of detail, the solid and admirably proportioned architecture of Mr Strachey's books are an inheritance from generations of civil servants. The Victorian iconoclasts were so taken up with attacking established religions that they never scrutinized established morals. They were, indeed, Puritans of a very grim order, enormously anxious to show that the destruction of Christian dogma did not entail any weakening of Christian morals. In this they were illogical and, in the persons of their descendants, they are now completing their task. Never were novels less propagandist, less *romans à thèse*, than those of Mrs. Woolf. But the ethic implicit in them and in Mr Strachey's book, is a pagan ethic. Similarly Mr Huxley shocks the conventional by trying to apply to personal morals that hard light of reason with which his grandfather illuminated biology and religion. Mr Aldous Huxley, however, remains a preacher, though his creed is different from his grandfather's. Mrs Woolf and Mr Strachey, on the other hand, remain fastidious and remote.

[A discussion dealing exclusively with Strachey has been omitted.]

Now, let us look for a minute at Mrs Woolf's books. Her first novel, *The Voyage Out*, was written, I believe, when she was only twenty-four, but it was some years before it was published in a revised form.

It is fairly traditional, technically, and resembles more than anything the novels of Mr E. M. Forster. (He is an old and intimate friend of Mrs Woolf.) But already essential qualities destined to branch exuberantly out in her work are here in bud—a runaway imagination and a hypertrophied sensibility to the variety and simultaneousness of human life. Thus, the scene of the book is in South America where she had never been, and one of the most remarkable chapters describes a hotel and specifies, moreover, what each of its inhabitants from attic to basement is doing and feeling and thinking at a particular moment. Her next book, *Night and Day*, is a failure, as if Matisse had tried to paint a still life in the style of de Heem. In a sense it can be taken as a protest against the heavy atmosphere of reverent culture in which the author had been educated. (There is a story that she and her sister Vanessa Bell, the painter, were brought up never to speak unless they had something to say.) But the chief point of the book is that it was a serious attempt to adapt her mind to the exigencies of the academic novel. Meanwhile, she was writing front-page articles for the dignified *Times Literary Supplement*, reading deeply, widely, passionately and learning Greek—she was never at a university. She married Leonard Woolf, who had been a civil servant in Ceylon and who was now writing on co-operation in industry and on economic imperialism.

Mr and Mrs Woolf started a press and an early publication was a little book called *Monday or Tuesday*. It was illustrated with wood cuts by Vanessa Bell, the ink of which came off on the text opposite; for it was printed in the most amateur way, I presume by the author and her husband. But it was the *Quatorze Juillet* of the Edwardian novel. In one story Mrs Woolf looks at a mark on the wall of a room, in another at a woman in a railway carriage and in each case she unleashes her imagination and creates a history. With *Monday or Tuesday* she emerged definitely with the liveliest imagination and most delicate style of her time. But these were only sketches. *Jacob's Room* was the first full-size canvas. It is the life of a man told by the effect he has on the persons and objects with which he comes into contact—a sort of detective story in which the particularities of the protagonist are deduced from the tracks he has left in the snow. There is no plot. *Mrs Dalloway* is an even more gallant and successful experiment. We follow two persons, a fashionable hostess and a melancholic clerk, through their day. A word is given to every person they see—I think about one hundred and fifty are actually given names—and, though the two never meet, we perceive at the end that they are the obverse and reverse of a single soul. Technically, this is Mrs Woolf's most remarkable novel. But *To the Lighthouse* is probably her best. Here for the first time, some of the characters become solid, particularly the old man, in whom one may fancy one recognizes the nobly eminent features of Sir Leslie Stephen himself. And in a transitional passage of extraordinary virtuosity, time passes. It is as if each book contained the seed of its successor—Mrs Woolf's work is a dynasty, interrupted by one pretender. For in *Orlando* time keeps passing. We are swept from Queen Elizabeth to 1928.

The first thing to say about the book is that it is a lark. The preface is a parody of prefaces and the whole book is written in tearing high spirits. The style modulates, sings tunes by Sterne, by Browne, by Emily Bronte, by De Quincey, yet remains individual to Mrs Woolf. Sometimes it even breaks into verse; look at page 270 in the American edition and strip the typographical disguise.

Let us go, then exploring,
This summer morning
When all are adoring
The plum blossom and the bee.
And humming and hawing,
Let us ask of the starling . . .

[The remaining eight lines of Mortimer's 'poem' have been omitted.]

The book is listed as biography. And it is no secret that *Orlando* is a portrait of Mrs Harold Nicolson, who writes under her unmarried name, V. Sackville-West. The book includes not only a quotation from her poem *The Land*, but photographs of her as well as of the ancestors from which she shows herself so evidently descended.

The rich historical background of the Sackvilles has awakened a thousand associations in Mrs Woolf's mind. For Knole, their house that is like a town, is English history made visible in stone and velvets and silver. A race of poets, these Sackvilles, who are patrons when they are not writers. (The first English tragedy, *Gorboduc*, was the work of one of them.) The accretion of generations which you find at Knole is something peculiarly English. One Sackville flaunted an Italian mistress in the face of Europe, another a Spanish dancer, but more characteristic is the fact that a third, at Harrow, was Byron's fag. Knole has a high banqueting hall, paved with stone, in the medieval way. Van Dycks hang upon its panelled walls, but there is a singular lack of pomp about the house. The rooms are not grandiose or in the

Italian taste, like those of Blenheim. A parvenu like Marlborough might astonish Europe with his splendors and call his house, with good reason, a palace. The Sackvilles lay perdu among their ancient trees, in their rambling and interminable labyrinth of sober stone, the ladies working at their tapestry, the men talking to Dryden or Reynolds.

Vast, yet unostentatious, sumptuous yet never brilliant, fortified yet marvellously peaceful, Knole is not a palace. It is just Knole and Orlando is an embodiment of this proud tranquillity, at once a house and a person. The present heir, a first cousin of Mrs Nicolson, Edward Sackville-West, is also a writer with a fantastic imagination and a deliciously personal sense of comedy. His last novel, *Mandrake Over the Water Carrier*, is a most brilliant affair and in *The Ruin* he has fine descriptions of Knole. But it is in *The Land*, placid and slow moving as a deep river, that we find the literary counterpart of this ancient house. And the author of *The Land* is Orlando. The portrait Mrs Woolf has given of her must be judged as a painting, not as a likeness. Perhaps it should be put on record that the likeness is remarkable. But not, of course, photographic. Mrs Woolf is always free and easy with her facts. She will take Claridge's out of Brook Street and place it in Piccadilly. She will look through the club windows in St James's Street and see the old gentlemen sitting at tables with soda-water siphons by them, when a London club is one place where a siphon is never to be seen. And *Orlando* is full of anachronisms. Old St Paul's is given a dome and dahlias flower in England in the Seventeenth Century; but, then, does she not deliberately make the mountains of Wales, the spires of London, and the sea, all visible from one point? Mrs Woolf believes in the imagination. She takes a glance at the world. The horses of her fancy bolt and she throws the reins over their heads. Literature is not an imitation of life, it is another life.

I was reading the other day the enchanting letters of Lady Ritchie, who was Thackeray's daughter and a sister-in-law of Sir Leslie Stephen. (Her books, I may say, are very well worth reading.) And I came on this passage: 'Except the statues, all the things I tell you aren't the things I specially like, which are just the odds and ends which I forget again as I drive by. There was the King of Naples yesterday, there was an onion shop—there was a little marble seat in the corner of a palace where we sat—a dab of blue through a door—and a girl whirling her arm.'

Just such odds and ends provide much of the material which Mrs Woolf orders into a significant relationship by the rhythm of her prose.

From the first, she has been in love with life. Everything excites her, beggars and duchesses, snowflakes and dolphins. She cuts a wall from a house, like the men you see demolishing with pickaxes, and the old wall-papers show, with marks where the pictures have been, and the bed. At once it is peopled with all the odd varieties of human fauna. I do not know what writer has ever had this Midas touch so developed —every object she touches becomes iridescent, every word she uses is alive and pulling like a trout on a line.

The resulting texture is so dazzling that some readers turn away from Mrs Woolf's work; its virtuosity blinds them to its integrity. To others it seems literally too exquisite; they fancy they smell the lamp, where I can perceive only a delicate flavour of scholarship. Evidently the style is the result of years of experience. We can see it developing as we follow the chronological order of her works. But this long apprenticeship has left her a complete mistress of her medium. Her line, like a great painter's, is now spontaneously artful. When she scribbles a note to her bank, we may be sure it is in individual and prismatic sentences. The outcome of her long schooling is a style which follows with marvellous closeness the rhythm of her speech. It is, therefore, a natural style in the fullest sense, that is, not the ready-to-wear stuff which is the easiest to come by, but a vesture exactly fitting her in every idiosyncrasy. I know only one other person whose writing and whose talk are so closely related, and that is Jean Cocteau. Neither he nor Mrs Woolf talks like a book; but their books talk like a person. Incidentally, among the people I know, whose company is a delight, I consider these two in a class apart.

I should like to end this article by showing what it is that Mrs Woolf and Mr Strachey have in common. But I do not know how, not because it is non-existent, but because it is indefinable. In a sense the pictures of Botticelli and Pontormo are profoundly different, yet put them by the side of Venetian or Sienese pictures and their kinship becomes obvious. So it is with the authors of *To the Lighthouse* and *Queen Victoria*. One book is fiction, the other biography. In style they are a world apart but in mind the authors have this mysterious quality in common which we do not find in Wells or Bennett or Lawrence. It has some relation to a voice that is never too loud, a scepticism that remains polite, a learning that is never paraded and a disregard, that never becomes insulting, for the public taste. It is a quality of inherited culture. Genius and taste can only come to terms by something approaching a miracle. In these two writers this miracle is accomplished.

77. Storm Jameson, from 'The Georgian Novel and Mr Robinson', *Bookman* (New York)

July 1929, 449–63

Storm Jameson (b. 1897). British novelist. In this article she created Mr Robinson, an 'ordinary' man, who is trying to pick his way through Georgian literature.

Then, if not Aldous Huxley (or not yet) why not Virginia Woolf? There are moments when, blushing for the difficulty he finds in saying suitably what he deeply feels, little Mr Robinson puts his money on her rather than on Mr Huxley. One of these moments happened to him after he had read *Orlando*. He read it with delight, with awe, disturbed, enchanted, exalted. And yet wondering.

Mrs Woolf is, beyond comparison, a master of language. The word *style* has a faintly disreputable flavour. It has come to mean a quality which can be imposed on a novel from the outside, a trick, in which the quickness of the hand deceives the eye. The *style* of *Orlando* is imposed on it from within—the spirit made articulate. It is just, flexible, and lovely. Add that it owes to Sir Thomas Browne, to Defoe, more to Sterne, and confess that Mrs Woolf apprenticed herself to masters who were good enough to teach her what she already divined. 'We must shape our words,' thought Orlando, 'until they are the thinnest integument for our thoughts.' In one light, the book resembles a tapestry of which every detail is carefully contrived, the grass enamelled with flowers, the stones of a castle, the branches of the candlesticks, the folds of a gown, and the feathers in a young man's cap. It deals with space and time in the arbitrary fashion of tapestries—a century dropped between one group and the next. In another light, everything, flowers, houses, candles, plumed hats, streets, cities, clouds, all have become translucent, a lucence stained with thought. What we see is a process, the very chemistry of thought and action. In another and less favourable light the book has the air of a strange and lovely *pastiche*. In no light does it cease to be strange, subtle, exciting, and lovely. It enters the soul of the reader through his ears. To turn, immediately on reading *Orlando*, to a book by any other living English novelist, is to find his beauties commonplace, his style poor and flat.

And yet (we are back again with little Mr Robinson, now fairly wringing his hands in an anguish of self-abasement)—Something is missing. What is missing? Why is it that the author of *Orlando* is not a very great novelist?

It may be, I think, because she lacks humanity. She is in some way, or by some word laid on her, outside humanity. She sees as an artist sees, listens as a musician does, to common suffering, crying, laughing, doing good and doing mischief. Doubtless she suffers, weeps, laughs, herself—but not as a man does. As a fallen angel might. Or a changeling. She has no roots in our common earth. Her genius, carefully tended, pruned, enriched, has no roots in our common earth.

She can reproduce a scene with the fidelity to detail and clear colouring of a Breughel. And think about it until she has destroyed it. She is cursed with double vision.

[Quotes p. 290 'She looked there' to 'chequer of light and shade.']

Yet Mrs Woolf remains the most remarkable figure among all those to whom Mr Robinson's insistent respectful gestures have, bless the man, been drawing our attention for the last hour.

78. From *The Voyage Out* to *Orlando*: two French surveys

1930

(a) Jean-Jacques Mayoux, from 'Le roman de l'espace et du temps—Virginia Woolf', *Revue Anglo-Americaine* (Paris), April 1930, 312–26.

There is a remarkable continuity in the work of Virginia Woolf, masked by great differences in technique. She is entirely dedicated to spritual things, to understanding and expressing profound realities, which are at the same time intimate and universal. She seems in certain ways singularly detached from an epoch of low brows and strong jaws which has Action for its goddess. Nothing is a matter of indifference to her, except for social problems. Virginia Woolf's major concerns are life and the soul, and she is courageous enough not to shrink from highly charged words. She seeks to project a vision of the world rather than reflect the age or fabricate characters and situations. One cannot conceive of her other than giving to her epoch, whatever it may be, a benevolence tinged with irony, the safeguard of her independence.

Her predominant concerns also characterise that which she terms 'the Russian point of view'. The soul: Dostoievski and his persistent questioning and passionate search for the hidden springs of action and the depths of human character. Tolstoi's work is full of life seen as the complex knot of creation, with its joy and anguish mixed, as though they were only different intensities; life shot through with time, surrounded by space. The Tchekhovian mixture. Russian point of view? The 'Cimetière Marin' is no different from all this. But we must admit that it is to the Russians that we owe a novel dominated by such preoccupations....

The German critic Curtius points out, as characteristic of Proust, a similar feeling of the way in which of all values, physical and moral, are relative to distance (which is by this very description almost identified with time). What a strange difference between Albertine's head close up, and the same head at some distance. And what a fantastic rondo the three spires of Martinville dance between the movement of the hero and the horizon.

What particularly distinguished Virginia Woolf's approach is the importance she gives to the non-rectified perspective, to its bizarre errors, the even-handed justice of its ironies, the unique impartiality of its indifference, and the artistic value of this momentary triumph of appearance:

From a distance the *Euphrosyne* looked very small. Glasses were turned upon her from the decks of great liners, and she was pronounced a tramp, a cargo-boat, or one of those wretched little passenger steamers where people rolled about among the cattle on deck. The insect-like figures of Dalloways, Ambroses, and Vinraces were also derided, both from the extreme smallness of their persons and the doubt which only strong glasses could dispel as to whether they were really live creatures or only lumps in the rigging. Mr Pepper with all his learning had been mistaken for a cormorant.

Dwarfing and other effects of perspective seem to falsify the romantic aspect of distance. Because they belong to an opposing conception of reality, these neglected and doubly ironic effects are the inverse of the romantic transfigurations which distance allows:

At night, indeed, when the waltzes were swinging in the saloon, and gifted passengers reciting, the little ship—shrunk to a few beads of light out among the dark waves, and one high in air upon the mast-head—seemed something mysterious and impressive to heated partners resting from the dance. She became a ship passing in the night—an emblem of the loneliness of human life, an occasion for queer confidences and sudden appeals for sympathy.

But it is in *Jacob's Room* that Virginia Woolf for the first time creates space using her own methods. On the beach, when the book opens, Jacob's mother is writing; opposite her, at some distance, a painter uses her to build up his own picture-space; Jacob is invisible in the rocks, and his little brother calls:

'Ja—cob! Ja—cob!' shouted Archer. . . .
The voice had an extraordinary sadness. Pure from all body, pure from all passion, going out into the world, solitary, unanswered, breaking against the rocks—so it sounded.

By means of a few significant points and the links which we necessarily make between them, space is created for our imagination. Space is created directly, and described in its effect, it is no longer a question of mere assertion. The great marquee woven of lives and destinies, in which our restless strivings are consumed and so often wasted, is held up by these few pegs. This expanse, in which the child on the shore cannot join the child on the rocks, is too great. Its resemblance to time, which, contrary to appearances, is more inexorable, is suggested at the end of the book, when Jacob dies:

'Jacob! Jacob!' cried Bonamy, standing by the window. The leaves sank down again.
'Such confusion everywhere!' exclaimed Betty Flanders, bursting open the bedroom door.
Bonamy turned away from the window.

Jacob's room is at Scarborough, Cambridge, London, Athens—one can see that it is not a Balzacian 'frame'. There is a Jacob who is, above all, a series of moments in life, moments in successive rooms. For, Anima replacing Animus, the great emotions are brought into play much less than the emotion of living itself—than 'Life' which is Virginia Woolf's true subject. And life, in her vision of it, is essentially formed of groups of complex units which one might call space-moments. The linking together of objects in the same moment, in the same corner of space, gives them a meaning and forms between them a singularly strong bond. This constitutes what the animal or primitive being within us apprehends—or rather, let us say simply what the living being apprehends. Our conscious habits of thought obstinately turn us away from this apprehension towards a logical connection and continuity in time, towards something which at least holds the promise of a logical meaning. This continuity of space, which is an unacknowledged aspect of our reality, tends always to be reconstructed from fragments. And the least 'important' fragments are the most likely to reconstruct the totality and to give us an immediate and, as it were, intuitive reality (intuitive, because we do not distrust it). And the central, I might say, the human, reality (which we distrust so much when anyone tries to communicate it to us directly) is here made familiar to us in a manner that we would have thought beyond the power of the novel. Here is a moment at the beginning of *Jacob's Room*, around the sleeping Jacob:

[Quotes pp. 11–12 'Mrs Flanders has left' to 'violently beside it.' and 'Outside the rain' to 'trying again and again.']

Where does this space end, on which our existence depends? Where does Jacob's multiple room come to an end, this room which his imagination, his conscious or unconscious self, continues to cling to obscurely? At what point, if one ascends high enough, does space begin to belong less to Jacob than Jacob belong to space? What special importance does the 'hero' have, after all? Though he might be in Athens, cannot we, for a moment, turn our myopic attention away from him in order to see night and day traverse the countryside, spread over London, and effortlessly harmonise innumerable other lives with his?

In its extreme form, this vision, which becomes implicit after *Jacob's Room* recalls the panoramas of *The Dynasts*. This distant view, from high in space is an ironic commentary on the action. . . .

Orlando seems to stand clearly apart. It is the fantastic biography (with Victoria Sackville-West, the poetess, as its very real basis) of a hero who lives three hundred and fifty years, and who becomes heroine halfway through (and we know for certain that we are all more or less bi-sexual). How can we discover in all this the urgent reality of the other works? Should we say it: yet another book about time and duration, last born of the innumerable progeny of Bergson-Croce-Spengler, the last manifestation of an intellectual fashion which is becoming boring. . . .

Orlando is a witty fantasy. But that is not the true interest and reality of the book. *Orlando* is the portrait of an imagination, the symbolic painting of duration considered as an image store, and of the way in which the past reappears in the present. *Orlando* in one sense is a *Time Regained*, with a radical difference, a difference in tone. The painful tension in Proust's work comes from the anguish which passing time causes him and the importance he attaches to regaining it. The total lack of dramatic pressure, of emotive tonality in *Orlando* comes from the absence of the flow of life and of the peril of death. *Orlando* is the happy solution to a problem which is not posed. . . .

What distinguishes the poet is that for him everything is memory. By that, I mean to say that only sensation finds in him a ready interpretation, and evokes an image which is so intimate that it seems to be a recollection. Thus Orlando taking a lift in a department store:

[Quotes p. 270 'Now the lift' to 'in a treasure sack!' and p. 274 'How strange it is!' to 'filled with tears.']

It is here that I see the most striking comparison between *Orlando* and *Time Regained*, two very dissimilar works. If Proust insists so much in all his work, on the summoning of an image at sensation's bidding, it is because he feels that in this way all real images arise, both those which come from the biographical past and those from what one might call the poetic past. Here are two passages from *Time Regained* which are almost a commentary on Virginia Woolf's work:[1]

(Sometimes an impression hides) not ... an earlier experience but a new truth, a precious image which I was trying to discover by efforts of the kind one makes to remember something, as though our loveliest ideas were like musical airs which might come to us without our having ever heard them and which we force ourselves to listen to and write down....

Is not the most beautiful part of the *Memoires d'Outre Tombe* assimilable with my sensations relative to the madeleine.... Finally, in the case of Baudelaire, such reminiscences are still more numerous, evidently less fortuitous and consequently, in my opinion, decisive. It is the poet himself who with greater variety and leisure seeks consciously in the odour of a woman, of her hair and of her breast, those inspiring analogies which evoke for him 'l'azur du ciel immense et rond' and 'un port rempli de flammes et de mâts'. I was seeking to recall those of Baudelaire's verses which are based upon the transposition of such sensations.

Is it not a sign of real value in Virginia Woolf's work that it is so rich in universal ideas? Is it not a good indication of the quality of her writing that such important and difficult subjects as the dimensions of all existence have been with so much flexibility and variety transposed into an aesthetic order, that vision has been made from thought? We are not sure of having always demonstrated this. The critic deviates towards ideas as if drawn by an irresistible vice; and it is the last, least glorious, but perhaps not the least useful of his duties, to warn against his deformation.

(b) Paul Dottin, from 'Les Sortilèges de Virginia Woolf', *Revue de France* (Paris), April 1930, 556–66.

Paul Dottin (b. 1895). French university teacher of English. Literary critic, author of a study of Daniel Defoe.

All the novels of Mrs Virginia Woolf will soon be available to the French public: Stock have undertaken to publish all of them and have recruited a really excellent team of translators. *Mrs Dalloway* appeared

[1] *Time Regained*, translated Stephen Hudson (1931), 1968 (Chatto & Windus), 224, 276–7.

a few months ago with an enthusiastic preface by André Maurois. *To the Lighthouse* is in the press, and French translations of *Jacob's Room* and *Orlando* have been announced. *Mrs Dalloway*, it may be added, has been included in the syllabus for the degree in English, alongside the masterpieces of Jane Austen, George Eliot and Emily Brontë. Of the contemporary English writers we believe few will have the good fortune to find such zealous and persuasive champions on this side of the channel.

Does Mrs Woolf deserve so much devotion, dedication and enthusiasm? Yes, considering that it is the prime duty of translators to introduce the *avant garde* literature of England—that which has freed itself most completely from classical moulds and from the traditional rules, and which is farthest from French conceptions. For the novels of Mrs Woolf are as far as possible from the Latin habits of clarity, precision and order, in a word, from the Latin genius.

That is to say that reading a book by Mrs Woolf will be an arduous, at times repellent task, even for those who love Giradoux or Paul Morand. But Mrs Woolf is no prophet in her own country: only the admirers of Dorothy Richardson and Marcel Proust appreciate her—those who regard themselves as members of the intelligentsia and whom the ordinary sensible man has dubbed 'highbrows'. As for the Americans, their impression of Mrs Woolf and her works is summed up in the terse formula: 'a tough proposition'.

And yet Mrs Woolf's novels are worth the trouble involved in understanding them. In the first place, her language is very beautiful, as sober and clear as the thought is complex and obscure: the very able translations of S. David and M. Lanoire lose nothing of this precious quality. Secondly, Mrs Woolf has talent, a peculiar talent which delights in symbolism and reverie. . . .

> 'I will come,' said Peter, but he sat on for a moment. What is this terror? what is this ecstasy? he thought to himself. What is it that fills me with extraordinary excitement?
>
> It is Clarissa, he said.
>
> For there she was.

These are the last words of the novel (*Mrs Dalloway*). What do they mean? Probably that Clarissa Dalloway too kills herself. Logically, this seems to be Mrs Woolf's idea. Clarissa, like all the other characters in the book, has never ceased to deplore the void in her existence, and desire the strength to re-shape her life. In death she will find at last calm and serenity, just like Septimus, who was tortured by the impossibility of embracing his chimerical visions. Mrs Woolf is as nihilistic as the most sombre of the Russian novelists.

But one can also accept, with André Maurois, that Clarissa, having got over her exhaustion, resumes, sheerly by routine, the monotony of fashionable life. In which case, the novel is yet more pessimistic, the conclusion still more desperate: Man caught up in the wheels of social conventions no longer has the energy to make the gesture which will liberate him from ennui; the madman alone has the courage necessary to adopt the only possible solution: the leap into the void.

Whatever the conclusion may be, one sees how far Mrs Woolf's novel is from our classicism. The only link that one can find between one episode and another is that of a strict synchronism: the characters are close to each other in time and space and lead apparently different lives which are really similar because equally vain and empty.

In the main, the novel takes place in the minds of the three principal figures, Clarissa, Peter and Septimus. But the method of interior monologue does not avoid artificiality, for it involves an abuse of the flashback technique. At the precise moment that they enter upon the scene, the characters feel the need, as if by chance, to go over in their memory all their youth and career, all that the reader needs to know about them and their circle.

As for the absence of form, so alien to the French manner, that belongs to the oldest tradition of the English novel. It stems directly from the *Essays* of Addison, and from Fielding, who felt obliged to slip into *Tom Jones* moral disquisitions or discussions with his readers. In this respect Mrs Woolf—*horresco referens*—is completely conservative and traditional.

To the Lighthouse is clearly superior to *Mrs Dalloway*, for now and then it releases intense feelings which were completely lacking in the earlier novel. One comes across delightful passages on the joys of motherhood, the worries of a good hostess, and especially the occupation and dreams of children:

[Quotes pp. 94–5 'She heard them stamping' to 'in the garden.']

. . . Perhaps the French reader will be wearied, after a while, by the almost exclusive use of the nuances of the indirect style. Perhaps he will be irritated by certain odd reflections. Thus, whenever two characters meet, their first thoughts are: 'He smells of soap' or 'she is wearing those nice shoes which allow more room for her toes.' But just when boredom and irritation make one wish to put the book aside, a light, humorous touch reconciles us, for example, a 'slating' of English cooking:

[Quotes pp. 156–7 'It is putting cabbages' to 'English cook throws away.']

And yet the satirical element is never dominant, whereas the preceding novel, *Mrs Dalloway*, is in many respects a vast satire on London high society.

Like *Mrs Dalloway*, *To the Lighthouse* is a book constructed from a single sentence, which reappears like a leitmotif. There, it was, 'Don't forget my party.' Here, we have: 'If it's fine tomorrow we'll go to the lighthouse.'

. . . What is this symbol? What does the lighthouse represent, eternally lighting up the house when living and when dead? No one can say with any certainty. No doubt it is the human ideal, the perfect end which men strive to obtain in their dreams. At all events, the moral of Mrs Woolf's story is obvious: her nihilism has never appeared so clearly. 'No longer does anything mean anything to me.' James reaches the lighthouse at last, but he finds stone instead of diamond. Lily at last completes her painting, but it is a daub, not a masterpiece.

And yet Lily does not despair: she has had her vision. She has had a brief glimpse of the truth: happiness can exist, not of course in the quest for an impossible grail, but in performing humble everyday duties. Only Mrs Ramsay had been fully happy, for she had fulfilled her mission, that of a perfect mistress of the house. James, however, had a mystic ideal which was too elevated: he wished to reach the source of light, but comes to realise that he has been the victim of a mirage.

One can fancy that at the end of the novel the weary Lily retires from the world to lead a vegetating life, turning entirely to the past, and that the visitors to the lighthouse, after they have seen the nothingness of their illusions, are engulfed by the sea and the darkness.

The latest major work of Mrs Woolf, *Orlando*, is equally symbolic, but the totally new mode indicates a prodigious power of self-renewal in the author. What is life? The question is asked continually by the hero of the book. And the reader is tempted to reply: a simple external change, for the mind of man never changes! . . . There is a little of everything in *Orlando*. 'The English disease, love of nature' inflicts its ravages here to the great delight of the reader. The satirical element is abundant . . . there is, in the chapter where Orlando changes sex, a pastiche of the 'passionate style' of De Quincey which is particularly successful.

Yet, although it contains some magnificent pages, for example those which describe the Great Frost in the times of James I, Mrs Woolf's novel leaves the impression of something incomplete, disappointing and imperfect. Undoubtedly, this is because Mrs Woolf has allowed a fault to develop which was already evident in *Mrs Dalloway*: the mania of gossiping without rhyme or reason to her reader. She appears to feel the need for commenting on or explaining the least gestures of her characters. No doubt she is here in the purest tradition of the English novel, that of Fielding. But in her own novel she multiplies these intrusions excessively, arresting the action and appearing to take a perverse delight in irritating the reader. It is all the more annoying in that *Orlando* is full of anachronisms, most of them deliberate. Mrs Woolf loves to mystify to the point of spoiling her singular talent and harming her reputation as an artist. Many readers will not pause to notice the beauties of *Orlando*, persuaded as they will be that it is simply a piece of mystification.

To sum up, apart from *To the Lighthouse*, which deserves to go down to posterity as a whole, it is probable that only extracts of Mrs Woolf's work will appear acceptable to future generations. But she has not said her last word, for *Orlando* marks a considerable effort towards clarity, an almost complete renunciation of the Joycean pattern. If she keeps the originality of her form and thought whilst renouncing her taste for fantasmagorias and mirages, Mrs Woolf can write an immortal book. But she must remember that the self is hateful and that the modern reader is a big enough boy to understand all by himself that novel which his predilections have induced him to choose.

A ROOM OF ONE'S OWN

24 October 1929

79. From an unsigned review, 'Women and Books', *Times Literary Supplement*

31 October 1929, 867

'How she was able to effect all this is surprising, for she had no separate study to repair to, and most of the work must have been done in the general sitting-room, subject to all kinds of casual interruptions.' These unobtrusive words have grown familiar; Jane Austen, the surprising person, has emerged into what to her would have been an inconceivable fame. Mrs Woolf quotes the sentence in her essay, and it must have suggested the image for her title. It seems, certainly, to make a room of one's own look superfluous. But though there may have been men of letters, and perhaps women, who have been unperturbed by the chatter of their families, they probably did not feel obliged to hide their writing from the eyes of servants or visitors as Jane Austen did. By a sort of pre-established harmony within her she achieved the perfect result; the chief wonder lying, as Mrs Woolf observes, in the entire absence from her books of any signs of fear, protest or resentment aroused in her by doing something which it seemed not quite creditable to do. For 'a room of one's own', like the *arrière-boutique* of Montaigne, seems the natural symbol of detachment and calm; and it will stand as well for the material minimum of freedom, means and opportunity which is essential to a writer.

But—to keep to the main path of a delightfully peripatetic essay—these necessaries, spiritual and material, have been long in coming within the reach of women. It is common knowledge, no doubt, but it sparkles into life again as Mrs Woolf describes what might have happened to an imaginary gifted sister of Shakespeare. . . .

[An expository paragraph has been omitted.]

But the most interesting, if less diverting, points are those in which it touches the art of writing. It is certainly of interest to find an artist who has (one is tempted to say) so masculine a sense of literary form as Mrs Woolf remarking that women must devise a 'sentence' of their own, as the weight and stride of a man's mind are too unlike theirs to be useful. And since 'the book has somehow to be adapted to the body', theirs should perhaps be shorter and more concentrated than men's books. Their fiction, too, has counted for more than their poetry, even if the first impulse was poetic. Here, among other causes, may be the straits of poverty—one thinks of the tragic case of Charlotte Mew. However, in her work or Emily Dickinson's, as in the higher and more accomplished art of Christina Rossetti or Alice Meynell, a certain concentrated quality reappears. So it does in Katherine Mansfield's stories, where at times one feels the point is almost too exactly made. Perhaps such concentration in little is women's equivalent to masculine grasp. 'Grasp' seems to imply both a wider surface and a trenchancy not so much of emotion as of brain.

But here it is a question of the imaginative reason. Coleridge, who said that he had known strong minds 'with Cobbett-like manners' but never a great mind of that sort, believed that all great minds must be androgynous. And it is that thought of his which Mrs Woolf persuasively develops. There is nothing very startling in the belief that, with artistic natures at least, the man's mind has a share of the feminine and the woman's of the masculine, and that the two elements must fuse with and fertilize each other to produce a complete creation. So to Mrs Woolf Shakespeare seems the type of the androgynous unimpeded mind, 'though it would be impossible to say what Shakespeare thought of women'. It would be amusing, and at times perplexing, to go on with illustrations. Coleridge, for instance, pronounced Wordsworth to be '*all* man'. But we can hardly suppose that he excluded him from the great minds in consequence. Mrs Woolf may provoke some surprise when she says that Mr Galsworthy has not a spark of the woman in him. But though we may dispute cases, the principle itself bridges those divisions of sex-consciousness which are disastrous to our age and have led men, in Mrs Woolf's opinion, to write only with the male side of their minds. And her essay, while it glances in a spirited and good-tempered way over conflicts old and new, is really always bent on more intrinsic matters. These, one might say, are a love of life, a love of freedom and of letters; meeting in the conviction that if a writer does what he should he will bring us into the presence of reality.

80. V. Sackville-West, from a review, *Listener*

6 November 1929, 620

V. Sackville-West (1892–1962). Novelist and poet. A very close friend of Virginia Woolf. Her life and family history formed the basis of *Orlando*.

Mrs Woolf, as you probably know, is a critic as well as a novelist; but this little book, which is not a novel, is not pure criticism either. In so far as it is 'about' anything at all, it is a study of women, their circumstances (especially in the past), and the effect of those circumstances upon their writing. . . .

The burden of Mrs Woolf's exhortation to women is that they should be themselves, and should exploit their own peculiar gifts instead of trying to emulate the gifts proper to the masculine mind; and you will see also from these quotations that the book is not only full of ideas but also of commonsense. Mrs Woolf has perhaps never been given sufficient credit for her commonsense. Airy, fantastic, brilliant—all these adjectives have been lavished on her, till you might think her work as coloured but as empty as an iridescent bubble; you might overlook the fact that the fluttering leaves on the tree to which I compared her just now are tethered to solid boughs which in their turn are tethered to a solid trunk; you might forget that her extravagances, if they have imagination and poetry for grandparents on the maternal side, have also sense and erudition for grandparents on the paternal. I make this allusion to the ancestry of Mrs Woolf's creative genius all the more confidently because she herself, in this essay, indicates the need for something of the sort in reference to literature. No less a critic than Coleridge, she reminds us, said that a great mind is androgynous. She tells us a little parable of a man and a woman getting into a taxi and driving off together, and then she adds, 'Certainly when I saw the couple get into the taxi-cab, the mind felt as if, after being divided, it had come together again in a natural fusion. The obvious reason would be that it is natural for the sexes to co-operate.' Mrs Woolf is too sensible to be a thorough-going feminist. There is no such thing as a masculinist, she seems to say, so why a feminist? And she goes on to wonder (amateurishly, she says) whether there are two sexes in the mind corresponding to the two sexes in the body, and whether they also require to be united in order to get complete satisfaction and happiness? I know of no writer who fulfils this condition more thoroughly than Mrs Woolf herself. She enjoys the feminine qualities of, let us say, fantasy and irresponsibility, allied to all the masculine qualities that go with a strong, authoritative brain; and it is precisely this combination added to her profound knowledge of literature which fits her so admirably to discuss women in general, and women who write in particular. I hope all men will read this little book; it will do them good. I hope all women will read it; it will do them good, too.

81. Arnold Bennett, from 'Queen of the High-Brows', *Evening Standard*

28 November 1929, 9

I have often been informed by the elect that a feud exists between Virginia Woolf and myself, and I dare say that she has received the same tidings. Possibly she and I are the only two lettered persons unaware of this feud. True, she has written a book about me and a mythical Mrs Brown. But I have not read the book (I don't know why). True, I always said, until she wrote *To the Lighthouse*, that she had not written a good novel. But I have said the same of lots of my novelist friends. True, she is the queen of the high-brows; and I am a low-brow. But it takes all sorts of brows to make a world, and without a large admixture of low-brows even Bloomsbury would be uninhabitable.

One thing I have said of her: she can write. *A Room of One's Own* is a further demonstration of this truth. (She has her private notions about grammar, See p. 50.) And I have said that you never know where you are in a book of hers. *A Room of One's Own* is a further demonstration of this truth also. It is stated to be based on two papers read to the Arts Society of Newnham and the One-Damned-Thing-After-Another Society at Girton. On p. 6 she refers to herself as a lecturer. On p. 6 she suggests that you may throw 'it' into the waste-paper basket. Well, you can't throw a lecture into the waste-paper basket. You can only walk out from a lecture, or treat your ears as Ulysses treated the ears of his fellow-mariners.

The book has a thesis: namely, that 'it is necessary to have five hundred a year and a room with a lock on it if you are to write fiction or poetry.' With the implied corollary that women, being usually without five hundred a year of their very own, and liable to everlasting interruption, are at a serious disadvantage as novelists and poets.

The thesis is disputable. Dostoevsky wrote some of the greatest novels in the world while he was continually distracted by terrible extra-artistic anxieties. And I beg to state that I have myself written long and formidable novels in bedrooms whose doors certainly had no locks, and in the full dreadful knowledge that I had not five hundred a year of my own—nor fifty. And I beg to state further that from the moment when I obtained possession of both money and a lockable door all the high-brows in London conspired together to assert that I could no longer write.

However, Virginia Woolf's thesis is not apparently important to her, since she talks about everything but the thesis. If her mind was not what it is I should accuse her of wholesale padding. This would be unjust. She is not consciously guilty of padding. She is merely the victim of her extraordinary gift of fancy (not imagination). If I had to make one of those brilliant generalisations now so fashionable, defining the difference between men and women, I should say that whereas a woman cannot walk through a meadow in June without wandering all over the place to pick attractive blossoms, a man can. Virginia Woolf cannot resist the floral enticement.

Some will describe her book as a feminist tract. It is no such thing. It is a book a little about men and a great deal about women. But it is not 'feminist'. It is non-partisan. The author writes: 'Women are hard on women. Women dislike women. Women—but are you not sick to death of the word? I can assure you that I am.' Admirable attitude! And she comes to no satisfactory conclusion about the disparateness of men and women. Because nobody ever has and nobody could.

You may walk along Prince Consort Road, and through the open windows of the Royal College of Music hear the scrapings, the tinklings and the trillings of a thousand young people trying to make themselves professional musicians. And you may reflect that ten years hence nine-tenths of the girls among them will have abandoned all scraping, tinkling and trilling for love, domesticity and (perhaps) cradles. And you may think that you have discovered the origin and explanation of the disparateness of men and women. Not so! Great opera-singers have borne child after child, and remained great opera-singers.

82. M. E. Kelsey, from 'Virginia Woolf and the She-Condition', *Sewanee Review*

October–December 1931, 425–44

The writer, drawing on the explicit comments in *A Room of One's Own*, discusses the 'feminine' aspect of Virginia Woolf's work. It is a long article, with illustrations drawn from all of Virginia Woolf's work then published. The following brief extracts indicate the general line of the argument.

It is the feminine sides of life which motivate the greater part of Mrs Woolf's fiction. The root of plot and character and setting reach deep into a rich feminine soil. Such a statement demands careful definition, for Mrs Woolf's attitude is far from the polemics of traditional Feminism. From the ashes of those bitter conflicts has arisen a new conception of the whole problem, to which Mrs Woolf gives a form and a voice.

. . . She explains in *A Room of One's Own*, 'Different though the sexes are, they intermix. In every human being, a vacillation from one sex to the other takes place'. Not only that, but such duality is a necessity; 'It is fatal to be a man or woman pure and simple; one must be woman-manly or man-womanly.' For the mind, in order to accomplish its best work, must possess 'some stimulus, some renewal of creative power which it is the gift only of the opposite sex to bestow.'

. . . 'the feminine' is made up of all the delicate, the indefinable, the impalpable elements of existence; it is the surge of feeling as opposed to the balance of intelligence; it is mystery, not clarity; spirit, not matter. It is the transfiguring light that distinguishes one experience from another, happening from experience; it is poetry, not prose, life itself before thought has shaped it. The 'feminine' is universal and yet transitory, and it can be expressed only by brittle half-phrases, symbols, poetry.

. . . That Mrs Woolf's books should be built for and upon this side of existence seems peculiarly striking, for her own mind is, I think, more manly-womanly than woman-manly. Or perhaps it is not peculiar, but natural, that one sex-principle should be primarily interested in the other. At any rate—here is Mrs Woolf, possessed of as keen a critical mind, as masculine a wit, as any purely male writer of the day. Yet, in her creative work she interests herself in 'feminine' manifestations; yet she herself reacts to 'feminine' phases in a 'feminine' way. It is difficult to obtain much information explanatory of such a situation.

. . . Enter, here, the Spirit of the Age, bringing in its train whole barges full of Stream of Consciousness Novelists, of Impressionists and Expressionists and Vorticists and Fantasists and Painters of Abstractions, all endeavouring to express the inexpressible, to give form to the formless, with all Cassandra's eagerness and all William's critical interests. But Mrs Woolf has managed to compromise with the Spirit of her Age quite as successfully as did Orlando. The transaction is 'one of infinite delicacy, and upon a nice arrangement (of it) . . . the whole future of [her] works depends.' Mrs Woolf has been, no doubt, wafted towards her absorption with the 'feminine' or spiritual sides of life, in some degree by the trends of the age, which lead away from detail-for-detail's sake, from fact-for-fact's sake. But she has managed to remain herself for all that, with her own theories and methods and conceptions. Mrs Woolf has kept to those emotions and reactions to which her Cassandra-side responds instinctively; she has outlined entirely the 'feminine' aspect of such experiences as she has never felt, of situations with which she has no sympathy. The one-sided world thus created feels a bit strange, until one remembers that selection is the essence of any art. Mrs Woolf is connected with the 'she-condition': namely, in the very deepest wells of her own subconscious purpose. In those underlying places below rational or even instinctive recognition, every writer's ruthless aim is to justify his perception and conception of things, and to force people to see as he sees, perhaps to see *why* he sees. It is the crying need of the individual to prove the existence of his own world, in a life of bewildering variety and of deceiving appearances. In this 'life *is* like that' connotation, he sets forth his idea of living by creating a little model world, governed by his own selections from the actual universal laws (if such there be). And it is here, in this fundamental phase, that Mrs Woolf's conception of life still seems to conform to her own definition of 'the feminine'. All the points previously discussed are, of course, integral parts of her basic conception of life, as well as illustrations thereof. But speaking more generally, one can say: to her, living is enormously complex, enormously difficult; it is not simple, it is not logical, it is not focused on one point, as she conceives 'masculine' phenomena to be. There are myriad elements, all churning and turning and frothing and surging, and the wonder is that anything ever rises clearly to the top, long enough to be defined, for everything is somehow inextricably mingled with everything else. Life is mysterious, indefinable. The most one can do with explanation is something like this: (*Monday or Tuesday*) 'Life's what you see in people's eyes; life's what they learn, and, having learnt it, never, though they seek to hide it, cease to be aware of—what? That life's like that, it seems'. . .

And any experience, any perception thus pointed, thus transfigured, is worth life itself; here, in living intensely in the moment, in sensing Reality, in holding it to one's heart, is value—infinite value. By this feeling of significance is the incident and the world itself 'stabilized, stamped like a coin indelibly, among a million that slip by imperceptibly'. Each one of the novels is reducible to a series of such Pater-like moments. . . .

So Mrs Woolf tries to re-create the breath of the impalpable as it passes; and sometimes she succeeds, and we feel the breath on our face, and agree with Clarissa Dalloway and Septimus Warren Smith that this is all that matters—this ecstasy—and that death is better than its loss; and sometimes she fails, and leaves us with an exquisite metamorphic shred of chiffon in our hand, wondering what it is all about.

THE WAVES

October 1931

83. Unsigned review, *Times Literary Supplement*

8 October 1931, 773

Virginia Woolf was surprised at this reviewer's praise for her characters (see Introduction, p. 23).

What kind of book does one write after *Orlando*? That was an exception and a prodigy in more ways than one. Here, in *The Waves*, is something visibly in the line of Mrs Woolf's novels, and a return to the life we live, yet so singularly unconventional in its texture and form that one might fancy Orlando's vivid flashes of the past were the real, and this the dream and the prodigy.

For the book is, as it were, a piece of subtle, penetrating magic. The substance of life, as we are accustomed to see it in fiction, is transposed and the form of the novel is transmuted to match it. The six characters, a band of friends—three of each sex—reveal themselves from childhood's spring to the autumn or winter of their lives; but all they feel or do is given to us from their own lips, each taking up the one before in a kind of tranced, yet impetuous soliloquy. Each is alone with himself and yet aware of the others; in the middle and again at the end we see them reunited as a group, and finally Bernard, the man of words and contacts, gathers up the whole perspective. Such, in the barest words, is its scheme, which, fluid as it appears in the reading, has the nicest symmetry of arrangement. Its substance is not to be divided from its form; the form has been evoked by the essence—for substance seems too ponderous a word for the gleaming, darting drops of light which these lives are, as one sees them. As one of the girls says in an excited moment:

I see every blade of grass very clear. But the pulse drums so in my forehead, behind my eyes, that everything dances—the net, the grass; your faces leap like butterflies; the trees seem to jump up and down. There is nothing staid, nothing settled, in this universe. All is rippling, all is dancing; all is quickness and triumph.

It is a glittering rain of impressions and reactions, then, to which Mrs Woolf has reduced the experience of her characters? Not quite, though she seldom or never eschews the medium of the five senses. Their moods and selves are shown by a gesture, an image, a perception, but these are filaments in the consciousness of each speaker. Each of them is much more conscious than we habitually are—this sharpened and dramatized consciousness is the 'convention' of the novel—and utters not merely his sense of the moment, but, again and again, his secret individuality. Here, for instance, one of them enters a room:

[Quotes p. 91 'I smoothed my hair' to 'something once splendid'.]

and here another

[Quotes pp. 157–8 'The leaves might have hidden me' to 'I never join you happily'.]

One might say that in Mrs Woolf's novel life has turned into what she once described it as being—'a luminous halo, a semi-transparent envelope surrounding us from the beginning of consciousness to the end'. And the novel has turned into something very like a poem. This incisive and unflagging prose is as rapid as verse, and the utterances follow one another with a sort of rhythmical incantation. Sometimes they are frankly antiphons, and one always has that sense of a response; the book moves to that measure. This formal effect recurs with the further settings which have given it its title; prefixed to each movement of it there is a background of the sea, with changes from dawn to sunset. Here, it seems to us, the effect of a complete detachment does not quite succeed. It may be because Mrs Woolf does not keep our eyes on the sea, but diverts them to birds and fields and gardens; or it may simply be that these elaborate, often exquisite, passages are too deliberate altogether.

A poetic novel, as it certainly is, it is still—however peculiarly—a novel. The six people all have their idiosyncrasy of nature; Bernard, with his communicative, affable receptiveness; Louis, very conscious of humiliations, but with a kind of ruthless romanticism below his business efficiency; Neville, who lives with a concentrated inwardness and makes, we infer, a name; and the women—Jinny, who lives for her body and the sparkle of life; Susan, embedded in the country rhythm and motherhood; and Rhoda, a flying nymph of solitude. We watch them unfolding, and are aware of the silence under their speech, movement without action, and the flickering of that inmost flame of personality—call it spirit or ego—whose place is often vacant even in a novel of character. Mrs Woolf's uncommon achievement is to have made this visible, and it is hardly less of a feat, perhaps, to have shown life in a texture which matches it. It seems a proof by example that the matter of fiction can be changed and distilled to a new transparency. Yet there is as certainly a cost in the process. The book, with all its imaginativeness and often poignant feeling, leaves some sense of a void behind, if not of an actual desolation. It is not merely, perhaps, that we have been deprived of the usual comfortable upholsterings but that creative experience in life is of a closer tissue than this and demands a fuller view of its attachments. Alive as the novel is with the vividness of things, one feels in more than one sense that its spirits roam through empty places. Yet it is simpler, after all, to be grateful for a book that achieves its own aim and that no one else could have written.

84. Harold Nicolson, review, *Action*

8 October 1931, 8

Harold Nicolson (1886–1968), diplomat and writer. Married to V. Sackville-West, and a great friend of the Woolfs. He also gave a radio talk on Virginia Woolf's work and published 'The Writing of Virginia Woolf' in the *Listener*, 18 November 1931, 864. His best-known work is probably *Some People* (1927), which Virginia Woolf reviewed for the *New York Herald Tribune*.

A new novel by Virginia Woolf is always an event of importance. I prophesy that this morning's publication of *The Waves* will cause a literary sensation. For in this, her latest book, Mrs Woolf has carried 'the internal monologue' a stage further than was dreamt of even by Joyce. It forms the entire apparatus of her story. It expands the lyrical note which lurks always as the undertone to her writings into something antiphonal, sacerdotal, vatic. There is a note in this book which has never yet been heard in European literature.

As the symbol of her theme, Mrs Woolf has taken the flux and reflux, the strange purposelessness, of the sea as viewed from above and at a distance. Continually does this symbol cut across her vision, intruding into her images its battering restlessness, its unplumbed mobility, its incessant renewals of shape and energy.

Her whole intention is to depict the fluidity of human experience, the insistent interest of the inconsequent, the half-realised, the half-articulate, the unfinished and the unfinishable. She succeeds triumphantly. Her book sparkles with a thousand diamonds, and at times it is shrouded with solemn cloud-reflections.

Mrs Woolf has not attempted to give a consecutive narrative or to isolate distinct characters. Her aim is to convey the half-lights of human experience and the fluid edges of personal identity. Her six characters fuse, towards the end, into a synthesis of sensation.

It is important that this book should be read twice over. The book is difficult. Yet it is superb.

85. Frank Swinnerton, review, *Evening News*

9 October 1931, 8

Like Arnold Bennett, Swinnerton disliked Virginia Woolf's whole conception of the novel (see his comments on 'Mr Bennett and Mrs Brown', No. 40).

Something a good deal more valuable than skill is shown by Mrs Virginia Woolf in her new novel—or prose poem—*The Waves*, which is a series of rhapsodies, linked and contrasted, by which the spiritual life of half-a-dozen people, from childhood to maturity, is presented. I am not a great admirer of Mrs Woolf's work, and I find the present book as bloodless as its predecessors; but it would be idle to deny great distinction to the style, great beauty to many of the similes, and much subtlety and penetration to the author's intuitions. If to these qualities life had been added, I should have been lost in admiration of Mrs Woolf's gifts.

The scheme of the book is one which it must have been very interesting to plan, and one which it is interesting to consider. But the book itself is not very interesting to read. Partly this may be because all the six characters whose thoughts are communicated to us seem to think in the same tone, so that it is hard to remember which of them is which. But whatever the cause, the incessant chanting effect grows monotonous, and I found my attention distracted or exhausted as I read, even though, a moment before, I had been conscious of magic.

In the end, Mrs Woolf, too, seems to discover that she has failed; for she allows one of her rhapsodists to become an apologist and narrator. He tells us, too late, what the book has been about—the story. Hating story, denying story, Mrs Woolf tries to do without story. Her apologist says:

> It is a mistake, this extreme precision, this orderly and military progress; a convenience, a lie. There is always deep below it, even when we arrive punctually at the appointed time with our white waistcoats and polite formalities, a rushing

stream of broken dreams, nursery rhymes, street cries, half-finished sentences and sights—elm trees, willow trees, gardeners sweeping, women writing—that rise and sink even as we hand a lady down to dinner!

That is quite true; but if you remove outlines you are left with something approaching mush. Though we ourselves may be lost in sensations and reveries, we are not therefore, to others, the amorphous creatures of the Woolfian novel. And the characters in *The Waves* have, for the reader, no such personalities as those known to their friends. Seen, as it were, as receptive sensationalists, from within, they never live. Once, therefore, one is past the beauty of the author's writing, and the ingenuity of her associative power, one is conscious only of a luminous transparency which bears no relation to flesh and blood. Yet these characters are offered as human beings.

86. Gerald Bullett, review, *New Statesman and Nation*

10 October 1931, Literary Supplement, x.
'Virginia Woolf Soliloquises'

Because it is her constant endeavour to record the psychological minutiae of experience, to snare in words an incommunicable secret, and to show the bubble of consciousness shining, expanding, reflecting—in its depths and on the surface—the changing colours of the universe around it, Mrs Woolf's writing has always been 'difficult': by which I mean that it will yield its motive, its clear and luminous core, only to a reader who is ready to empty himself of preconceptions and to become in the highest degree receptive, patient, searching. In her fidelity to this austere purpose she has discarded one by one, as distractions, the various devices which most writers, and nearly all readers, have held to be not merely aids but obvious necessities of narrative. She does not, as Henry James did, starve the visual sense; her drama does not, as his did, take place in a sort of cerebral twilight where no sound ever falls (I exaggerate in the interests of definition). Indeed, it is precisely by a series of significant images, both visual and aural, that she seduces one's immediate attention; and the spell is reinforced by the exquisite cadences of her prose. But though she is lavish of imagery, having the poet's instinct for the concrete phrase, this imagery does not, for the most part, relate to the physical world from which it is borrowed: it is merely a translation, into terms of that world, of apprehensions not otherwise suggestible. Consciousness, the immediate experience, is her quarry: the objective universe is no more than a hypothesis. Reading her books in their order, one observes that she becomes increasingly jealous of the space given to the description of 'action'. From *Jacob's Room* onwards (except *Orlando*, which was an experiment in another kind) this 'action'—the physical behaviour of her characters—is more or less parenthetical, and outward phenomena—storms and sunsets, stars and flowers, the pageant of human bodies—are seen only as reflections in the moving mirror of consciousness, moments in a continuing time-sensation. In short, Mrs Woolf is a metaphysical poet who has chosen prose-fiction for her medium.

In her new book, *The Waves*, she pursues her peculiar technique to its logical extreme, and comes, in a sense, full circle. Six characters, three men and three women, speak in soliloquy against the background of the sea. We see them abstracted from time, lifted out of the circumstances of daily life. They have each a name, each a private and independent existence; but in one important respect they are all Virginia Woolf. Every novelist must create his people out of his own psychological substance; they live with his life; the book is an extension of his being. The ordinary novelist, however, in support of his conceit that these characters are separate from each other and from him, is at pains to differentiate them by describing their individual appearance, gestures, circumstances, physical habits, and above all by endowing each with an idiom of his own. But here, in Mrs Woolf's book, all these aids to illusion are deliberately dispensed with. Every novelist speaks through his various masks; but her masks on this occasion—Bernard, Susan, and so on—are confessed as such, and the voice speaking through them never varies, never disguises itself, speaks always in its own subtle literary idiom, and gives utterance to thoughts which the character in question (a child, let us say) could not, in nature, have had. It is not as if the author said: 'Here are certain people in this or that situation. And this is what they are thinking'. It is not even: 'This is what, though they are not thinking it, they have in their minds.' It is rather: 'If they were aware of themselves as I, their creator, am aware of them, and if, further, I were to lend them all the resources of my mind and art, this is what they could tell us.' Nothing, it is evident, could be more remote from naturalism than that. The quest for an ultimate personal reality, the resolve to pare away from the psyche all adhesive irrelevancies, has led this writer to adopt a purely non-representational convention, a classical formalism. No literary convention is more artificial, or in appearance more absurdly naive, than the soliloquy; and what Mrs Woolf does with it here is little short of miraculous. We see her people as personal essences. They mature; they grow old. The use of the first person singular is a transparent device; it is even, if you like, a kind of cheating, since, once we have accepted it, it gives us just that illusion of intimacy which, in logic, the method cannot for a moment support. But this only means that Mrs Woolf has solved, for herself, the problem of how one may eat one's cake and have it. It is impossible to describe, impossible to do more than salute, the richness, the strangeness, the poetic illumination of this book. The characters are not analysed, as in a laboratory: they are entered into, intuited. In each soliloquy in this pattern of soliloquies we ourselves are at the centre. We *are* Bernard, we *are* Susan, but with this difference: that we have borrowed, for a moment, the lamp of genius, and by its light may read the secrets of our private universe.

87. G. Lowes Dickinson, 'Your book is a poem', from a letter to Virginia Woolf

23 October 1931

Goldsworthy Lowes Dickinson (1862–1932), Cambridge don and writer on historical and philosophical themes. A close friend of some members of the Bloomsbury Group, especially Roger Fry and E. M. Forster. Virginia Woolf knew him only slightly. Reading his works some time after his death she came to the conclusion that he was always 'theorising about life; never living'. (*A Writer's Diary*, 261). But his comments on *The Waves* pleased her, and she replied: 'What you say you felt about *The Waves* is exactly what I wanted to convey. Many people say that it is hopelessly sad—but I didn't mean that. I did want somehow to make out if only for my own satisfaction a reason for things . . . But I did mean that in some vague way we are the same person, and not separate people. The six characters were supposed to be one'—(27 October 1931).

Quoted in E. M. Forster, *Goldsworthy Lowes Dickinson* (1934), 1962, 230–1.

Your book is a poem, and as I think a great poem. Nothing that I know of has ever been written like it. It could I suppose only be written in this moment of time. And now I understand or think I do to what you have been leading up all these years. The beauty of it is almost incredible. Such prose has never been written and it also belongs to here and now though it is dealing also with a theme that is perpetual and universal.

Oh dear what words, and even so only touching the least essential. For there is throbbing under it the mystery which all the poets and philosophers worth mentioning have felt and had their little shot at. I have only read it once and I see and know that it ought to be read often.

88. L. P. Hartley, from a review, *Week-end Review*

24 October 1931, 518

L. P. Hartley (1895–1973). Literary journalist, and later novelist.

[The characters] do not speak what is in their minds, they speak what is at the back of them: their inner consciousnesses are rendered articulate, but not dramatic, nor even coherent; they proceed from association to association, from speculation to speculation borne up on bubbles of pure aesthetic emotion. Surely never were so many moments of vision, so many flashes of arrowy insight, gathered together between the covers of a novel.

But vision of what? Insight into what? The page flickers before one's eyes like a pointillist picture, alive with golden notes, but so much has been disrupted, standards overturned, ideas blown skywards, the great body of knowledge has been punched so full of deadly holes that there is, it seems, no authority to whom we, or they, can refer for an answer to the simplest question. They ask rhetorical questions of the universe: 'Why turn one's head hither and thither?' 'Who is he?' 'Who is she?' But the universe, dissolved in the crucible of their minds, no longer exists; it is not an idea even. 'We have destroyed something by our presence,' says Bernard. 'A world perhaps.' True enough; they have even dimmed the sense of their own identities; it is the printed page that speaks; phrases and sentences of perfect beauty, strains seraphically free from taint of personality.

. . . The paradox of Mrs Woolf's book is that although she is suspicious of 'meaning', and finds conventional explanations hollow, she stars her pages with 'significance', isolated examples of significance, apprehended by the senses but bewildering to the mind. Her genius is like a shaft of sunlight breaking into a room—a golden medium in which float a million fiery particles but beyond that enchanted area the darkness is darker than it was.

89. Louis Kronenberger, *New York Times Book Review*

25 October 1931, 5

An interesting comparison between the method of *The Waves* and other forms of stream of consciousness writing and a discussion of the strengths and dangers of Virginia Woolf's new method (see Introduction, p. 24).

'About this time Bernard married and bought a house . . . His friends observed in him a growing tendency to domesticity . . . The birth of children made it highly desirable that he should augment his income.' That is the biographic style, and it does to tack together torn bits of stuff, stuff with raw edges. After all, one cannot find fault with the biographic style if one begins letters 'Dear Sir,' ends them 'yours faithfully' . . . though one may be humming any nonsense at the same time—'Hark, hark, the dogs do bark,' 'Come away, come away, death.'

So speaks one of Mrs Woolf's characters in *The Waves*, much as once before Mrs Woolf herself, in 'Mr Bennett and Mrs Brown', spoke in derogation of superficial realism in the novel and in defense of a less hackneyed, a less 'probable', a less restricted presentation of life. Her own break with traditional fiction of the Arnold Bennett school, a break due equally to her temperament and her talent, came early; and with each successive novel it has become more pronounced. Indeed, considerable as the distance is from *Clayhanger* to *Jacob's Room* it is even greater from *Jacob's Room* to *The Waves*. And the distance traversed is not merely in method; the very substance of her novels has undergone an ever increasing change. In creating new forms, she has found new materials to fit them. What precedent is there for the interlude called 'Time Passes' in *To the Lighthouse*, for the exact kind of jeu d'esprit accomplished by *Orlando*? But all these innovations have been but steps leading up to *The Waves*, where Mrs Woolf, so far as the novel is concerned, has almost reached the jumping-off place.

She has not done so in *The Waves* for what would appear to be the simplest reason: its form. In form, to be sure, *The Waves* is possibly original in fiction—it is told entirely in soliloquies. All that we know of the six characters whose destinies we follow from childhood to old age is conveyed by them in a succession of speeches addressed only to the reader; there is no conversation between them and no direct narrative. But the use of the soliloquy in fiction (it has already been done on a smaller scale by other novelists) does not in itself drastically alter the sphere of the novel: it has always been used on the stage exactly as stream-of-consciousness or interior monologue have come to be used in the novel—to convey, directly, the workings of a character's mind. Used for the same purpose in the novel, highly artificial though it is, it can have the advantage over interior monologue of permitting a more articulate, because more rhetorical, utterance. Characters are not only thinking; they are also expressing themselves, and there is no reason why the author should not express their thoughts for them with an art that is frankly his rather than theirs. What is more, these people have a formal existence wholly in keeping with the idea of a novel—they go to school, they go to work, they marry, they have love affairs, they grow older, they die. What could be more traditional?

But this existence is formal only, and the real reason why *The Waves* comes close, as a novel, to going out of bounds is that its true interests are those of poetry. Mrs Woolf has not only passed up superficial reality; she has also passed up psychological reality. She is not really concerned in *The Waves* with people, she is hardly concerned in the prosaic sense with humanity: she is only concerned with the symbols, the poetic symbols, of life—the changing seasons, day and night, bread and wine, fire and cold, time and space, birth and death and change. These things treated separately, as facts, are indeed the stuff of a novel; but treated collectively, as symbols, they are the stuff of poetry. In spirit, in language, in effect *The Waves* is—not a poetic novel but a poem, a kind of symphonic poem with themes and thematic development, in prose. It is as weak in genuine perceptiveness as it is rich in sensibility; and even when a character seems most skilful in penetrating himself, it is the essence of a mood that he captures, not a truth. Mrs Woolf does not give us her characters as men and women; she gives them to us clearly in seed (Rhoda, for example, is 'frightened and awkward') and in seed they remain throughout the book. Their thoughts, their words, their preliminary differences from one another become stylized and they themselves fit, at length, into a verbal pattern, half ornamentally. They are not six people but six imagist poets, six facets of the imagist poet that Mrs Woolf is herself.

This prose, this imagery, is not in other words a medium, but an end in itself. The texture of the prose is a warp of sensory impressions woven into woof of poetical abstraction. As prose it has very often a high distinction—it is clear, bright, burnished, at once marvellously accurate and subtly connotative. The pure, delicate sensibility found in this language and the moods that it expresses are a true kind of poetry. And since literature comes before the novel, and *The Waves* reaches the level of literature, whether it is a good or bad novel, or any novel at all, is not really important. Bernard's summing up at the end, for instance, of what their lives have meant—a cohesive, exquisite and sometimes moving stretch of writing—must be allowed, if no precedent exists for it, to set its own.

The question still remains, however, as to just how good this book is, not if you please as a novel, but as a kind of poetry, as literature. Certainly it has seductive form (how smoothly, for example, the time-sense operates in carrying these people through life); certainly it contains much distinguished and beautiful writing; certainly it reveals exquisite sensibility. These qualities make it good enough to deserve the most careful scrutinizing, when high standards of comparison must be brought into play. And measured by those standards, though it survives as something rare and unique enough, it emerges as minor writing. It cannot satisfy the demands of either important fiction or of important poetry. There is something pale, mild, wistful, sentimental about its poetic feeling—it voices too facilely, almost (despite its fine prose) too conventionally, man's feeling about himself in the universe, his longings for the past, his regret at time passing, his fear of death. No one has ever described better than Mrs Woolf has here our common wish to imprint on our memory all the detail of a scene before it changes, to arrest a moment in time; and yet it is simply a marvellous description, it is not quite vision. And all along the line it is a nostalgic, not quite a visionary, quality that she has captured; it is always sensibility she has, never passion; we never get, in a mystical flash, the universe, only the many separate things in nature. On an extensive scale she has written imagist poetry of the first order—a very far cry from the 'biographic style.' But a very far cry, also, from greatness.

90. Storm Jameson, review, *Fortnightly Review*

November 1931, 677–8

Storm Jameson disliked the 'cleverness' of the book's method, but thought its essential value remained in spite of this. She also pointed out the inadequacy of the 'stream of consciousness' label (see Introduction, p. 24).

When I had read a dozen pages of this book I said: 'I shall begin my review with some such phrase as this: Criticism of Mrs Woolf's work is difficult because of the reverence one feels for it, and for her immitigable integrity.' After that I thought I should try to find careful respectful words, to say that the convention which Mrs Woolf has adopted for this book is one that a clever writer might have thought of and a great writer would have rejected as—clever. Before long I had abandoned this superficial judgment with the conviction that the book's especial quality made any undergraduate cleverness in its scheme of no importance.

Six characters are revealed at varying periods in their lives from childhood to old age. They reveal themselves, speaking in soliloquy, a few strands from the thoughts of each mind being woven in with the thoughts of the other minds to form the invisible web that holds them together in division. The change of time is marked, struck, by the recurrent image of the sea, from dawn to night. The progression is only in Time, since the characters, though their movements are described, remain static.

There are two ways by which this book can be approached. Looked at directly, it allows itself to be labelled as a novel in the 'stream of consciousness' method. The label is inadequate. It describes only the surface of the book, which is a succession of flashes, some long, some brief, as if the bird skimming the stream were now impatient, darting down and away again, and now content to fly for long minutes directly above the water, noting every stone on the bed and every blade bent by the current. Images recur, as a turn of the stream recalls an earlier one.

The other way of approach brings us nearer the hard core of the book. Mrs Woolf's preoccupation as a writer is not, after all, with appearances—despite the exquisite care with which she describes natural beauty:

> Rivers became blue and many-plaited, lawns that sloped down to the water's edge became green as birds' feathers softly ruffling their plumes. The hills curved and controlled, seemed bound back by thongs, as a limb is laced by muscles; and the woods which bristled proudly on their flanks were like the curt, clipped mane on the neck of a horse.

Appearances, and the relations between appearances, form the subject matter of almost all novels. Writers can be divided into honest or dishonest (romantic, sentimental, melodramatic, etc.) by their attitude to these. The impulse of the writer is to record, to place some scene, some moment, out of the reach of time. The pleasure given to the reader is that of recollection, or the sight of something new and strange. Once in a long while a writer appears whose interest is less in the appearance then in the essence. Such a writer comes very early to the point where the labour of recording events and conversations, of portraying characters who go through all the motions of everyday life, becomes intolerably wearisome and futile. Mrs Woolf seems to have reached this point. In this book she is striving—without the concessions made in her earlier books—to convey a *whole* vision, the essence of life, not a story-full of scattered and fragmentary forms.

The effort shows itself in her prose, which in this book has become more incisive and sinewy. A more profound effect is that on her passages of natural description. Descriptive prose is generally a sort of bastard writing which tries to paint with words. It tries to make you see a sunrise—which is the proper work of a painter—as the work of a musician must be to make you hear it. Mrs Woolf's way with a sunrise is to try to make you *think* it. The words she uses to describe it are not the equivalent in speech of the actual scene (description of colours, changes of light, etc.) but the image suggested to her mind by the picture-words and written down in their place. Thus the sunrise is a woman 'couched beneath the horizon' who raises a lamp.

In order to strive for a whole vision (to achieve it is ultimately impossible) Mrs Woolf has made enormous sacrifices. She is like a woman who has turned her back on life and watches it passing in a mirror, so that nothing shall shake the steadiness of her glance, none of those distractions, those sudden blindings, that come from touching what one sees.

91. Two opposing American views

1931

(a) Robert Herrick, from a review, 'The Works of Mrs Woolf', *Saturday Review of Literature* (New York), 5 December 1931, 246.

Robert Herrick (1868–1938). American novelist and Professor of English at Chicago University. In this article he was reviewing the American Uniform Edition of Virginia Woolf's works as well as *The Waves*. He argued that there was a development in her work from the particular to the general, culminating in *The Waves*, in which style is emphasised at the expense of content. In the same issue of the *Saturday Review* a letter appeared deploring precisely this kind of approach to *The Waves* and criticising American reviewers for their unenthusiastic reception of the novel (see next item, No. 91b).

With dispassionate despair, with entire disillusionment I surveyed the dust dance; my life, my friends' lives, and those fabulous presences, men with brooms, women writing, the willow tree by the river—clouds and phantoms made of dust, too, of dust that changed, as clouds lose and gain and take gold or red . . . mutable, vain. I, carrying a notebook, making phrases, had recorded merely changes; a shadow, I had been sedulous to take note of shadows. How can I proceed now, I said, without a self, weightless and visionless, through a world weightless, without illusion?

So Bernard, the most definitely loquacious of the phantoms in *The Waves*, phrases the dilemma of the modern world. But here we are concerned less with the dilemma and Bernard's reaction to it than the effect of such an attitude on the creative artist, on Mrs Woolf's various volumes where life is projected for our inspection imaginatively. To quote again the candid Bernard:

[Quotes pp. 59–60 'Now begins to rise in me' to 'make me what I am.']

Such an intense consciousness of futility commonly leads to sterility, as in Bernard's case. Let us see.

'Nothing exists outside us' (says another phantom—the Solitary Traveller in *Mrs Dalloway*) 'except a state of mind.' Mrs Woolf, therefore, has been concerned almost wholly with different 'states of mind' from *The Voyage Out* to *The Waves*, which aspires to summarise all states of mortal mind. It is a curious progress from the particular to the general.

[Survey of Virginia Woolf's fiction from *The Voyage Out* to *To the Lighthouse* omitted]

She has achieved a style, her style. Which in itself becomes a temptation to further experimentation, and the results we have in *Orlando*, which is almost purely a stunt, and in *The Waves*, which is style and very little more. In these two books the appeal of the universal has quite overwhelmed the sense of the particular. The seed of *Orlando* is to be found in the earlier books, e.g.:

[Quotes *Jacob's Room*, p. 96 'The lamps of London' to 'millions of pages?']

As for *The Waves*, it cries out page upon page for quotation, so easy, abundant, sure is the flow of words on which the burden of its theme is borne. 'Words and words and words, how they gallop—how they lash their long manes and tails!'

As a vehicle of expression the English novel has moved a long way from the ponderous work of George Eliot, testimony to the accelerated pace of our intellectual life. It is more open to question how far the novel has moved, is moving in content; as, let us say, a record of the lives lived at any given time. For this last, surely, is one of the proper functions of literature, an inevitable function, to be the record of that civilization from which it springs. If instead of the traditional visitor from Mars we substitute a convinced communist, someone from Russia informed and acute enough to perceive differences, what can we imagine would be his reflections on the world (the English-speaking part of it) as gleaned through the pages of Mrs Woolf's novels? He might smile benignly at the picture of Percival in *The Waves*, one of the phantoms who never speaks but whose existence nevertheless seems to have a profound influence on the more vocal phantoms of the tale. Percival, 'lounging on the cushions, monolithic', is the ideal of English imperialism:

[Quotes *The Waves*, p. 97 'Time seems endless' to 'he is—a God.']

(Gandhi seated at the council table in London would surely smile!) Our communist critic might pass over the mystical silence that falls on a London street when royalty (or mayhap a prime minister) puts his face to the window of a passing motor car as merely a playful gesture on the part of the novelist, possibly (but improbably) ironic in intention.

But he would surely not overlook the fact that practically every one of the novelist's characters existed on the exertions of others, on some unearned increment of society, for which they pay, if they pay at all, by being ornamental, loyal, or serviceable in small routine ways. Nor —what is far more important—that, although these characters chatter a great deal about literature and art and cognate matters, none of them is distinguished in action or in thought, and, most damnatory of all, they assume the futility, and the inevitability of their world. One would not need to be a communist to become convinced that no society composed of such human beings as Mrs Woolf has projected can possibly long endure whether in England or elsewhere.

The multiple reflection of a dying race, this twilight of small souls, may very well be the dramatized intention of the novelist. But one doubts it. One feels rather that in the case of Mrs Woolf the novelist has been hypnotized by the flow of lives around her, and that her progress from concern with the dreary particulars of her forlorn universals is but the rationalization of the intellectual in face of futility.

Is it possible that, in order to have a literature with a more vital sense of life than that I have been describing, we shall have to suffer a revolution of some sort, so that *homo sapiens* (or his successors) can regain that primitive, passionate, unreasoned conviction of the reality and the significance of the life he is living, which he is so rapidly losing? It may be so. Meantime, it is a pity that our cleverest writers—those whose words are most eagerly caught up by the quick youth of the day, who are recognized as their guides—do not seek to appeal to more of their fellow men. It is always a pity when the head becomes separated from the heart and the instincts, and no longer leads! It has not been thus in the past, Shakespeare (whose name comes so often to the lips of Mrs Woolf's characters) is an instance, where the best mind of his age found an expression that appealed, still appeals to myriad lesser minds. There have been many others. But not a Joyce, a T. S. Eliot, a Proust... Mrs Woolf, so richly endowed, so admirably equipped for the novelist's widest appeal, should not be content with the acclaim of a clique, however distinguished its members may be.

(b) Earl Daniels, letter to the editor, *Saturday Review of Literature* (New York), 5 December 1931, 352.

Earl Daniels. American university teacher. Here he gives a diametrically opposite view to that of Robert Herrick in the previous item, which appeared in the same issue of the *Saturday Review*.

In America we incline to make much of the condescension of British critics toward our literature. I wonder if our treatment of Mrs Woolf's latest novel may not be an indication that American reviewers are likely to look and pass by on the other side, where British fiction is concerned.

So far as I have seen them, reviews of *The Waves* have been little more than casual. There has been talk of style, which one who knows is ready to take for granted with Mrs Woolf, although here, it seems to me, she has come nearer to fusing prose and poetry into an expression of unapproached beauty than she has in any of her previous writing. There has been talk of experiment, of the absence of plot, of vagaries of punctuation and sentence structure, of a hundred other superficial things which don't very much matter. And there has been enough comment on difficulty to warn off any reader who doesn't happen to agree with St Thomas Aquinas that beauty—even like truth and goodness—is one of the most difficult things in the world, demanding a strenuous effort, which, in the end, is more than adequately rewarded.

But who has spoken clearly out to pronounce *The Waves* one of the most important novels of our day, as it so certainly is, worth any number of meretricious best-sellers and book club selections; a book which, on its appearance, should have met with a 'hats off' respect from the critics?

In the first place, it is life caught from the angle of one of life's sharpest mysteries—the sense of time passing. Mrs Woolf has experimented with time passing in *To the Lighthouse* and in *Orlando*. In *The Waves* she passes beyond experiment to mature accomplishment, so that I venture the verdict that better than any other novelist she has solved one of the major problems of fiction, and has actually given the reader a full realization of the time element. Secondly, Mrs Woolf has subtly shown the changes wrought by the movement of time. They are not changes to be easily apprehended, to be realized as one realizes that a friend is today wearing a brown suit where yesterday he wore a blue one. But they are none the less real for our inability to see. We do not see; but we feel the changes which quite defy our efforts to account for them. So Bernard, in the final section of the book, adding up the differences in his personal appearance, must admit, baffled by the problem, that the whole is more than the sum of parts.

Time and change, the impinging of time and experience upon individuals make up the important substance of *The Waves*. And the power and significance of the novel is in the effects wrought by time and change, until Louis becomes the practical man of affairs, Susan the matron of domesticity. Jinny the hard-surfaced sophisticate, and so on . . . And yet the summary is only tentative. Mrs Woolf is too wise to believe that the subtleties of human personality can be defined in a label, and she makes Louis, Susan, and Jinny more, even to themselves, than the convenience of a ticket can define. Perhaps Bernard best illustrates the point of view. Phrase-making *littérateur*, man of pose, only in the end does he succeed in putting off pose and phrase to face the real self, able triumphantly to declare, 'Against you I will fling myself, unvanquished and unyielding, O Death.' Then only is it time for the waves, as they do in Mrs Woolf's final sentence, to break on the shore.

The value of *The Waves* is in its significant presentation, to a generation which has largely forgotten, of what literature, when it has known itself, has always regarded as of first importance: man in the midst of things, man set upon by things, man confused, facing that inner real self of whose existence he feels sure. Whereas the Psalmist turned outward to God and queried, 'What is man that Thou art mindful of him?' Mrs Woolf's characters turn to that inward self and question, 'What then is this *I*, and for what does it count?' And so the book, based as it all essentially is on the elemental dualism of reality, becomes the eternal drama of subject and object, of inner and outer, of the eternal and the flux. Being that, and being written out of all of Mrs Woolf's mastery of her craft, *The Waves* is a novel of first importance; one of the few which have come in our own day with so much as a small chance to survive the vigorous test of time.

92. Unsigned review, *San Francisco Chronicle*

6 December 1931, 2b

Most people are going to find *The Waves* extremely difficult reading—all people, in fact, excepting those who are prepared to accept the author's highly artificial trick in writing it for the sake of the poetic images she invokes. Those readers being certainly in the minority, it is hard to see why Mrs Woolf chose so odd a manner to convey what she had to say.

In itself the trick Mrs Woolf uses is not new; it is simply the trick of soliloquy, long the exclusive property of the stage, excepting for brief and occasional fictional appearances. In *The Waves*, the reader is permitted to follow the fortunes of six closely associated characters from youth to old age, entirely through listening to them talk to themselves about themselves—'think' to themselves about themselves might be better. What those people do is directly in the tradition of the novel (although nothing they do is more than mildly exciting); the newness consists merely in the author's chosen vehicle of expression.

It cannot be denied that through her method she has obtained some richly poetic effects. Of a symbolist turn of mind she sees things—even her characters and the vicissitudes that befall them—as symbols; she is extraordinarily sensitive to impressions; she has imaginative talent; she has a subtle and brilliant way with words.

But after all is said and done, her people remain poetic reflections.

They are simply six Mrs Woolfs, they are not more than attenuated shadows—brilliant, many-sided, tricky, but still shadows—of the real people the reader has a right to expect.

The Waves, then, is more like a poem than a novel, but it is not quite either one. It is more an exercise in words and impressions and ideas—an exercise in images perhaps. No doubt it is a beautiful exercise, but it lacks the reality, the passion, the association with life that would bring it into relation with those who must read it. And lacking that passion, that association, it lacks the significance that would make it a fine book.

93. Gerald Sykes, review, *Nation* (New York)

16 December 1931, 674–5

Gerald Sykes (b. 1903). American novelist.

The word 'modern' has more significance today than it probably ever had before. No century can have been so conscious of its difference from other centuries as the twentieth. To go into this consciousness, this 'modernism', would require a great deal of space; but if we confine ourselves to the arts, and to a very brief glance at them, we observe, beginning several years ago, a considerable number of clever people—not necessarily artists—who nevertheless desired to 'express themselves'. (Some began in poetry or painting and ended in advertising or lampshades.) They were much too ingenious, too renascent to be content with the art forms that they found. Change, unconventionality, experiment were in the air. In literature, in prose, the old novel form displeased them. They wanted 'new forms'. It irked them to be confined to realistic narration, which precluded a language like that of the Elizabethans, which they envied.

The present volume is one of the culminations of that movement. In *The Waves* Mrs Woolf has carried her well-known experiments to their farthest. It is unquestionably a new form, a novel told entirely in soliloquies. The six characters, close friends, never speak to each other from childhood to old age. The only direct narration describes the symbolic journey of the sun, between chapters, from east to west. It is a novel, as every page testifies, that hangs upon a theory. This theory is that by not bothering to be natural the author will be enabled to deal with life and beauty as her ancestors dealt with them, and the lost resources of English literature, particularly its exalted language, will be reclaimed.

The story of *The Waves* is schematic, frankly inconsequential. It is a book that quotation will describe best. Neville has received word that Percival, whom he loves, has died:

> Oh, to crumple this telegram in my fingers—to let the light of the world flood back—to say this has not happened! But why turn one's head hither and thither? This is the truth. This is the fact. His horse stumbled; he was thrown. The flashing trees and white rails went up in a shower. There was a surge; a drumming in his ears. Then the blow; the world crashed; he breathed heavily. He died where he fell . . . Come, pain, feed on me. Bury your fangs in my flesh. Tear me asunder. I sob, I sob.

Some sacrifice must be made, of course, for so much grandeur of speech and emotion. Genuineness, reality, is too much to hope for under circumstances like these. No one can be expected to believe in Neville's grief; it is obvious that he (like all the other characters, in all the other situations) is striking an attitude. In order that Mrs Woolf may write like her ancestors it is necessary that her book be hollow throughout. There is irony, therefore, in her choice of the soliloquy form, which, since of all forms that is the most susceptible to self-consciousness, was the one best suited to betray this hollowness.

Culturally, despite its lofty traditionalism, *The Waves* suggests a pretty lampshade—a well-educated lampshade, smart, original, advanced. Not an ordinary lampshade by any means, but one that has been a mode of self-expression. A confusion peculiar to our country makes it necessary to point out the important differences between a desire for self-expression and the true creative urge. It is not the latter, it is not an artist's passion, that we discern in *The Waves*. There is beauty—one has the sensation of being smothered in beauty—but it is synthetic. Unfortunately, criticism of new imaginative literature is in such bad shape today that most people, hearing that *The Waves* has a 'new form', will lump it indiscriminately with the rest of 'modernist' fiction, and particularly with *Ulysses* by James Joyce. No two books could better exemplify the difference between a desire for self expression and the true creative urge. In *The Waves* we see what happens to an amiable talent that lacks an inner drive; we see virtuosity that has finally become disconnected from inspiration, virtuosity therefore that has lost its original charm and turned into a formula; we see a torrent of imagery because the imagist tap has been left running. In *Ulysses* we see a genuine work of art. It has nothing to do with the tea-room modernism that we have been discussing.

Anyone will perceive that the matter did not necessitate the form of *The Waves*. The form was born simply of restlessness, whim, a desire for novelty. And the novelty is not new; in every preening sentence we hear—we are expected to hear—a cadence of old. Isn't it odd that an appetite for experiment should be blended with an appetite for the past, that modernism should lead to archaism? Perhaps this kind of modernism was conceived not in the midst of modern life, but far removed from it, in a hushed, luxurious library, surrounded by the classics.

94. Edwin Muir, review, *Bookman* (New York)

December 1931, 362–7

Mrs. Woolf's first novel was *The Voyage Out*; *The Waves* is her latest. There is little in common between those two books, one is tempted to say, except the sea, which is in them both. The sea indeed is in all Mrs. Woolf's books, either as a background or a memory, and not even the walls of London can keep it out. Her mind appears loath to travel quite beyond sight or sound of it, and she employs it by preference as a reservoir of similes and metaphors. It appears in the opening page of

Mrs. Dalloway, which is a novel whose very theme is London, and one remembers also that other passage describing the heroine sewing a silk green dress. She 'collected the green folds together and attached them, very lightly, to the belt. So on a summer's day waves collect, overbalance, and fall.' The simile is recondite and yet strangely apt; it could have occurred only to a writer who thought often about the sea, so often that it came to hold more and more unexpected and abstruse correspondences. In *To the Lighthouse* the sea has actually grown dangerous, becoming something very like a symbol, a fact which may help to explain the occasional unreality of that book. It may help to explain also why in *The Waves* one of the characters damns symbolism so heartily. There is no symbolism, however, in *The Waves*; there is, on the contrary, something in comparison with which symbolism appears a mere makeshift.

But without trying to discover what the sea is a symbol for in Mrs. Woolf's books, it is clear enough that it stands for something in her imagination, and it is this something that connects her first book with her latest, and at the same time, taking advantage of the privilege of an ocean, explains the great distance between them. *The Voyage Out* was at least innocently symbolical; it was at once a very remarkable first novel in the conventional style of the time, owing a little to Chekhov, as most good novels did just then, and also a first voyage out over unknown seas where, at least as a possibility, lay the islands which Mrs. Woolf later discovered.

There is, for instance, in *The Voyage Out* as in its immediate successor *Night and Day*, that sense of a confusion of categories, of tragedy and comedy coexisting in the same situation, which she found such original ways of expressing in her later books. At first she conveyed this mixture of comedy and tragedy as certain of the English novelists had done before her; Sterne in particular, the supreme master in this style; and Scott, a writer whose name recurs persistently in her books, almost like a refrain; but she did not permit herself their wholehearted resignation to a shamelessly luxurious emotion; it brought her troubled thought rather than care-free effusion. In this she complied with the spirit of the age. For one reason or another—perhaps it is the spread of a more scientific way of regarding everything, including our emotions, perhaps it is merely that the emphatically unemphatic code of the public schools is extending everywhere—a novelist nowadays who values his or her intelligence is reluctant to deal in tears, far less therefore in tears and laughter in the same breath. We are so much more austere in such matters than our ancestors that scenes which were to them an opportunity for people of sensibility to evince the delicacy of their feelings now disgust us by their indelicacy. We are repelled indeed by quite a number of things in these half-comic, half-pathetic scenes: by the unnecessary piling on of the agony, the almost nonsensical clash between two zones of emotion, two worlds of emotion, and by the conduct of the novelist, who makes not the slightest effort to square them, but instead is transparently pleased at having arrived at such a happy sentimental conjuncture, and wishes us to admire him for his punctuality.

Tears are a solvent, laughter is a catharsis, but in an age when people analyze their emotional responses, these particular ones too must lose something of their authority, until it becomes doubtful whether they can claim even to be legitimate. So the sort of emotional complex which once evoked them, either singly or simultaneously, and in doing so apparently resolved itself, nowadays continues to burden the writer's mind, which in turn has to work at high pressure to resolve it and get rid of it. In other words the art of fiction has become more intellectual. So that what was a glorious opportunity a hundred or even fifty years ago has turned into a tormenting problem, which, sometimes much against his will, leads the novelist on through a whole series of questions: How can such contrasts exist? What are tragedy and comedy? What is experience? and finally, Why am I asking all these questions at all, seeing that I know there is no answer to them? Mrs. Woolf's questions begin, I think, from this problem of the coexistence of comedy and tragedy, at any rate from a perceived fundamental ambiguity in life, to which laughter and tears, even in solution, are not a sufficient or even an apposite reply. Starting from this problem, and it is formulated in her first two books, the progressive development of Mrs. Woolf's art, up to its crown in her latest book, is quite comprehenisble.

Yet in spite of that her first two books are very unlike their successors. In them she conscientiously accepted the novel as it was; she treated its limitations with solicitous respect; she seemed resolved above all to avoid the characteristic virtues which we recognize now as hers: she refused to take any short cuts, and she eschewed not only lightness, but the very appearance of it. Parts of *Night and Day* are actually dull, and not with a naturally outpouring dulness, but with the more deadly sort secreted by a writer resolved to concentrate on her job and carry it out according to given rules whatever the spectator may think; it is a kind of dulness that may almost be called disinterested, even self-sacrificing. From the writing of *Night and Day* Mrs. Woolf must have learned a very great deal, but apart from that the book is a fine one; if the mould did not suit the author's genius, what she poured into it was entirely her own. There are scenes in it which persistently linger in the memory: the meeting between Denham and Rodney on the Embankment, and Katherine's wanderings through London on the evening that she broke her appointment. There is also that exquisite interior, the Hilbery household, and the delightful Mrs. Hilbery. The strange thing about *Night and Day* as about *The Voyage Out* is the general not displeasing grayness as of a winter's day in London; the light which irradiates every scene she touched later is quite absent.

It began to tinge her work as soon as she entered on what may be called her experimental stage. There is a glimmer of it in *Monday or Tuesday*, a small volume of sketches; it flickers brilliantly but fitfully in *Jacob's Room*, shines steadily in *Mrs. Dalloway*, fades considerably in *To the Lighthouse*, but in *The Waves* gives a more intense light than ever before, a light from which veil after veil has fallen. *The Waves* is so greatly superior to anything else of Mrs. Woolf's that one is tempted to consider the rest of her work, even the exquisite *Mrs. Dalloway*, as irrelevant, and to take this as the sole measure of her genius.

But that would be unjust, for Mrs. Woolf is one of those writers whose very failures and half-successes are valuable as marking a line of development. So *Jacob's Room* and *To the Lighthouse* with their hesitancies, their occasional dulnesses, their traces of falsity, are more to be admired than the easy success of *Orlando*. *Orlando* is a charming and unreal trifle; a little too deliberately charming, perhaps, and a little irritatingly unreal, for it is never quite unreal. But it is difficult for Mrs. Woolf to rid herself of all seriousness when Time is her theme; it is the problem that has occupied her ever since *Jacob's Room*. The idea of *Orlando* was a witty one; a character who survives for several centuries, maintaining his identity, but changing his attributes so radically that, beginning as the hero of the story he ends as its heroine: this was an admirable invention for incarnating the impartiality of Time's mutations. Yet as Mrs. Woolf cannot take such things merely wittily or merely fancifully, the wit is less detached than wit should be, and the fancy has never quite the freedom of fancy. The book is a success in an illegitimate style; the comparative failures of *Jacob's Room* and *To the Lighthouse* are worth a score of such triumphs.

In *Jacob's Room* Mrs. Woolf recreated a character through memories and associations, and gathered the limbs of Osiris imbedded in various strata of time and space. The separate limbs are exquisitely articulated, but one has the impression that some have not been retrieved, and that the others have been assembled somewhat haphazardly. The book is fragmentary. In *To the Lighthouse* she strove rather to evoke Time itself both directly and through the characters. The book consists of three parts. The first describes a summer's day in the Hebrides; it is followed by a short section called 'Time Passes'; then there is another summer's day several years later in the same, now changed, setting. As a single achievement the middle section of this book is perhaps the best thing Mrs. Woolf wrote before *The Waves*. It describes the gradual dilapidation of the house where the action has passed and will pass again. The house is beset by countless great and little forces, by wind, rain, mice, dust, neglect, its own age. A very powerful sense of time is conveyed in this way. But when Mrs. Woolf writes about time she is carried away; the middle section of *To the Lighthouse* is consequently far too strong for the other two: it did not need all this, one feels, to make a few characters a few years older. The time she evokes has hardly anything to do with individual human life at all, except accidentally, like evolution, for example; it is so much too powerful that it seems to have no effect at all, like an electric charge which, multiplied a thousand times, passes through one's body without one's feeling it, whereas, reduced to the right voltage, it would act devastatingly.

Mrs. Dalloway, which came between *Jacob's Room* and *To the Lighthouse*, is more perfect than either. In it, instead of scattering her characters through time, Mrs. Woolf gathers them into a single summer's day in London, and in doing so gathers time there too, thus producing for us another of its ambiguous facets. Everything in this book is steeped in time, either as a memory or a property of this one day, so that it is difficult to tell what the figures are which move about in it, whether they are mere aspects of a day, or human characters who would be as solid in sullen and foggy weather. There is something more dreamlike, one imagines, than the author intended, in those figures whose names one forgets so soon, while remembering their little mechanical gestures, and the bright rooms and streets, the sounds of bells and traffic that surround them. But if they are more than commonly perishable it is at least partly the author's almost clairvoyant sense of time that makes them so; they fade when subjected to it as certain colours do in an intense light. So that all the undoubtedly deft characterization which Mrs. Woolf lavishes on them seems wasted, and is sometimes tiresome; it is as if she were trying to characterize eleven o'clock in the morning, or four in the afternoon, for the characters might almost have been called after the hours. As parts of the changing moods of one day they are charming, they are even real; it is when the author tries to give them the attributes of independent entities that everything becomes false. Her characterization is skilful, understanding, sensitive, and the only thing that keeps it from being masterly is that it is not applied to characters; there are none in the book.

Mrs. Woolf quite discards characterization in the ordinary sense in *The Waves*, and her vision of life at last stands out clearly. She seems no longer concerned with temporal attributes in this book, but with permanent things: the problem of time which she has pursued for so long has yielded her here a resolution. The six figures whose monologues make it up are beings freed from the illusions of time. They stand beyond time and see themselves within it; they incarnate something in the spirit which in the midst of change is not deceived. They have been blamed for not being characters, and very ignorantly; for to such beings character is merely a costume they put on, and have to put on, before they go on the temporal stage to play their parts. If they are to be called characters at all, then they are characters who have awakened.

It is difficult to find any parallels in literature for these six figures, or for the dimension in which they move. One may be reminded now and then of Pirandello's much overpraised *Six Characters in Search of an Author*; but the resemblance is only a surface one. For Pirandello merely presents schematically a few aspects of illusion, whereas Mrs. Woolf has pierced to something deeper, to that part of us which refuses to be deceived. Is there a part of us which refuses to be deceived? If there is, it exists where consciousness is most intense, alert and magnanimous. It exists also at a level where laughter and tears, whether singly or simultaneously, are no longer apposite responses. These six figures are something new in literature, so new that a critic may legitimately refuse to try to find a formula for it. The book is a continuous revelation on a level rarely touched by the novelist.

In conception, however, it is quite simple. Six characters, three men and three women, tell in alternate monologue their stories from childhood to middle age. The whole is written in the present tense, the response of the monologist accompanying every event as it happens, the awake character who regards and the somnambulist character who acts being indissolubly attached and yet separate. Seen by this passionate observer all action, all emotion, all change becomes a series of pictures. 'There is a hill striped with houses. A man crosses a bridge with a dog at his heels. Now the red boy begins firing at the pheasant. The blue boy shoves him aside. "My uncle is the best shot in England. My cousin is Master of Foxhounds." ' 'The cart grows gradually larger as it comes along the road. The sheep gather in the middle of the field. The birds gather in the middle of the road—they need not fly yet. The wood smoke rises. The starkness of the dawn is going out of it.' In a stream the pictures follow one another. 'And when evening comes and the lamps are lit they make a yellow fire in the ivy.' 'A child playing—a summer evening—doors will open and shut, will keep opening and shutting, through which I see sights that make me weep. For they cannot be imparted. Hence our loneliness; hence our desolation. I turn to that spot in my mind and find it empty.' 'There is the puddle, and I cannot cross it. I hear the rush of the great grindstone within an inch of my head. Its wind roars in my face. All palpable forms of life have failed me. Unless I can stretch and touch something hard, I shall be blown down the eternal corridors forever. What, then, can I touch? What brick, what stone? and so draw myself across the enormous gulf into my body safely?' 'It was only for a moment, catching sight of myself before I had time to prepare myself as I always prepare myself for the sight of myself, that I quailed. It is true; I am not young.' 'So I went out. I saw the first morning he would never see—the sparrows were like toys dangled from a string by a child.' Why are all those pictures so strangely vivid, like windows violently broken in the closed wall of experience? Because they are seen not by the acting character, but by his other self who watches him from beyond time. 'All these things,' one of the six says, 'happen in one second and last forever.' Such sufferings and pleasures are like those of bound spirits to whom has been left the liberty to look and judge.

Mrs. Woolf's conception of life in this book is a pessimistic one lightened only by the supersensual pleasures of the contemplating self. 'All these things happen in a second and last forever.' 'If there are no stories, what end can there be, or what beginning? Life is not susceptible to the treatment we give it when we try to tell it.' (Incidentally this has not prevented her from trying to tell it.) 'But now I made the contribution of maturity to childhood's intuitions—satiety and doom; the sense of what is unescapable in our lot; death; the knowledge of limitations; how life is more obdurate than one had thought it.' And in a description of a meeting of all the six figures: 'We saw for a moment laid out among us the body of the complete human being whom we have failed to be, but at the same time, cannot forget.' It is in intellectual formulations such as these that the grief of Mrs. Woolf's ideal observers finds its keenest edge. That grief is very keen, but it is not a grief that can be solved by tears; it is hostile to them.

Nothing is stranger in modern literature, and nothing probably could tell us more about it, than this hostility to tears, the mark at which once even the greatest writers aimed. All that one can do is to note it. The modern writer, no matter how passionately or deeply he may feel, is never concerned with the tears in things. D. H. Lawrence was a man who felt and wrote with conspicuous passion; George Eliot, let us say, was a woman who felt and wrote not with conspicuous passion; yet in her calm way she tapped the fount of tears, whereas D. H. Lawrence, while arousing many emotions in our breasts, quite ignored this immemorial source of relief. In spite of all his anti-intellectualism he was more penetrated by what he himself called the virus of intellect than George Eliot, though she was as powerfully resolved to be intellectual, as he to be 'instinctive'. Indeed almost all modern novelists are more intellectual in a certain sense than any of their predecessors of fifty years ago: in the sense that the intellect conditions their emotional responses more decisively, making those responses less naïve and immediately satisfying. More deliberate and unsure, also, however; for it is difficult to achieve, where the intellect is in part control, any effort possessing the simple inevitability of a burst of tears. This may partly account for the sense of emotional frustration, of indefinite postponement, which so many modern novels produce. It may account, for instance, for Lawrence's equivocal operation on us. The old catharsis was definitely impossible; the new one was difficult to find. In *The Waves* a new catharsis has been found. Its art is at once modern and complete.

The great step forward that Mrs. Woolf made in *The Waves* is reflected also in the style. *Mrs. Dalloway* was a wonderful piece of writing, but its grace had a touch of hesitation, even of fussiness, with all those clauses and sentences ending in 'ing'. But the passage describing Clarissa sewing the silk dress is one of the finest in the book, and may serve for a test of comparison:

So on a summer's day waves collect, overbalance, and fall; collect and fall; and the whole world seems to be saying 'that is all' more and more ponderously, until even the heart in the body which lies in the sun on the beach says too, That is all. Fear no more, says the heart. Fear no more, says the heart, committing its burden to some sea, which sighs collectively for all sorrows, and renews, begins, collects, lets fall. And the body alone listens to the passing bee; the wave breaking; the dog barking, far away barking and barking.

How different the rhythm of that is from that of the passages I have quoted from *The Waves*. It is a fluttering rhythm, a rhythm in which a thousand almost imperceptible hesitations are concealed. In *The Waves* this prose has put away all hesitation, and cuts out images and thoughts in one sweep. It is impatiently, almost violently immediate. What it recalls most strongly is Rilke's superb prose, which was a sort of inspired shorthand. And one imagines that it has changed in this astonishing way because Mrs. Woolf is dealing directly now with immediate and essential truths of experience. The result is an authentic and unique masterpiece, which is bound to have an influence on the mind of this generation.

95. Gabriel Marcel, review, *Nouvelle Revue Française* (Paris)

February 1932, 303–8

Gabriel Marcel (b. 1889). French philosopher and man of letters.

Mrs Virginia Woolf is without doubt one of the most remarkable prose writers of our time. Her latest book—towards which all her previous works converge—is a wonderful bundle of phrases and verbal melodies expressing special moments of feeling. And yet it would hardly be correct, I feel, to describe the author of *Orlando* as a novelist of genius. The perpetual concern with technical innovation as revealed in her latest books is enough to show how anaemic her sense of the novel is. Surely we are right in believing that creative minds of a high order, in this field as in others, have made technical innovations only because they *had* to? They make these innovations unawares and, as it were, unwillingly, simply because their vision of man and the world could not accommodate itself to the traditional means of expression. One feels that Mrs Virginia Woolf is capable of that disdainful pity with which an artist of my acquaintance used to treat painters who are prompted by the ridiculous ambition of 'representing' something.

I notice here and there the same impatience, the same claim to transcend the limits of an art. But should we not distrust these 'goings beyond' which seem more than once to disguise an impotence and a lassitude pushed, in the oddest way, to such a point that they do not recognise themselves for what they are? Mrs Virginia Woolf's admirers will no doubt reply that in order to translate the relations of individuals with others and with themselves in their elusiveness; in order to represent the unfulfilled in life and the overlapping of related consciousnesses, she was constrained to break the very rigid framework of the orthodox novel. Is this quite certain? The human constellation is given to us in *The Waves* as a shifting pageant. If I compare it with that which sparkles in the first book of *Dusty Answer*, I should have to admit, at the risk of provoking violent disagreement, that Rosamond Lehmann appears to me to have captured in a more adroit and assured manner, the musical quiver which courses through a group of adolescents, and this without recourse to any unusual methods. Besides, the method which Virginia Woolf uses in *The Waves* appears to me extremely awkward. Could anything be more tiresome than those six (interior?) monologues which constantly break off and so fragment indefinitely? One thinks of a musician who, assigning one part to the flute, another to the violin, yet another to the violin cello or the harp, simply joins the parts together. I am quite aware that we cannot ask a writer to orchestrate the parts like a composer, who superimposes them, and that there cannot be any question of our being made to apprehend simultaneously the outpourings and lyrical asides of Bernard, Susan and Rhoda. But the fact that this is impossible reveals precisely the irrationality of lifting arbitrarily certain technical devices from among the structural resources of one art and transposing them to a quite different art. Moreover, in obedience to a fatal dialectic, language tends here to lose itself in a 'fluvial' element which is distinct from it and which undoubtedly flows out into pure silence.

What is the phrase for the moon? And the phrase for love? By what name are we to call death? I do not know. I need a little language such as lovers use, words of one syllable such as children speak when they come into the room and find their mother sewing and pick up some scrap of bright wool, a feather, or a shred of chintz. I need a howl; a cry . . . Nothing that comes down with all its feet on the floor. None of those resonances and lovely echoes that break and chime from nerve to nerve in our breasts, making wild music, false phrases. I have done with phrases.

How much better is silence; the coffee-cup, the table. How much better to sit by myself like the solitary sea-bird that opens its wings on the stake. Let me sit here for ever with bare things, this coffee-cup, this knife, this fork, things in themselves, myself being myself.

What pathetic incoherence in this invocation which repudiates itself.

If only Virginia Woolf had managed to individualise the tone of the six alternating voices so as to render them as distinct for our mental ear as that of an oboe or a horn! But no. Despite an obvious effort to invent various leitmotifs, the author does not, in my opinion, succeed in detaching herself from her protagonists. She never realises that the very attempt at depersonalisation confers a unique, definite, and personal accent on her incarnations. Perhaps Percival alone will touch us as a real thing, because he never appears, and by not giving him a voice—her own voice—Mrs Woolf has saved him from herself. It was hardly a brilliant inspiration to place as a background to her book a seascape whose aspect changes as the hours of the day go by. Once one rejects the facile developments which this contrivance suggests, and one sees the book for what it is rather than what it was intended to be, I doubt if one could discern (except in the final pages), a tangible relation between, on the one hand, the spatial and temporal framework which falls into several episodes, and, on the other hand, an action which is spread across the entirety of lives whose development we are asked to grasp. There is something arbitrary in all this, an absence of inner necessity, which makes the reading of *The Waves* infinitely painful, and even, if I might risk the conjunction of words, almost *inexecutable*.

I might add that one shudders to think what similar methods will produce when clumsy imitators attempt to employ them. The overwhelming odds are that it is the young writers most destitute of skill or creative power who will be most completely seduced by this adventurous technique—let's say it—by this brazen facility.

As it happens, Mrs Woolf, almost in spite of herself, has found a way of escaping from the prison of form to which she has condemned herself. There is the enchanting beauty of the chapter in which the six characters express the various incommunicable emotions aroused by the death of Percival, whom they all love in one way or another. But most of the time the reader rebels against the constant recourse to a factitious perspective which tends to show us events happening in six lives, either transparently, or, as it were, indistinctly, at the end of some avenue or other which disappears as soon as one tries to travel down it. It is true that Mrs Woolf has brought her book to a close with an uninterrupted monologue of one of her characters, Bernard, the novelist, who gives us, after a fashion, the concentrated substance of what we have as yet been able to gather only in bits and pieces. We find ourselves wondering if Bernard without our knowing it has been the only 'I' of this strange pleiade formed by himself and the five friends of his childhood.

[Quotes p. 205 'And now I ask' to 'this identity we so feverishly cherish, was overcome.']

But would it not have taken an infinitely more subtle art to direct our attention indirectly, and not in this crudely explicit manner, to this retrospective knowledge? Actually, it appears to me, that Mrs Virginia Woolf's technique, like that of Joyce, (though in a rather different sense) implies a radical misconception of the very conditions of attention, or, what amounts to the same thing, a naive belief in the changeable nature of these conditions. There is here, I sincerely believe, an inner weakness, and it will not be long before we recognise its effects.

Nevertheless, I confess that this assessment of *The Waves* does not give a full account of the impression the book has made on me: it has left out an element of doubt and something like an uneasy admiration. When Bernard observes that life does not quite lend itself to the treatment we give it when we endeavour to narrate it, he raises metaphysical problems the importance of which I am far from being unaware. Does the biographical representation of characters interpose itself as an opaque screen between us and their actual, that is to say 'unhistorical' reality? Something irresistibly forces us to admit this. I cannot help being at times deeply conscious of anguish before the unknown and impenetrable in life—and this is something which makes itself felt on nearly every page of *The Waves*. Only what disturbs me in Mrs Woolf's book is the confusion, perhaps a systematic and fully conscious one, which she makes between the purely sensory (something which lies within the range of biography) and the apprehension, in flashes, of a world which would transcend biography. One meets again here the ambiguity, transposed, to be sure, but essentially the same, which is at the heart of Proust's work. Bernard, who is from the beginning to the end the author's mouthpiece, says

> There is nothing one can fish up in a spoon; nothing one can call an event. Yet it is alive too and deep, this stream . . . The crystal, the globe of life as one calls it, far from being hard and cold to the touch, has walls of thinnest air.

All these metaphors have to-day an undeniable prestige. And yet one should be on one's guard, for surely nothing is more fallacious than the idea of dematerialisation. A solution is no less material than the crystals which form imperceptibly at the bottom of the phial containing it. It is true that Mrs Woolf is haunted by the mystery of the spirit, but it would be an odd piece of self-deception if we persuaded ourselves that this sort of phosphorescent stream into which, in her hands, our lives, our human lives, seem to be transformed leads us to any decisive revelation. The truth is that this is an illusory path, a will o' the wisp with which a sick and probably desperate woman diligently bewitches herself.

96. Floris Delattre on Virginia Woolf and Bergson

1931

From 'La Durée Bergsonienne dans le roman de Virginia Woolf', *Revue Anglo-Americaine*, December 1931, 97–108.

Although a number of reviewers had hinted at the comparison, this was the first detailed analysis of similarities between Virginia Woolf's writing and the philosophy of Bergson. This article was incorporated in Delattre's *Le Roman psychologique de Virginia Woolf*, which appeared in 1932.

Instead of considering time as an insert homogeneous *quantity*, something which is not at all distinct from space, being composed like the latter of identical, unchanging units and lending itself to mathematical measurement, Bergson concentrates his attention on the *qualitative* character of time—on time as made up of heterogeneous elements, varying with each individual, changing ceaselessly. It is this which he calls 'real duration', that is, something which does not belong to the world of things that can be recorded, added to or divided, but is a whole into which many forces and complex influences meet and fuse. Considered thus, the hours, minutes and seconds into which 'duration' is cut up by our intelligence and senses, are only a simple translation in terms of time—and with an eye merely to practical action—of the total reality which comprises, in fact, the creative activity of our psychological life.

This conception of duration, through which Bergson has sought to understand the bases of the immediate self in all their integrity, lies at the heart of Virginia Woolf's novels. She too has placed herself altogether within 'real duration': she has firmly linked psychological experience, the whirling confusion of which she observes with an acute and penetrating eye, with the notion of a continuous 'qualitative and creative' duration, which is simply consciousness itself. She shows especially the unique, unpredictable mental states of her characters, in which there is no recurrence of identical conditions, and no possible prevision of the future. Again, the 'action' in her novels, consisting entirely of an incessant flux of emotional moments, is only, and Bergson's words are once more perfectly adequate, 'a duration in which the past, always in motion, enlarges itself ceaselessly into a present that is absolutely new';[1] and the reality which she describes is 'a perpetual growth, a creation which is endlessly pursued'.[2] Normal time divides the days which characters live into regular spaces. Big Ben chimes the hours for Peter Walsh and Septimus Warren Smith, for Miss Kilman and Elizabeth Dalloway, as for Clarissa herself, casting into the London sky 'the warning, musical; then the hour irrevocable', 'the leaden circles dissolved in the air'. But there it is only a question of 'clock time', as the novelist shows clearly in *Orlando*

> The mind of man, moreover, works with equal strangeness upon the body of time. An hour, once it lodges in the queer element of the human spirit, may be stretched to fifty or a hundred times its clock length; on the other hand, an hour may be accurately represented on the timepiece of the mind by one second.

Clock time is thus only a spatial interpretation, only abstract space. Duration, on the other hand, is altogether concrete. It dilates or contracts according to the variable intensity of human experience. It is a continuity of the facts of consciousness, not accomplished, but accomplishing themselves. It is a spiritual reality, that is to say a uniquely subjective relation between the spirit and external reality. It is a 'psychological notion' 'belonging to the order of quality', 'duration and consciousness are one'—so many of Bergson's theses—indeed, his very words—express precisely Virginia Woolf's standpoint throughout her work, human life being in her eyes, and following another of Bergson's definitions, 'a succession in which there is no repetition, where every moment is unique'.

[1] *L'Évolution créatrice,* p. 218.
[2] Ibid., p. 216.

97. Two scrutinies

(a) William Empson, 'Virginia Woolf', in *Scrutinies by Various Writers*, collected by Edgell Rickword, 1931, vol. 2, 204–16.

William Empson (b. 1906) was one of the pioneers of this type of criticism, his *Seven Types of Ambiguity* having appeared the previous year (1930). In its final chapter he discussed the need for, and the problems raised by, a 'machinery of analysis':

On the face of it, there are two sorts of literary critic, the appreciative and the analytical; the difficulty is that they have all got to be both. An appreciator produces literary effects similar to the one he is appreciating ... The analyst ... sets out to explain, in terms of the rest of the reader's experience, why the work has had the effect on him that is assumed. As an analyst he is not repeating the effect; he may even be preventing it from happening again. Now, evidently the appreciator has got to be an analyst, because the only way to say a complicated thing more simply is to separate it into its parts and say each of them in turn. The analyst has also got to be an appreciator; because he must convince the reader that he knows what he is talking about (that he has had the experience in question); because he must be able to show the reader which of the separate parts of the experience he is talking about, after he has separated them; and because he must coax the reader into seeing that the cause he names does, in fact, produce the effect which is experienced; otherwise they will not seem to have anything to do with each other (Peregrine edition, 1961, 249–50).

Shakespeare was like Nature; we have been saying it for three centuries. There were more echoes in his work than he knew; he wrote from his Preconsciousness; any work in hand formed a world he was living in, so that he could find his way about in it as if by habit; any of his stones may have been made bread, and repay turning. Novelists have seldom been called Nature in this sense; at any rate they have not been commented on in such detail; and by way of showing that the same claim might be made for Mrs Woolf I shall try to pick up, turn in my hand for the moment, two quite small stones from the road to the lighthouse, till they catch the light, and are seen to be, if not bread, at least jewels.

Mrs Ramsay feels tired at the beginning of her dinner party.

> . . . the whole of the effort of merging and flowing and creating rested on her. Again she felt, as a fact without hostility, the sterility of men, for if she did not do it nobody would do it; and so, giving herself the little shake that one gives a watch that has stopped, the old familiar pulse began beating, as the watch begins ticking—one, two, three, one, two, three. And so on and so on, she repeated, listening to it, sheltering and fostering the still feeble pulse as one might guard a weak flame with a newspaper.

Watches don't beat up to three, they beat up to two, or four in pairs. Before calling this a harmless small mistake, however, one must consider an earlier passage. James has just gone to bed; she feels at peace over her knitting.

> Not as oneself did one rest ever, in her experience (she accomplished here something dextrous with her needles), but as a wedge of darkness. Losing personality one lost the fret, the hurry, the stir; and there rose to her lips always some exclamation of triumph over life when things came together in this peace, this rest, this eternity; and pausing there she looked out to meet that stroke of the Lighthouse—the long steady stroke, the last of the three—which was her stroke, for watching them in this mood always at this hour one could not help attaching oneself especially to one of the things one saw; and this thing, the long steady stroke, was her stroke.[1]

The Lighthouse becomes a symbol of energies at the basis of human life, which support and exclude the understanding; Mrs Ramsay sets herself going like the Lighthouse to sustain her party, and it is for this reason that the pulse is like a flame. Or one may say that the Lighthouse has at times been the symbol of reason and male power of setting large-scale things in order (for it is in sight of the Lighthouse that Mr Bankes and Mr Tansley go and talk politics on the terrace after dinner, as if they had gone on to the bridge of the ship to take up their bearings), and it is then with a sort of feminist triumph that it becomes a symbol of Mrs Ramsay. The complex working of her symbols continually involves devious motivations of this kind; one must remember with some alarm (thinking of feminism) a moment in Jacob's room, when Betty Flanders, that good and generous woman, remembers in passing how she did not like red hair in men, and how she had the cat castrated that was given by one of her admirers.

1 There are a couple of errors in Empson's quotation (from p.100 of *To the Lighthouse*).

The other example is more controversial; it comes in the second part of the *Lighthouse*, when Mrs Ramsay is dead and time is passing in the empty house. (The War is mentioned two pages later.)

Nothing it seemed could break that image, corrupt that innocence, or disturb the swaying mantle of silence which, week after week in the empty room, wove into itself the falling cries of birds, ships hooting, the drone and hum of the fields, a dog's bark, a man's shout, and folded them round the house in silence. Once only a board sprang on the landing; once in the middle of the night with a roar, with a rupture, as after centuries of quiescence, a rock rends itself from the mountain and hurtles crashing into the valley, one fold of the shawl loosened and swung to and fro.

Some people, when you tell them that this patch is of rare excellence, say that it is not true; that a shawl, especially only one fold of it, does not roar; perhaps even that this is a neurotic cultivation of hyper-sensitivity for hyper-sensitivity's sake. The image in any case speaks very truly about such small domestic changes, startling both because apparently uncaused and because of the gulfs of time that surround them; but it is relevant to the shawl for a reason you have to remember; because of what Mrs Ramsay said when she put it there. Cam was frightened of the boar's skull in the night nursery, so Mrs Ramsay wound her shawl round it and said how lovely it looked now: 'it was like a bird's nest; it was like a beautiful mountain such as she had seen abroad, with valleys and flowers and bells ringing and birds singing and little goats and antelopes . . .'

It is only if you have remembered this fancy that you realise with how terrible an irony it has come true. Mrs Ramsay is dead and the house empty; even her most domesticated and personal piece of matter has become monstrous and inhuman, like a mountain, like matter in astronomy. But you have had to remember the words for a long time, and it seems as if Mrs Woolf herself was not so much remembering them as finding her way about the book as if by habit; it is this sort of small correspondence, used so often, that makes up a full and as it were poetical attitude to language such as would gain by an annotated edition.

A more serious objection, I think, can be brought against the sentence about the mantle of silence weaving things into itself. Mrs Woolf can show very brilliantly how the details of her characters' surroundings are woven into their moods; this is an important part of a novel, and what I have just called her poetical use of language is the best way of doing it. But here the whole point of the situation is that *no* character is in the room; what is eerie about the sounds is precisely that they are *not* being woven into anybody's mood; and the sentence seems to have the falsity that comes from always using a single method. As long as this sort of method is being used dramatically, to show how a character felt, it is excellent if only because it is true; people's minds do work like that; it may really be the only way to deal adequately with motivation. But when it is being used to show merely how Mrs Woolf is feeling about what she describes the result is not always formal enough to be interesting. One thing reminds her of a lot of others, and the story is held up while they are mentioned; but one feels that the reasons why she thought of these things at the moment of writing are not part of the book.

When the shawl made her think of a rock it was, I believe, part of the book, for the reason I have given; but such a method makes extraordinary demands on the author's sincerity; he must be living in his work very completely if he can indulge in free association and be sure that it will be relevant. Of course you may say that an author must always attempt this condition, regardless of consequences; this, I take it, is the main doctrine of surrealism, but it has an air of putting the cart before the horse. A novelist's wit (of which Mrs Woolf has so much) is likely to carry its own setting and explanation, but his personal poetry is not reliable in the same way.

It is necessary in talking about Mrs Woolf to consider these problems of form, because her solution of them is so closely connected with her choice of subject; if in her later novels she treats them high-handedly it is not so much from indifference or undue concentration as from a change of emphasis. I shall look, for example, at the way she makes a novel stop.

Night and Day and *The Voyage Out*, if one thinks of the earlier ones, end respectively with marriage and death; these, of course, are the traditional, and might seem the only reliable methods. But for stopping *Mrs Dalloway* these ways would be no use, because of the particular sort of person whose functions and modes of thought are being described. For the person now in the centre of the stage is a sensible and highly sensitive married woman, not concerned to lead the life of independent intelligence, who is the sun of her world, who acts as clearing-house for the emotional needs of her household, who is always intensely aware of the mood of everybody in the room, and who frequently does not listen to the conversation. Such a person has, in a sense, renounced her private drama, so that one does not wish it to be brought to either of these climaxes. For one thing, we are only shown the day of Clarissa's party; the map is on too large a scale to include the coast as well as the central towns. *To the Lighthouse* is a story about Mrs Ramsay, but in a sense her death is a minor incident brought in to show how her influence lived after her; things centre round her in the third part just as continuously, with just as little natural climax, as they did in the first. You might indeed say that it is hopeless to look for an orderly plot about such a heroine, because the things that are interesting about her make a plot irrelevant. And yet it is a mistake to suppose that you can say even those things in a novel without a plot.

Mrs Woolf's later style is very beautifully adapted to the requirements of this subject; so much so as to attack very directly the problem of motivation. Indeed I think it is for this that she will chiefly be remembered; in this administrative but domestic setting, by the very structure of the sentences, we are made to know what it felt like for the heroine to make up her mind. Of course in itself this is not new; it is the main business of a novelist to show his reader, by slow accumulations, all the elements and proportions of a decision, so that the reader knows how the character felt about it; but Mrs Woolf, so as to be much more immediately illuminating, can show how they are at the back of a decision at the moment it is taken.

We arrive, for instance, with some phrase like 'and indeed' into a new sentence and a new specious present. Long, irrelevant, delicious clauses recollect the ramifications of the situation (this part corresponds to the blurring of consciousness while the heroine waits a moment to know her own mind; and it is here, by the way, that one is told most of the story); then by a twist of thought some vivid but distant detail, which she is actually conscious of, and might have been expected to finish the sentence, turns her mind towards the surface. From then on the clauses become shorter; we move towards action by a series of leaps, each, perhaps, showing what she would have done about something quite different, and just at the end, without effort, washed up by the last wave of this disturbance, like an obvious bit of grammar put in to round off the sentence, with a partly self-conscious, wholly charming humility in the heroine (how odd that the result of all this should be something so flat and domestic), we get the small useful thing she actually did do.

Most of the important things for a critic to say about Mrs Woolf have been said by herself in *A Room of One's Own*, and centre round a peculiar attitude to feminism. For instance, she says there that women novelists must be expected to do something entirely new in describing the mental attitudes of women, and their relations with other women, which male novelists do not know about. This seems a large claim; surely Richardson knew how women talked when there wasn't a man in the room; and when you have said, as Mrs Woolf does say, that every complete author must be spiritually hermaphrodite, you seem to have quelled this aspect of the sex war as vehemently as you called it into being. But her best work is certainly illuminated by this notion; in particular, it has a sort of submissive sensitiveness to immediate circumstances (helpless sensitiveness, one might say, except that it is just this quality that improves them) which gives her work both the delicacy with which she can seize on a shade of domestic atmosphere and (so as to raise the formal questions I am talking about) the peculiar evanescence of her designs as a whole. One might also put down to this a concentration on to domestic details as dramatic; Mrs Flanders, for instance, not knowing what to do with her dead son's boots; but again it is no use saying it could only be done by a woman novelist. Shakespeare is full of details of this sort, which would be humorous if they were not terrible.

Not, by the way, that he would have used the detail as a means of ending a long work; there is a sort of self-consciousness in the way it is thus thrust upon you as peculiarly good, and you have to decide it is peculiarly good if it is to make a satisfying ending at all. Still, there is no doubt about the finality of the situation; the end here is Jacob's death. The end of *To the Lighthouse*, though much more arbitrary, is as satisfying, and leaves one remembering the whole book, partly by the unifying and mystifying effect of the symbol, chiefly because there is nobody left at the end about whose future behaviour you feel immediately curious. On the other hand this is almost shockingly untrue of *Mrs Dalloway*: most of the book has been leading up to what happens just after the last page. Of course Clarissa did not allow the situation to become melodramatic; if you thought she would Mrs Woolf is snubbing you. But I do not know how she carried it off, or what effect it may not have had on Peter; and even if I ought to, I feel the snub is a harsh one. Certainly the book stops (like a dance tune) at one of the possible stopping places, at one of the minor apotheoses of Clarissa; but so far as one has any sense of finality it is for more or less arbitrary reasons. The party for which she has prepared all through the day of the book is over; the shell-shock case is dead; and he has been connected with the main story in some degree since she has heard of him from Sir William Bradshaw. None of these outweigh our curiosity about the meeting of Clarissa and Peter.

The influence of the Chekov short story, I think, has been misleading in England; Chekov can afford to stop in the middle of a conversation because you know how it would go on. He is hopeless about his characters; they will never do any better; and one stops in the middle as with a final gesture of despair. But a novel in which the characters are capable of dealing with many different situations must stop either when they are dead or when they will from then on have to deal with different situations, and have brought to some order the ones they were dealing with before. So that once you abandon death and marriage the sea is uncharted. For instance, Proust's great novel, you might say, could not stop, because the descriptions of motive were too minute and the interconnections too many; it rolled on by its own weight to end in a rather cumbrous series of universal reconnecting generalisations. On the other hand, Mrs Woolf's early short stories—'Kew Gardens', for instance—use what may be called the Vase of Flowers method; things seen in the same mood are described together, and there they are; two lovers and a slug; so you stop. This seems inadequate, whether derived from Chekov or not; the range of interest (identifying oneself with all the characters and so forth) in the crudest melodramatic story is much greater than the range of interest (mainly contrast and correspondence) in a vase of flowers. Indeed the impressionist method, the attempt to convey directly your own attitude to things, how you connect one thing with another, is in a sense fallacious; it tries to substitute for telling a story, as the main centre of interest, what is in fact one of the by-products of telling a story; it tries to correlate sensations rather than the impulses that make the sensations interesting; even tries to define the impulse by an accumulation of the sensations it suggested to the author. Even those delicate interconnections on which the impressionist method depends (those two I consider at first, for instance) need a story to make them intelligible, and even if Shakespeare (since I have dragged him in) could afford to abandon himself to these delicious correspondences he had first to get a strong and obvious story which would be effective on the stage. I think myself, at any rate, that Mrs Woolf's most memorable successes come when she is sticking most closely to her plot.

Still, of course, the trouble about sticking closely to a plot is that in that case (for the more interesting plots) you can't deal adequately with motivation; Defoe's method only worked because his characters were undomestic people in dire need of money, so that their motives were fairly plain. All one can say against the wilful and jumping brilliance of Mrs Woolf's descriptive passages is that, as part of a design, they come to seem unsatisfying; however delicate and brightly coloured they seem cut in low relief upon the great block she has taken for her material, and even when you are sure that some patch is really part of the book you often cannot (as you can in my two examples) see why it should be. Of course her methods catch intensely a sense of period, of setting, of the immediate person described; are very lifelike, in short; and I do not know how far it may be due to just this quality; to the fact that so many of her images, glittering and searching as they are, spreading out their wealth of feeling, as if split, in the mind, give one just that sense of waste that is given by life itself. '. . . the great revelation perhaps never did come. Instead, there were little daily miracles, illuminations, matches struck unexpectedly in the dark.'

'How far that little candle sheds its beams'; but still it is the business of art to provide candelabra, to aggregate its matches into a lighthouse of many candlepower. If only (one finds oneself feeling in re-reading these novels), if only these dissolved units of understanding had been co-ordinated into a system; if only, perhaps, there was an index, showing what had been compared with what; if only these materials for the metaphysical conceit, poured out so lavishly, had been concentrated into crystals of poetry that could be remembered, how much safer one would feel.

(b) M. C. Bradbrook, 'Notes on the Style of Mrs Woolf', *Scrutiny*, May 1932, 33–8.

M. C. Bradbrook (b. 1908). Professor of English, Cambridge University. This article caused Virginia Woolf to examine her attitude towards criticism:

> What is the right attitude towards criticism? What ought I to feel and say when Miss B. devotes an article in *Scrutiny* to attacking me? She is young, Cambridge, ardent. And she says I'm a very bad writer. Now I think the thing to do is to note the pith of what is said—that I don't think—then to use the little kick of energy which opposition supplies to be more vigorously oneself. It is perhaps true that my reputation will now decline. I shall be laughed at and pointed at. What should be

my attitude—clearly Arnold Bennett and Wells took the criticism of their youngers in the wrong way. The right way is not to resent; not to be longsuffering and Christian and submissive either. Of course, with my odd mixture of extreme rashness and modesty (to analyse roughly) I very soon recover from praise and blame. But I want to find out an attitude. The most important thing is not to think very much about oneself. To investigate candidly the charge; but not fussily, not very anxiously. On no account to retaliate by going to the other extreme—thinking too much. And now that thorn is out—perhaps too easily (*A Writer's Diary*, 179–80).

In reading any of the later novels of Mrs Woolf, a curious and persistent trick of style obtrudes itself on the attention.

'But for women, I thought, looking at the empty shelves, these difficulties are infinitely more formidable.' (*A Room of One's Own*)

'The mind is certainly a very mysterious organ, I reflected, drawing in my head from the window, about which practically nothing is known.' (Ibid.)

'There is a coherence in things, a stability: something, she meant, is immune from change and shines out (she glanced at the window with its ripple of reflected light). Here, she felt, putting down the spoon, here was the still space that lies about the heart of things.' (*To the Lighthouse*)

The first two passages are ratiocinative, the last a description of a mood. Yet the little asides serve the same purpose in all three: by stressing time and place, they deflate the statement: the affirmation is given a relative value only: neither the reader nor the writer is implicated: they are not trapped into any admissions, or required to endorse anything in more than a qualified way. The effect has been described by T. E. Hulme: 'The classical poet never forgets the finiteness, the limit of man . . . If you say an extravagant thing, there is always the impression of yourself standing outside it and not quite believing it.'

Mrs Woolf refuses to be pinned down in this way, and consequently she is debarred from a narrative technique, since this implies a schema of values, or even from the direct presentation of powerful feelings or major situations. In *Mrs Dalloway* the most powerful feelings depend on more powerful feelings long past: the old relationships between Clarissa, Peter, and Sally Seaton, the war experiences of Septimus Warren Smith. They are reflected, indirect, 'the reward of having cared for people . . .' (*Mrs Dalloway*). In *To the Lighthouse* the feelings are peripheral: they are minor manifestations of powerful forces: as for instance when Mrs Ramsay reassures her husband on the terrace. The success of the book is due to the fact that the reader accepts the implication of the major forces behind the small situations. But even then the real nature of the subject is cloaked by Mrs Woolf's method of description through a kind of metaphor which has a highly abstracting effect.

Whenever the direct presentation of powerful feelings or major situations is inescapable, Mrs Woolf takes refuge in an embarrassing kind of nervous irony (as in the bracketed passages in *To the Lighthouse*, part two).

'This violent kind of disillusionment is usually to be expected of young men in the prime of life, sound in wind and limb, who will later become fathers of families and directors of banks.' (*Jacob's Room*)

'Here a girl for sale: there an old woman with only matches to offer' (Ibid.)

'A shell exploded. Twenty or thirty young men were blown up in France, among them Andrew Ramsay, whose death, mercifully, was instantaneous.' (*To the Lighthouse*)

That 'mercifully' at least might have been spared.

For Doris Kilman and Charles Tansley (who are parallel figures) Mrs Woolf reserves her heaviest satire. Miss Kilman's feelings for Elizabeth or Tansley's sensations at the dinner party are analysed with a brutality that is faintly discomforting. They are both devoid of the social sense, scholars who have developed the intelligence at the expense of the arts of living.

The heroines on the contrary live by their social sense: they are peculiarly sensitive to tone and atmosphere: they are in fact artists in the social medium, with other people's temperaments and moods as their materials. Mrs Ramsay is the complement of Lily Briscoe, 'Mrs Ramsay, saying *Life stand still here:* Mrs Ramsay making of the moment something permanent (as in another sphere Lily herself tried to make of the moment something permanent) . . . In the midst of chaos there was shape: this eternal passing and flowing was struck into stability. *Life stand still here*, Mrs Ramsay said.' (*To the Lighthouse*).

It is the arresting of a single 'moment', a significant spot in the temporal sequence that is Art for Mrs Ramsay and Mrs Woolf. In The Spot on the Wall (sic) Mrs Woolf describes her technique, which is essentially static. A single moment is isolated and forms a unit for the sensibility to work on. The difficulty lies in relating the various moments. Intensity is the only criterion of a detached experience and there is a consequent tendency for everything to be equally intense in Mrs Woolf's works. Everything receives the same slightly strained attention: the effect is not unlike that of tempera painting, where there is exquisite delicacy of colour, but no light and shade. (The connection of this with the refusal to assent to a statement absolutely is too obvious to need any stressing.)

Mrs Woolf's difficulties have always been structural. In *Jacob's Room* she hardly attempted a solution: in *Mrs Dalloway* she began the rigid telescoping of the time sequence which was developed in *To the Lighthouse*. A series of echoes and cross references form the real framework of the book; they are of the kind Joyce had used in *Ulysses*, but there is nothing to correspond to the more bony support which in *Ulysses* is provided by the structure of the episodes. The precarious stability of *To the Lighthouse* dissolved into the muddle of *Orlando* (in any case a *jeu d'esprit*), and the futile counterpointing of *The Waves*.

Mrs Woolf's books seem to be built up in a mosaic from the 'moments': scenes, descriptions, odd names recur from time to time. Here is a typical case:

'Already the convolvulus moth was spinning over the flowers. Orange and purple, nasturtium and cherry pie, were washed into the twilight but the tobacco plant and the passion flower over which the great moths spun were white as china.' (*Jacob's Room*)

'How she loved the grey white moths spinning in and out, over the cherry pie, over the evening primroses.' (*Mrs Dalloway*)

Moll Pratt the flowerseller and the Reverend Edward Whittaker, figures who appear for a moment only, are in *Jacob's Room* and *Mrs Dalloway*; and the Dalloways themselves are of course from *The Voyage Out*.

This kind of thing developed into the subtler correspondence between parts one and three of *To the Lighthouse*, as for instance, Cam's recollections of the stag's head. (*To the Lighthouse*, 117, 313)

The significant moments, the units of Mrs Woolf's style are either delicate records of the external scene, expressed in epigrammatic metaphor usually ('The whole platefuls of blue sea', 'The dragon-fly paused and then shot its blue stitch further through the air') or the presentation of a mood such as Mrs Ramsay's reverie on the terrace (*To the Lighthouse*, 29–30). These moods are hardly ever dramatic, i.e. bound by the limitations of the character who experiences them. The personality of Mrs Ramsay on the terrace or of Mrs Dalloway in her drawing room does not matter: neither their individuality nor the plot is of any relevance. The mood is in fact an isolated piece of pure recording, of a more complex kind but not essentially different from the epigrammatic metaphor. It is less an emotion than a sensation that is presented: the feeling is further depersonalised by Mrs Woolf's use of metaphor: for instance in the description of Mr Ramsay appealing to his wife (*To the Lighthouse*, p. 61).

These two elements of Mrs Woolf's style, the observation of the external world and the description of moods, are separated out in her last book, *The Waves*. The interchapters describe the movements of sun and tides (the sea is for Mrs Woolf a symbol of the eternal and indifferent natural forces) (*Mrs Dalloway*, 64; *To the Lighthouse*, p. 30): this movement forms a kind of parallel to the development of the lives of the characters. But the effect of a page or two of epigrammatic metaphor is very fatiguing: the myopic observation, the lack of variations in the tension impose a strain on the reader. Sometimes phrase-making conquers accuracy: 'the lark peeled his clear ring of song and dropped it through the silent air' suggests the long call of a blackbird, but hardly the trills and twitters of the lark.

In the main portion of the book, there are no solid characters, no clearly defined situations and no structure of feelings: merely sensation in the void. Without any connections of a vital sort between them, with no plot in the Aristotelian sense, the sensations are not interesting. Emotions are reduced to a description of their physical accompaniments: the attention is wholly peripheral. This for example is the equivalent of the experience of being in love:

> Then there is the being drawn out, eviscerated, spun like a spider's web, twisted in agony round a thorn: then a thunder clap of complete indifference: the light blown out: then the return of measureless inexpressible joy: certain fields seemed to glow green for ever (*The Waves*).

There had been hints of this danger even in the earlier works: 'how could one express in words these emotions of the body? To want and not to have, sent up all her body a hardness, a hollowness, a strain.' (*To the Lighthouse*). Physical sensations, which are immediately present, and have no relations to any schema of values, are all that Mrs Woolf dares to assume in her readers.

All attempt to order and select has gone. 'There is nothing that one can fish up with a spoon, nothing that one can call an event . . . How impossible to order them rightly, to detach one separately or give the effect of the whole . . . Nevertheless, life is pleasant, life is tolerable. Monday is followed by Tuesday, then comes Wednesday.' (*The Waves* cf. *Monday or Tuesday*, her first attack on the problem of the time sequence.)

Mrs Woolf never, as is so frequently asserted, attempts to reproduce the process of thinking. Such generalised activity does not interest her: moreover, thinking implies a thesis which one is ready to defend. Mr Ramsay, who is a philosopher, 'thinks' with the most helpless particularity: the progress of human thought is symbolised for him by an alphabet, just as, for Lily Briscoe, a large kitchen table stands for the mental pursuits of Mr Ramsay himself. Their mental atmospheres are indistinguishable: and in both cases, the mood is not one of thought but of reverie.

The heroines are astonishingly ingenuous. Their tact and sensitiveness are preserved in a kind of intellectual vacuum. Mrs Dalloway 'muddled Armenians and Turks: and to this day, ask her what the Equator was and she did not know.' (*Mrs Dalloway*). Mrs Ramsay ponders 'A square root? what was that? Her sons knew. She learnt on them: on cubes and square roots: that was what they were talking about . . . and the French system of land tenure . . . She let it uphold her, this admirable fabric of the masculine intelligence,' (*To the Lighthouse*). Compare the dependence of Mrs Flanders and even of Lady Bruton.

The camouflage in *A Room of One's Own* serves the same purpose as this nervous particularising: it prevents Mrs Woolf from committing the indelicacy of putting a case or the possibility of her being accused of waving any kind of banner. The arguments are clearly serious and personal and yet they are dramatised and surrounded with all sorts of disguises to avoid an appearance of argument.

The shrinking of the heroines is too conscious, as the playfulness of *A Room of One's Own* is too laboured. To demand 'thinking' from Mrs Woolf is clearly illegitimate: but such a deliberate repudiation of it and such a smoke screen of feminine charm is surely to be deprecated. Mrs Woolf has preserved her extraordinary fineness and delicacy of perception at the cost of some cerebral etiolation.

98. William Troy on Virginia Woolf's poetic method

1932

William Troy, from 'Virginia Woolf', *Symposium* (Concord, New Hampshire), January–March 1932, 53–63 and April–June 1932, 153–66.

William Troy (1903–61). University teacher and literary critic.

The essential difficulty with the poetic method as used by Mrs Woolf is that it renders impossible the peculiar kind of interest which we are accustomed to derive from narrative. By the poetic method is meant the method of substituting poetic symbols for an ordered pattern of human action. The important thing about symbols is that they are used to stand for something else; the important word in such a definition is the word *stand*. Whatever activity in the mind or sensibility has gone on to produce them, symbols themselves are fixed, permanent and static. They may be considered, therefore, as the effort of the imagination to fix itself somewhere in space. The symbol may be considered as something *spatial*. Symbols are thus ordinarily used in lyric poetry, where the effort is to fix ideas, sentiments, or emotions. By themselves, of course, symbols in poetry are no more than so many detached, isolated and unrelated points in space. When projected separately, as in the poetry of the Imagist school, or in too great confusion, as in most contemporary poetry, their meaning is too special to have any value to the intelligence. The worlds which they indicate are either too small or too large to live in. But whether separate or integrated into a total vision symbols are capable of being grasped, like any other objects of space, by a single and instantaneous effort of perception. The interval of time between their presentation in a poem and our response to them is usually no longer than the time required for our grasp of their significance. Even when their presentation is like a gradual exfoliation, as in certain poems by Donne and Baudelaire, for example, that time is never allowed to be too greatly prolonged. We do not require Poe's axiom that all lyrics must be brief to understand why they must be so. The symbols on which they are constructed can be perceived in a moment of time.

When narrative based itself on a simple record of action progressing in time it was assured of a certain degree of interest. When later it based itself on an arrangement of action which corresponded to a consistent view of life or reality, it attained to the very high interest of a work of art. As long as it based itself firmly on action according to one pattern or another, it was certain of some degree of interest. To understand the nature of the satisfaction which we seem to take in the representation of reality in a temporal order we should have to know more about certain primitive elements of our psychology than science has yet been able to discover. It is enough to recognize that whatever the reasons this satisfaction is rooted in our sense of *time*. It is enough to realize that this is the basis of the appeal which narrative has made through the whole history of fiction, from the earliest fables of the race to the most complex 'constructions' of Henry James. For this reason, for example, description has always occupied a most uncertain place in fiction. Description, which deals with things rather than events, interposes a space-world in the march of that time-world which is the subject of fiction. For this reason the use of poetic symbols in fiction, as in all Mrs Woolf's work since *Monday or Tuesday*, seems to be in direct contradiction to the foundations of our response to that form.

99. Virginia Woolf in Italy

1933

Salvatore Rosati, from 'Litteratura Inglese: Virginia Woolf—Aldous Huxley', *Nuova Antologia*, Rome, 16 December 1933, 636–45.

Salvatore Rosati (b. 1895). Italian literary critic.

The three novels (*Jacob's Room*, *Mrs Dalloway* and *To the Lighthouse*) are three moments in the tendency towards an increasingly rigorous interiorisation. All scaffolding is eliminated from them; there is no plot and no framework imposed on the characters from outside. The inner life is formed by the succession of mental facts and sensations, and of emotions and thoughts which arise in reaction to them: a character consists essentially in this succession, this continuous flow, of consciousness.

In this way Virginia Woolf reverses the existing situation. In Victorian and post-Victorian art the 'optical centre' of the novel—to use the expression once again—seems to form itself in external reality. In Virginia Woolf's novels, on the other hand, the spirit is not reflected in the facts, but the facts in the spirit, and the optical centre is an internal one. Although Virginia Woolf proposes to follow 'the pattern . . . which each sight or incident scores upon the consciousness', this fidelity to experience has never prevented her from attempting a selection from amongst particulars. What is more important, this has not prevented her from paying attention to the form and unity of her work. Her psychological observation is never crude; on the contrary, it is always transformed by what may be called her psychological impressionism. Being quite independent of facts, she aims not at reproducing life but at creating it. It is this aesthetic transformation of keen observation which led critics to speak of her 'scientific mysticism'. All this is achieved with greater artistry in *Mrs Dalloway* and *To the Lighthouse*. The latter, though less successful than *Mrs Dalloway*, nevertheless has secondary characters which are more intimately conceived as spiritual extensions of the central personage. In the last section, in particular, the interpenetration of the present with past memories creates, in a dream-like atmosphere, a continuity of psychological texture and an evocative power which shows a close relationship between the art of Virginia Woolf and that of Katherine Mansfield. Developing from the narrative method of the earlier novels, the writer succeeds in creating, in *To the Lighthouse*, an intense lyricism and poetry.

Having reached this point, Virginia Woolf, as though looking back on the path she has travelled, and meditating on the lyrical element which gives life to her works, has written a poem of poems (it cannot be called anything else), *Orlando* (1928). The book has a place of its own in relation to all her earlier and later works: it forms, so to speak, a parenthesis. The line characterising the three major novels will then be resumed again and taken yet further, though perhaps with less power, in *The Waves* (1931). In these notes we shall, however, be compelled to limit ourselves to *Orlando*, and attempt a brief discussion of it, because of all Virginia Woolf's books it is considered to be the most enigmatic and disconcerting. A useful discussion of it will naturally involve an interpretation of its meaning. . . . Although there are patches of verisimilitude, Virginia Woolf transports the reader from the opening pages into an atmosphere remote from realism. . . . This conception of time—consistent as we have seen, with that in Virginia Woolf's earlier novels, reveals itself fully, on a symbolic plane, in the life of Orlando, who is the embodiment of the principle cited above: 'some are hundreds of years old although they say they are thirty-seven.' All the more so if we consider that though the duration of his life changes, his contact with one of the arts—poetry—remains unbroken. And it is poetry that the oak tree on the hill symbolises, the tree under whose shade the adolescent in search of solitude found refuge:

[Quotes p. 20 'He loved, beneath all this' to 'his floating heart.']

These are indeed the beloved and clairvoyant fantasies of art which preserve and perpetuate in the human heart the visionary stages of one's earliest years. All his life, through the loves of queens and gallants, through changes of landscapes, wanderings, spells of idleness, change of sex, Orlando will go on working at a poem with the title 'The Oak Tree'. At the end of the book, after the change in sex, after the experience of motherhood which is glorified in the poem, the soul which has in the course of thirty-seven years lived through centuries, will return to the old oak tree still standing on the hill. It will recover intact all the sensations and fancies of childhood . . . Orlando's poem —we can certainly call it that—is a high oak tree on a hill, on which the world turns as if on an axis . . .

[Quotes pp. 289–90 'Yes, she thought,' to 'everything was partly something else.']

These words, quoted from the last few pages of the book, signify the end of the long journey; the conquest and possession of poetry as a mode of existence; only thus having reached the final steps of knowledge ('I am on the point of understanding') does the poet find all the universe and all life harmonised in his own spirit in an organic unity. Hence the indifference towards external reality which forms the basis of Virginia Woolf's art, and in which we recognise the liberation of poetry from a dependence on facts.

. . . The beginning and the end are both marked by the oak on the hill. This symbolic tree and many scenes and events return in these pages like musical motifs. And indeed it is more appropriate to speak of musical structure than plot in the ordinary sense of the term. The oak, that is, poetry, is the leitmotif and the entire book is, as it were, the elaboration of a musical phrase which returns in the end to the note on which it began. And it is significant that Orlando is one of the most clear-cut and precise of Virginia Woolf's characters, in spite of the variations in age and environment.

Treated by a less skilful artist, many of the episodes, the transitions from one to another and the changes of scene and setting, might easily have lapsed into worn-out tricks such as one finds in fairy tales. Instead, the spiritual nature of the events allows the writer to present them without recourse to the sensational. She retains throughout, except perhaps in the episode of sex change, an inspired lightness of touch, a poetic equilibrium, in which the more concrete particulars have their existence, as it were, in an intensely visionary atmosphere. On almost every page of the book Virginia Woolf is confronted by situations in which any emphasis or extravagance would have spoiled the tone. On almost every page she has had to put subtle movements of the mind into words and execute difficult patterns of colour and shade. This lightness and grace of manner has been combined, without incongruity, with a lucidity and concreteness in which we can see the cultivated heritage of the best prose writers of the 18th century, particularly Sterne. Virginia Woolf not only explicitly refers to the author of *Tristram Shandy* in her essay 'Mr Bennett and Mrs Brown', she has also edited the Oxford *Sentimental Journey* and written a prefatory essay. Virginia Woolf's prose is distinguished by a great wealth of vocabulary. It is often rhythmic and sometimes employs assonance and rhyme. But all these resources, including the slightly archaic touches which occur now and then, are used with great discretion. The equilibrium is never disturbed, not even by the similes, abundant though brief, which, despite their simplicity, acquire from the prevailing tone their suggestive power. Virginia Woolf has been compared to Sterne by many critics, chiefly for the impressionism which, to a certain degree, is common to both; but while Sterne's strong point is his humour, that of Virginia Woolf—although she is not lacking in the best English humour—is lyricism.

FLUSH

5 October 1933

100. Peter Burra, from a review-article, *Nineteenth Century*

January 1934, 112–25

Peter Burra (b. 1909). Literary and art critic. Author of *Baroque and Gothic* and *Van Gogh*. This is a survey of Virginia Woolf's work rather than a review, but the writer begins his article with some remarks about *Flush*, which he sees as a 'necessary pause' in Virginia Woolf's development. There are also some interesting remarks on certain psychological aspects of her novels—a line of enquiry taken in more recent criticism.

'What kind of book does one write after *Orlando*?' asked one of Mrs Woolf's reviewers at the outset of an article on *The Waves*. And during the two years that have passed since then the great question has been, What kind of book does one write after *The Waves*? Each of Mrs Woolf's works has been a literary career in itself. Each has been something perfect, but at the same time so original that her readers, if they are successful in following one of her adventures, must needs preoccupy themselves with the further question of what it is leading to next. *The Waves*, one might be thinking, was the limit of her development. There her early experiments are carried to their logical conclusion—so extremely that it is hard to see what will follow unless it is to be repetition. True, the method is so beautiful, so fitting a medium for the expression of Mrs Woolf's thought, that she might well remain content with it. But she has never led us to expect anything but surprises, and there is probably still something new ahead. Meanwhile,

Flush calls a halt. The whole process of writing so complicated a work as *The Waves* must have been exhausting, and in her new book Mrs Woolf allows herself a deliberate simplification of narrative by telling a story through the figure of one who cannot be expected to experience streams of mental consciousness, nor to interpret the significance of events philosophically, or psychologically—namely, Mrs Browning's cocker-spaniel, Flush.

Flush, like *Orlando*, is called 'A Biography', but is almost as much more than that as *Orlando* was. As biography it is an excellently full character-study, supplying all available details from all available sources (such as Flush's dislike of the smell of eau-de-Cologne, implied in Mrs Browning's poem) and gives dates for all the principal incidents. But the story of the dog—so beautifully and lovingly told—is perhaps to be taken only as the frame, the convention for the telling of another story which is greater than itself. It so happens that the years of Flush's life coincide with the meeting, the elopement, and the early married years of Elizabeth Barrett and Robert Browning. Flush and Wilson, the maid, were the only witnesses of the whole story. Mrs Woolf might almost as well have chosen Wilson to write a biography of, but 'since Miss Barrett never wrote a poem about her', she says in a charming note 'her appearance is far less familiar than his' (the dog's), and Flush's life has the advantage of being shorter and confining itself to the relevant years; and above all, Flush was a dog. For Flush, the convention, like Mrs Woolf's earlier convention, permits the omission of all the tiresome details and irrelevancies which in 'materialist' fiction annoy her so much. Flush sees and understands only as much of the story as Mrs Woolf wishes to tell. He may also think and feel as much or as little as is convenient, since, though an animal, he is capable of some simple human emotions, as all dogs are, which in his case were strengthened through years spent on the bed of an invalid. 'His flesh was veined with human passions.' He is the chorus, the commentary on the story, the observer whose detachment from it makes its significance sharper. Yet he is more than that. Mrs Woolf uses him almost as Swift used the Houyhnhnms, but without anger, rather with the gentlest irony, weaving together the lives of beast and man.

Flush is entirely beautiful; but it is a necessary pause, it is not a *tour de force* as its predecessor was.

Mrs Woolf's art is that of the psychologist. She does not direct our steps into new ways of life, but suddenly reveals to us in the piercing light of her poetic imagination things which have long been latent in the dark places of consciousness, hitherto unrealised by any power of explicit speech. She has, in fact, assimilated into her art all that modern psychology has to offer, and this poetry, these fictions of loveliness, have a firm basis in the latest discoveries of science. Rachel's *angst* dream, for example, James Ramsay's behaviour with his father and mother, the retention by the people of *The Waves* of their childhood's impressions into old age, are direct expositions of what we have learned from Freud. The whole of her books are constructed round such knowledge, which accounts largely for the amazing strength of her writing and the sureness of her touch on life.

One other important point she seems to have taken deliberately from psychology—the use of 'substitution-symbols'. Orlando, for example, knew that 'girls were roses, and their seasons were short as the flowers! Plucked they must be before nightfall.' Yet it scarcely matters whether this imagery, this poetry, this inevitable tendency to see 'everything as something else', comes to us when we sleep or when we are awake. It is the fabric of Mrs Woolf's writing. She is a poet. And for this reason her books cannot be hurriedly read for the story's sake, like many novels, but must be treated with as much care as is given to poetry, so that the symbols and refrains—which are never casual, but planned with utmost care and interrelations—can be remembered and recognised. Some of these symbols are of universal application—for example, Laurels for Triumph, Violets for Death, Snails for Self-seclusion. Others, which are harder to follow, are personal ones for certain characters, generally due to some experience in childhood, such as the 'immitigable tree' which Neville could not pass, since as a child he had overheard the cook speaking of a man whose throat had been cut, while he was looking at an apple tree, and the tree became a symbol in his mind of objects which he could not surmount. Mrs Woolf never explains or reminds us of these symbols, but leaves them to recur and to be recognised exactly like the Wagnerian *leit-motif*. And in this absence of explanation and our joy of recognition lies one of the secrets of her charm for us. Nor does she employ this austerity only with direct symbols. When Cam, sitting alone in the bow of the boat, looks back to their house on the island just before they reach the Lighthouse, this passage occurs:

But as, just before sleep, things simplify themselves so that only one of all the myriad details has power to assert itself, so, she felt, looking drowsily at the island, all those paths and terraces and bedrooms were fading and disappearing, and nothing was left but a pale blue censer swinging rhythmically this way and that across her mind. It was a hanging garden; it was a valley, full of birds, and flowers, and antelopes . . . She was falling asleep.

Where, for a moment we wonder, have we heard those words before? Then slowly we remember; they are the very words which Mrs Ramsay had used to send her to sleep in the nursery, that night years before, when they had been disappointed in their wish to go to the Lighthouse. Just because Mrs Woolf does not remind us directly of that scene, but leaves it to us to recognise like a returning tune, we are enchanted.

Of such art, finally, is composed the prose in which she writes. Mrs Woolf has used prose as few or none have ever used it before. She has successfully used it as a vehicle for poetry. It is the style of music rather than of reason. She has finally emancipated English from the unnatural yoke of classical construction and yet replaced that yoke with something which is as strong as it is beautiful. But our last consideration of her should be as of one who has enriched our ideas about life. She has disdained to give us a gallery of infinitely various characters as the novelists of the eighteenth and nineteenth centuries did, though her first two books prove that she could have done so had she wished. But to her such characterisation is little more than a display of virtuosity. And yet we feel that she is one whose imagination has known all men in all places; that she has felt intensely the significance of our life as it moves inevitably towards death, and knows how while we live we long for things which we cannot touch, striving passionately to become 'the complete human being whom we have failed to be, but at the same time cannot forget'.

101. Maud Bodkin on archetypal patterns in Virginia Woolf's work

1934

From *Archetypal Patterns in Poetry*, 86–8, 299–307.

Maud Bodkin, writer on philosophical and psychological themes, died in 1967. Her argument is more subtle than many psychological studies of literature, and her appeal, as we can see in the following extract, is to the 'concrete impression' which the work under discussion has had on the reader.

Perhaps to each individual reader or spectator these communications come differently. If he attains sincerity to discern the spontaneous choices of his own heart, he will find that certain images and phrases pre-eminently serve him as instruments of reference to the intimate discoveries that his own life has yielded.

The mode of this traditional participation in collective tradition is beautifully illustrated in a book that has the distinctively present-day form, of a novel that is both less and more than a novel as understood in the past, showing in its texture and construction a new development both of the artistic and of the psychological interest. In Virginia Woolf's novel, *Mrs Dalloway*, one seems to recognize an expression of that same impulse of scientific curiosity, to discern and record impartially the inner flow of thought and feeling, that led Galton to make the experiments referred to at the beginning of this chapter.

Writing elsewhere of the aim that in some modern writers is changing the form of the novel, Mrs Woolf says: 'Let us trace the pattern, however disconnected and incoherent in appearance, which each sight and incident scores upon the consciousness.' In passing from mind to mind tracing this pattern, Mrs Woolf presents, as poetry or music may present, a sensuous element recurring, entering into ever new combinations, becoming ever more charged with emotional significance; and reveals this form as true both of the daily flow, and of the age-long development, of the inner life.

In accompanying the main character of the novel in this intimate fashion through parts of the experience of a single day, we find certain lines of poetry recurring amid the vital flux and reflux of feeling, with the power of an individually unconsciously appropriated symbol. 'But what was she dreaming as she looked into Hatchard's shop window? What was she trying to recover? What image of white dawn in the country, as she read in the book spread open':

> Fear no more the heat o' the sun
> Nor the furious winter's rages.

When these lines come to Clarissa in the morning of the recorded day, they come between a thought of the life of the London streets—so loved that it seemed that somehow after death she must survive in their ebb and flow—and a thought of the stoical bearing 'this late age of the world's experience' had bred in men and women. The line comes again in one of the alternations of vital rhythm—a backward, inward turning of libido following the outward flow—such as Jung describes as repeating itself unconsciously in our lives 'almost continually'.

> 'Fear no more,' said Clarissa. Fear no more the heat o' the sun; for the shock of Lady Bruton asking Richard to lunch without her made the moment in which she stood shiver . . . she feared time itself, and read on Lady Bruton's face, as if it had been a dial cut in impassive stone, the dwindling of life . . . feeling herself suddenly shrivelled, aged, breastless.

So, for minutes, for an hour or two perhaps, the tide of life sets backward and each object on which her eyes fall is caught into the ebb—her attic bedroom, the sheets stretched tight across the bed. 'Narrower and narrower would her bed be.' Thoughts come of the relations of life in which she has failed. But, as she muses and her day wears on, the tide of sensibility turns again. Calm descends on her. 'Fear no more, says the heart, committing its burden to some sea, which sighs collectively for all sorrows, and renews, begins, collects, lets fall.'

These fragments may recall to the reader who knows the book how lightly and inevitably it portrays the recurring, amid the flux of an individual sensibility, of symbols of a group tradition—a tradition here mediated by no institutional or dogmatic religion, no profound literary study, only by lines from casual reading that have become means of reference to ideals diffused through personal relationship.

It would seem that the function fulfilled by such symbols in the life of an individual to-day is the same that was performed by the images and dogma of institutional religion, more widely in the past—and still in the present for those who feel no inward barrier to the acceptance of religious symbols . . .

The consideration of our psychological patterns from the angle of contemporary fiction gives opportunity for recurring to a question put aside at an earlier point of our discussion. The attempt to trace the form assumed in poetry by the archetypal images of man and woman suggested the inquiry whether one could find in the poetry of women writers any imaginative representation of man, related to the distinctive inner life of a woman in the same manner as an image of woman appearing in poetry shows relation to the emotional life of man. In classical poetry no figure could be found fulfilling this condition. Within the field of contemporary literature, with the range of women's work in fiction open to us, it should be possible to choose an example illustrative of the form a type-image of man may take, in relation to the course of a woman's inner life.

The example I choose is from the imaginative work of Virginia Woolf: the fantasy entitled *Orlando, a biography*.

The character of this tale, the mingling of mockery and mystification with whatever it may possess of serious meaning, makes its attempted analysis a hazardous undertaking. The critic, laying hold on subject-matter of such lightness and shifting iridescence, risks the change of breaking a butterfly upon his wheel. But this risk is incurred in some degree by every attempt at psychological analysis of works of imagination. In accepting it, where most imminent, one can only endeavour to handle one's elusive subject-matter not too heavily; confirming, perhaps, the hints found in it by reference to stabler material.

For our purpose, the tale of Orlando is attractive in its rejection of a matter-of-fact framework for the more imaginative mode of conveying truth. It presents a woman's experience through the fantasy of a life running through centuries; beginning with the adventures of boy and man, but later, suffering—with some spasm of bewilderment though with no undue shock—transformation to a woman's state. Such a fantasy gives opportunity for moments of survey arrestingly truthful to the experience of any woman whose imaginative life has been largely shaped by the thought and adventure of men. These moments are rendered with gay fidelity to the scattering glimpses that any reflective mind may know, of a past compounded from both personal and communicated experience; where, among the fragments that 'the hussy, Memory' agitates before us, there is always the chance that some casual-seeming image may prove of deep personal significance.

In one such moment of survey, the woman Orlando recalls from her Elizabethan boyhood the single encounter she had enjoyed with Shakespeare—seen pen in hand, with fixed eyes, as though behind the domed brow deep thoughts were revolving. The image, revived by the sight of the marble dome of St Paul's—at a time when Orlando, voyaging in state to England, has been realizing exciting potentialities of her womanhood—calms her emotion. 'The distractions of sex, which hers was, and what it meant, subsided.' She is recalled to her faith in the office of the poet, whose magic of words, that 'reach where others fall short', she is to pursue amid the diversions of life in eighteenth-century London.

The manner in which the reference to Shakespeare recurs, in the tale, at one critical point and another of the flow of thought and incident, gives to the image a special significance . . . The psychologist may term the poet-figure that can function thus in the inner life a form of the father-imago . . . The gain of considering in a context literary, rather than medical, such intimately reverenced images is that we more easily recognize other aspects than the negative, inhibiting ones stressed by the medical analyst. The communicated experiences of poetry bear witness to a positive, creative aspect which the figure of poet or father may possess within the inner life, mediating to the individual those social values which can be assimilated by his own nature. As to the child the father may appear pre-eminently the being that has command over speech, material contrivance, and all forms of the world's stored magic, so, with the development of the inner life, other figures—by chance, the poet—take the father's place, as charged with that same *mana*.

The realization of such a personal symbol one may find suggested in *Orlando* by the description of the early encounter with the poet:

> Orlando stopped dead . . . 'Tell me' he wanted to say, 'everything in the whole world' . . . but how speak to a man who does not see you? who sees ogres, satyrs, perhaps the depths of the sea instead? So Orlando stood gazing . . .

A little later, the rising of this memory was the signal for an 'insurrection' in Orlando's mind, whereby the admired deeds of his ancestors, all their hunting and fighting and spending, compared with the poet's glory, seemed dust and ashes. Of the poet thus raised to supremacy, of Shakespeare, we are told in the passage already quoted 'whenever she thought of him, the thought spread round it, like the risen moon on turbulent waters, a sheet of silver calm.'

[There follows a description of the figure of the sea-captain, Orlando's husband-lover, and of the wild-goose symbol.]

. . . Of any reader to whom these quoted fragments recall a concrete impression of the book, I would ask the question whether this play of images of poet and lover, in relation to the wild-goose symbol, and to the suggested course of a woman's life, evokes any aura of emotional memory, within which, at a venture, associations might be discerned to other figures of literary tradition. Limiting our search by the question concerning significant figures of men in women's writings, one might ask concerning the Heathcliff of Emily Bronte's *Wuthering Heights*—a figure that, with the abundant commentary it has called forth, might well have been made a starting-point for study of the Hero, in Satanic phase, in relation to woman's emotional life—do we feel any significant association between Heathcliff and the conjunction in Orlando of the wild-goose symbol, the haunting image of the poet and the lover rounding Cape Horn? . . .

A medical psychologist has suggested that the relation between man and woman, as determined by racial history, might be diagrammatically rendered by two concentric circles, man having his place on the outer, woman on the inner circle.*

When man looks outward he sees the world, when he looks inward he sees woman and her child. His escape from her is into the world. The woman, however, looking outward sees the man, through whom only she touches the outer world of reality and whose favor she must seek to gain her wishes.

At the time when the Brontes wrote, this historically determined relation was strongly enforced by existing social conditions; and we may agree with Romer Wilson's assertion in her study of Emily Bronte,† that the evil aspect of Heathcliff as a 'dark hero' is due, in part, to the frustration in Emily's secluded life of her masculine qualities of pride and self-assertion. In the life of a woman of to-day, as portrayed by Virginia Woolf in *Orlando*, there is no such persistent restraint of masculine qualities. A woman may play an independent part in the

* Beatrice M. Hinkle, *The Recreating of the Individual* (Allen & Unwin, 1923), 306.
† *All Alone* (Chatto & Windus, 1928).

world, which she may find herself recalling, like Orlando, with a shock of incongruity, at some moment when the seduction of masculine attentions has merged her in an ostentatiously feminine role. Yet even Orlando, in her character as woman-lover, reaches out, as does Catherine Earnshaw, to an existence of her own beyond her; and finds this existence, her creator declares, in the guise of a sea-captain braving the perils of the Horn. It is over his head—the aeroplane having now supplanted the ship—that there springs up the winged wild thing by which the woman finds herself haunted and lured.

Here, as always, it is hard to force the meaning conveyed by imaginative speech into terms more precise than that speech itself. Only through comparison can we sometimes sharpen the edges of the intuition conveyed, urging it a little way toward the definiteness of a concept. With Catherine Earnshaw's cry of need for the existence beyond her, we may compare the more subtly elaborated representation of Orlando calling up in turn her many varied selves, settled and stilled only when, in thought of an existence beyond, those selves 'communicate' and fall silent. With the type-figure of the sea-captain perpetually braving the world's storms, we find related, through the wild-goose symbol, the figure of the poet, master-adventurer and treasure-seeker in the realms of the mind; and we may hazard the conclusion that in this tale—whatever its other purport—we have incidentally a modern rendering, from the woman's standpoint, of that intuition, communicated from man's side by Dante's *Comedy* and Goethe's *Faust*, that through the immortal and ever-elusive Image formed in each of the other, man and woman alike find a way of approach to Reality, or to the Divine.

102. An enemy: Wyndham Lewis

1934

(a) Wyndham Lewis, from Chapter V 'Virginia Woolf', *Men Without Art*, 1934, 158–71.

Wyndham Lewis (1886–1957). Satirical novelist and 'Vorticist' painter.

In *Time and Western Man* (1927) Lewis had attacked 'time writers' like Gertrude Stein and Joyce. He was the self-styled 'Enemy' of artists who created work which he thought 'fluid' or 'internal'. When *Men Without Art* was announced, Virginia Woolf noted:

In today's *Lit. Sup.*, they advertise *Men Without Art*, by Wyndham Lewis: chapters on Eliot, Faulkner, Hemingway, Virginia Woolf... Now I know by reason and instinct that this is an attack; that I am publicly demolished; nothing is left of me in Oxford and Cambridge and places where the young read Wyndham Lewis. My instinct is not to read it. And for that reason: Well, I open Keats and find:

> Praise or blame has but a momentary effect on the man whose love of beauty in the abstract makes him a severe critic on his own works. My own domestic criticism has given me pain beyond what *Blackwood* or *Quarterly* could possibly inflict... This is a mere matter of the moment—I think I shall be among the English poets after my death. Even as a matter of present interest the attempt to crush me in the *Quarterly* has only brought me more into notice.

Well: do I think I shall be among the English novelists after my death? I hardly ever think about it. Why then do I shrink from reading W.L.? Why am I sensitive? I think vanity: I dislike the thought of being laughed at: of the glow of satisfaction that A., B. and C. will get from hearing V.W. demolished: also it will strengthen further attacks: perhaps I feel uncertain of my own gifts: but then, I know more about them than W.L.: and anyhow I intend to go on writing. What I shall do is craftily to gather the nature of the indictment from talk and reviews; and, in a year perhaps, when my book is out, I shall read it. Already I am feeling the calm that always comes to me with abuse: my back is against the wall: I am writing for the sake of writing, etc.; and then there is the queer disreputable pleasure in being abused—in being a figure, in being a martyr, and so on (*A Writer's Diary*, 227–8) (see *Introduction*, p. 26).

In the present chapter I am compelled, however, to traverse the thorny region of feminism, or of militant feminine feeling. I have chosen the back of Mrs Woolf—If I can put it in this inelegant way—to transport me across it. I am sure that certain critics will instantly object that Mrs Woolf is extremely insignificant—that she is a purely feminist phenomenon—that she is taken seriously by no one any longer today, except perhaps by Mr and Mrs Leavis—and that, anyway, feminism is a dead issue. But that will not deter me, any more than the other thorny obstacles, from my purpose: for while I am ready to agree that the intrinsic literary importance of Mrs Woolf may be exaggerated by her friends, I cannot agree that as a symbolic landmark—a sort of party-lighthouse—she has not a very real significance. And she has crystallized for us, in her critical essays, what is in fact *the feminine*—as distinguished from the femininist—standpoint. She is especially valuable in her 'clash' with what is today, in fact and indeed, a dead issue, namely nineteenth-century scientific 'realism', which is the exact counterpart, of course, in letters, of French Impressionism in art (Degas, Manet, Monet).

But the photographic Degas, he is literally the end of the world, luckily—he is more than off the map; and following forty years behind the French mid-nineteenth century realists, the late Mr Bennett was such a dead horse (dragging such a dead issue) that Mrs Woolf was merely engaged in an undergraduate exercise in her pamphlet about him, it might be asserted. In spite of that, so long as prose-fiction continues to be written, the school of 'realism' will always have its followers, in one degree or another. . . . We are probably on the threshold, according to all the signs and portents, of a great period of imaginative satire—the times are propitious. And, establishing as I am here the theoretic foundations for such work, I have found that the criticism of 'realism' is of very great use for a full illumination of my subject. And that is why I have considered it worth while to dissect in detail the Woolf-versus-the-realists controversy: and this of course is, as I have said, especially indicated, owing to the part that the feminine principle plays in this debate.

Equipped with this explanation, I think we may now proceed. Well then, when Mrs Woolf, the orthodox 'idealist', tremulously squares up to the big beefy brute, Bennett, plainly the very embodiment of commonplace *matter*—it is, in fact, a rather childish, that is to say an over-simple, encounter. It is a cat and dog match, right enough: but such 'spiritual' values as those invoked upon Mrs Woolf's side of the argument, are of a spiritualism which only exists upon that popular plane, as the complement of hard-and-fast matter. The one value is as tangible, popular and readily understood by the 'plain reader' as the other. I doubt if, at bottom, it is very much more than a boy and girl quarrel (to change the metaphor from dog-and-cat). I believe it is just the old incompatibility of the eternal feminine, on the one hand, and the rough footballing 'he' principle—the eternal masculine—on the other. There is nothing more metaphysical about it than that.

'If we try to formulate our meaning in one word we should say that these three writers (Wells, Bennett, Galsworthy) are materialists. It is because they are concerned not with the spirit but with the body that they have disappointed us,' writes Mrs Woolf. Is it so simple? Or rather, were we compelled to decide upon the respective merits of a person, of the same calibre as, say, Bennett, but who was as delicately mental as he was grossly material, and of Bennett himself, should we not have to say, that in their respective ways, their masculine and feminine ways, they were much of a muchness—indeed, *a good match*? The preoccupations of Mrs Dalloway are after all not so far removed from the interests of Mr Bennett's characters. One is somewhat nearer to 'the Palace', the other to the 'Pub'. But does not that even suggest a subtle kinship, rather than an irreconcilable foreignness? . . .

I must assume that you do not know, or I must recall to your mind, the parable of Mrs Brown and Mr Bennett. Mrs Woolf tells us, in a skilful little sketch, how she enters the carriage of a suburban train, and in so doing intrudes unwittingly upon the rather passionate conversation of two people—one, *very large*, a blustering, thick-set, middle-aged bully of a *man*: the other, *very small*, a very pathetic, poor little old lady (not *quite* a lady—'I should doubt if she was an educated woman', says Mrs Woolf—but none the less to be pitied for *that*!). The big bully had obviously been bullying the weaker vessel: and Mrs Woolf calls the former Mr Smith, the latter Mrs Brown. As to make conversation before the inquisitive stranger in the other corner, or else dreaming aloud, the little old woman asks her *vis-à-vis* if he could tell her whether, after being the host for two years running of caterpillars, an oak tree dies. And while Mr Smith (who is a shamefaced coward, as are all big bullies come to that) is eagerly replying to this impersonal question, glad to be able to mask beneath an irrelevant stream of words his blackguardly designs upon the defenceless old lady, Mrs Brown begins, without moving, to let fall tear after tear into her lap. Enraged at this exhibition of weakness on the part of Mrs Brown (which he probably would refer to as 'waterworks' or something brutal of that sort) the big bully, ignoring the presence of a third party, leans forward and asks Mrs Brown point blank if she will do, yes or no, what he asked her to do just now, and poor Mrs Brown says yes, she will. At that moment Clapham Junction presents itself, the train stops, and the big bully (probably jolly glad to escape from the eye of public opinion, as represented by Mrs Woolf we are told—for he had little streaks of decency left perhaps) hurriedly leaves the train.

Now the point of this story is, we are told, that Mrs Woolf, being born a novelist of course, and this episode occurring apparently before she had written any novels (1910 is the date implied) is in a quandary as to what to do. She would have *liked* to write a novel about Mrs Brown, she tells us. But how was she to do it? For after all Wells, Galsworthy and Bennett (the only novelists apparently that, true child of her time, she knew about) had not taught her how to do it: the only tools (she apologises for this professional word) available were those out of the tool-box of this trio. And alas! they were not suitable for the portrayal of Mrs Brown. So what was poor little she to do?

She then enlarges upon her dilemma—which she tells us was also the dilemma of D. H. Lawrence, of E. M. Forster and the rest of the people she recognises as the makers and shakers of the new-age (*all*, to a man, ruined by the wicked, inappropriate trio—I need not repeat the names).

Finding himself in the same compartment with Mrs Brown, Wells would have looked out of the window, with a blissful faraway Utopian smile on his face. He would have taken no interest in Mrs Brown. Galsworthy would have written a tract round her: and Bennett would have neglected her 'soul' for her patched gloves and stockings.

This was really a terrible situation for a novelist to be in, in 1910: and everything that has happened since, or to be more accurate, that has *not* happened since, is due to the shortcomings of this diabolical trio (but especially, we are led to understand, to the defective pen of the eminent Fivetowner) . . .

What Mrs Woolf says about the three villains of this highly artificial little piece is perfectly true, as far as it goes: 'the difference perhaps is,' she writes, 'that both Sterne and Jane Austen were interested in things in themselves; in character in itself: in the book in itself'. Of course, of course! who would not exclaim: it is not 'perhaps' the difference—[it] is as plain as the nose was on Hodge's face. Of course Sterne and Jane Austen were a different kettle of fish, both to Mrs Woolf's three sparring partners or Aunt Sallies, and to Mrs Woolf herself.

And then Mrs Woolf goes on to tell us that we must not expect too much of Messrs. Eliot, Joyce, Lawrence, Forster, or Strachey either. For they all, in their way, were in the same unenviable position. All were boxed up with some Mrs Brown or other, longing to 'bag' the old girl, and yet completely impotent to do so, because no one was there on the spot to show them how, and they could not, poor dears, be expected to do it themselves! Do not complain of *us*, then, she implores her public. Show some pity for such a set of people, born to such a forlorn destiny! You will never get anything out of us except a little good stuff by fits and starts, a sketch or a fragment. Mr Eliot, for instance, gives you a pretty line—a solitary line. But you have to hold your breath and wait a long time for the next. There are no 'Passion flowers at the gate dropping a splendid tear' (cf. *A Room of One's Own*) —not in *our* time. There are just disjointed odds and ends!

> We must reconcile ourselves to a season of failures and fragments. We must reflect that where so much strength is spent on finding a way of telling the truth, the truth itself is bound to reach us in rather an exhausted and chaotic condition. Ulysses, Queen Victoria, Mr Prufrock—to give Mrs Brown some of the names she has made famous lately—is a little pale and dishevelled by the time her rescuers reach her (*Mr Bennett and Mrs Brown*).

There you have a typical contemporary statement of the position of letters today. Its artificiality is self-evident, if you do no more than consider the words: for *Ulysses*, however else it may have arrived at its destination, was at least not *pale*. But here, doubtless, Mrs Woolf is merely confusing the becoming pallor, and certain untidiness of some of her own pretty salon pieces with that of Joyce's masterpiece (indeed that masterpiece is implicated and confused with her own pieces in more ways than one, and more palpable than this, but into that it is not necessary to enter here). As to the 'strength spent in finding a way', that takes us back to the fable of Mrs Brown, and the fearful disadvantage under which Mrs Woolf laboured. Anyone would suppose from what she says that at the time in question Trollope, Jane Austen,

Flaubert, Maupassant, Dostoievsky, Turgenev, Tolstoy, etc., etc., etc., etc., were entirely inaccessible to this poor lost 'Georgian' would-be novelist: it is as though she, Bennett, Wells and Galsworthy had been the only people in the world at the time, and as if there had been no books but their books, and no land but England.

The further assumption is that, prior to *Prufrock*, *Ulysses* and Mr Lytton Strachey's biographies, there had been either (1) no rendering of anything so exclusive and remote as the 'soul' of a person: or else (2) that the fact that there was not much 'soul' in the work of Mr Bennett made it very very difficult for Mr Joyce to write *Ulysses*: and that by the time he had succeeded in some way in banishing Mr Bennett, he had only strength enough left to concoct a 'pale' little 'fragment', namely *Ulysses*.

But, again, it is obviously the personal problems of Mrs Woolf getting mixed up with the problems of Mr Joyce above all people! For it is quite credible that Clayhanger, astride the island scene—along with his gigantic colleagues, Forsyte and Britling—was a very real problem for the ambitious budding pre-war novelist (especially as she was a little woman, and they were great big burly men—great 'bullies' all three, like all the men, confound them!) . . .

Those most influential in the literary world, as far as the 'highbrow' side of the racket was concerned, have mostly been minor personalities, who were impelled to arrange a sort of bogus 'time' to take the place of the real 'time'—to bring into being the imaginary 'time', small enough and 'pale' enough to accommodate their not very robust talents. That has, consistently, been the so-called 'Bloomsbury' technique, both in the field of writing and of painting, as I think is now becoming generally recognised. And, needless to say, it has been very much to the disadvantage of any vigorous manifestation in the arts; for anything above the *salon* scale is what this sort of person most dislikes and is at some pains to stifle. And also, necessarily, it brings into being a quite false picture of the true aspect of our scene.

So we have been invited, all of us, to instal ourselves in a very dim Venusberg indeed: but Venus has become an introverted matriarch, brooding over a subterraneous 'stream of consciousness'—a feminine phenomenon after all—and we are a pretty sorry set of knights too, it must be confessed—at least in Mrs Woolf's particular version of the affair.

> I saw pale kings, and princes too,
> Pale warriors, death-pale were they all . . .

It is a myopic humanity, that threads its way in and out of this 'unreal city', whose objective obstacles are in theory unsubstantial, but in practice require a delicate negotiation. In our local exponents of this method there is none of the realistic vigour of Mr Joyce, though often the incidents in the local 'masterpieces' are exact and puerile copies of the scenes in his Dublin drama (cf. the Viceroy's progress through Dublin in *Ulysses* with the Queen's progress through London in *Mrs Dalloway*—the latter is a sort of undergraduate imitation of the former, winding up with a smoke-writing in the sky, a pathetic 'crib' of the firework display and the rocket that is the culmination of Mr Bloom's beach-ecstasy). But to appreciate the sort of fashionable dimness to which I am referring, let us turn for a moment to Mrs Woolf, where she is apeeping in the half-light:

> She reached the park gates. She stood for a moment, looking at the omnibuses in Piccadilly. [*Mrs Dalloway*] She should really have written *peeping* at the omnibuses in Piccadilly!—for she would not say of anyone in the world now that they were this or were that. She felt very young: at the same time unspeakably aged. She sliced like a knife through everything: and at the same time was outside, looking on. She had a perpetual sense as she watched the taxicabs, of being out, out, far out to sea and alone: she always had the feeling that it was very, very dangerous to live even one day.

To live *outside*, of course that means. Outside it is terribly *dangerous*—in that great and coarse Without, where all the he-men and he-girls 'live-dangerously' with a brutal insensibility to all the *risks* that they run, forever in the public places. But this *dangerousness* does, after all, make it all very *thrilling*, when peeped-out at, from the security of the private mind: 'and yet to her it was absolutely absorbing: all this, the cabs passing.'

Those are the half-lighted places of the mind—in which, quivering with a timid excitement, this sort of intelligence shrinks, thrilled to the marrow, at all the wild going-on! A little old-maidish, are the Prousts and sub-Prousts I think. And when two old maids—or a company of old maids—shrink and cluster together, they titter in each other's ears and delicately tee-hee, pointing out to each other the red-blood antics of this or that upstanding figure, treading the perilous Without. That was the manner in which the late Lytton Strachey lived—peeping more into the past than into the present, it is true, and it is that of most of those associated with him. And—minus the shrinking and tittering, and with a commendable habit of standing, half-concealed, but alone—it was the way of life of Marcel Proust.

But it has also, in one degree or another, been the way of life of many a recent figure in our literature—as in the case of Marius the Epicurean, 'made easy by his natural Epicureanism . . . prompting him to conceive of himself as but the passive spectator of the world around him.' Some, not content with retreating into the ambulatories of their inner consciousness, will instal there a sort of private oratory. From this fate 'the fleshly school' of the last century was saved, not much to its credit certainly, by the pagan impulses which still lingered in Europe. And it became ultimately the 'art-for-art's-sake' cult of the Naughty Nineties. Walter Pater was, of course, the fountainhead of that cult. And he shows us his hero, Marius—escaping from that particular trap, waiting upon the introverted—in the following passage:

At this time, by his poetic and inward temper, he might have fallen a prey to the enervating mysticism, then in wait for ardent souls in many a melodramatic revival of old religion or theosophy. From all this, fascinating as it might actually be to one side of his character, he was kept by a genuine virility there, effective in him, among other results, as a hatred of what was theatrical, and the instinctive recognition that in vigorous intelligence, after all, divinity was most likely to be found a resident.

That is, from the horse's mouth, the rationale of the non-religious, untheosophic, pleasure-cult, of which—in that ninetyish pocket at the end of the nineteenth century, in full, more than Stracheyish, reaction against Victorian manners—Oscar Wilde was the high-priest. And there is, of course, a very much closer connection than people suppose between the aesthetic movement presided over by Oscar Wilde, and that presided over in the first post-war decade by Mrs Woolf and Miss Sitwell. (Miss Sitwell has recently been rather overshadowed by Mrs Woolf, but she once played an equally important part—if it can be called important—in these events.) It has been with considerable shaking in my shoes, and a feeling of treading upon a carpet of eggs, that I have taken the cow by the horns in this chapter, and broached the subject of the part that the feminine mind has played—and minds as well, deeply feminized, not technically on the distaff side—in the erection of our present criteria. For fifteen years I have subsisted in this to me suffocating atmosphere. I have felt very much a fish out of water, very alien to all the standards that I saw being built up around me. I have defended myself as best I could against the influences of what I felt to be a tyrannical inverted orthodoxy-in-the-making. With the minimum of duplicity I have held my own: I have constantly assailed the swarms of infatuated builders. So, having found myself in a peculiarly isolated position, I had begun to take for granted that these habits of mind had come to stay, in those about me, and that I must get used to the life of the outlaw, for there was nothing else to do.

(b) Stephen Spender, a defence of Virginia Woolf.

Stephen Spender, review of Wyndham Lewis's *Men Without Art*, *Spectator*, 19 October 1934, 574, 576.

Spender (b. 1909) was one of the younger generation of left-wing poets whom Virginia Woolf met through John Lehmann and the Hogarth Press.

In the first two chapters of this book Mr. Wyndham Lewis, as a critic, is at his best. Messrs. Hemingway and Faulkner are evidently writers for whom he has respect and whom he can attack without losing his sense of their proportions. Various sanitary and necessary ideas are ventilated through the other chapters, with all the draughtiness of Mr. Lewis's style. None is better than his analysis of a Hemingway hero, the character who lives a violent life in violent surroundings but who is essentially acted upon by events, and is incapable of acting or of thinking for himself. The essay entitled 'The Greatest Satire is Non-Moral' should be read by everyone who imagines that a satiric writer should be a moralist, and the chapter on the 'Terms Classical and Romantic' is a genuine contribution to that argument.

Moreover, the book is full of brilliant hits and amusing skirmishes. Two sentences on D. H. Lawrence have the air of tying Lawrence in a knot. 'My objections to Mr. D. H. Lawrence were chiefly concerned with that regrettable habit of his incessantly to refer to the intestinal billowing of "dark" subterranean passion. In his devotion to that romantic abdominal Within he abandoned the sunlit pagan surface of the earth.' His account of Mr. Eliot's attitude towards his own works—'Did the author of *The Waste Land* believe in God?' 'How can I say?' drawls Mr. Eliot testily—is amusing. So is the burlesque account of Mrs. Woolf's essay 'Mr. Bennett and Mrs. Brown'.

One would have little but admiration for Mr. Lewis's habit of successfully tying people into knots were his own criticism as rigid as one might expect from a writer with such high standards of taste, and such contempt for both the taste and the work of others. But it is distressing to find that Mr. Lewis himself occasionally, as it were, curls round, and makes a knot as fantastic as any of his victims. An excellent example of the Lewis knot is provided in the essay on Mrs. Woolf. Twelve well-filled pages of malice and ill-temper—often amusing examples of both—are devoted to attacking Mrs. Woolf for her remark that 'we must reconcile ourselves to a season of failures and fragments.' It may be remembered that Mrs. Woolf, in her essay, 'Mr. Bennett and Mrs. Brown', attributes this fragmentariness of imaginative fiction to the false lead given by her three contemporaries —Wells, Bennett and Galsworthy. Mr. Lewis quite pertinently (though not altogether justly) remarks: 'Anyone would suppose from what she says that at the time in question Trollope, Jane Austen, Flaubert, Maupassant . . . &c., &c., &c., were entirely inaccessible to this poor lost "Georgian" would-be novelist: it is as though she, Bennett, Wells, and Galsworthy had been the only people in the world at the time.' This common-sense point of view is doubtless salubrious, though it provides no real answer to Mrs. Woolf. But the end of the chapter is really surprising. After more hits at Miss Sitwell, Mrs. Woolf, Mr. E. M. Forster and everything he labels Bloomsbury, Mr. Lewis concludes: 'It has been with considerable shaking in my shoes that I have taken the cow by the horns in this chapter. . . . For fifteen years I have subsisted in this to me suffocating atmosphere. I have felt very much a fish out of water.' This is totally unexpected. Why should Mrs. Woolf seem to suffocate Mr. Lewis? And, if he feels suffocated by Mrs. Woolf, why should he object to her being suffocated by Messrs. Bennett, Wells and Galsworthy? He ought to be pleased. And where now are Tolstoy, Maupassant, Flaubert, &c., &c.?

The more one reads of this book the more such knots are tied, and do such questions occur to the reader. For instance, why, if Mr. Lewis makes violence a criterion of badness in novels, does he show such an admiration, in a later chapter, for the extremely violent novels of Mr. Wyndham Lewis? Why, when in one chapter he ridicules the criticism of Mr. T. S. Eliot, is he content in later chapters to appropriate his critical conclusions?

Except in the first two chapters, this book is almost lacking in any serious critical appraisement of any writer. Apart from his vigorous enemy attack, in the names of satire and the great without, there seems almost no constructive side to Mr. Lewis's criticism. He will occasionally throw a bouquet to some author—a few are thrown to

Mr. Auden—but to say that Mr. Auden is 'brilliant and interesting', and to misquote a line is not criticism. It would be easiest to assume that Mr. Lewis has no good opinion of any other living writer, but unfortunately there is one high light in this book which does little credit to his taste: 'Mr. Roy Campbell, in his *Georgiad* has produced a masterpiece of the satiric art, which may be placed beside the eighteenth-century pieces without its suffering by that proximity.' This is a book in which *The Waste Land* is referred to with contempt, as are also the novels of Mr. E. M. Forster, and in which Mrs. Woolf is attacked with a great deal of malice and without any show of evidence that Mr. Lewis has read either of her best works, *The Waves* or *To the Lighthouse.*

(c) Wyndham Lewis, letter to the Editor, *Spectator*, 2 November 1934.

On reading this, Virginia Woolf noted in her Diary '. . . opened the *Spectator* and read W.L. on me again. An answer to Spender. "I am not malicious. Several people call Mrs. W. Felicia Hemans." This I suppose is another little scratch of the cat's claws: to slip that in, by the way—"I don't say it—others do".'—(*A Writer's Diary*, 231).

The reiterated statement in a book-review (namely that of October 19th, by Mr Stephen Spender) that the literary criticism contained in *Men Without Art* is 'malicious'—specifically that I 'attack' Mrs Woolf with 'a great deal of malice'—compels me to reply, since the phraseology can scarcely be unconsidered or accidental, seeing that 'malice' in England does not signify the same thing as *malicieux* in France. So it is the principle of free speech that I am defending as well as myself. Handicapped as we are under a super-individualist legislation—which allows the utmost licence in criticism of the State, in contradistinction to the Individual—it should be a matter of honour, among writers, at least, to refrain from taking advantage of these oppressive laws. I should indeed be 'suffocated by Mrs Woolf' (to quote from a very muddled sally of Mr Spender's)—though in no other sense that I could imagine—were I to be threatened with the policeman should I happen to mention her *Lighthouse* with disrespect! And others would be 'suffocated' by me, if, referring to my *Paleface* with disapproval, the same threat were levelled at them.

Mrs Woolf appears to be the principal difficulty for Mr Spender. But in *Men Without Art* I have everywhere stressed that my criticisms are rather a writer's than a reader's. It is the internal creative *machinery* that I expose: not the footlight illusion of the *prima donna*, so much as the latter in process of slimming, voice-production, and make-up. Criticism of this nature is 'destructive', of necessity, from the standpoint of pure publicity—especially where a reputation is so flimsy as to be peculiarly susceptible to 'destruction'.

If Mr Hemingway I said, as I was bound to do, that he had lifted intact, for his rather different he-man purposes, the early manner of Miss Stein. But in doing that I was 'at my best', it seems: I was behaving with critical decorum (though Mr Hemingway, I suppose, might hold another opinion, in this respect, to that of Mr Spender or Mrs Woolf). But when I refer to the obvious imitation of episodes in *Ulysses* to be met with in *Mrs Dalloway*, then I am showing 'a great deal of malice'.

But this is absurd. Anyone has a right to their opinion of the books of Mrs Woolf—as also of those of Mr Roy Campbell: though both these rights are denied me by Mr Spender. To admire Mr Campbell's books 'does little credit to one's taste', I am told: whereas *not* to admire overmuch those of Mrs Woolf is simply 'malicious'.

My reason for assuming that my misdemeanour, in the case of Mrs Woolf, can only relate to my references to *Mrs Dalloway*, is that afterwards I am so paradoxically accused of 'appropriating' Mr Eliot's—of all people's—criteria (which is self-evident I could not do if I wished, seeing how greatly I differ from him). But I fail completely to follow the sensitiveness on the score of Mrs Woolf's 'originality' displayed by *all* her supporters. Mr Ezra Pound—a literary figure as much esteemed as Mrs Woolf—has, for example, never disguised the fact that he is mainly a translator—an adapter an arranger, a *pasticheur*, if you like. And Mr T. S. Eliot has even made a virtue of developing himself into an incarnate Echo, as it were (though an *original* Echo, if one can say that). This imitation method, of the *creator-as-scholar*—which may be traced ultimately to the habits of the American university, spellbound by 'culture'—and which academic *unoriginality* it was Mr Ezra Pound's particular originality to import into the adult practice of imaginative literature—does not appeal to me extremely, I confess. But at least no amateurish touchiness on the score of 'originality' is involved in it.

Mrs Woolf is charming, scholarly, intelligent, everything that you will: but here we *have* not a Jane Austen—a Felicia Hemans, rather, as it has been said; for there are some even more 'malicious' than I am, I am afraid. Would not anybody, to conclude, in reading Mr Spender's article, come away with the impression that, as quoted by him, my quip of 'taking the cow by the horns' referred to Mrs Woolf? Yet the same reader should he turn to p. 170 of my book, where the expression occurs, immediately would discover that this expression refers to the Feminine Principle—specifically stated as equally belonging to those 'not technically on the distaff side'—and not to any individual, whether Mrs Woolf or another.

103. The artist and politics

1933, 1935, 1936

(a) R. D. Charques, from 'The Bourgeois Novel', in *Contemporary Literature and Social Revolution*, 1933, 108–14.

The author stated his position modestly in the preface to his book:

> There is no intention here of questioning the virtues of formal criticism, still less of claiming for an enquiry along the lines of the present book that it makes for a superior understanding of literature. But it is hoped that it may make for a better understanding of the influences from without which affect the contemporary writer and of the conditions of society which favour good literature.

If Mr Aldous Huxley is a very detached writer Mrs Virginia Woolf is by comparison aloofness itself. Not, of course, that her novels are lacking in human sympathy. They are too much in love with life to be misanthropical, they have too much imagination to be unfeeling. But Mrs Woolf's is a reticent and rarefied sympathy: she has her novelist's being somewhere in the heights of contemplative fantasy. She skims as lightly as a bird—as lightly as Clarissa Dalloway with her touch of the jay about her—over the ordinary preoccupations of men and women. No other contemporary novelist is so far removed from trivial or worldly things, so delicately poised above the common earth of fiction. No other novelist, it is true, achieves the sudden grace of Mrs Woolf's downward flight into the air we normally breathe; nor are such descents any the less enchanting for being rare. But it is a bright and shining world of fantasy rather than the common light of common hours which this novelist evokes for us.

It may seem at best superfluous to introduce theories of literature into the serene and illuminated world of Mrs Woolf's invention; and certainly theories, which are apt to be two a penny at most times, can do little to enhance its magic or explain it away. The attempt to apply a political yardstick to *Orlando* or *The Waves* may well suggest an inability to take any pleasure in them. For it is pleasure of a peculiarly unmixed kind that these novels offer. If we forget everything that the poets and the metaphysicians have said about beauty, it is in *Orlando* or *The Waves* that we get an impression of beauty that is quite complete and self-contained. Truth and the rest of the hierarchy of aesthetic values have nothing to do with it, and poetry as a criticism of life seems a rather empty maxim. Practically the whole of Mrs Woolf's work, indeed, conveys, though in varying degrees, this impression of completeness and self-containedness. Her refusal to lend a hint of symbolism to the strange tropical setting, the wholly imaginary country, of *The Voyage Out*, her first novel, and the keen, fine-drawn integrity with which the tragedy is presented are also characteristic of her later work.

Mrs Woolf's manner changes altogether in her next novel, *Night and Day*, and changes once again and still more drastically in *Jacob's Room*; but her peculiar reticence, her aloofness remains. She stands entirely apart from her characters, apart from their experience. 'She sliced,' Mrs Woolf says in the following novel, of Clarissa Dalloway, 'like a knife through everything; at the same time was outside, looking on. She had a perpetual sense, as she watched the taxi-cabs, of being out, out, far out to sea and alone.' That sense of isolation is very marked in Mrs Woolf's novels; it is the mainspring of her play of fancy, her evocation of wonder, to which the commonest scene or sight lends itself. What is it, a fish, the blade of an oar, a spar of some shipwreck?—for the most familiar things are after all the remotest and, like Mrs Dalloway, like Lily Briscoe, like Bernard and Susan and Jenny[1] and Louis and Rhoda and Neville in *The Waves*, one can be sure of nothing. Of people least of all; for beneath the surface of people there is layer upon layer of mystery. Not, indeed, that nothing and nobody is obvious, even though one is far out to sea. Not, that is to say, that Mrs Woolf is without a strong literary vein of realism. She has, to begin with, an instinctive and very humorous eye for character. The little roomfull of miniatures in the pages of each of her novels is vivid with the colours of life. Familiar greys and drab tones mingle with the sharper colours. There is Mrs Kilman in her mackintosh coat, hot and protesting her grievance, her superiority. There is Charles Tansley, 'the little atheist'—the perfect little atheist. There is Mr Bankes and his passion for preserving the salts in vegetables. These are real; these belong, so to speak, to life. But they are not important in Mrs Woolf's scheme of things. Foibles do not matter. Doubts and difficulties do not matter greatly, nor people who are excessively distracted by them. What is important is the secret, the fantastic glow in which things are enveloped. What matters is the moment of contemplation from afar.

For life has its vexations and disappointments, may be dull or difficult, but there is always refuge or immunity from the worst in contemplation of—what shall we say?—a mark on the wall. Mrs Woolf's little fantasy, 'The Mark on the Wall', gives us something of the quintessence of her imaginative method. That mark above the mantelpiece—is it a nail, a rose-leaf, a crack in the wood? One could, of course, get up and look. But even so could one be certain? Meanwhile, since it is pleasant to wonder, to what dizzy heights of speculation and uncertainty—the Greeks, Shakespeare, the whole past of human history, the laws of Nature—a mark on the wall may take us! Always there is something to dispel the hard, separate facts on the surface of existence, something to remind us of its mystery. What if the mark turns out to be a snail? One can think as well sitting still as standing up; perhaps better.

Thoughts as swift and allusive and sparkling as Mrs Woolf's are clearly worth an infinity of doubts about marks and snails. And to be aloof, perhaps, is merely to ignore one set of appearances and create another. Only in one of her novels, *To the Lighthouse*, does Mrs Woolf abandon the habit of detachment and the sense of looking on; and this is the loveliest of her books and Mrs Ramsay the nearest and the most

[1] Jinny.

intimately communicated of her characters. In the other novels there is more light than warmth; the fineness and playfulness of Mrs Woolf's sensibility seem to restrict passion. Lit by a strange splendour of poetry, *The Waves* is in an obvious sense very remote from human circumstance, and it almost defeats its purpose as a result. Life has there been abstracted of all its material reality and only a metaphysical essence remains. The world of appearances in *The Waves* is so thin and impalpable, so fragile a structure, that a coarse word would shatter it.

It seems useless to look for a statement of hard, separate facts in Mrs Woolf's novels. But the facts are implicit in her themes and characters; and in their social bearing they are summed up in a score of contrasts in the novels—not merely the too obvious contrast of Septimus Warren Smith with the rest of the people in *Mrs Dalloway*, not merely the 'real differences' which Mrs Ramsay, though she despaired of 'elucidating the social problem', ruminated as she wrote down in carefully ruled columns wages and spendings, employment and unemployment—but the more subtle contrast of Mrs Dalloway, for instance, who graces society but is always a little less than essential to society, with Mrs Ramsay, who is at the heart of life, who is at all times necessary. In that kind of contrast, however unconscious, Mrs Woolf makes her contribution to social criticism. 'Oh! thought Clarissa, in the middle of my party, here's death, she thought.' Mrs Ramsay would surely not have thought that.

For the statement of fact there is, of course, *A Room of One's Own*, which is full of admirable good sense. It is necessary, Mrs Woolf says, to have five hundred a year (if you are a woman) and a room with a lock on the door if you are to write fiction or poetry. Whoever can doubt it? 'Intellectual freedom,' Mrs Woolf concludes briefly, 'depends upon material things.' Who will demur, and where is truth to be found if not here? But Mrs Woolf's novels leave only the narrowest opening for truth of this kind to enter. They enclose a hundred virtues other than the most prosaic. Mention ignorance, dirt, vulgarity, want—and the serene and lovely world of her making vanishes, as though a bubble had burst. There is no place in it for commonplace reality, for the crude strife of material desires, for the harshness and bitterness of class struggle. Mrs Woolf's novels turn aside from all this. Inevitably there clings to her work something of the decadence, the refinement of decay, like a fragrance that is too prolonged, of the culture of her period. When all praises have been sung, Mrs Woolf's art remains the art of a governing class in English society.

(b) Dmitri Mirsky, from 'The Highbrows, 6: Bloomsbury' in *The Intelligentsia of Great Britain*, trans. Alec Brown, 1935, 111–20.

D. S. Mirsky (1890–1939). Russian aristocrat who escaped from Russia after the Revolution. He returned in the 1930s and was 'liquidated' by Stalin, though whether in the precise manner predicted by Virginia Woolf, we will probably never know. Leonard Woolf gives the following description of him in his *Autobiography*:

I always felt that he was fundamentally one of those unpredictable nineteenth-century Russian aristocrats whom one meets in Aksakov, Tolstoy, and Turgenev. Sometimes when one caught in a certain light the vision of his mouth and jaw, it gave one that tiny little clutch of fear in the heart ... In all our relations with him he seemed an unusually courteous and even gentle man, highly intelligent, cultivated, devoted to the arts, and a good literary critic. He had, at the same time, that air of profound pessimism which seemed to be characteristic of intellectual Russians, both within and without the pages of Dostoevsky. Certainly Prince Mirsky would have found himself spiritually at home in *The Possessed* or *The Idiot.*

One day Mirsky came to us in Tavistock Square and told us that he was going back to Russia. This must have been in 1931. By that time one knew something of the kind of life (or death) that an intellectual might expect in the Russia of Stalin. It seemed madness, if not suicide, for a man like Mirsky voluntarily to return to Russia and put himself in the power of ferocious fanatics who could not possibly have the slightest sympathy with or for him. We knew Mirsky well enough to say so. He was extemely reticent, shrugging it all off with some platitude, but he left us with the impression of an unhappy man who, with his eyes open, was going not half, but the whole, way to meet a nasty fate. We never saw him again (*Downhill All the Way*, 23–5).

According to Virginia Woolf's *Diary* it was June 1932, not 1931, when this meeting took place. She set down the following little sketch and prophecy:

Mirsky was trap mouthed: opened and bit his remark to pieces: has yellow misplaced teeth: wrinkles his forehead; despair, suffering, very marked on his face. Has been in England, in boarding houses, for 12 years; now returns to Russia 'forever'. I thought as I watched his eye brighten and fade—soon there'll be a bullet through your head. That's one of the results of war: this trapped cabin'd man (*A Writer's Diary*, 181–2).

With all this distinction between the old and the new emancipation, the 'progressive' and the esthetic, they have not remained two distinct and separate currents, but have mingled their waters, and the turbid patch where those waters meet has become one of the most striking features of the intelligentsia of Great Britain. Indeed, it is the very group which first used the word *intelligentsia* and was first dubbed *highbrow*.

This group is specially connected with Cambridge, the university which by long tradition, from Newton to Rutherford, and from Spenser right down the line, has been the university of great pioneers of the exact sciences and of the greatest English poets. Particularly at the commencement of the twentieth century, Cambridge contained a brilliant group of young men who combined a political radicalism with an interest in the most 'intriguing' abstract problems, and further an extremely refined taste produced by study of English poetry and French painting. One of these was Bertrand Russell, another J. M. Keynes. It was in their time that the student society known as 'The Heretics', was founded for the purpose of discussing and spreading unorthodox ideas in all fields of culture.

This Cambridge circle produced a group of intellectuals bound together by personal ties and resident in the district of London known as Bloomsbury—the same district contains the British Museum and the oldest college of London University, founded in 1827 by pupils of Bentham—and the group has become famous under the same name, *Bloomsbury*. The principal figures of this group were the abovementioned Keynes, the biographer and essayist Lytton Strachey, the novelist Virginia Woolf, and two art critics, Roger Fry and Clive Bell. This group established its own weekly, *The Nation*, financed by Keynes, and a publishing house, the Hogarth Press, founded by Virginia Woolf and her husband.

The basic trait of Bloomsbury is a mixture of philosophic rationalism, political rationalism, estheticism, and a cult of the individuality. Their radicalism is definitely bourgeois, a product not even of Shaw's new progressivism or the fabians, but of the old bourgeois radicalism and utilitarianism. Thus the weekly *Nation* (now dead) did not support the labourist movement, but the liberal left wing. Bloomsbury liberalism can be defined as a thin-skinned humanism for enlightened and sensitive members of the capitalist class who do not desire the outer world to be such as might be prone to cause them any displeasing impression.

The atmosphere of Bloomsbury is extremely aristocratic, the atmosphere of gentlemen in well-furnished studies. Bloomsburians live amid books, 'great minds' of the past (as assessed according to their outlook, of course), and move in the best intellectual and esthetic circles (as assessed, etc.) of the day. They avoid all extremes and abnormalities, though they treat everything which is original and 'inspired' with great respect.

The rationalism and liberalism mark them off very sharply from the common or garden esthetic bohemians of modern times, and also very sharply from the Russian modernism of the opening of the century. Being theoreticians of the passive, dividend-drawing and consuming section of the bourgeoisie, they are extremely intrigued by their own minutest inner experiences, and count them an inexhaustible treasure store of further more minutious inner experiences. They have a high opinion of Dostoievsky and of Freud.

But even these writers are taken by them without any trace of common bohemian gluttony. They are agile-minded, and of Freudian concepts they make a very special kind of mental discipline; I may say that a prominent bloomsburian once told me how he had trained himself, every time he wakes in the night, be it only for a single minute, immediately to take up his pencil and record all dreams experienced up to that point.

Yet the interest these people show in Dostoievsky and Freud is quite equalled by their interest in Voltaire and Spinoza. They believe (or should I say, they hope?) that reason plus education will some day bring an age in which people will be enlightened ladies and gentlemen much like themselves, and there will be no more wars or revolutions. But it must not be thought that they are in the least degree democrats. They see civilisation as the privilege of people who are well brought up and enjoy leisure. Having 'one's own room' in which one can escape from the outer world and its racket is, so we are informed by a book written by Virginia Woolf on the emancipation of women, the first condition of civilised creative work. And Clive Bell has written a book which constitutes a kind of manifesto. It deals with 'Civilisation'. He informs us that the only civilised epochs in history have been the age of Pericles in Athens, the Italian Renaissance, and the Eighteenth Century in France (*les salons*!). He lays it down that the indispensable condition of this civilisation (in the given periods), was that there was an 'enlightened class' which was relieved of earthly cares by having an income for which it did not have to work.

The favourite, one might almost say the national, authors of Bloomsbury are—Proust and Chekhov. It goes without saying that the first would satisfy them. His passive but so persistent and well-disciplined introspection, free from any wild fantasy, is a perfect expression of the psychology of the 'enlightened' dividend-drawer. The cult of Chekhov is a little more unexpected. Chekhov reached Great Britain as the last word in Russian literature, and was judged against a background of Tolstoy and Dostoievsky. This explains it. Bloomsbury had found a Russian writer who was completely bourgeois, completely devoid of those distressing rough corners in which, as a result of serfdom, Russian writers used to abound, and when they read him they felt quite at home.

Moreover, what was especially attractive in Chekhov was his technical perfection, the discreet lyricism of his art, and the way in which he built up his story from passive experiences and kept action outside. Finally, in Chekhov they discovered an ethical system which was just like that gentlemanly ethical system of Samuel Butler, only expressed with far more discretion and finesse.

The influence of Bloomsbury has passed far beyond its confines. The chief propagandist of Bloomsbury, Middleton Murry, is a person in many respects the very opposite of all that Bloomsbury holds dear. The creative influence of Chekhov was particularly marked in Middleton Murry's short-lived wife, the talented New Zealand writer, Katherine Mansfield. But we should say that in the real bloomsburians we do not find so much an influence of Chekhov as a spiritual identity. The study of Chekhov did not begin till after the war, but the pre-war novels of two exemplary bloomsburians, Virginia Woolf and E. M. Forster, are completely chekhovian in spirit.

Of these two Forster is the less true to type. He first published in the nineteen-hundreds, in the period of the social-realistic novel, and the construction of his novels is more reminiscent of Tourgeniev than of Chekhov. The liberalistic individualistic chekhovian psychology appears in them in rather a naive form. Forster is a modest, direct writer who has not soaked himself in Proust and does not care a damn about estheticism. But that element of psychological hair-splitting runs like a thread through all his work. Everything is reduced to a matter of personal relationships, of human kindliness and delicacy.

The most interesting of his novels is the latest one, *A Passage to India* (1924), a typical colonial novel of a bourgeois intellectual, in which the relationships between the colonisers and the natives is brought down to a question of personal decency in the treatment of others. The principal figure in the book is an Indian intellectual, a character sketched with real goodwill, but yet all the time from the lofty standpoint of European greatness.

But Virginia Woolf may be described as the principal literary expression of Bloomsbury. She is unquestionably a great artist. She has created her own method, a lyrical kind of exposition of her leading characters—what might be described as an esthetisation of the method used by Chekhov in *The Three Sisters*. Virginia Woolf is even more thin-skinned than Forster is, and she experiences the suffering of others acutely. But the sufferings with which she deals are limited to purely physiological suffering, as that of a woman growing old, and to individual psychological sufferings caused by the breakdown of personal bonds. Wherever they do appear as socially conditioned sufferings, they are, as in Proust, without exception the sufferings of the parasitic cream of the bourgeois. One of the lyrically most powerful passages in her work is one describing the inward experiences of a society woman who accompanies her husband to a lunch with another society woman —to which lunch she is not invited.

But what is most striking in Virginia Woolf is the purpose of her lyric method. This is devised in order to master the particular suffering and dissolve it away. The suffering is wrapped up in self-contained rhythms and sublimated from the world of reality to a world of esthetics. Her lulling rhythms are a fine example of the narcotic function which art takes on in the hands of liberal esthetes, who turn it into a new and more perfect form of dope, though of course one not intended for the people.

We have a much smaller artist, though no less typical of Bloomsbury, in Lytton Strachey, author of 'artistic' biographies . . .

Thus did the liberal estheticism of Bloomsbury reach the season of moulting; its ironical feathers disappeared and the world beheld it in a banal senile coat of imperialist worship of 'greatness' and 'grandeur' and 'the picturesque'. But then that end was only to be expected, since the cultured leisure of those enlightened children of the bourgeoisie is ensured them by what shekels come in from colonial and other dependent lands.

(c) Philip Henderson, from *The Novel of To-day*, 1936, 23–28, 87–91.

Philip Henderson (b. 1906). Poet, novelist and critic.

The first part of this extract refers to Forster's comparison between Virginia Woolf and Sterne (No. 67).

Reviewing this book, George Orwell described it as 'a weaker version of Mirsky's *Intelligentsia of Great Britain*', this latter being the 'archetype of Marxist literary criticism' (See No. 103b.). Orwell attempted to analyse the difficulty of combining propaganda and criticism:

> But unfortunately the notion of art for art's sake, though discredited, is too recent to be forgotten, and there is always a temptation to revert to it in moments of difficulty. Hence the frightful intellectual dishonesty which can be observed in nearly all propagandist critics. They are employing a double set of values and dodging from one to the other according as it suits them. They praise or dispraise a book *because* its tendency is Communist, Catholic, Fascist or what-not; but at the same time, they pretend to be judging it on purely aesthetic grounds. Few people have the guts to say outright that art and propaganda are the same thing. . . . Most of the time Mr Henderson is keeping up a pretence of strict critical impartiality, but it is strange how invariably his aesthetic judgments coincide with his political ones. Proust, Joyce, Wyndham Lewis, Virginia Woolf, Aldous Huxley, Wells, E. M. Forster (all of them 'bourgeois' novelists) are patted on the head with varying degrees of contempt. (*New English Weekly*, 31 December 1936, reprinted in *The Collected Essays, Journalism and Letters of George Orwell*, vol. 1 (1968), Penguin ed., 1970, 288–91.)

'History changes, Art stands still.' Sterne thought that his door-hinge wanted oiling in the eighteenth century and Mrs Woolf in the twentieth thought for a long time about a mark on the wall that finally turns out to be a nail. While so engaged their minds ran parallel for a short time. See, says Mr Forster, art has stood still for nearly two hundred years! It is true that Virginia Woolf uses a ruminative, fragmentary method reminiscent of the author of *Tristram Shandy*, but there the resemblance quite definitely ends. 'Would Shakespeare's manners have obliged us to leave the room?' she asks in *The Common Reader*. That observation alone reveals a world of difference between the more than easy-going eighteenth-century country parson and sensitively-nerved daughter of the librarian Sir Leslie Stephen. It is a difference between the more robust outlook of eighteenth-century England and that spiritual home of thin-skinned liberal enlightenment known as Bloomsbury, whose members, as Mirsky says, 'do not desire the outer world to be such as might be prone to cause them any unpleasant impression' (*The Intelligentsia of Great Britain*).

As we should expect, therefore, Mrs Woolf in her essay on the proper approach to the novel, *Mr Bennett and Mrs Brown*, is actively engaged in the same metaphysical game of hide and seek as Mr Forster. Arnold Bennett, she tells us, accused the novelists of the post-war generation of being unable to create characters that are real, true and convincing—terms the use of which in Mrs Woolf's view only prove the crassness of Bennett's mind. Her reply to this charge is to cut the ground from under Bennett's feet by asserting that, whatever compromises we make for all practical purposes to bridge over the gulf of our ultimate loneliness and isolation, we can never really know any other human being at all. According to her, the novelists of the pre-war generation, Galsworthy, Bennett and Wells, shirked this problem by laying enormous emphasis on 'the fabric of things'. 'They have given us the house,' she says, 'in the hope that we may be able to deduce the human beings who live there. . . . To give them their due, they have made that house much better worth living in. But if you hold that novels are in the first place about people and only in the second place about the houses they live in, that is the wrong way to set about it.' Therefore, she says the post-war generation had to begin by destroying these houses of literary convention before they could get at the people inside them. The point is, however, that having destroyed the old houses they did not bother their heads about building new ones and took it for granted that houses would always be somehow provided for them to live in. But having been born inside the old houses, the 'fabric of things' bequeathed by their fathers, says Mrs Woolf, weighed so heavily upon their spirits that, like E. M. Forster, James Joyce and D. H. Lawrence, they had to break a few windows before they could breathe. Nevertheless Mrs Woolf complains that E. M. Forster and D. H. Lawrence spoilt their early work by trying 'to combine their direct sense of the oddity and significance of some characters with Mr Galsworthy's knowledge of the Factory Acts and Mr Bennett's knowledge of the Five Towns'. For Mrs Woolf tells us how much she resents it when a novel of Bennett or Galsworthy makes her feel impelled 'to join a society or, desperately, to write a cheque'. She does not want to be reminded that the world does not consist entirely of Mrs Dalloways shopping in Bond Street and giving dinner parties in Westminster. The great novelists of the past, she says, do not have such a disturbing effect upon her. 'The difference perhaps is that both Sterne and Jane Austen were interested in things in themselves; in character in itself; in the book in itself'—and not, she implies, in social relations and the oppressive 'fabric of things'. If only the middle-class paradise of Jane Austen's world could last for ever!

Now, however, we are continually being pestered with these outside problems, even within our own preserve. Importunate young people, 'bleak young intellectuals' down from the universities, come along, rubbing the bloom off life, telling us that we've got to worry about the working class, and the coolies, who, they say, work in the plantations and cotton mills of India at an average wage of three farthings a day (but, of course, those Indians can live on so little!), civil disobedience campaigners and their aged relatives mercilessly flogged, their hair burned off with petrol by the police, thousands of Congress men imprisoned without trial, all this in the Corner Stone of the Empire, the Brightest Jewel in the British Crown, fascist atrocities in Germany, Austria, Bulgaria, Jugo-Slavia and Spain, where men and women and boys are at this very moment being dismembered, burned alive, hewn in pieces, their nails torn out and red-hot irons thrust into their stomachs in the name of law and order and to 'save the world from Bolshevism'—completely spoiling our dinner parties with their tactlessness, till we feel that we've got to join a society or, desperately, to write a cheque.

After all, says Mrs Woolf, are we not all just sitting in a railway carriage, rushing towards our final destination in time, and all we can hope to do is to gaze about us, bewildered by the world and the complexity and confusion of our own emotions. Know anything? Make decisions? Act? How can we?—not, at least, till our dividends begin to drop off. All we can really know is the suffering of our lonely souls. Far better identify one's outlook with a literary lap-dog!

Nevertheless, some of us begin to get a bit restive sitting in our railway carriage, hearing all about the rarefied emotions of our friends. We begin to look away from old Mrs Brown, sitting opposite in her respectable poverty, and glance out of the window at the street upon street of hovels converging upon London, that seem rather the approach to hell than the outskirts of the richest city in the world, and begin to realize, perhaps, that all this is not just an aesthetic, not just 'shapes of grey paper', but places where people have to spend their lives, where they are born, where they return tired after a day's work, where they rot without work, where they love and marry and bring children into the world and where, finally, they die without ever having lived . . .

The method of Joyce, combined with the attitude of Proust, may be seen applied on a smaller scale in the novels of Virginia Woolf. Mrs Woolf has avoided the pitfalls of prolixity and the magnification of trivialities into which both these writers have fallen, being concerned with what might be called the musicalization of reality. From *Jacob's Room* to *The Waves*, her style has progressed more and more towards the rhythm and texture of music. And by this I do not mean mere lyricism, for her writing has a counterpointed quality with clearly-defined motives woven into a continuously flowing musical texture. This is not, needless to say, a method adapted to either a very deep exploration of individual problems, or to anything like a comprehensive view of the real world, such as we find in the greatest writers. But within their self-imposed limitations, her novels achieve a clear and balanced perfection. That hers is a drawing-room world liable to be shattered as soon as its doors and windows are thrown open to the rumours of a greater and more turbulent life outside, that she deliberately creates this seclusion from the world, is evident enough:

[Quotes *To the Lighthouse*, pp. 29–30 'But here, as she turned' to 'impulse of terror?']

Such a passage is highly significant as it reveals in essence the writer's whole attitude to life. What fills her with a terror is the sudden realization that the external world will not always play the convenient part of a soothing accompaniment to her thoughts, that it cannot for ever be relegated to the position of a background, that at some time or other it will suddenly assert itself with a brutal importunity, and that then the seas of this world will rise like a ghostly roll of drums and engulf the island of serenity and detachment from which Mrs Woolf is still able, for a little while, to view them. Then all the delicate texture of her subjective values vanish, as ephemeral as a rainbow. 'When one gave up seeing the beauty that clothed things,' thinks Mrs Ambrose in *The Voyage Out*, 'this was the skeleton beneath.'

It is true that in *Mrs Dalloway*, Virginia Woolf, seizing upon 'London, this moment in June', achieves a more stable and realistic balance between her imagination and the objective world. For that reason *Mrs Dalloway* is not only a better novel than *To the Lighthouse*, for all its exquisite lyricism, but Mrs Dalloway herself is a far more real character than Mrs Ramsay. All the same, it may not be altogether out of place to wonder whether these ladies would be quite so detached had they to cook their own dinners and wash up the plates, dishes and pans afterwards, instead of momentarily interrupting their reflections to give instructions to cook and parlour-maid.

As the philosophical Mr Ramsay reflects, during one of his solitary promenades on the terrace of their house in the Hebrides, 'possibly the greatest good requires the existence of a slave class.' By 'the greatest good', of course, Mr Ramsay means the comfort and leisure of his own class. 'In any case,' muses this philosopher, 'is the lot of the average human being . . . the criterion by which we judge the measure of civilization?' The answer to that question depends upon what Mrs Woolf means by civilization, though possibly more than an indication is provided by Clive Bell, one of the principal Bloomsbury aestheticians. In his book *Civilisation*, Mr Bell lays it down that the only really civilized epochs in history were the age of Pericles in Athens, the Italian Renaissance, and eighteenth-century France, where culture was the expression of the lives of an enlightened leisure class.

104. Frank Swinnerton, 'on the whole creatively unimportant'

1935

From *The Georgian Literary Scene*, 1935, 392–4.

Swinnerton refers to 'four poetic somethings' in *The Waves*, an error which drew this reproof from Professor Guiguet: 'as there are obviously six voices in the novel, this inaccuracy, which is more than just a slip, gives some idea of the quality of his criticism.' (Jean Guiguet, *Virginia Woolf and Her Works*, trans. J. Stewart, 1965, 51n.) Virginia Woolf noted 'I have had three severe swingeings lately: Wyndham Lewis; Mirsky; and now Swinnerton. Bloomsbury is ridiculed; and I am dismissed with it. I didn't read W.L.: and Swinnerton only affected me as a robin affects a rhinoceros—except in the depths of the night' (*A Writer's Diary*, 240).

Some readers of Virginia Woolf apparently obtain a satisfaction from her work which they do not find elsewhere. For me, this work seems very clever, very ingenious, but on the whole creatively unimportant. It is all done with the wits; there is nothing in it for those who do not pride themselves upon intellectual superiority to the herd. There is nothing in it which is not offered to merely current middle-class culture, the culture in which—post-Freud, post-Jung, and so on—all our younger minds are preoccupied by self-analysis. With the cleverness of young minds, they recognise in Virginia Woolf's characters leaps and states mental familiar to themselves, and in that sense, making allowance for the difference of class, are doing no more than poor people do when they read novelettes. For if, recognising a state of mind, or a whim, or a learned allusion, one self-complacently acclaims in these books no more than recognisable phenomena, what is then left of Virginia Woolf's creative genius? She certainly does not purge by pity and terror.

What Arnold Bennett meant, I feel sure, in charging Georgian writers with ignoring the first essential of novel-writing, the creation of character, was that in the novels he had in mind (let us say that one of them was a book by Virginia Woolf, although I have no knowledge that he ever read a book she had written) there was no person seen and presented, as they say, in the round. In a book about Mrs Brown, there was, for the reader, no Mrs Brown. Virginia Woolf replied that in life itself there never was a Mrs Brown, only a 'Mrs Brownness', the essential something which to Mrs Brown is all that Mrs Brown knows when she goes about her day's life. She claimed to be presenting not Mrs Brown, but Mrs Brownness. That sounds splendid. But in order to discover the Mrs Brownness Virginia Woolf is forced to write solely of ruminative or introspective persons, and when she had carried her exploration to the four minds in *The Waves* she had reached as far as that particular method would take her. There were four poetic somethings; but they all thought alike. The reason for this, in my opinion, is that Virginia Woolf is essentially an impressionist, a catcher at memory of her own mental vagaries, and not a creator. She is aware, too, of many of the latest scientific facts and theories about human beings, but she is unable to imagine, to create, a human being who is not exactly like herself. Such a person as Arnold Bennett or Frank Swinnerton she could not—would not wish to—imagine. Nor Mrs Brown either, I believe; for her Mrs Brown is but a dream-jumble of odds and ends. She thinks she is pursuing the essential, but in fact she is too sensitive, highly intelligent, and playful in mind, to have the emotional depth of an imaginative person. Psychologically she is as much at fault as the so-called realist, in thinking that if she chases every detail she will find truth. That is not the way to write great novels. Jane Austen was wiser and less anxiously exploratory; but Jane Austen had more creative imagination than cultivated brains. How odd that Virginia Woolf cannot see this.

And since I have mentioned Jane Austen, I must again refer to the charming book, *A Room of One's Own*, which is a mingling of feminism with reverie and invention. In this book Virginia Woolf traces, as well as the available material will allow her to do, the history of the education of women. Saying nothing of the Pastons, she looks through English literature and letters for news of the way in which through the centuries women learned to write and then, in time, came to write books and plays. She says nothing of several people who would possibly have been unhelpful to her examination, such as Maria Edgeworth,

Mrs Inchbald, Mrs Gaskell, and Mrs Trollope; but comes to the conclusion that until a woman has a private income of five hundred pounds a year and a room of her own of which she can lock the door she cannot hope to be free to write good books—or do anything else. For the writing of good books, says Virginia Woolf, needs leisure, and no woman in the past has had any life of her own, neither liberty nor opportunity to do what she would best do.

With the argument of this piece I have no concern, for I am not here discussing feminism (I only object specifically to the statement that no genius ever came from the working class, because even if genius is confined by Virginia Woolf to literature there is always D. H. Lawrence, who never had a room of his own); but with the assumption that fiction is only to be written by educated women I must deal because it has a larger application. It is the view of Virginia Woolf, and those who think as she does, that no literary work done by any but highly educated persons of their own kind of culture can or should be interesting. This I must point out to be educational snobbery, which in Bloomsbury has succeeded the social snobbery of pre-Georgian days. In every small town in England there are some few persons who think they are better than the rest of the inhabitants; they restrict their familiar acquaintance to the few, and condescend to the many. We who do not belong to their number may rub our eyes at an antediluvianism, but they take it very seriously, and have no notion that they represent a smugness, based upon inexperience, which is altogether ludicrous.

105. 'Feminine fiction': two contrasting views

1937

(a) F. B. Millett, from 'Feminine Fiction', in *Cornhill Magazine*, February 1937, 234–5.

F. B. Millett. Teacher at a number of American universities.

But certainly the most brilliant woman novelist of the post-War period is Mrs Virginia Woolf. Mrs Woolf's major concern seems to be the creation in fiction of a sense of reality, but her conception of reality differs fundamentally from the realism of the older generation of Moore and Bennett. She is persuaded that reality, as distinct from realism, is an inward and subjective thing, that to communicate a sense of life the novelist must abandon the construction of an external world brick by brick and devote himself to the construction of character through the complexity of the contemporary consciousness. She sees consciousness, as all but the behaviouristic psychologist sees it, as a complex of bodily sensations, feelings, emotions, and ideas, and through her rendition of that complex, she attempts the creation of a sense of being alive. Perhaps no other novelist of this period, not even Dorothy Richardson who may be said to have initiated this method for the English novel, is so skilled in communicating this sense of life being lived. For she brings to her work the most highly individualized of gifts—hyper-sensitiveness on the sensory side, the most refined observation of the thought and feeling processes, and a deep and tender response to the pathetic evanescence of the reality she has dedicated herself to adumbrating.

On the technical side, as well, no novelist of this time is more conspicuously gifted. Like Huxley and Joyce, she usually abandons plot as a principle of structure, but she knows that the stream of consciousness must be supplied with banks lest it inundate author and reader alike. In *Jacob's Room* (1922), the principle of unity, the personality of Jacob, seemed inadequate to bind together the disparate impressions of him seen subjectively and objectively, but in *Mrs Dalloway* (1925) the same principle is used with greater effectiveness, for the personality of that not too profound but singularly charming woman is kept sufficiently steadily in the centre of the reader's interest to furnish a point of reference for the other persons of the story, even though they touch the life of Clarissa Dalloway only fleetingly. Even more daringly, in her beautiful novel, *To the Lighthouse* (1927), Mrs Woolf uses a personality as the integrating principle of her singularly poignant pictures of transient human existence. Mrs Ramsay is seen, not merely as the singularly unself-centred centre of her existence, but (not only in her life, but, after her physical death, in her spiritual persistence) as the focus of a concentric series of existences more or less intimately involved with hers. Added to Mrs Woolf's constructive power is the charm of her style, a style freshly redolent, delicately poetic, and rhythmically subtle. If there is in the contemporary period any novelist whose every word any critical reader must heed, that novelist is Virginia Woolf.

(b) Herbert J. Muller, from 'Virginia Woolf and Feminine Fiction', *Saturday Review of Literature* (New York), 6 February 1937, 3–4, 14–16.

Herbert J. Muller (b. 1905). American critic and scholar, Professor of English at Purdue University.

As I am using the work of Virginia Woolf chiefly as a springboard from which to plunge into disagreeable generalization, simple justice demands a prefatory tribute to her many admirable qualities, and particularly to her real importance to all collectors of the blessed 'tendencies' in modern fiction. She is a conspicuous figure in the reaction against a literal, pedestrian realism: a realism that in the light of the new views of personality and consciousness—not to mention the new notions about time and space, cause and effect—seems atavistic or absent-minded. She protests against the neatness, above all the solidity and rigidity of life as represented by an Arnold Bennett. 'Life is not a series of gig lamps symmetrically arranged,' she writes; 'life is a luminous halo.' And this halo cannot be rendered by mere inventory or analysis.

Mrs Woolf is, in short, of the large, significant, often misunderstood company of impressionists, and hence is related to such novelists as Conrad, Lawrence, Joyce, and Proust. She has made it her business to render immediately the actual feel of life: to convey the essence of experience by subtle intimation and not by analysis or comment, by evocation of atmosphere and not by formal narrative, in general by direct realization and not by mere description. The conventional realists, she declares, give 'a vast sense of things in general, but a very vague one of things in particular'; and life does not necessarily exist more fully in apparently big than in apparently small things.

Let us record the atoms as they fall upon the mind in the order in which they fall, let us trace the pattern, however disconnected and incoherent in appearance, which each sight and incident scores upon consciousness.

Hence the minimizing of plot in her novels, as in so much modern fiction. Matthew Josephson once announced that the novel is approaching the saturation point because of the limited number of 'situations' available, the sameness of most story material; he finds the chief significance of Virginia Woolf, Joyce, and others in that they are confronting the problem of 'how to write a novel without telling a story'. But Josephson forgets that the same objection might be made to life itself—yet people go on living, and seem to find life on the whole as strange and exciting as ever. The invincible popularity of the risqué anecdote alone makes nonsense of the notion that we have grown weary of familiar situations. The real reason for the contemporary's exaggerated distrust of 'story', his sophisticated contempt for 'mere story-tellers', is rather a conviction that neither the whole immensely intricate truth nor the actual sensation of living can be adequately rendered by tidy narratives with a definite beginning, middle, and end. It is an insistence that life itself does not narrate. Plot has gone the way of the other trappings of conventional realism and for similar reasons; the gist of the objection to this realism is that it is not real enough.

This central intention explains all the striking characteristics of Mrs Woolf's methods: the myriad sensory impressions, the stream of consciousness, the deliberate discontinuity, what Gide calls the 'breadthwise cutting' of the slice of life; and all have many parallels in modern fiction. She is especially indebted to James Joyce. *Mrs. Dalloway*, the most successful of her novels, is like *Ulysses* the record of a single day; and like Joyce, Mrs Woolf introduces a host of unconnected characters and incidents. Apparently she has more confidence in the legitimacy of this intention, for she employs none of the artificial devices by which Joyce uneasily sought to unify his scattered material. She is content simply to give the full sensation of living during her day in London; and without the play upon all the human organs that is one of his devices, her novel is more clearly organic. She manages to create a whole that is greater than the sum of its parts and that at every point determines these parts; she establishes a subtle kind of unity and completeness that should satisfy all readers but those who must have a full stop to their symphony, a resounding chord that leaves no doubt as to the propriety of clapping and reaching for one's hat.

Now, almost all readers are impressed by the exquisite artistry of Virginia Woolf. It is revealed immediately in a prose style that has few equals in modern fiction. Always delicate, supple, shimmering, cadenced, it is at once lovely in itself and splendidly expressive. Inevitably one speaks of 'nuances', the precision with which she renders the elusive shades of thought and feeling, sight and sound. With so fine an instrument at her command, Mrs Woolf hence achieves brilliantly the end she set for herself: the imaginative re-creation rather than the formal dissection of human experience.

By her highly selective art, moreover, she manages to skirt the more obvious dangers implicit in her methods and materials. She filters and canalizes the stream of consciousness, presenting a vivid illusion of the life of the mind that is more meaningful than a literal reproduction; she gains all the advantages of intimacy and immediacy at the minimum cost of triviality, irrelevance, incoherence, or mere messiness. Above all, she does not explore consciousness and record sensation for its own sake, as Joyce does. Her stream flows somewhere and does not simply flow; if she presents no dramatic struggle and resolves nothing, at least she refers the sensations of her leading characters to fundamental problems of conduct—the problem of the meaning of their lives with which they are all intensely preoccupied.

Finally, one should be grateful for the mellowness of Mrs Woolf—a mellowness, unlike that of some of her British contemporaries, neither self-conscious nor premature. She is one of the few important literary personalities of this unquiet age that seem in no way maimed or poisoned by it. Her art is no sublimation of her private woes or compensation for her private frustration. Although novelists today are less prone to a cold hatred of their characters than they are reputed to be, none remains on more affable terms with his characters while yet keeping so clear of them. She has all the easy familiarity of the great

Victorians without their habit of taking liberties with it. In short, her fiction like her criticism consistently displays a spirit serene, tolerant, humane, civilized.

So much at least must be granted Virginia Woolf. She is on one of the forefronts of modern fiction; she is one of the most distinguished of living women writers. It seems almost ungracious, indeed, to point out deficiencies in so urbane, charming an art. Yet serious deficiencies there are; and her very eminence sharpens the issue raised by her work.

What finally impresses me in Mrs Woolf's fiction is its insubstantiality. This exquisite art somehow grows thin, this 'luminous halo' somehow grows wraithlike. Her novels have nothing of the elemental force of Dostoievsky, Hardy, or Dreiser; among their own impressionistic kind they have little of the intensity and glow of Conrad, Proust, or Lawrence. Behind all their subtlety and vividness is no real passion or energy. With her unfailing acuteness Mrs Woolf has stated exactly the limitations of the art of Arnold Bennett; Bennett was himself as just when he remarked, with masculine bluntness, that her novels 'seriously lack vitality'.

This deficiency is in part the price of her method and creed. To 'record the atoms as they fall', to 'trace the pattern . . . which each sight and incident scores upon consciousness,' is inevitably to give disproportionate emphasis to separate moments, and hence likely to leave an effect of inconsequence. Mrs Woolf flits about her subject, throws a flashing light from many angles, darts in to capture bright bits of truth; but by the very nature of this method she never comes to grips with a situation. She does not confront steadily a deep emotion or really plunge into it. A brilliant butterfly, swift in flight, she settles unerringly on the choicest flowers and extracts their choicest essence; but she never gets to the roots. Hence even the lovely style—dipping, sparkling, rippling, at any given moment a marvel of expressiveness—ultimately palls. The constant flutter and glimmer become monotonous; at the end it suggests preciosity or mere fussiness.

Similarly Mrs Woolf pays the penalty of her too constant immersion in the inner life. In reacting against the excesses of laborious documentation, she has contracted a kind of horror of externals. Too often the reader is straining his eyes at a mist. In actual experience, the halo that is her constant concern surrounds a solid, earthy substance; but of this substance she gives us only fleeting, sidelong glimpses. Hence, as Elizabeth Drew remarks, 'we feel rather as if we were trying to construct the plot of a Greek play from nothing but the remarks of the chorus.' Fragile and anaemic to begin with, her characters come finally to seem disembodied spirits—wispy, evanescent, despite their spiritual essence perishable. And this refining away of the solid substance of character becomes even more fastidious in the later novels of Mrs Woolf. *Mrs Dalloway* is set against the living background of London; in *The Waves* the outside world fades into a backdrop, leaving six minds quivering in a sensitized vacuum, six characters in search of an author: an author to give them flesh, blood, a home, a world—anything to clothe their precious spirits.

What sucks the blood out of Virginia Woolf's novels is not entirely, however, this ultra-refined technique. Even her early, more conventional novels, written before she had arrived in this rarefied realm where material circumstance is a kind of vulgar illusion, are wanting in vitality. They are less memorable, in fact, than her later novels, and plainly suggest that her later manner is more natural and becoming to her. And so one must look into her temperament, her whole equipment as a novelist, to discover the final explanation of her limitations.

In reviewing *To the Lighthouse*, Conrad Aiken paid a poet's tribute to the old-fashioned fragrance of Mrs Woolf's spirit, the odour of old lavender that comes off her work despite the ulta-modernity of her technique and her insight. Her characters are all gentle folk framed in a beautiful little picture in a cloistered gallery; and this tightly circumscribed scene is what gives her novels 'their odd and delicious air of parochialism, as of some small village-world, as bright and vivid and perfect in its tininess as a miniature: a small complete world which time has somehow missed.' Here is the charm of her work—and it is much the charm of Mrs Gaskell's *Cranford*. Here is also the reason why it is little more than charming. As creatures of shelter, her characters are too delicate to participate in a really big or intense drama. They never worry about vulgar necessity or the intrusion of rude, elemental emotion. They hear only as off-stage rumbles and rumours the great, terrifying, destructive forces of the outside world—as Clarissa Dalloway experiences the World War, a very horrid thing for a lady to have to think about. Their struggles come to seem a shadow-boxing in a hothouse. 'I am all fibre. All tremors shake me,' declares one of the six soliloquists of *The Waves*. 'I dance. I ripple. I am thrown over you like a net of light,' says another. 'Now,' declares less fortunate phantom No. 3, 'I will wrap my agony inside my pocket-handkerchief.' This is an almost complete summary of the perfected art of Virginia Woolf. These are indeed children speaking, but when they are grown up as ladies and gentlemen their accents are as highly mannered, their responses as tremulous, their feelings as refined. None has an emotion that cannot be wrapped up in a pocket-handkerchief.

This is not to say that Mrs Woolf is herself tender-minded and merely genteel—she clearly sees through her Mrs Dalloway. Neither is it to deny her the right to her materials—the world is infested with Mrs Dalloways. Yet one may fairly comment that out of such material at most only minor classics can be woven. In the world she has chosen to create, neither robust comedy nor deeply moving tragedy is possible. And what clearly defines her limitations is that this is apparently the only kind of world she is able to create. In *Mrs Dalloway*, to be sure, she introduces one Septimus Smith, a shell-shocked veteran, to supplement the narrowness of Clarissa's range of experience. His madness and suicide would appear to symbolize the brutal realities of the outside world, set Clarissa's party in its right perspective, provide the complement necessary for a whole picture of London. But even this madness has been toned down, purged of all terrifying elements. It is a very gentle, tender, wistful madness, nothing like that represented by Shakespeare and Dostoievsky. It is merely touching, at worst disturbing. It is indeed almost pretty.

To this extent at least Mrs Woolf shares the frailty of her characters: like them she never surrenders herself to life. She is seemingly as afraid to pull out all the stops and let go. The penalty of her culture and refinement is a too highly self-conscious art, an almost fearful aloofness, in Aiken's words a 'dextrous holding of the raw stuff of life at arm's length.' Conrad was equally concerned with the 'semi-transparent envelope' about human experience, but he strove to penetrate it, sink his teeth in the solid emotional experience from which it emanates: she gives us simply the envelope. She shies away from any experience so uncouth that it cannot be reduced to the tidy proportions of her drawing-room world, so powerful that it might break through the gossamer web of her art. It is, once more, a brilliantly woven web; but it is too fine-spun to contain any big emotion, any violent conflict, any profound or tumultuous experience.

In *A Room of One's Own* Virginia Woolf wrote a notable preamble to a kind of feminine Declaration of Independence. She asked that women writers be granted the same freedom as men, the same right to follow their calling in retirement without being asked to perform more mundane duties. Although her well-mannered plea scarcely created a furor, it was still a challenge; and no doubt it helped to secure a privilege already more generally taken for granted. Mrs Woolf now has a room of her own. But what does she do in it? She sits and embroiders. She does water colours in pastel shades. She plays minor chords with the soft pedal down. In short, her room might as well be the drawing room of a parsonage, and she serving tea to the ladies of the parish. Essentially, she writes like that busy housewife, mother, and soft-eyed model of Victorian womanhood, Mrs Elizabeth Cleghorn Gaskell . . .

[A general survey of contemporary women novelists is omitted.]

Precisely because they are chiefly concerned with immediate realities, the women writers are less likely to be distracted or thwarted by the profound uncertainties of this era. Yet for this same reason they are less significant for the critic concerned with the deeper issues of modern literature and life. These issues have no doubt given to many men a sickly and oppressive self-consciousness; but they are nevertheless urgent, they must somehow be met. Virginia Woolf and her sisters contribute little but their incidental refinements of method and manner.

THE YEARS

13 March 1937

106. Theodora Bosanquet, from a review, *Time and Tide*

13 March 1937, 352–3

Theodora Bosanquet had been Henry James's secretary.

Theme: the passing of the last fifty years reflected in the everyday life of separate individual members of a family. Is it, can it be, possible that Mrs Woolf, having considered with attention and some astonishment a few of the family chronicles now in fashion, caught the echo of a challenge? Did she, putting her ear to an acoustically curved shell, hear a voice, the assembled voice of other English novelists, murmuring: 'Now it's your turn. You who have tossed time about like a shuttlecock, disdained and defied the tolling of the hours, come off that lofty cloud. Let the years pass in the order of their chronological procession. Bridge your abysses in something more like the ordinary manner'?

Whether she asked that voice, or whether she just wanted to assure herself that any form can be successfully exploited by a sufficiently intelligent and accomplished writer, there can be no doubt that Mrs Woolf has brought off her trick. This shimmering succession of illuminated shots of the thoughts and words, the feelings and poses, of the members of the Pargiter family, these vivid fragments of seasons, days and moments, detached from a few of the years between 1880 and the present day, fall into a composition so lucid, coherent and significant that very few readers will find themselves honestly able to keep up any pretence of invincible ignorance about the author's intention....

The reaction of the class-conscious and guilt-ridden propagandists of the present age to this novel, as indeed to most of Mrs Woolf's work, is quite likely to be indignation. Her persistent preoccupation with the luminous glory of life and the value of the individual prisms through which it shines in such varying colours and proportions looks to them like the attitude of a callous Nero playing exquisite music while the human race toils and starves, piles up investments and armaments, drills in gas masks, perishes in dark alleys. Money and politics *must*, they maintain, be all our thought and talk until liberty and equality are safely established in the Constitution. If Mrs Woolf does not agree it is not because she is unaware of these problems and miseries, but because she knows that not even justice and liberty are ends in themselves. They are not life. Life is a fountain of living water within us. What will it profit us if we eliminate all the causes of war, equalize everybody's income, sterilize all the unfit, if the jet of that fountain is plugged up?

In *The Years*, celebrating the recurrent rebirth of the beauty of the visible world and the marvel of the minds that recognize it, we are in contact not only with a first-rate novelist, who can summon human personalities to her page in the flick of a sentence, but also with a great lyrical poet. It is not a poet's function (*pace* Mr Auden & Co) to offer us a sociological tract but to give us more abundant life.

107. From an unsigned review, *Times Literary Supplement*

13 March 1937, 185

Has life a pattern or is it a formless flux? Can we shape it, for ourselves or others, or do we and they float like driftwood down the stream? Which is the true aspect of age, its inward illusion of plasticity and youth or its external petrifaction? These eternal questions must afflict all novelists in varying degrees, particularly those who have long retrospects, and to their different approaches many well-known titles bear witness—*The Old Wives' Tale*, *The Way of All Flesh*, *The Forsyte Saga*, *Jean Christophe*, *A la Recherche du Temps Perdu*. And now Mrs Woolf, who has throughout her work been fascinated by the problems of change and continuity, makes time the hero of a long and beautiful novel which might have had for its title one that was chosen for a translation from Louis Couperus, *Old People and the Things that Pass*. That she has done it her own inimitable way needs no saying: the objective study, the ill-concealed autobiography, the leisurely chronicle, Proust's mixture of nostalgia and irony, Romains's brilliant *reportage*—these are not for her. To her keen sensibility the illuminating moments of life are discontinuous, and the questions that they ask are never answered. Are the recurring gleams true? Do the hints of refrains—say, the cooing of pigeons or the fall of rose petals—mean that there is a song? Are we what we look, at seven years old or seventy, or what we feel? When is anything true—then, now or never?

In composing this novel, which needs more than one reading, Mrs Woolf constructed a more elaborate framework and allowed history to play a more obvious part than usual. . . . Mrs Woolf's chronology is not very exact, as divers fluctuations in stated ages and one obvious discrepancy prove; but the only importance of these small inexactitudes is that they reinforce a certain impression of discontinuity in the writing of this book, as though the author, having selected the epic form, had found that it irked her, so that she was driven back to her true form, the lyric.

Indeed, some critics are likely to remark that, having chosen the epic form, she has too studiously refrained from filling it out with events. After the death of Mrs Pargiter nothing dramatic occurs, except the War, which no novel of to-day can avoid; and even that is little more than a backcloth for a very striking scene of family contacts. The excitement, in fact, is either wholly lyrical—especially in the exquisite vignettes of London sights and sounds—or lies in the developments and dialogues of certain characters. The important characters are women, notably Eleanor, the Colonel's eldest daughter, and Sara, Digby's younger child; and in Kitty Malone, a cousin of the Pargiters, there is a certain *dédoublement* of Eleanor, while Sara, who seems to live in some odd world of fancy, has towards the end a foil in Peggie, Eleanor's niece, a rather downright and embittered young doctor. . . .

If the reader occasionally, at first reading, wonders what exactly is being expressed in this penetrating but uneventful chronicle, he must have patience. The finale, with its several meetings leading up to the gathering of the whole family in Delia's flat, is inspired throughout—a brilliant fantasia of all Time's problems, age and youth, change and permanence, truth and illusion. It sums up certain aspects of an age, and may perhaps be the conclusion of an epoch in fiction, to which a new age and a new epoch are now succeeding.

108. Basil de Selincourt, review, *Observer*

14 March 1937, 5

Basil de Selincourt (b. 1876). Regular *Observer* reviewer.

When she read this review, Virginia Woolf commented:

> I am in such a twitter owing to two columns in the *Observer* praising *The Years* that I can't, as I foretold, go on with *Three Guineas*. Why I even sat back just now and thought with pleasure of people reading that review. And when I think of the agony I went through in this room, just over a year ago . . . when it dawned on me that the whole of three years' work was a complete failure: and then when I think of the mornings here when I used to stumble out and cut up those proofs and write three lines and then go back and lie on my bed—the worst summer in my life, but at the same time the most illuminating—it's no wonder my hand trembles. What most pleases me though is the obvious chance now since de Selincourt sees it, that my intention in *The Years* may be not so entirely muted and obscured as I feared. The *T.L.S.* spoke as if it were merely the death song of the middle classes: a series of exquisite impressions: but he sees that it is a creative, a constructive book. Not that I've yet altogether read him: but he has pounced on some of the key sentences. And this means that it will be debated; and this means that *Three Guineas* will strike very sharp and clear on a hot iron: so that my immensely careful planning won't be baulked by time of life etc. as I had made certain. Making certain however was an enormous discovery for me, though (*A Writer's Diary*, 278).

Everything that Mrs Woolf does is individual. *The Years* is rather nearer the norm of the novel than *The Waves* was; yet it blends Nature and Human Nature similarly, and no one could have written it who had not already written *The Waves*. Being a much easier book to read, it may well, for that very reason, have been even more difficult to write. *The Waves* reminded me of one of those puzzles with glistening silver balls and a maze of passages on a tray, which you must tilt to make them pass, by one route or another, through a small round hole at the bottom. The fascination of the brightness of those balls, as well as of their mobility, brought me over and over again to the attempt; yet I never managed to put more than four or five of them through the hole: while I was at work on the sixth the others always got away. Now, with *The Years*, though I have read it but once, and cannot have counted more than a twentieth of its treasures, all the balls (there are a great many of them—three families—a score or more, perhaps) have gone though the hole submissively and neatly. In fact, you could hardly call it a puzzle-board at all.

In general, though the method is different, the guiding motive in *The Years* is the same as in *The Waves*: that is, if I am right in thinking *The Waves* to have been inspired by a sense of the paradox of Time, or of our consciousness in Time, the paradox of its equally affirmable continuity and discontinuity.

' "I see a ring," said Bernard, "hanging above me. It quivers and hangs in a loop of light".' He is but a child, waking with other children, in bed, in his nursery; but it is as if he had said at once, 'I see and am eternity and all the world.' It is not what any child would have said: but it presents in words the dream-like integrity of his womb-enfolded awareness of dawning day, dawning life; so do the first remarks of the other children. And yet, while each remark affirms the whole, each also vividly isolates the passing moment. The significance of life, we soon begin to feel, is gathered for each of us into this present pulse of consciousness this *now*, this glistening point of light which is ours and ours alone unshareable. Our days are made up of these dew-drops of experience, in their swift succession, and, as the years pass, memory loops the brightest of them together like flowers, and the daisy-chain they make is our life's history. Well, call them a daisy-chain if you will, so long as you still remember that the whole world is in each of them, that they are, indeed, a chain of worlds. What is vividest may seem individual and isolated; yet, if the dewdrops were really separate, how should we ever unite them? If they were entirely ours how could we ever describe them to a friend? Somehow they are communicable, somehow their significance accumulates. For here we are, living and living together, and life has more meaning than its moments, and the shared life more than all.

I might compare *The Waves* to a rosette of daisy-chains. Each of the characters made his or her peculiar chain, as they dipped for their daisies into the same bowl, and these chains would unite and fit together, you could feel, as petals make a flower, if you could but grasp them wholly or pierce through them to the enclosing truth. The impulse in *The Years*, without being any less concentrated, is more kaleidoscopic. It is the history of a family—The Pargiters—in three branches through three generations; and again the sense of a single experience, of the family (perhaps) behind its many members, never entirely leaves us, though on every page and in every sentence attention is centred on some vivid event in Eleanor's or Morris's or Martin's separate experience. The technical problem, no doubt, is to find combinable separateness, to construct out of these flashing indirections a solid plot. But the method itself and something, too, in the instinct of the writer drives towards disjunction. Death is a recurring motive: and so are dinners. The entire existence of the children we first meet is dominated by a sick mother's slowly impending death; their cousins lose mother and father in quick succession; old Crosby's last comfort dies, the family dog; the deaths of Parnell and of King Edward are symbolical background events. When the time comes at last to wish the whole family good-bye, we do it at an evening party, a party given by Delia, who in her teens had had a passion for Parnell: the time is the present day, and the family is now so large that the tale of their disjointed impressions makes a little novel by itself—covering nearly 150 pages.

As I said, Mrs Woolf's method itself tends to dictate casual scenes and meetings. It is the method of concrete imaginative reconstruction. There is no description, in the old sense of preparations and wrappings; all is action, all is immediate contact with some one moving mind. The novel consists entirely of tiny cubes of live experience. Since the colonel has a mistress, you must go and stand with him on the dingy doorstep, first taking a quick glance to right and left, you must even help him put his hand down Mira's neck. You hear directly and summarily what the world and the weather are about, for that is part of all our business (though I do think the weather varies locally more than Mrs Woolf can always allow), and then what Edward and Kitty are doing in Oxford, or Milly and Rose in London, while the same stars look down and the same rain begins to fall, and the scenes change as fast as in a play of Shakespeare. And this is where the occasional lunch or dinner comes in. You are so close to each of the characters while you are with them that you cannot stay with them long; your characters must meet and part; also while they are together their conversation must be relaxed—a condition which nothing produces so comfortably as a glass or two of wine, even if there is nothing to be washed down but stringy mutton. I am arguing that the exceptional vividness and concreteness of the method inevitably tends to isolate the characters and heighten their self-consciousness. In passage after passage we come back to the question: What is this 'I'?

[Quotes p. 184 'All talk would be nonsense' to 'Rose protested.']

. . . So the paradox of time, or consciousness, implied in the theme of the novel, repeats itself in its form. No writer of our time is gifted, as Mrs Woolf is gifted, with power to divine and express the quality of infinity in all experience, in every detail of it; in this book, as in so many of hers, you may find whole pages in which each sentence is a little poem, a shining drop of dew. This is the very quality on which the continuity of each life and all our lives depends; this is continuity, this is unity. And yet the narrative or presentational form in which she gives it to us seems elaborately calculated to emphasise the isolations and separations of the framework, conditions, machinery of our existence. It is almost as if separateness were a bugbear of her own, a thing which in her creative writing she was determined to objectify and overcome:

> Yes! in the sea of life enisled
> With echoing straits between us thrown,
> Dotting the shoreless watery wild,
> We mortal millions live *alone*.

Poetry, in one mood, tends to insist on it, just because the desire of the poet is always for closer realisation of the actual solidarity which is both ultimate religious truth (we are all members one of another) and present economic fact. Poetry may insist on it, but the fact of poetry is its direct and final negation. And no one, I think, has come so near as Mrs Woolf to showing that every movement of consciousness is poetical.

However that may be, the development of her new book, to the very end, is of a kind to throw our human cross-purposes into the highest possible relief. Not only is its whole last act an evening party, with guests arriving and departing, most of the talk made up of half-finished sentences, and no one ever saying all he means to say; more than this, the party has a double climax—first, a speech which the slightly tipsy speaker is not allowed to make, but which he intended to have dedicated to the future of the race:

> 'The human race, which is now in its infancy, may it grow to maturity! Ladies and gentlemen!' he exclaimed, half rising and expanding his waist-coat, 'I drink to that.' He brought his glass down with a thump on the table. It broke.

second, a song heard only by the few last lingering guests, a song sung in raucous voices by the two caretaker's children, a song of morning. Mrs Woolf prints every word of it:

> Etha passo tanno hai
> Fai donk to tu do, etc

It is not Japanese: it is English. And the point is, that of this morning song, sung by the ecstatic, ugly children, not one syllable is recognisable.

[Quotes p. 465 'Nobody knew what to say' to 'thinking of the same thing.']

Is it a parable figuring the skein of misgivings, mistakings, misconceptions, misapprehensions, out of which we somehow manage to knit together these half-intelligible lives of ours? Or is it more particularly a comment on our actual human predicament, in this modern world, with its more than common clash of irreconcilable ideals? Whatever it means exactly, there can be no doubt of Mrs Woolf's deeper intention: 'The sun had risen,' her last words run, 'and the sky above the houses wore an air of extraordinary beauty, simplicity, and peace.' There is an inner peace and beauty corresponding to that pure heavenly brightness; to establish it, to live in it, is to realise that separation and solitude are mere appearances.

109. Howard Spring, review, *Evening Standard*

18 March 1937, 10

Howard Spring (b. 1889), after working on a number of newspapers, joined the *Evening Standard* in 1931. In the year following this review of *The Years* he published his best-seller *O Absalom!* (1938), published in the US as *My Son, My Son!* (see Introduction, p. 27).

Ever since Mr Noel Coward showed us in *Cavalcade* how to write history with a barrel-organ, novelists have turned eagerly to the method.

Take any family, preferably middle-class, round about the time of Victoria's Jubilee. Trace its vicissitudes through fifty years, bringing in Mafeking, Dolly Grey, the Suffragettes, Edward, George, the Great War, Tipperary; old Edward Ramsden, or whatever his name may have been, a curly-headed child who said something good about Victoria's funeral, standing stiff as a ramrod at the end, his hand at the salute, a tear in his eye, his grandson's medal on his chest, a game 'un, and, Gad sir, British.

That's the method: history clanking its spurs and jingling its medals, like a picture trying to subsist by virtue of a few high lights.

Now high lights can only subsist by virtue of low lights. When you have said that you have got to the heart of the method which Mrs Woolf uses in *The Years.* I do not often feel about a book that it has in it the stuff of immortality, and when you do feel like that about a book it's as well to shut up about it in this cynical world; but that is how I feel about *The Years.*

The book begins in 1880, it ends in the present day, and its theme is the progress through that space of time of the Pargiters of Abercorn Terrace, their families and friends.

So the time covered is the same as that required by the *Cavalcade* school of fiction and drama; but when you have finished this book you will feel, if you have any sensitivity at all, that here are the very flesh and bones, the blood and marrow of history—the thing itself, not an effigy for children, dressed in fancy ties and pin-striped trousers, with a few tear-making wisps of demure black crêpe.

You may judge the author's sense of what is important, of what really matters to the ordinary man and woman, from this: the Jubilee is not mentioned, the Boer War is not mentioned, the Suffragette movement is satisfactorily dealt with by a casual remark about a woman being in gaol for having thrown a stone through a window.

During the Great War there are no telegrams from the front, no medals, no mentions in despatches.

Just as Mrs Woolf will not allow the few occasions when the kettle boils over to obscure the truth that a lot of comforting and unobtrusive tea is made in between whiles—just as she will not allow this to happen with 'history' so she will not allow it to happen with her individuals.

There are no descriptions of courtships or marriages: you have to assume these high spots. Now this person is single; in the next section she is married and perhaps has several children.

The title is extraordinarily apt. You get to feel not the men and women spaced here and there along its flow, but time—the years themselves—are the 'heroes' of the book.

'The years changed things,' Kitty reflected, 'destroyed things, heaped things up'. That's it: that's what we feel: the change, the destruction, the heaping-up, microscopically manufacturing the gigantic from second to second. We seem to subsist in this book not on the bright surface of time, with its sallies and bubbles, its bickering round rocks that look immense but never stay the flow; but in the apparently still yet irresistible undercurrent of things that lie too deep for tears.

But though Time itself is here the primary force, enigmatic and inscrutable, against which all these lives have their transient being, with what vitality Mrs Woolf invests the little lives themselves, their affairs and their habitations!

The characters are numbered in dozens, but not one of them is blurred. This is the more remarkable because so many of them are evoked by the merest hints, thrown out without heat or stress.

There is old Colonel Pargiter, whom we meet at the beginning. His wife is dying—she is too long a-dying. He is solacing himself with a mistress. There is little more than a page devoted to that side of Pargiter's life, yet it is enough to make us aware of whole tracts of hidden and forbidden territory.

And as with people, so with houses, so with weather, so with everything the author's pen touches. A summer sunset as the guests at a Dorsetshire country house sit on the terrace and smoke their cigars and drink their coffee; a titled woman who has travelled by train all night, reaches her Yorkshire home in the dawn and walks through the May morning among the gardens and the woods; the same woman as hostess at a great London reception; an old servant saying good-bye at the door of a London house where she has worked for forty years: these are a few of the things that remain in the mind with an extraordinary clarity, as though one had been present and seen them.

But would one have seen them? 'Kitty's eyes alone registered what she saw. After the talk, the effort and the hurry, she could add nothing to what she saw.'

Ah! That adding to what is seen! That makes the artist! 'Flags flew taut as trout in a stream,' Mrs Woolf writes. There's adding for you!

And this extraordinary clairvoyance that sees simple things with a dewy and unsullied and virginal directness applies the same complete integrity of the spirit to the regard which is here cast upon the whole spectacle of men and women beating their way through the mists and confusions of time.

110. Richard Church, review, *John O' London's Weekly*

19 March 1937, 1019, 1021

Richard Church (1893–1972). English poet and critic. This review was headed 'A Poet Who Writes in Prose'.

How much nervous concentration of remembered sensuousness has gone to the making of *The Years*, Mrs Virginia Woolf's new novel! It demands close and leisurely reading, like a long poem. Indeed it is a poem, for every phrase in it is presented upon the mind's edge, keen and intense. There is not an insignificant sentence in this long work of some hundred and fifty thousand words. The sentences, the paragraphs, link up together into waves of emotion, and tides of recollection, a movement that swings on throughout the book, carrying all the substance of this artist's life; her personality, her environment, her culture, her crowded associations through a life that began in the 'eighties, and is still flowing on through the tortuous labyrinth of to-day.

The result is a book which one reads, as one reads certain long poems, with such a concentration of attention that at times one has to stop, overborne by the mood of beauty which the work engenders in one; to stop and unravel the complicated strands of pleasure. This queer trick of one's consciousness is something which I have always marvelled at, and have never been able to explain or arrest. It occurs, for example, when reading *Prometheus Unbound*, or *The Paradiso*, or in moments when reading Turgeniev's stories, or Hardy's. I found it happening to me in Mrs Woolf's *The Waves*, a book which to me remains as something quite lovely in its astonishing experiment with the slowing down of time. The same experiment, in a lesser and more realistic degree, occurs in *The Years*.

The Spirit of Time

That, I think, is the first reaction on reading it. It presents itself, as a whole, in the form of a stately, slow *pavane*, a dance of the spirit of time, and of the mortal and material creatures affected by time; all moving, perpetually moving, in this funereal measure, somewhat slower than life moves, but gradually acquiring a momentum until in the final section, called *Present Day*, the pace has quickened towards the giddy rhythm of our time, and the characters who have grown old in the book are clustered together, brave still, but bewildered by the speed and strangeness of an age that they cannot understand, and from which their cooling blood recoils.

As an accessory to this fugal shape, Mrs Woolf introduces a symbolism of wind. Nearly every section, especially in the earlier part of the book, opens with a description of wind blowing over England, and the narrowing down of this general effect to the places and the protagonists where the story is exfoliating. This symbolism, so emphatic in the early stages of the tale, adds to the impression of the Laocoon-like effort to wrest the Time-spirit to the author's will, as she drags back out of the past the vitality which once made it a vivid present and a womb of a future which in turn becomes a present and a past during the course of the story.

Wind over England

Here is one of these opening prose-poems, chosen especially because it contains a device which I shall discuss in a moment.

[Quotes p. 94 'The autumn wind blew' to 'roll over and snatch a rope.']

The casual reader will ask how birds in Trafalgar Square can soil the statues in Parliament Square. He will re-read and realize that the author has telescoped a whole mass of descriptive writing into this one phrase. Remember that the fierce wind is blowing, a fierce northern wind in the year 1891. What could be more graphic than the implied picture of Whitehall swept horizontally by the gale?

The Imagination Challenged

This method, the poet's rather than the prose-writer's method, is used throughout. Again and again the imagination is challenged by that of the author. Little prose-poems (but never 'fine writing') float past in the movement of the *pavane*, and lovely detached phrases such as that describing autumnal October as 'the *birth* of the year'; or that picturing an invalid woman lying in her room, having 'entered the private world of illness'; or later, when she lies dead on the day of the funeral, how as one entered the house the 'hall smelt with the amorous intensity of a hothouse' as the mutes carried down the wreaths.

This purely poetic exuberance affects also the creation of characters. There is one, a slightly crippled woman, whose conversation has a touch of divine irresponsibility, a fey-ness. 'Running water; flowing water. May my bones turn to coral; and fish light their lanthorns; fish light their green lanthorns in my eyes.' Even in the purely mechanical moments which every novel must have, moments when the characters are being moved on the board, the poet flashes out, giving us a passing glimpse of unasked-for beauty, just as Shakespeare did in his reference to Mariana of the Moated Grange. Here is one: 'On they swept again. Now they were passing the grey stone house where the mad lady lived alone with her peacocks and her bloodhounds.' A gratuitous flash, whetting the reader's appetite both for story and for detached ecstasy. It suggests how deep, how resourceful is the mind of the writer.

A Book of Rare Beauty

I have no room to say much more about this book. I have left my readers to discover for themselves the fundamental, human solidity of the tale, the gradual sanity of its growth, its firm roots in social experience and sophistication, its shrewd ability to estimate and present a thousand facets of human character and the cheat of fear, ambition, love, and appetite.

I can say nothing about the wonderful harmonizing of those developing characters with the music of time sweeping through the scenes and the hearts of the people. We see people born, flourish, age and die; and we never question the process, so perfectly articulated is it, detail by detail, both in flesh and spirit. I can only conclude by submitting the book, with joyous humility and astonishment, to my readers, as a thing of rare beauty.

111. David Garnett, review, *New Statesman and Nation*

20 March 1937, 481

David Garnett (b. 1892). Novelist, closely associated with the Bloomsbury Group. His novel *Lady into Fox* (1923) was a best-seller. There are some reminiscences about Virginia Woolf and Bloomsbury in his autobiography.

The Years, by Virginia Woolf, is a novel of 469 pages divided, not into chapters, but into dated sections. Thus, 1880 has ninety pages, 1891 forty-four, 1907 nineteen, 1908 fifteen, 1910 thirty-four, 1911 twenty-four, 1913 eleven, 1914 sixty, 1917 twenty-four, 1918 four, while one hundred and forty are devoted to the present day. I have given these figures in detail, because they reveal that the weight of the book is at each end and it seems reasonable to assume that Mrs. Woolf's mind moved with its greatest happiness and ease over the events of the present and of the distant past, which means over her reconstructions of Victorian childhood and her portraits of old age. The 'main business of life', as people call falling madly in love, getting married, and having children, the main business of life with all its agonising jealousies, ecstasies, and terrors, is there of course, but only because in fact it is always there and has to be included. The main business of life is not what stimulates Mrs. Woolf's imagination; it is not what she feels impelled to tell us about. Indeed her attitude is rather like that of Miss Eleanor Pargiter, one of the characters in her book.

> She could not hear what he was saying, but from the sound of his voice it came over her that he must have a great many love affairs. Yes—it became perfectly obvious to her, listening to his voice through the door, that he had a great many love affairs. But who with? and why do men think love affairs so important? she asked as the door opened.

Since, however, there has never been any shortage of writers who deal almost exclusively with courtship and love, it is rather a blessing to have one of the major English novelists preoccupied with other things.

The object filling Mrs. Woolf's pages is a family with all its ramifications and changing characteristics: a family which socially is not so very different from the Forsytes. Indeed an amusing essay might be written contrasting and comparing Galsworthy and Mrs. Woolf who, belonging to much the same class, have chronicled much the same set of people. The strict Communist would no doubt lump Mrs. Woolf and Galsworthy together, giving the preference to the latter, since he was more continually preoccupied with questions of social injustice. Yet it would be obvious, to someone living much farther than Moscow—to an observer in Mars—that the two writers have aesthetically nothing whatever in common. Galsworthy is a novelist of immense historical importance. He tells us how a certain class lived and made their money; he records the main business of life, how they made love and married and sentimentalised their emotions. The historian and the anthropologist of the future will find, in the *Forsyte Saga*, all his work done for him. There will be no need for him to warn his pupils that any of the facts in it are unreliable. Whereas what sort of a picture could they get from reading *The Years*? Only, I think, a totally false impression of an extraordinarily high degree of civilisation, but having as much likeness to reality as *As You Like It* had to social life in Elizabethan England, or *The Birds* to that of Ancient Athens. Mrs. Woolf had no doubt been at some pains to avoid the sort of anachronisms which the English teacher points out so triumphantly in the works of Shakespeare—'mounted to the very chimney tops to see great Caesar pass': *Note that the Romans did not have chimneys on their houses*—for such percipient critics were able to point to comparable errors in *Orlando*. But in *The Years* they will not find much, except possibly a meal in which brussels sprouts appear to follow the tart. The anachronisms here are more serious: they are those of omission. Nothing marks and dates society more than its ideas. Yet Mrs. Woolf does not seem to have asked herself what her characters were reading in 1891, or in 1918. Had she done so, she could have shown us the difference between the generation who read Meredith because they believed, like the critic in *Chambers Encyclopedia*, 1891:

Meredith is the foremost novelist of the day and one of the most invigorating and stimulative thinkers of his generation. It is believed that Mr. Meredith is, for the present at least, more extensively read by men than by women; and this, if a fact, may perhaps be partly accounted for by the purpose which he has so deliberately expressed, and so consistently carried out, of bringing philosophy into the domain of fiction.

—and the generation who, with equal fatuity, believed the same of D. H. Lawrence. Had Mrs. Woolf indicated that the minds of her characters were filled with such changing materials she would have given us a more convincing objective picture, but she would have been forced to describe them from the outside. It would be folly to wish for this. Mrs. Woolf is not an objective writer at all. We must read *The Years* not as we read *Pride and Prejudice*, but as we read *The Prelude*.

It would be impossible to over-praise the beauty of Mrs. Woolf's prose in *The Years*. There is, to my mind, an immense advance from the wild disjointed poetry of *Orlando* or *Flush*; a greater gravity, a ripeness and richness and warmth in the descriptive passages which she has achieved nowhere else and which marks her as the greatest living master of English.

She came out on the top. The wind ceased; the country spread wide all round her. Her body seemed to shrink; her eyes to widen. She threw herself on the ground, and looked at the billowing land that went rising and falling, away and away, until somewhere far off it reached the sea. Uncultivated, uninhabited, existing by itself, for itself, without towns or houses it looked from this height. Dark wedges of shadow, bright breadths of light lay side by side. Then, as she watched, light moved and dark moved; light and shadow went travelling over the hills and over the valleys. A deep murmur sang in her ears—the land itself, singing to itself, a chorus, alone. She lay there listening. She was happy completely. Time had ceased.

The unsophisticated directness of sense impression, of a child, of a poet, runs through the whole book. The only realities are the things she has seen that touched her imagination and that are lighted up in her mind. Scraps of paper blowing from a dustcart, a man's face who has made an assignation with a girl and feels himself on the brink of a love affair, the tea-urn sliding past the moving train—these are symbols pieced together like a patchwork quilt made from the scraps of a hundred old frocks: each little hexagon is the tangible symbol of a whole flood of emotions and of memories. There is richness and beauty and artistry in the quilt, and there is the harmony of music running through it—but it is fragmentary, discontinuous, not a woven fabric. There are indeed repetitions which may irritate. Too many characters are always talking aloud; conversations are always interrupted; people rarely hear what each other say; the mind and the eye dart off at a hundred angles. And this continual interruption comes to seem like a trick; the talk has the lack of smoothness of a conversation in *Alice in Wonderland* without its logic. It is an emotional shorthand—but what, the reader asks himself, would it be like if it were written out in long? And though this discontinuous world is moving, the people in it remain almost stationary. One is aware simultaneously of time and of timelessness. Such criticisms might damn another writer; they cannot be considered as implying drawbacks in Mrs. Woolf and I have made them because it is easier to describe what she is not than what she is, which is unique. She is a supreme imaginative artist, of extraordinary originality and, in my opinion, *The Years* is the finest novel she has written. It is altogether on a bigger scale than *Jacob's Room*, and has a fullness and richness in conception and execution which were lacking in *To the Lighthouse*. There is an awareness of old age, and of sympathy with it, in the last part of the book which is new. And her humour is of a kind which spoils one for anyone else's. Above all, her special quality, for me, is something I can only compare to a child's first visit to the pantomime—of finding myself in an enchanted world.

112. Edwin Muir, review, *Listener*

31 March 1937, 622

Muir thought *The Years* a step backwards after *The Waves*, a judgment supported by most subsequent critics. Virginia Woolf commented:

> I was so damnably depressed and smacked on the cheek by Edwin Muir in the *Listener* and by Scott James in the *Life and Letters* on Friday. They both gave me a smart snubbing: E.M. says *The Years* is dead and disappointing. So in effect did S. James. All the lights sank; my reed bent to the ground. Dead and disappointing—so I'm found out and that odious rice pudding of a book is what I thought it—a dank failure. No life in it. Much inferior to the bitter truth and intense originality of Miss Compton Burnett. Now this pain woke me at 4 a.m. and I suffered acutely. All day driving to Janet and back I was under the cloud. But about 7 it lifted; there was a good review, of 4 lines, in the *Empire Review*. The best of my books: did that help? I don't think very much. But the delight of being exploded is quite real. One feels braced for some reason; amused; round; combative; more than by praise (*A Writer's Diary*, 280).

The title of Mrs Woolf's new novel probably indicates what she wishes us to look for in it—that is, not so much a picture of manners as a graph of time; but if that was the problem she does not give the impression of having solved it with her usual skill. The years, we know, are indifferent to us; we grow old whether we are ambitious or lazy, married or single, good or bad. In leaving so much out of her story, in ignoring love, for instance, a striking omission in a novel containing about a score of characters, Mrs Woolf ignores what the years ignore, and this might seem right if the years did not ignore everything: they have no story. There is certainly a change in the life of everybody which is not merely the change brought about by his own experience, by what he has felt and thought and what has been done to him by the world; a change which comes over us at moments or at least that is how we feel it and that is the only way in which we can describe it. This feeling is very strongly conveyed in *War and Peace*, and it is conveyed mainly by Tolstoy's unique apprehension of the simultaneity of life. His picture shows us all the generations at once, childhood, youth, middle age, old age, a changeless picture modified by ceaseless change: and it is this completeness that gives us the measure and the sensation of the passing of time. It also gives time its continuity. Mrs Woolf does not attempt continuity. She shows her characters in 1880, 1891, 1907, 1908, 1910, 1911, 1913, 1914, 1917, 1918 and at the present day. One cannot say whether in doing this she wishes to say that life is discontinuous; the recurring pattern of the story seems to indicate the opposite: but the effect, in spite of that, is one of discontinuity. Almost everything has been abstracted from these characters except the fact that at certain dates they are certain ages. To make them feel and think in accordance with their ages (they hardly act at all) required a fine and discriminating imagination. But they do not become real, they only become old. One has the feeling that Mrs Woolf has almost left them out.

There are brilliant scenes in the story such as only Mrs Woolf could have written, the scene, for instance, where Eleanor reads a letter from her brother Martin in India while she is driving to the Law Courts in London: Mrs Woolf is incomparable when she is evoking a sense of simultaneity in time. But the pattern which she stretches over the story strikes one as cold and artificial, and mainly external. Sometimes it is employed with fine effect:

> 'Can't one live in more places than one?' Rose asked, feeling vaguely annoyed, for she had lived in many places, felt many passions, and done many things.
> 'I remember Abercorn Terrace', said Maggie. She paused. 'There was a long room; and a tree at the end; and a picture over the fireplace, of a girl with red hair.'

Where this comes it has the effect of poetry, perhaps because we know the long room and the tree and the picture only from Mrs Woolf's own description of them, and when Maggie speaks of them she re-creates them in another dimension. But the necessity to complete the pattern drives Mrs Woolf on to follow Rose's thoughts past this stage:

> She saw them sitting round a table; and a detail that she had not thought of for years came back to her—how Milly used to take her hair-pin and fray the wick of the kettle. And she saw Eleanor sitting with her account books; and she saw herself go up to her and say: 'Eleanor, I want to go to Lamley's.'

The first passage describes a natural memory, and being a natural memory it can surprise us; but the second is a careful fragment of Mrs Woolf's pattern, and it merely makes us wonder why, out of thousands of memories, Rose should be made to remember the particular one which was needed for that pattern: the natural surprise is gone. But we feel the pattern more persistently here than in any of Mrs Woolf's other books. The long last chapter on the present day is by far the best; but after *The Waves* this is a disappointing book.

113. Pamela Hansford Johnson, review, *English Review*

April 1937, 508–9

Pamela Hansford Johnson (b. 1912). Authoress, married to the novelist C. P. Snow.

The Years, as its title would indicate, is a biography of Time. In the lives of the Pargiter family in their actions, in their thoughts, and in their eyes the years pass; and the events, political and emotional, of half a century are reflected in their being. The major happenings of 1800–1937 are barely touched upon, but the human background of the story changes with infinite subtlety as a painting will change with the dust and damp, fires and bare hearths of a decade.

Each member of the Pargiter family is strengthened or devitalised, as the case may be, by the influence of externals hardly realized subjectively. With her deliberate, fluid skill, her boundless vision, her sudden, startling perception, Mrs Woolf re-creates not only the colour and life of days within old memory, but the very scent exhaled by the years as they dropped and fell into the earth of memory itself.

The Pargiters, though sketched with mordant clarity, never step from the backcloth of the story. However separate or sharp their entities, they are eternally subordinated to the Titan Years, who trail their shadows behind them as they go, sometimes obscuring a face, sometimes sharpening it to an old and glorious beauty. Of all Mrs Woolf's novels, this is the most nostalgic, the most austere, the most impressive. There is a certain divorce from life as we see it, a certain groping towards a dignity and peace too often denied us, a certain expression of wish-fulfilment. But it does present for the first time in full clarity the hypothesis that change and readjustment are the great externals, with power to touch the flower but never the root.

114. Peter Monro Jack, from a review, *New York Times*

11 April 1937, Section 7, 1 and 27

Mrs Woolf's novel, her first since *The Waves* of 1931, is rich and lovely with the poetry of life. It might be called a chronicle novel, since it begins in 1880 and ends in the present day, or a 'family' novel, since it narrates the fortunes of the large and representative Pargiter family. But it eludes both classifications. Though the founder of the present family, old Colonel Pargiter, who lost two fingers in the Indian Mutiny—is, in habit and class, a bit of a Forsyte, there is nothing of the careful solidity of Galsworthy's saga, with its verifiable genealogy, interludes and corroborative detail.

Rather this is a long-drawn-out lyricism in the form of a novel, with flying buttresses to sustain its airy and often absent-minded inspirations. There is the minimum of substructure. But there is everywhere, on one lovely page after another, a kind of writing which reveals a kind of feeling that is more illuminating than a dozen well-made and documented novels. Mrs Woolf has made, or unmade, her novel in the form of a poem or a piece of music,

And so not built at all
and therefore built forever,

and it is this subtle and oblique composition, though we may perhaps exaggerate its durability, that gives whatever she writes its distinction.

She has not continued from *The Waves*, which was the furthest the novel could go in the way of freedom, or even license, of reverie and the stream of consciousness. Instead she has turned back to earlier forms of her own. *The Years* resembles somewhat the general motive of *To the Lighthouse* in its marking of time as the chief protagonist of recorded life. But sometimes there is the traditional form of narration that she mastered so easily in the early *The Voyage Out*. There is also the discontinuity of *Jacob's Room*. There is also the unity and singleness of *Mrs Dalloway*, with the years of five decades tolling instead of the chiming of a day's hours. In short, Mrs Woolf has written her longest novel, her richest and most beautiful novel, out of many years in the practice of writing . . .

So far as the book is a chronicle of family life, we must note that it has a perfect beginning and a perfect end, and almost no middle. The development of character, the process of growing up, the movie-life of fiction, so to speak, has never been easy to Mrs Woolf; or perhaps she distrusts its genuineness. The childhood in the house in Abercorn Terrace, opening at tea-time with Milly taking her invalid mother's place at the tea-kettle which works so badly, and the family coming in from here and there: Martin from school, Eleanor from being kind to the poor, the Colonel from his club and his mistress, Morris from his law office; and the dinner that follows and is interrupted with the death of the long-ailing mother—this opening is so brilliantly composed that one looks back with dismay to the opening of another novel of about the same year and time of afternoon, Galsworthy's *The Man of Property*, so full of upholstery and exposition. Mr Galsworthy himself wrote of 'pickling' and 'embalming' his characters. But Mrs Woolf's persons are alive with the excitement of life. No one, I believe, has quite her immediacy of effect, her recklessness of sensation, tempered by breeding and intelligence, turned into pure expressibility.

. . . Between the beginning and end there is a sort of stasis, possibly more true to life than the dynamics of other novelists; but still part of a criticism of Mrs Woolf's method. The characters were young; now they are old: and both Mrs Woolf can render to perfection. In the meantime events happen, and they are arbitrarily selected. Eleanor at a committee meeting, Rose in prison because of Votes for Women, Eleanor at dinner with her cousins during an air raid; these are pictures, vividly painted but without a frame, unless one's own experience supplies one. It is here that one recalls Galsworthy again, who charted the course of each character. Mrs Woolf lets them wander at will, forgetting and remembering, as one does really in life, moving slowly or standing still and musing while new inventions and policies clamour for attention. Her people live in the past, in the family, in all the rôles of Victorian decorum; and yet with a sense of fun and intelligence and common sense and uncommon sensibility; and, above all, with the eccentricity of personality, so that no category quite contains them: they are as likely to burst into poetry as politics, or to qualify the army with a quotation from Horace. There is no cataloguing them, and no way of regimenting them into the customary form of fiction.

It is this, really, that gives Mrs Woolf's novels their utmost delight, a quality of pleasure in living, a lovely sense of people thinking and feeling and brooding by themselves, with vague memories and sharp present sensations, with bits of song and odd poetry; and still their contact with life, in 1880 or 1920, is quite definitely realised . . .

Lovely as *The Waves* was, *The Years* goes far behind and beyond it, giving its characters a local habitation and a name, and expressing Mrs Woolf's purpose in the novel more richly than it has ever been done before.

115. William Troy, review, *Nation* (New York)

24 April 1937, 473–4

In this review Troy continues a line of argument begun in his *Symposium* article (see No. 98).

By this time so little that is fundamental remains to be said of the merits or limitations of Mrs Woolf's narrative method that a review of her new novel, which is a reshuffling of elements already familiar to all readers of her work, is doomed to the same sort of repetitiousness from which that work itself has for some time suffered. Her admirers, writing in a style too suspiciously like her own to be altogether convincing, will revive the phrases about the beauty and the distinction and the ultimate truth to life of everything that Mrs Woolf has written. And a few others, still disturbed by the persistence of these claims, will take the trouble to point out that each of them is capable of a little more exact definition—particularly the reference to the truth about life. They will doubtless protest that what we probably get in these distinguished novels is not so much life as a special vision of a special kind of life—a vision, moreover, that has been largely created, nurtured, and corroborated by the conditions of this life. 'We receive but what we give,' in Coleridge's well-known formula; and if Mrs Woolf's impression of the years is what it is, it may be only because she has superimposed on them an impression that was, in the first place, the kind of impression that the Ramsays, the Pargiters, and the rest were forced to draw from their own experience. From this maddening shuttle of cause and effect, this rankest of determinisms, we are never released through that vigorous act of imagination by which the writer attempts to transcend the limiting conditions of his materials: the deep voice of Coleridge mumbling of the fusion of '*sum*ject' and '*oom*ject' is stilled like everything else by the resounding waters of time. So also in the set pieces of beautiful writing—precisely distributed here at the beginning of each of those divisions by which the immeasurable is arbitrarily measured—what we get thrown back at us, in this charming evocation of a summer day, this clever impersonation of a March wind, are images and words and phrases so hoarily incrusted in the characters' collective consciousness that nothing really fresh is added to our perception. And it is undoubtedly the total effect of language of this sort that is referred to by the somewhat vague term distinction. It is now apparent that final evaluation of Mrs Woolf's work must revolve monotonously around the question of the experience and the attitude toward experience of her typical characters. This is a standard imposed by her faithful refusal to oppose any attitude of her own by which we can measure them within the perspective of her work. And it is, needless to say, a standard that cannot be very successfully applied beyond a certain point. Either these people will be found to glow with a still potent charm of well-bred sensitivity or they will emit a most unpleasant smell as of something already quite dead and decayed.

All that is perhaps necessary in this review, therefore, is to consider the reshuffling that has taken place in the light of its possible consequences on the theme. For the book is of course another celebration of the flux, another slow passage down the most traversed river in modern fiction, another extended prose gloss on *Eheu fugaces, anni labuntur.* But where in *Jacob's Room* and *Orlando* the theme was rendered in terms of a single individual, and where in *Mrs Dalloway* and *To the Lighthouse* the period covered was relatively short, we have here a chronicle of a whole typical middle-class English family, with their accumulating host of relatives and friends, from 1880 to the present. Such distinctions should not, however, be stressed too much; for in *The Waves* also Mrs Woolf was concerned with tracing the destinies of a group of people over the whole course of their lives. The great difference would be that for the first time she is trying to maintain something like a balance between the outer and the inner reality, between the public and the personal, between the mechanical ticking of Big Ben and the sound of time's passing in the mind's ear. In this effort she has returned somewhat to the form and style of her very earliest novels; she has adopted a simple chronological order; and she has practically put a stop to the direction which reached its climax in *The Waves.*

The most immediate changes to be observed will be in fact the reduction of those prolonged subjective improvisations that have been so much admired in all Mrs Woolf's more recent novels. From another point of view of course, this shift to a neater, more rapid, less mannered style will be welcomed. It promises, at least at the beginning, a corresponding modification of other important things—most notably the conception of human character as little more than a highly sensitized instrument for registering impressions. But this is unfortunately a promise that recedes in exact proportion to the characters' uniform failure, through the unfolding years, to exhibit anything resembling moral progress. Time goes on and on, but the Edwards, the Delias, the Eleanors, and the Kittys retain the same niceties, the same frustrations, the same terror of existence with which they began. All suffer from a malady of will that makes them as inappropriate to the purposes of fiction as to the bustle and dirt of the London street.

Of all the symbolical scenes in the book none is more symbolical than the one in which a member of the Pargiter clan, looking out from the tastefully furnished room in the slums which she shares with her sister, is made to exclaim: 'In time to come . . . people, looking into this room—this cave, this little antre, scooped out of mud and dung, will hold their fingers to their noses'—she held her fingers to her nose—'and say, "Pah! They stink!" ' With characters possessing such a view of themselves, Mrs Woolf is hardly able to do very much that she has not already done, with consummate perfection, in the past. The present book merely throws into new relief the fact that no expansion of scale, no experimentation with method can lend meaning and significance where neither is implicit in the experience. It seems more than ever unlikely that Mrs Woolf's talents, which are considerable in so many different departments of fiction, will develop to their full measure while she persists in limiting herself to purely formal variations on the same old dirge-like tune.

116. W. H. Mellers, review, *Scrutiny*

June 1937, 71–5

W. H. Mellers (b. 1914). Professor of Music and literary critic. The review is a characteristic statement of the *Scrutiny* case against Virginia Woolf.

Mrs Woolf, we all know, is a Poet in Prose; or rather she has—perhaps one should say had—a range of sensuous impressions which would have stood a great poet in good stead. But sensuous impressions, though they are immensely important and perhaps the only means whereby a poet can make his apprehensions and his attitudes concrete and comprehensible, are not an end in themselves; if they were, most normally sensitive children would be great poets. Of course, Mrs Woolf is an 'intelligent woman', but, as a reviewer in the *Calendar* pointed out ('Towards Standards of Criticism', 48ff.) on the publication of *Mrs Dalloway*, her intellectual capacity is oddly disproportionate to, and immature compared with, her sensitiveness, and, if she ventures outside the narrow range imposed on her by her sensuousness, she becomes a child. Since the range of experience implied in sensuous apprehension purely and simply, is, indeed, necessarily so limited, it is perhaps significant that the only occasion when she has been able to use her impressions, in their various subtle inter-relations, to form an organisation, a whole, has been when she was concerned, to some extent at least, with personal reminiscence; and it is probable, moreover, that what she did in *To the Lighthouse* could only be done once.

In this book, anyway, Mrs Woolf used her impressions triumphantly as imaginative concepts, and she perfected an original technique to express the order which she apprehended within these impressions. As she is a sensuous artist, and what the senses perceive is transitory and mutable, she saw them as dominated by Time; and she found a central symbol for her theme so just and integral that it is not as oversimple as it may superficially appear, to say that what differentiates *To the Lighthouse* from Mrs Woolf's other books is precisely that in this work alone *something really happens*—the trip to the Lighthouse. And here, because she has kept within her limitations, her conception of human relationships and of moral values is delicate and sure. (Mrs Ramsay has positive life, is something compelling and potent.) But how limited this conception nevertheless is, is suggested by the somewhat suspicious easiness of the middle section (Time Passes). Even in this book, where her poetry is so consummately incarnated, her attitude is ultimately that of the 'sensitive' young girl who, growing old in years, looks back and remembers.

When she had written *To the Lighthouse* there were three courses open to Mrs Woolf. Either she could enlarge her scope, do something fresh; or she could stop writing altogether; or she could cheat by way of technique. She chose the last of these alternatives. In *The Waves* there is a fatal falsification between what her impressions actually are and what they are supposed to signify—they are pinned to her prose like so many dead butterflies. Mrs Woolf goes through the appropriate gestures (doors open, doors shut), uses the appropriate formulae (the rose blossoms, the petal falls), but the champing beast on the shore confesses itself a mechanical toy, and the artificially artful parallel with the waves hardly pretends to be anything more than a parallel. The artfulness of the method makes the immediacy and hence the quality of the impressions themselves deteriorate. The rhythm loses the subtle flexibility of the earlier books falling at times to the bathos of the magazine story:

> But if one day you do not come after breakfast, if one day I see you in some looking-glass perhaps looking after another, if the telephone buzzes and buzzes in your empty room, I shall then after unspeakable anguish, I shall then—for there is no end to the folly of the human heart—seek another, find another, you. Meanwhile, let us abolish the ticking of time's clock with one blow. Come closer.

While many of the 'poetical' images betray only too patently their genesis. ('A crack of light knelt on the wall'.) A rudimentary analysis of any characteristic passages suffices to prove, indeed, that, shorn of the 'original' technique, what Mrs Woolf has to say about the relationship between her characters, about the business of living, is both commonplace and sentimental.

The hero-worship of Percival (a 'great master of the art of living') is perhaps a minor point, though symptomatic; but the radical weakness and falsity of the book is revealed in the central position occupied by

Bernard, the maker of phrases. 'Now you tug at my skirts, looking back, making phrases . . . I shall be a clinger to the outsides of words all my life . . . There is some flaw in me, some fatal hesitancy, which if I pass it over, turns to foam and falsity.' There could be no more accurate description of what Mrs Woolf is doing in *The Waves*; essentially her attitude is that of the undergraduette—or Bloomsbury—poet. 'There are stories, but what are stories? What is the thing that lies behind the semblance of the thing?' Our lives are shrouded in obscurity and knowing nothing we turn on our wistfullest smiles and tread our way to the grave. It is difficult to see how an honest reader can discover any more 'profundity' in *The Waves* than this; and if there *is* any form in these multiple incoherencies the trick lies in Bernard's 'I retrieve them from formlessness with words.' It is only a trick, and a pretty threadbare one at that. We must note, too, the complete disappearance of the irony that gave such subtlety of poise to *To the Lighthouse*; though Mrs Woolf is 'critical', there is no evidence that she hasn't, with Bernard, a sympathy which amounts to an implicit self-identification.

Whatever lingering doubts we may have entertained about the validity of *The Waves* are resolved with dismal finality when we consider Mrs Woolf's new novel, *The Years*, in which, without the superficial screen of Experimental Technique, she reveals the same sentimentalities and ineptitudes. Presumably the explicit theme is one which has been implicit in the earlier books, the inevitable theme of the sensuous impressionist, 'the passage of time and its tragedy'. Only, as Mrs Woolf presents it, it isn't tragic, but merely fatuous. It is impossible to find tragedy in the ageing of persons who are non-existent, and, far from having the rounded vitality of Mrs Ramsay, the characters in this novel have not even the factitious existence of the collections of phrases that make up the personae of *The Waves*. These people are phantoms; they grow old, but they cannot change because they have never been alive, in so far as they exist at all it is as a bundle of memories. The book is a document of purposelessness. Either life is supremely meaningless, or, as the years go by, there is perhaps a pattern (what has been, will be), yet there is no point in the pattern. The discovery of it entails, indeed, a degree of falsification, The repetitions, the cooing doves and the bonfire smoke, are sly and artful, the jig-saw of the litterateur. 'Does everything then come over again a little differently? she thought. If so, is there a pattern, a theme, recurring, like music . . .? who makes it? Who thinks it? Her mind slipped. She could not finish her thought.' The atmosphere of uncertainty, of ambiguity, is of course, traded upon. Conversations are misunderstood, thought is incommunicable. 'Who's right? Who's wrong? . . . We cannot make laws and religions that fit because we do not know ourselves . . . If we do not know ourselves how can we know other people?' And consequent upon this purposelessness is a sense of oppressive frustration. People are always having 'the truth' on the tip of the tongue, but are unable (and it is God alone that knows why) to utter it. The 'climax'—pathetic paradox—comes when Nicholas, attempting to make the speech that would at last reveal the secret of their lives, is prevented. 'It was to have been a miracle. A masterpiece! But how can one speak when one is always interrupted. . . . I was going to drink to the human race . . . He brought his glass down with a thump on the table. It broke.'

The long final section on the Present Day is, indeed, easily the best part of the book, and here the ambiguity and purposelessness, the frustration, becomes less artful and, paradoxical as it may seem, more sharply focussed with a quality of passive desolation which is comparable with the neurasthenic weariness and fatigue of Kurt Weill's queerly documentary ballet *The Seven Deadly Sins*, though it entirely lacks the negative intensity of Weill's music. 'Rest, rest, let me rest. How to deaden, how to cease to feel; that was the cry of the women bearing children; to rest, to cease to be . . . not to live; not to feel bearing children; to rest, to cease to be . . . not to live; not to feel; to make money, always money, and in the end, when I'm old and worn like a horse, no it's a cow . . .' The extraordinarily inert, incantatory rhythm of the prose, and the remotely reminiscent nature of the images—as though the scene were viewed not immediately but in retrospect, distantly as through a mirror or through the glass of an aquarium—produces an effect oddly similar to the gray, drab exhaustion, the unreal nightmarish atmosphere of Weill's music, but it is, of course, superficially more 'refined', more precious.

To speak of Mrs Woolf's refinement reminds us of her celebrated femininity, which quality seems to go hand in hand with the curiously tepid Bloomsbury prose into which she has always, in unguarded moments, been inclined to trickle. Here, anyway, it only enforces the feeling of weakness and sterility, and one can but reflect dismally on the inanity of a world in which the only positives seem to be 'silence and solitude'. These incoherently reminiscent mumblings seem purposely to ignore the human will and all it entails; and although we have no right to blame an artist for not doing what he didn't intend to do, the complete omission, in a work which embraces the passage of time during the last fifty years, of (for instance) physical desire may strike us at least as odd. Of course it is obvious enough that Mrs Woolf's social world is a minute one. The phrase 'feminine intuition', used in connection with Mrs Woolf, inevitably invites comparison with Jane Austen and if the latter has social decorum, Mrs Woolf can only be said to have social decorousness. But, even at her best, for all her air of abysmal profundity, is Mrs Woolf's spiritual world either quite as far-reaching as it seems? Some of us may perhaps think that, as a novelist, Mrs Woolf is too concerned about Life to be concerned, as was Miss Austen, very adequately about living. And if it be objected that Mrs Woolf is not using the novel *qua* novel but for a poetical end, we return to the point from which we started; and conclude that she is, in the long run, only a very minor sort of poet.

THREE GUINEAS

4 June 1938

117. From an unsigned review, *Times Literary Supplement*

4 June 1938

'Oh it pleased me that the *Lit. Sup.* says I'm the most brilliant pamphleteer in England' (*A Writer's Diary*, 294).

Mrs Woolf in her novels makes masterly use of the reflecting mind's haziness and inconsequence to build up, out of images, a brilliant picture; and admiring readers, stimulated by this poetic process, are sometimes misled into supposing that it constitutes her chief artistic equipment. It is in her criticism, whether of books or institutions, that the keen edge of her other tool becomes apparent; and that other tool is precision itself, consequence, logic, directed by an irony that is sharp but never inhuman. Mrs Woolf seldom writes a pamphlet, but she is the most brilliant pamphleteer in England. *Three Guineas* is a pamphlet which, in various ways, challenges every thinking mind to-day; so that all should read it, not only for their enjoyment of its admirable style and wit, but that they may define in their own minds their answer to her arguments.

The New Lysistrata

In essence, the question propounded is that of Lysistrata—how can women help to stop war?—but the simple levity of Aristophanes's answer naturally bears no resemblance to Mrs Woolf's treatment of a matter that brooks no laughter. Humour she uses, but her seriousness is profound....

Some of the notes which contain the quotations also contain the quintessence of the author's wit, for example, those about lectures on English literature, about the maid's part in English upper-class life and about the rage of the educated class for trying to improve the working class, to mention only a few. Many readers of this book will applaud, others grind their teeth; some will mostly enjoy the display of graceful wit, others mostly ponder the arguments; but none, either the convinced or unconvinced, will be impervious to the dextrous bodkin, against which the only protection is a disinterestedness of action and a clarity of mind equal to Mrs Woolf's. . . .

It needs more than one reading to enjoy the artistry, appraise the arguments and formulate such criticism as occurs. Nevertheless, we should like to have had Mrs Poyser's criticism and that of the mother who figures in *Sons and Lovers*. Also, in spite of the gulf, D. H. Lawrence might have had something to say regarding a matter not here touched on, the possessiveness of women in the private life; and the modern father of an emancipated daughter, with an allowance of her own, a flat of her own and an earned salary in addition, might observe that Mrs Woolf's continual quotations from the lives of a past generation of heroines do not really move him very deeply. Possibly, too, it might be said that Mrs Woolf cannot solve the whole problem if she only states it for educated women of a civilized *bourgeoisie*. Nevertheless, she limits her scrutiny with her eyes open, and it would be the grossest misunderstanding which accused her of intending to exacerbate the antagonism and mutual ignorance of the sexes which, in the end, she has ruefully to admit: 'as fighting thus is a sex characteristic which she cannot share, so it is an instinct which she cannot judge'. This is a fairer statement, and nearer to the truth, than the pleas of most believers in the perfectibility of mankind. Yet even Mrs Woolf seems hardly to appreciate the implications of this admission and its effect upon the fundamental problem. May it not be that the myth of the Fall expresses the truth that so long as there is flesh aware of flesh there will be conflict, and while there are bodies to hunger and desire, the poet's dream of universal, unbroken peace will never be realised? . . . to regain Paradise no number of guineas or societies will avail.

118. Theodora Bosanquet, from a review, *Time and Tide*

4 June 1938, 788–90

Three Guineas is the book of the year. Whatever other books may come, it is unlikely that 1938 will give us another volume by Mrs Woolf, and no other living English writer carries such an array of gifts and accomplishments under one bonnet or cap. Here, then, is this year's finest example of what England can produce in literature. Like all Mrs Woolf's works, it carries its author's signature on every page. It is made of vision translated by a subtle intelligence, passion lighted by wit, confident and easy control of words and phrases. It flows in a form which moves and gleams like the ripple of waves drawn by the irresistible magnetism of the moon. And as waves seem to return on themselves before each advance, so the movement of Mrs Woolf's mind seems to glide back, to catch up an earlier thread of the argument, only to gather momentum for flowing over a new crest to a higher level.

Yet for all the shimmer of its surface, *Three Guineas* is a revolutionary bomb of a book, delicately aimed at the heart of our mad, armament ridden world. Or, if not precisely at the heart, at an even more vital if less physiologically localized centre, the dark womb of the unconscious (or subconscious, as you will) where various undesirable eggs hatch into monsters which thrust their way to the surface in fears and oppressions, dictators and mass murders . . .

I hope I have made it clear that *Three Guineas* is a provocative and controversial book. Mrs Woolf is trailing not merely her coat, but a few delightfully and deliberately misleading scents. Quibblers can throw themselves hungrily on symbolic statements, special pleadings, extravagant flights of imagination. They can protest that 1919 is not the date she says it is, that Cambridge is not the only University, and that the Rev. Patrick Bronte may reasonably be held to have lengthened his daughter Charlotte's life, however unpleasantly he behaved about that affair of the curate. But Mrs Woolf is not writing as a lawyer, a professor, or any other educated man. She does not pretend to be impartial. Women, she might say, cannot be impartial. And although I do not suppose that Mrs Woolf would maintain in the teeth of much evidence, that jealousy, vanity, greed and possessiveness are found only in public life and exhibited almost exclusively by the male sex, it is a fact that she does not believe that 'God Almighty made women to match the men.' She has never thought as badly of women as that.

It is not as Amazons but as Antigones that Mrs Woolf sees the daughters of educated men. Their freedom should be not to break laws but to discover the Law, the true pattern of life. Creon, you will remember, had Antigone shut up in a tomb, and Creon is the false pattern of a dictator with death in his face. Since Mrs Woolf is a prophet, her vision will no doubt be fulfilled; but since prophets are notoriously unreliable in matters of days and centuries, the world may have to wait a long time for that fulfilment—to wait perhaps for the crest of another great wave and the worship of another form of the Bona Dea. But today the daughters of educated men, children of earth and of the starry heaven, will, if they are intelligent, read *Three Guineas* with close attention and consider in its brilliant light the comparative merits of the birthright which they are asked to claim and a precarious mess of pottage.

119. Basil de Selincourt, from a review, *Observer*

5 June 1938, 5

Only the other day I drew down *Literature and Dogma* from its honoured place on a distant shelf and, as I revived my memory of its caustic expostulatory cadences, reflected with sorrow on the narrow range of their effectiveness. Nonconformity and Establishment pursue the beaten path in much the same spirit now as fifty years ago, softened only too little by the truth that penetrates and unifies; we are still bound to the dead letter of our professional, our man-made creeds.

Mrs Woolf's reasonings and expostulations, her irony and ridicule, in *Three Guineas* have much the tone of Matthew Arnold's, and I am wondering whether the world will swallow them and acknowledge the justice of her cause, as once it did of his, and afterwards roll on in practical indifference, too set in its ways to realise that those ways need changing. Of course, the professionalism of religion has been man-made in almost every country. And is it because men have laid down the lines not of religion only, but of so many other things—industry, law, education—that those lines are apt to be hard and fast lines, conspicuously lacking the resiliency and adaptiveness which life and growth require? Who, you may ask me, could lay down these lines but men? We are surely not to suppose, wherever we require it, a deus ex machina, a divine messenger arriving in the nick of time to cut each knot? That is far from being Mrs Woolf's suggestion. Her point is that men, who constitute but half the world, persist in behaving as if they were the only half that mattered; as if they were by necessity the creators and directors. Yet if you look around you, if you consider, for example, the condition of Spain, can you be sure that the direction and the initiation are the best that could have been found? . . .

It is a hateful story and it is also an absurd story; Mrs Woolf has done the best she could for us in showing how absurd. But she has also words of deep wisdom on the principal question, the question where we should look if we wish to find the seeds of war. Of course, there is an obvious animal combativeness which is the glory of the male. Among the subtler human motives she specially denounces the pride of privilege and possession: mainly male, no doubt, at present; but I fear women, too, will always tend to succumb when the interests of their children or their loved ones are at stake.

120. K. John, from a review, *New Statesman and Nation*

11 June 1938, 995–6

The review was entitled 'The New Lysistrata'.

This writer cannot make a point heavily, or endure the bleakness of abstraction for half a page. Everything comes to life at her touch. She ranks as a highbrow; yet no penny-a-liner is more careful to avoid dullness, and meet attention halfway. And *Three Guineas* equals anything of the sort she has done, but the question is what to say about it. Should one call it simply a work of art, and hold up her method to the despair of all bunglers? Can one discuss its ideas, as though they were not involved with that enchanting presentment? Reviewers must have had the same difficulty with *A Room of One's Own*. . . .

If women were really solid for peace and freedom, I think they would have some chance of getting it, by whatever method—breaking shop windows, for example. For that matter, if they had been solid for the vote they would very likely have got it quicker. But a number of them were violent anti-suffragists—beginning with Queen Victoria, who was certainly not afraid to speak her mind, and whose mind was that the agitators should be well *whipped*. And to-day a number are Fascists: it may be unnatural and astounding, but there it is. Can we assume that in the moment of becoming independent they will veer round?

But they should be independent, in either case. There is no questioning the justice of Mrs Woolf's demands, or the beauty of her gospel—though it includes one or two hard sayings. I can't see, for instance, why she is so bitter on lectures, and on those who 'adulterate' their culture by mixing it with personal charm. All charming people of culture do this all the time, and can't help doing it. Mrs Woolf does it, inevitably, in every sentence of her personal style. Surely such 'adulteration' is one of the best things the world can offer?

121. Graham Greene, review, *Spectator*

17 June 1938, 1110–12

Graham Greene (b. 1904). Novelist. See Introduction, p. 29.

There is a mythical quality about Mrs Woolf. It is sometimes hard not to believe that she is a character invented by Mr E. M. Forster. Listen to him describing the Schlegel sisters in *Howards End* and think how it applies.

> In their own fashion they cared deeply about politics, though not as politicians would have us care; they desired that public life should mirror whatever is good in the life within. Temperance, tolerance, and sexual equality were intelligible cries to them; whereas they did not follow our Forward Policy in Thibet with the keen attention it merits, and would at times dismiss the whole British Empire with a puzzled, if reverent, sigh.

It must have needed courage (what would the post bring?) on the part of an earnest, middle-aged barrister to write to Mrs Woolf asking her how in her opinion we were to prevent war and inviting her to join a society for that purpose. She would not join the society, but she sent him (the Schlegels could never have refused such an appeal) a guinea and a letter. This is the letter.

The question—how are we to prevent war?—involved elaborate and subtle research in that brain which I have always pictured as a large whorled shell with intricate convolutions trapping somewhere within them the sound of the sea (the sea which Mrs Ramsay heard splashing round the lighthouse, as she turned the pages of the Stores catalogue) and stamped on the outside 'A Present from . . .' some family resort. It involves the whole social relationship between men and women: it involves an appeal she has received for the rebuilding fund of a women's college and another from a society 'to help the daughters of educated men to obtain employment in the professions'. Men are reminded of the sacrifices women made for centuries that *they* might be educated at the universities (has that education helped to prevent war?), of the opposition, often gross and physical in form, they raised to prevent women in their turn receiving a university education, and of the present unfair discrimination against women in the professions, particularly in the Civil Service. Yet now we turn to them and ask for their help. What can women do?—'What real influence can we bring to bear upon law or business, religion or politics—we to whom many doors are still locked, or at best ajar, we who have neither capital nor force behind us?'

The question is horribly just, and caught in that whorled shell goes echoing back. If man's university education, their professional life with its absurd pageantries, the wigs and ribbons and stripes, have done nothing for peace but rather encouraged competition and war, is it right to help women along the same road? Mrs Woolf's notes are crammed with the appalling utterances of our professional leaders—a judge interpreting England and the late Sir Ernest Wild on the proper influence of women, and her pages are illustrated with photographs—of the general, the judge, the archbishop, tinkling with trinkets. And though in the end Mrs Woolf does send a guinea each to the rebuilding fund and the society, to her latter gift she attaches a wise and austere condition. Biography—in the lives of such women as Florence Nightingale and Mary Kingsley—has taught her the value of the old unpaid-for education snatched with difficulty from the man-ruled home. 'We cannot deny that these, if not educated, still were civilised women.'

> This biography, when asked the question we have put to it—how can we enter the professions and yet remain civilised human beings, human beings who discourage war, would seem to reply: If you refuse to be separated from the four great teachers of the daughters of educated men—poverty, chastity, derision and freedom from unreal loyalties—but combine them with some wealth, some knowledge, and some service to real loyalties, then you can enter the professions and escape the risks that make them undesirable.... Such are the conditions attached to this guinea.

Chastity is given a very wide, very intellectual meaning: it has nothing—in Mrs Woolf's argument—to do with sexual experience; though it is hard to understand why Mrs Woolf should rule out the genuine chastity—as practised by Florence Nightingale and Mary Kingsley—from the value of their education.

It is here we come on the one defect of this clear brilliant essay. When Mrs Woolf's argument touches morality or religion we are aware of odd sounds in the shell. Can a shell be a little old-fashioned (quoting Renan), a little provincial, even a little shrill? Can a shell be said to lead a too sheltered life? Mrs Woolf discusses Christianity only in terms of the Church of England, and one cannot imagine the most agnostic Frenchwoman—a countrywoman of Maritain, Bloy, Péguy, Mauriac—writing of the moral laws: 'That such laws exist, and are observed by civilised people, is fairly generally allowed; but it is beginning to be agreed that they were not laid down by "God", who is now very generally held' (note the unusual stylistic chaos: is some emotion imperfectly suppressed?) 'to be a conception, of patriarchal origin, valid only for certain races, at certain stages and times.' And only a very good woman, living at a 'good address', could write in connexion with what Sir Ernest Wild so complacently considered to be a woman's proper influence ('every man who had a woman to care about him liked to shine in her eyes'):

> If such is the real nature of our influence, and we all recognise the description and have noted the effects, it is either beyond our reach, for many of us are plain, poor and old; or beneath our contempt, for many of us would prefer to call ourselves prostitutes simply and to take our stand openly under the lamps of Piccadilly Circus rather than use it.

It is all a little reminiscent of the words of that good man who would rather have given his daughter poison than a copy of *The Well of Loneliness.*

122. Q. D. Leavis, review, *Scrutiny*

September 1938, 203–14

Q. D. Leavis. University teacher and literary critic. Wife of F. R. Leavis. Her pioneering study *Fiction and the Reading Public* was published in 1932 (see Introduction, p. 29). When she read this review, Virginia Woolf commented 'I read enough to see that it was all personal—about Queenie's own grievances and retorts to my snubs' (*A Writer's Diary*, 301).

This book is not really reviewable in these pages because Mrs. Woolf implies throughout that it is a conversation between her and her friends, addressed as she constantly says to 'women of our class', though bits of it are directly and indirectly aimed at those women's menkind. What 'our class' is turns out to be the people whose fathers function at Westminster, who 'spend vast sums annually upon party funds; upon sport; upon grouse moors . . . lavish[es] money upon clubs—Brook's, White's, the Travellers', the Reform, to mention the most prominent.' Mrs. Woolf would apparently be surprised to hear that there is no member of that class on the contributing list of this review. On the other hand, readers of this review will be surprised to hear that Mrs. Woolf thinks this class—the relatively very few wealthy propertied people in our country—is to be identified with 'the educated class' and contains at this date the average educated man and the average student of the women's colleges of the older universities. This is the first of many staggering intimations for the reader that Mrs. Woolf is not living in the contemporary world: almost the first thing we notice is that the author of *Three Guineas* is quite insulated by class. What respectable ideas inform this book belong to the ethos of John Stuart Mill. What experience there is of domineering and hostile man (for that purports to justify the undertaking) is second-hand and comes from heresay.*

* Often unreliable. Mrs. Woolf instances as one burning injustice: 'Not a single educated man's daughter is thought capable of teaching the literature of her own language at either

It is no use attempting to discuss the book for what it claims to be, which is a sort of chatty restatement of the rights and wrongs of women of Mrs. Woolf's class, with occasional reflexions where convenient on the wrongs of other kinds of English-women. Mrs. Woolf, by her own account, has personally received considerably more in the way of economic ease than she is humanly entitled to, and as this book reveals, has enjoyed the equally relaxing ease of an uncritical (not to say flattering) social circle: she cannot be supposed to have suffered any worse injury from mankind than a rare unfavourable review. Writing this book was evidently a form of self-indulgence—altruism exhibits a different tone, it is not bad-tempered, peevishly sarcastic and incoherent as this book is throughout. As a reviewer I must say it impresses me as unpleasant self-indulgence, and as a member of a class of educated women Mrs. Woolf has apparently never heard of, I feel entitled to add that it is also highly undesirable. The reviewers have indeed all blessed the book, but any man who objected would lay himself open to the obvious charges of (a) being no gentleman and (b) expressing a resentment easily explicable in psychological terms, while any woman who refused to vote solid would of course be a traitress to the cause. Nevertheless I venture to voice what I know to be the opinion of many educated women, that Mrs. Woolf's latest effort is a let-down for our sex. *A Room of One's Own* was annoying enough, causing outpourings of disgust in the very quarters in which Mrs. Woolf, one gathered, expected to earn gratitude; but this book is not merely silly and ill-informed, though it is that too, it contains some dangerous assumptions, some preposterous claims and some nasty attitudes.

The method is a deliberate avoidance of any argument—its unity is emotional. She tries in fact to make a weapon of feminine inconsequence, and I felt sympathetic with another reader of *Three Guineas*, of course of the wrong sex, who remarked to me that Mrs. Woolf's mental processes reminded him of Mrs. Nickleby's. The result affects me like Nazi dialectic without Nazi conviction. Take pages 39 to 40. They run like this (I preserve Mrs. Woolf's wording where possible): men dress up in their professional capacities as warriors, lawyers, courtiers, dons; they forbid us women to wear such uniform, but

---

university.' There are at present six women regularly on the lecture-list for the English Tripos and I believe at no time in the last ten years has there been less than four—a generous representation for two colleges. Again: 'The great majority of your sex (Englishmen) are to-day in favour of war.'

don't let them suppose that they are anything but a ridiculous spectacle to us; preserving archaic costume for public ritual in the universities emphasizes the superiority of educated men over other people; this arouses competition and jealousy, emotions making for war; women therefore can help to prevent war by refusing to wear academic dress (though they have at present a legitimate grievance in not being allowed to wear it at Cambridge) or to accept public honours, and by openly despising the men who do. I cannot understand all this as anything but phrases which have no meaningful connection with each other, but it is a fair specimen of the rhetoric in which the 'argument' of *Three Guineas* is conducted. This passage moreover is illustrated with photographs, but as they are evidently selected with malice and as the thought perforce leaps to mind how a corresponding selection, probably as stupid-looking or ridiculous, could be compiled of eminent women's faces and persons in gala dress, the method defeats itself. As does another artifice. This is to write as though the defects of human nature existed only in the male branch (if deliberate it's bad tactics because it outrages common sense and if unconscious, as there seems reason to suppose, it discounts the whole undertaking). For example, Mrs. Woolf gives much space to the Victorian father who almost without exception, she thinks, kept his daughters in intellectual and economic subservience. I do not myself believe that the bourgeois fathers at any period were worse than the mothers, or that both varieties of parent are not at all times equally inclined to proprietary behaviour wherever unchecked by self-knowledge, whatever the state of the law and public opinion. Mrs. Woolf writes as though the Victorian fathers whom she adduces as jealous of their daughters marrying or achieving economic independence were not to be paralleled in many ages, including our own, by the common case of mothers who try to run their sons' lives (D. H. Lawrence's mother is a well-known type) and it is even arguable that the moral and emotional pressure exerted by mothers upon their children, particularly sons, is worse than the economic dependence of daughters and wives.

In fact the release of sex hostility this kind of writing represents is self-indulgent because it provides Mrs. Woolf with a self-righteous glow at the cost of furnishing an easy target for unsympathetic males, and at the still greater cost of embarrassing those women who are aware that the only chance of their getting accepted as intellectual equals by intelligent men (and so ultimately by the men who run the institutions and professions) is by living down their sex's reputation for having in general minds as ill-regulated as Mrs. Woolf's is here seen to be.* It is a reputation that will die the harder for *Three Guineas*.

For just think of the proposals made here for improving the position of educated women. There is her proposal for reforming the evils of the professions by women refusing to acquiesce in them. Instances given are: refuse to approve of academic dress and decorations because these somehow cause wars; accept University lectureships in literature and then refuse to lecture because all such lectures and all teaching of literature (except by creative writers to those itching to become such themselves) is 'vain and vicious',† refuse to pander to 'adultery of the brain' by writing for journals or publishers (alternative source of income for professional women writers not inheriting five hundred a

* Mrs. Woolf heaps contumely upon Mr. Joad for alleging that conversation—by which he presumably means, as many of us do, serious discussion—is ruined by the presence of women. Though he might have put it less irritatingly, a conscientious woman would often feel obliged to admit from her own experience that this attitude is understandable. I have frequently heard accounts from educated women of their discomfort at discussions which have been nullified or spoilt by shameless exposures of the limitations of female intellects. Such accounts have often ended with the formula 'I blushed for my sex.' The remedy is of course a more rigorous intellectual discipline and that acquaintance with standards which produces humility. Mrs. Woolf's idea however is to abolish that kind of education altogether—see below.

† There are notoriously perfectly worthless lectures on literature—the kind students call 'potted textbook,' and those which are summaries of texts, answering to Mrs. Woolf's account of 'sipping English literature through a straw'. But Mrs. Woolf does not apparently mean these. It seems curious that she does not make the obvious suggestion that women should show their mettle by offering the right kind of teaching (for there is a right kind, unless the opinion of the better students is negligible, and she might have satisfied herself that this is so by undertaking some field-research—a necessary preliminary, one would have thought, to voicing an opinion on a subject of which Mrs. Woolf can have no first-hand knowledge having, according to *Who's Who*, been educated at home). She alleges in general terms the danger of infection from 'a mature mind lecturing immature minds' on literature. This looks like a joke if you happen to know that the invariable complaint made by serious students of literature at *any* English university is that they suffer from working under lecturers who haven't the wherewithal for impressing a student with anything but boredom. The very marked objection of the run of such lecturers to a method of discussing literature that stimulates students to ask questions (I have heard of the objection being made in these words) is then understandable. And the objection of inferior or spoilt writers to the potential creation of a public capable of distinguishing between good and bad art is also understandable. By seeking information at the right instead of the wrong end of the process Mrs. Woolf could have learnt that the effective method of teaching literature does not tell young men and women what to approve or disapprove of (to do so, would of course merely antagonize) but develops in them individual sensibility—a capacity for discovering what is of value in art, and how those values can be usefully organized. Examinations then become not what Mrs. Woolf censures as 'the reduction of English literature to an examination subject' but a test whether a student has profited by his studies to become a person capable of discriminating, evaluating, and organizing his judgments, as well as whether he has studied widely enough to have acquired a sound basis for judging. 'Vain and vicious' seem to be the right terms for those who would prevent such genuinely educational work.

year and rooms of their own not indicated). Then there is the plan for abolishing the man-made university with its examinations, degrees, and distinctions based on native ability, and substituting the ideal college as conceived by and for woman. At a time when all responsible educationalists are expressing radical dissatisfaction both with the existing college system and with the accepted idea of university education this attracts our attention as a hopeful sign. But as a nice practical start Mrs. Woolf won't hear of university students being prepared in any way to earn a living, even by studying specialities. She thinks that adults from eighteen to twenty-one can justify their existence as burdens on the state by studying what she calls the art of living. Most people might feel that the art of living is best acquired incidentally to some discipline, either that given by brute circumstances when one is forced to stand on one's own feet (ideal: Robinson Crusoe) or that acquired in the pursuit of specialist studies—and many educationists now think it would be an improvement to combine the two. Without some such discipline the art of living becomes a pitiful affair. Mrs Woolf's conception of it turns out to be the variety implied in the prospectus of an Arts Theatre I once received which announced something like this, that it would be a place where people who appreciated the arts of dress, epicurism and conversation would be able, in appropriate surroundings, to feed a corresponding taste for the art of drama. It seems to me the art of living as conceived by a social parasite. Mrs. Woolf wants studies in her college to be pursued by 'the clever and the stupid' side by side, without any troublesome distinctions or standards to spoil things. But if an institution for the higher education of adults is to defend humane values, as Mrs. Woolf in theory at any rate desiderates, it can only do so by jealously maintaining the highest possible standards where the arts are concerned and conducting the most rigorous scrutiny of intellectual processes generally. Hence its very first duty would be to inculcate the critical attitude and its second to develop in its students the ability to discriminate, judge and reject, along with the practice of responsible thinking and conduct. Mrs. Woolf however feels even more strongly than about the wrongs of women of her class the wrongs of writers like Sir Edmund Gosse and Tennyson (specified along with Keats as objecting to criticism—a few instances of better-known objectors to criticism, such as Miss Edith Sitwell and Marie Corelli, would have made the point clearer) and her most cherished project of all is to uproot criticism root and branch in the Nazi manner. With access to some practical control Mrs. Woolf would evidently develop into a high-powered persecutor; this throws a pretty light on her conception of truth, freedom and intellectual liberty which she calls upon educated women to maintain. She wants to penalize specialists in the interests of amateurs, and so her university, in spite of a promise that learning should be studied there for its own sake, could only be a breeding-ground for boudoir scholarship (a term I once heard applied to the learning of one of Mrs. Woolf's group) and belletrism. I cannot believe that any one else would think this an improvement on the existing kind of university studies, or that such a higher 'education' would be more successful than the present kind in discouraging meanness of spirit, hostility to freedom of thought and hatred of disinterestedness. Mrs. Woolf's is no doubt a feminine conception of congenial study, as opposed to the existing masculine one of disciplined studies towards an end, but is it the kind of education women have struggled for admission to in the past? *Three Guineas* draws freely on the impressive biographies of the leaders of female emancipation, but from the quotations she gives I conclude the desires of these women were the same as mine and those of most men on entering college, the desire to continue a general education by disciplined specialist studies under the best available instructors (who, shameful admission, still happen to be men in most fields) and as far as possible in the company of those students able to set the highest standards and work with the greatest degree of maturity (who also happen to be men, which explains why sensible women would never dream of imitating Mrs. Woolf's feminist heroics). The least damning thing you might say about Mrs. Woolf's proposals is that they are irresponsible.

Out of these babblings the noble and dignified utterances of Josephine Butler, the vigorous good sense with which Sophia Jex-Blake pursued her reasonable demands, the humility of Anne Clough, appeal to Heaven against the context in which they find themselves. I think such women would rather not have had the claims of their sex advocated by Mrs. Woolf's methods. I myself stipulate that any piece of female writing advocating equality of opportunity for the sexes should prove its author to have a highly developed character and a respectable intellect, to be free from mere sex-hostility, to have an at least masculine sense of responsibility and that capacity for self-criticism which impresses us as a mark of the best kind of masculine mind, and over and above that to come from a woman capable of justifying her existence in any walk of life. There really are quite a number of women like that about. I would rather the kind of men who need converting from gross prejudice against women's abilities should read not *Three Guineas* but, among other recent women's books, *Highland Homespun* (Margaret M. Leigh), *Can I Help You, Madam?* (Ethyle Campbell), *I'm Not Complaining* (Ruth Adam), *Sex and Temperament in Savage Society* (Margaret Mead)—books which in varied ways exhibit women capable of doing a job (farming, business, education, social sciences) which demands sterling qualities of mind and character. These books are impressive documentation of women's right to share interests and occupations that have sometimes been considered suitable only for men.

But I have passed over Mrs. Woolf's plan for the complete emancipation of women of her class from the prison-house she considers every part of the home other than the drawing-room to be. To judge from *Three Guineas* Mrs. Woolf wants the women of her class to have the privileges of womanhood without the duties and responsibilities traditionally assumed by them, and to have the advantages of a man's education without being subsequently obliged, as nearly all men are, to justify it. Thus she urges the re-endowment of the almost extinct class of 'idle, charming, cultivated women' whose function would be to provide those dinner-tables and drawing-rooms where the art of living, as previously defined, is to be practised, and she is indignant that the early students of Girton and Newnham had to make their own beds and suffer plain living—though some responsible educationalists now advocate university reform in the direction of obliging even men to conduct their education in the more realistic surroundings provided by the absence of servants.

On the other hand, 'Daughters of educated men have always done their thinking from hand to mouth. . . . They have thought while they stirred the pot, while they rocked the cradle. It was thus that they won us the right,' etc. I agree with someone who complained that to judge from the acquaintance with the realities of life displayed in this book there is no reason to suppose Mrs. Woolf would know which end of the cradle to stir. Mrs. Woolf in fact can hardly claim that she has thus helped to win us the right, etc. I myself, however, have generally had to produce contributions for this review with one hand while actually stirring the pot, or something of that kind, with the other, and if I have not done my thinking while rocking the cradle it was only because the daughters even of uneducated men ceased to rock infants at least two generations ago. Well I feel bound to disagree with Mrs. Woolf's assumption that running a household and family unaided necessarily hinders or weakens thinking. One's own kitchen and nursery, and not the drawing-room and dinner-table where tired professional men relax among the ladies (thus Mrs. Woolf), is the realm where living takes place, and I see no profit in letting our servants live for us. The activities Mrs. Woolf wishes to free educated women from as wasteful not only provide a valuable discipline, they serve as a sieve for determining which values are important and genuine and which are conventional and contemptible. It is this order of experience that often makes the conversation of an uncultivated charmless woman who has merely worked hard and reared a family interesting and stimulating, while its absence renders a hypertrophied conversation piece like *Three Guineas* tiresome and worthless. Mrs. Woolf's plan for a new society intrigues me nevertheless. We are to have one kind of educated women, the idle charming cultivated women, who are to be subsidized as hostesses for the art of social intercourse (it is presumably to spare the sensibilities of these exquisite creatures that criticism of literature is to be prohibited—perhaps because they tend to dabble in letters themselves). Then we are to have a sterner kind of educated woman, the professional woman, for whose benefit the men's colleges are to be thrown open and all the available scholarship money divided equally between the sexes—the women who are to be just like men only more high-minded. Both these kinds are the five-hundred-a-year-by-right-of-birth-as-daughters-of-the-ruling-classes women. Then there are to be the base-born women who come in on the edge of the picture as drudges, to relieve both the other kinds of women of their natural duties (I mean of course nursing and rearing their own infants) as well as the routine of home-making. To impress hired labour for such work is enlightened ('remember we are in the twentieth century now,' writes Mrs. Woolf, and quotes a feminist writer to the effect that a mother is only incapacitated from pursuing her profession for two months per child) but Mrs. Woolf's ancestors who thought it advisable to send their daughters about London accompanied by a personal maid are the objects of much laboured irony (see p. 294). Then there are the unfortunate men who are to marry these daughters of educated men. If their wives choose to have babies—for women are to avert war by refusing to bear children, but apparently not indefinitely—they must from the start share the work of tending their offspring. A thoroughgoing revolution in their wage-earning pursuits, and so a regular social reorganization, unenvisaged by Mrs. Woolf, must take place to allow this. I like to think of the professional man hurrying home at four-hour intervals to spend upwards of half an hour giving the baby its bottle (for breast-feeding will only be able to survive among the uneducated) —among other duties; and presently he will have little time to give to his profession if he has any unenlightened doubts about trusting the growing mentality and sensibilities of his child to hirelings. But perhaps Mrs. Woolf does not mean to be taken as seriously as this. Or perhaps she is advocating the Soviet system of handing the child over to the State to rear at the earliest possible age. If so she should say as much and clear up her projects: they are at present all too nebulous.

I should like to end by making one part of them a little less so. It will be necessary to draw upon the disagreeable facts of experience instead of confining ourselves with Mrs. Woolf to assertions and wishful prophecy; but to import even a little reality into such a discussion should be a service. The position then with regard to further female emancipation seems to be that the onus is on women to prove that they are going to be able to justify it, and that it will not vitally dislocate (what it has already seriously disturbed—and no responsible person can regard that without uneasiness) the framework of our culture. It is no use starting all over again with the theory with which the Victorian emancipators began, we have to look at the results of fifty years of experience and consider facts which worry thoughtful women. One is that it is the exceptional and not the average woman student who is the intellectual equal of the average serious undergraduate in the same subject. 'Every year I have from one to two dozen men reading my subject [one of the humanities, taken by a comparable number of each sex, in which women generally get better preparation at school than men] with whom I can discuss it as equals. I have learned from long experience that among the women students there will be only one such in three years, if that.' Observations of this kind from perfectly open-minded witnesses are not unusual, and substantiate the regular complaint of outstanding women students that there is a dearth of congenial intellectual company to be found in college—whereas the men can always find such company. Either, that is, the women's colleges do not cream the country as the men's do, or else there is precious little intellectual cream available for them to skim off. In relation to this, we may examine Mrs. Woolf's implication that women are victimized because they are restricted to about ten per cent of the students at both Oxford and Cambridge. It is an open secret that even at present the entrance lists can hardly be filled without lowering the standard of admission undesirably—this may well be because it is harder for intelligent girls at the lower end of the economic scale to get to college than for their brothers, but Mrs. Woolf is concerned only with daughters of the well-to-do and she may rest assured that none of these if up to honours standard is ever prevented from entering Oxford or Cambridge because the quota is filled.* Again, Mrs. Woolf thinks it monstrous that the men's scholarship list at Cambridge is more than six times the length of the women's, but the general informed opinion seems to be that to throw all scholarships open to both sexes would mean that women would probably get fewer scholarships than at present, and rarely any in some subjects (scholarships being awarded on evidence of promise as well as of acquirements). To say that this is because women have not had the educational advantages of men, that is, of being taught by men at school, only puts the difficulty further back. The obvious course is to advocated co-education at an earlier stage than college, as a preliminary to women's storming the older universities.† Mrs. Woolf's guns should have been trained not on the protectionists of the men's colleges but on the women of her own class who don't give their daughters the chance to start fair with their brothers, but send them to conventional establishments where they never come up against masculine standards. Mrs. Woolf should logically be campaigning for two things—co-education from the primary to the boarding schools, and a change in the social structure which will allow the daughters of *any* men to enter upon the highest course of studies they are fitted for. As for the daughters of Mrs. Woolf's class, evidence suggests that they value the opportunities offered by the universities less than in the early days when these had to be struggled for. 'I am in the minority of those who go there to work and they think it funny,' the daughter of an educated man, in her first year at one of the Oxford colleges, remarked to me recently. Perhaps related to this is the complaint often heard from intelligent Oxford undergraduates that the women students there

* Though of course, on general principles the restriction of their numbers should be left to the wisdom of the women's colleges themselves, which could be trusted to do that in their own interests. But Mrs. Woolf does not take this line.

† If Mrs. Woolf were to reply that those who cannot take high honours may nevertheless profit from going to college and should have the chance of doing so, we should have to remind her of the existence of the modern universities, to which women, like men, have unrestricted access. I say 'remind', but the regular use of 'either university' in *Three Guineas* suggests that Mrs. Woolf has never heard of any but Oxford and Cambridge. To say that there is a case for keeping the older universities for those students capable of the highest standards in many specialisms is not to deny that it would be desirable for the modern universities to have much more of the atmosphere and educational method of the former. Here is another reform Mrs. Woolf might more reasonably have demanded in the name of women.

make themselves a nuisance. It suggests another reason for deploring the tone of *Three Guineas*. One hears there is still plenty of sex-hostility about in the common-rooms and combination-rooms; Mrs. Woolf only cites the indefensible manifestations of such an attitude, but women cannot afford to give such prejudice any grounding.

If from evidence of what limited progress we have made in equalizing the sexes we wish to move to a more profitable attack on theory than *Three Guineas* makes there is *Sex and Temperament in Savage Society*. Miss Mead's investigation of different kinds of societies where (a) the women are 'masculine' in temperament and activities and the men 'feminine,' (b) both sexes are 'masculine,' (c) both are 'feminine,' provides real evidence (assuming the other anthropologists have checked the sources) that many qualities and habits of feeling which we think sex-linked are the arbitrary results of social forms. If a competent social psychologist were to apply the findings of this book to the problems connected with emancipating women within our culture we might get somewhere at last. Certainly there is no longer any use in this field of speculation for the non-specialist like Mrs. Woolf.

ROGER FRY

25 July 1940

123. Herbert Read, review, *Spectator*

2 August 1940, 124

This review and that of Forster (No. 124) represent opposing attitudes towards Bloomsbury at this time.

In the circle to which Roger Fry belonged there were many brilliant people, and more than one of them would have been capable of writing his life. But Mrs. Woolf, as Fry himself seems to have realised in a prescient moment, was his only perfect biographer, and this book is in every respect what he would have wished it to be: honest, sympathetic, understanding and—prevailing against the bias of a long and intimate friendship—objective in its design and workmanship. Some of Mrs Woolf's readers, accustomed to the very personal quality of her imaginative writing, will perhaps be surprised at the cool and level stretch of this narrative; and if they have found her critical essays sometimes too oblique and coy, they will be pleased with a new firmness and directness. The material of a scholar's life is bound to be refractory: no action, no open glory, no plaudits. To make for continuity, for 'inscape', for the necessary tension, the biographer must pick up the golden thread of the spirit, and follow it through the mind's dark corridors. That is exactly where Mrs Woolf excels: her intuitive perception of values—human values, aesthetic values, moral—and her interest in what is called the drama of life enable her to convert the débris of memories, anecdotes, letters and records into the organic shape of a work of art.

The limitations are those of an inside point of view. Mrs Woolf belongs to the same set or coterie to which Roger Fry himself belonged. The public has given it a local habitation in Bloomsbury, but it was nourished at Cambridge and in reality it had an altogether wider ambience: it was (and is) a fairly common attitude to life. It was (the past tense is now inevitable) a cultured attitude; but its exponents would probably prefer the word 'civilized'. It was an *élite*—of birth no less than of education; its leading members were the sons and daughters of eminent Victorians, and they had passed through one or other of our public schools. Cambridge then gave them a scientific and inquiring temper. Historians, economists and philosophers belonged to this *élite* no less than writers and painters, and for that reason it could never be loosely identified with Bohemianism. But no less certainly it could never be identified with a true sense of reality. It turned with a shudder from the threatening advance of what it would call 'the herd'. Though it despised the moral pretensions and social prestige of the parent generation and hated the prevalent commercialism, it did not attempt to reconcile its own traditions of good taste and refinement with the necessary economic foundations of a new order of society. This was very obvious in Roger Fry's case: faced with the machine, mass-production and universal education, he could only retreat into the private world of his own sensibility. He did, more and more as time went on, attempt to find a universal philosophical justification for this private world, and he had at his command an ingenuous mind and a patient experience of his subject. But all this effort did not bring him into any very vital sympathetic relationship to his own age.

This came out very clearly in his only public venture—the Omega Workshops. This experiment was very nearly a success—a success, that is to say, with the small and snobbish public that can afford to buy individualistic art in a machine age. That it could not be more than this was evident in its early days to four of the most original artists whose services Fry had enlisted; they revolted with perhaps unnecessary violence, but one passage in their manifesto expressed a truth which is still not obvious to anyone within the charmed circle:

> The Idol is still Prettiness, with its mid-Victorian languish of the neck, and its skin of 'greenery-yallery', despite the Post-What-Not fashionableness of its draperies. This family party of strayed and dissenting Aesthetes, however, were compelled to call in as much modern talent as they could find, to do the rough and masculine work without which they knew their efforts would not rise above the level of a pleasant tea-party, or command more attention.

This brings us to the real problem of Roger Fry's life—a certain ambiguity which was due to his championship of Post-Impressionism.

His sincerity has more than once been questioned, but usually by forthright reactionaries like Dr MacColl, who could not understand why a man who knew so much about art could support such an abrupt break with tradition. Fry was quite capable of looking after himself in that quarter, but he was hurt and bewildered when the young men whom he had patronised turned against him. It would be absurd to suggest that Fry did not really appreciate artists like Cézanne, Matisse and Picasso; he had an inborn aesthetic sensibility which could not play him false. But he had been converted rather late in life—he was over forty when he first began to appreciate the significance of Cézanne—and much as his mind might react to the art of Matisse and Picasso, he was never able to follow them in his own painting. He might try to penetrate the secret of Cézanne, not only by analysing him as he did in his most brilliant essay in art criticism, but also by trying to repeat the old wizard's performance on canvas; but it would never have occurred to him to jump forward, in front, not only of Cézanne, but even of Matisse and Picasso. Painters with much less talent have ventured more: but Fry's deepest instinct was not adventurous—his point of view being that 'art as created by the artist is in violent revolt against the instinctive life, since it is an expression of the reflective and fully conscious life', a point of view which is the antithesis of that expressed by Matisse and Picasso and the artists who have come after them.

The explanation of this ambiguity probably lies in the traditions against which Roger Fry vainly revolted. The 'snailhorn sensibility' which manifested itself while he was still an undergraduate studying science was something that could not be denied: it made him give up a scientific career; it made him disappoint his eminent Quaker parents; it landed him in all sorts of financial and social difficulties; it gave him immense joy and stimulated him to endless intellectual research; but it could not prevail against the Inheritance—against the prettiness and the protectiveness of the Ivory Tower, against the benevolence of the Liberal outlook, against the intellect's pretensions to the final word.

124. E. M. Forster, review, *New Statesman and Nation*

10 August 1940, 140–1

Good book. If the exigencies of journalism permitted, a reviewer should confine his remarks to these two words. Good book; which the thousands who know Mrs Woolf's work, or Roger Fry's, will be reading, and about which, therefore, nothing need be said. Good book and sad, and here loquacity can start. For though Mrs Woolf does not stoop to the pathetic, though she keeps with dignity and disinterestedness to her theme, her readers are tempted to stray from it, and to reflect gloomily upon the abbreviation of civilisation and the failure of hope. All that Fry cared for, and worked for, is being destroyed. Good sense has gone, so have the pursuit of truth, peacefulness, and France. In their places stand pernicious idealism, propaganda, violence, Hitler. Courage has become the only virtue, mysticism the only victory. Sterile both of them. The steady determination of the civilised man to become slightly more civilised, and incidentally to benefit others, has been thwarted, at least for our generation. Fry was spared this disillusionment. He slipped on the floor of his flat in 1934, lucky fellow, and fractured his thigh, which saved him. Almost the last time I saw him, he was talking, in his sensitive yet tough way about the European situation. 'Things are going round a very nasty corner indeed,' was his conclusion. Then he turned to some more fruitful topic, to Khmer sculpture, I think. He did not know how nasty the corner would be, and our thankfulness that he has passed away is a measure for our present sense of insecurity.

'Found wanting!' say the prim barbarians. For them, Fry epitomises a way of life which has failed. Barbarians are prim, as he discovered. They are 'sour and melancholy elderly hypocrites full of sham modesty and noble sentiments' who have an instintinctive dislike of art but are obliged to endure it in peacetime, because of its snob-value. When the Omega workshop fails, they rush to buy its products at half-price, and commercialise its designs. They cannot endure independence. When he enjoys Cézanne and Van Gogh twenty years too soon (in 1913 instead of 1933) Sir William Richmond announces that 'he must not be surprised if he is boycotted by decent society.' When he will not buy trash for the Metropolitan Museum at New York, Mr Pierpoint Morgan sacks him. At the end of his life he appears to triumph over his enemies. His way of looking at things is tolerated. He wins the domestic happiness which the tragedy of his wife's illness had postponed. His authority as a critic stands higher than anyone's since Ruskin. He has friends and allies all over the globe. But the barbarians are waiting for war. 'Found wanting', they chant, if they remember his trifling career to-day. The standards he upheld, the very objects he liked to look at, have collapsed.

There is no facile retort to their sneers. If we say 'Beauty lives really, sanity must surely re-emerge' we fall flat. A reply must be hazarded, and on those very lines, but only a fellow artist can phrase it properly. So let us turn to Mrs Woolf and attend to what she says. She is the perfect defender, who defends by expounding. Here is her description of a visit to his studio in 1918, after the so-called Great War, the war which was to end all wars:

> He was huddled in an overcoat over the stove, writing. He was worn; he looked older; his cheeks were more cavernous; his face more lined than before. But he was as eager as ever to talk 'about all sorts of things', and the room was, if possible, still more untidy. Mrs Filmer had obeyed the command on the placard 'Do not touch'. Mrs Filmer had not touched. Rows of dusty medicine bottles stood on the mantelpiece; frying pans were mixed with palettes; some plates held salad, others scrapings of congealed paint. The floor was strewn with papers. There were the pots he was making, there were samples of stuffs and designs for the Omega. . . . But on the table, protected by its placard, was the still life—those symbols of detachment, those tokens of a spiritual reality immune from destruction, the immortal apples, the eternal eggs. He was delighted to stop working and to begin talking. But directly the friend was gone, the article would be finished, and directly the light dawned upon that very untidy room he would be at work upon his picture. Whatever the theory, whatever the connection between the rhythms of life and of art, there could be no doubt about the sensation—he had survived the war.

That is the only sound defence to 'Found wanting'. There will always be apples and eggs. They are more indestructible than France. Even if apples and eggs are abolished, there will still be lumps and lines, which will stimulate the artist while the rest of us mock. Presently we stop mocking; under the stimulus, the artist is making something which would not have existed otherwise; a whole way of life, in itself a surprise, has accreted around his passion, so that even if his actual picture bores us, we are obliged to stare and to ponder. Some critics say that Roger's apples and eggs were bad ones; they have certainly never sold like Cézanne's. But they still keep their value as symbols of civilisation. They and the life that grew round them—including the startled onlookers—survived one war, and will survive another. The art-impulse seems indestructible, in fact. This is not to say that it can be left to take care of itself. It is dormant until we wake it up. And Mrs Woolf's biography shows us how Fry was always waking up art, shaking it up, raking it up, right back from the days when he saw a red poppy burst in his parents' garden.

What form art will take next, I naturally don't know. Even Fry did not know, and he was very diffident in the midst of his self-confidence, and very ready to admit that he might miss the point in something new. But—and here he is our example—he never 'boycotted' anything which he did not understand. To be sensitive, to have an open mind—these are valuable qualities even in wartime, whatever the wireless says. Do they help us to conquer the Nazis? They don't. They are weapons in a larger and a longer battle.

So the book, besides being good and sad, is sustaining. Directly and indirectly, it counsels endurance. Directly, because Fry had a great deal of private sorrow to bear and surmounted it successfully and even gaily. Indirectly, because we see functioning through him one of the finer sorts of human activity. It functioned in the past; he himself often recognised it—for instance, in the Lectures of Sir Joshua Reynolds. It will function in the future provided we do not allow ourselves to be numbed by horrors. Like most of us, Mrs Woolf preaches best when she does not preach, and her accurate account of her friend's life, her careful analysis of his opinions, have as their overtone a noble and convincing defence of civilisation.

OBITUARY NOTICES

125. Stephen Spender, *Listener*

10 April 1941, 533

In these dark times, the death of Virginia Woolf cannot strike her circle of friends and admirers except as a light which has gone out. Whatever its significance, her loss is irreparable. Her strength—and perhaps also her weakness—lay in her rare mind and personality. Moreover, the quality of what she created had the undiluted purity of one of those essentially uncorrupted natures which seem set aside from the world for a special task by the strangest conjunction of fortune and misfortune.

Yet when one thinks of what Virginia Woolf achieved, her life appears far more a wonderful triumph over many difficulties than in any sense a defeat. In a different time or in different circumstances, she might well have died far younger and with far less finished. As it is, although she died at the height of her powers, she had completed the work of a lifetime. The history of other writers who have suffered from ill-health shows how much there is here to be grateful for.

Her best novels, or prose poems in the form of fiction, are *The Voyage Out*, *Jacob's Room*, *Mrs Dalloway*, *To the Lighthouse*, *Orlando*, *The Waves*. Although all of these novels have in common the qualities which distinguish her writing, they differ not merely in portraying different material, but in having different artistic aims. Indeed the artistic aims in Virginia Woolf's novels are far more varied than the material, which is somewhat narrow and limited.

Most novelists having achieved, by about their third novel, a mature style, continue to write novels in that style, but covering different aspects of experience. With Virginia Woolf, however, style, form and material are indivisible. With every new novel she was 'trying to do something different', especially with time. For example, the whole action of *Mrs Dalloway* takes place in one day; the first long section of

To the Lighthouse describes a scene lasting for perhaps an afternoon; this is followed by a very short section describing the passage of several years, illustrated by the decay of an empty house. *Orlando*, is a fantastic account of someone who lives for several hundred years, beginning as a man and turning into a woman. *The Waves* is a poetic account of people seen through each other's minds through all their lives, speaking their thoughts in poetic imagery to each other. A new way of writing a book was simply a new way of looking at life for Virginia Woolf: she held life like a crystal which she turned over in her hands and looked at from another angle. But a crystal is too static an image; for, of course, she knew that the crystal flowed.

It is a well-known device of composers to take a theme and write variations on it. The same tune which is trivial in one light passage in a major key is profound in a minor key scored differently; at times the original tune seems lost while the harmonies explore transcendent depths far beyond the character of the original theme; now the tune runs fleetingly past us; now it is held back so that time itself seems slowed down or stretched out. This musical quality is the essence of Virginia Woolf's writing. The characters she creates—Mrs Dalloway, Mrs Ramsay, Mr Ramsay—are well defined to be sure, but they are only the theme through which she explores quite other harmonies of time, death, poetry and a love which is more mysterious and less sensual than ordinary human love.

A passage from *To the Lighthouse* will illustrate the peculiar beauty which she could achieve. Mr Ramsay, who is a philosopher—almost a great Victorian—faces the sense of his own failure:

> And what are two thousand years? (asked Mr Ramsay ironically staring at the hedge). What, indeed, if you look from a mountain top down the long wastes of the ages? The very stone one kicks with one's boot will outlast Shakespeare. His own little light would shine, not very brightly, for a year or two, and would then be merged in some bigger light, and that in a bigger still. (He looked into the darkness, into the intricacy of the twigs.) Who then could blame the leader of that forlorn party which after all has climbed high enough to see the waste of the years and the perishing of stars, if before death stiffens his limbs beyond the power of movement he does a little consciously raise his numbed fingers to his brow, and square his shoulders, so that when the search party comes they will find him dead at his post, the fine figure of a soldier. Mr Ramsay squared his shoulders and stood very upright by the urn.

This passage has all Virginia Woolf's virtues, and perhaps some of her defects. It starts off by being very faithful even in its irony to the thoughts of Mr Ramsay. She takes one of those plunges beyond the present situation of her character into the past and the future which strikes one often in her writing as a flight of pure poetic genius. But then the focus shifts and the writer has forgotten her character's thoughts, or perhaps she is regarding him from the outside. But the image of the leader of the expedition in the snow is a little too general, and one begins to wonder whether she hasn't strayed too far from the particular.

As with the impressionist painters, there are opposing tendencies in her novels. The one is centrifugal, the tendency for everything to dissolve into diffused light and in the brilliant detachment with which their surroundings flow through her characters' minds. The other is centripetal—the tremendous preoccupation with form which nevertheless holds her novels together and makes them far more significant than if they were just the expression of a new way of looking at life. This doubtless reflects an acute nervous tension in her own mind between a too great sensitivity which tended to disintegrate into unco-ordinated impressions, and a noble and sane determination not to lose hold of the central thread.

To have known Virginia Woolf is a great privilege, because it is to have known an extraordinary and poetic and beautiful human being. Some critics describe her as forbidding and austere. Her austerity was not that of a closed-in or a prudish mind. As with all genuinely intelligent people, one could discuss anything with her with the greatest frankness; she was far too interested in life to make narrow moral judgments. Perhaps she was a little too impatient towards stupidity and tactlessness; it is a gift to writers to suffer fools gladly. To be with her was a joy, because her delight and her awareness of everything around her communicated themselves easily and immediately to her friends. What was written on her beautiful unforgettable face was not severity at all, though there was some melancholy; but most of all there was the devotion and discipline which go with the task of poetic genius, together with the price in the way of nervous strain and physical weakness which doubtless she had to pay.

126. T. S. Eliot, *Horizon*

May 1941, 313–16

It has only been under peculiar conditions that I have ever been able to interest myself in criticizing—except in the currents of conversation—contemporary writers. In the case of authors whose work one considers pernicious, or whose work has been treated with an uncritical adulation which is pernicious, one figures to oneself occasionally an obligation to denounce or ridicule. In the case of authors whose merits have been ignored or misunderstood there is sometimes a particular obligation of championship. But when an author of unquestionable importance has received due tribute, and is not in the slightest danger of being overlooked or belittled, there is no compulsion to criticize: what chiefly matters is that his writing should be *read*. As soon as one generation has been succeeded by another, the endless labour of revaluations which will be in turn revalued must begin. It is not at the moment when a particular author dies that this work begins, but when a whole generation is gone.

There must, however, be some right point of reference for the moment of death, other than that of the formal obituary which is at best an attempt to say too much in too little space. It seems to me that when a great writer dies—unless he has already long outlived his life—something is in danger of vanishing which is not to reappear in the critical study, the full-length biography, or the anecdotal reminiscences. Perhaps it is something that cannot be preserved or conveyed: but at least we can try to set down some symbols which will serve to remind us in future that there is something lost, if we cannot remember what; and to remind a later generation that there is something that they do not know, in spite of all their documents, even if we cannot tell them what. It is something which Virginia Woolf, with all her craft and genius, failed to convey in her life of Roger Fry: and if she failed who, if anyone, should have been successful with a lesser figure, I doubt whether we can do much about her, however we try. It is what someone, I forget who, must have meant when he wandered about saying simply: 'Coleridge is dead.' I mean that it is neither regret that an author's work has come to an end nor desolation at the loss of a friend, for the former emotion can be expressed, and the latter one keeps to oneself; but the loss of something both more profound and more extensive, a change to the world which is also a damage to oneself.

While this feeling cannot be communicated, the external situation can to some extent be outlined. Any dead author of long ago, an author on whom we feel some peculiarly personal dependence, we know primarily through his work—as he would wish to be known by posterity, for that is what he cared about. But we may also search and snatch eagerly at any anecdote of private life which may give us the feeling for a moment of seeing him as his contemporaries saw him. We may try to put the two together, peering through the obscurity of time for the unity which was both—and coherently—the mind in the masterpiece and the man of daily business, pleasure and anxiety as ourselves: but failing this, we often relapse into stressing the differences between the two pictures. No one can be understood: but between a great artist of the past and a contemporary whom one has known as a friend there is the difference between a mystery which baffles and a mystery which is accepted. We cannot explain, but we accept and in a way understand. It is this, I think, that disappears completely.

The future will arrive at a permanent estimate of the place of Virginia Woolf's novels in the history of English literature, and it will also be furnished with enough documents to understand what her work meant to her contemporaries. It will also, through letters and memoirs, have more than fugitive glimpses of her personality. Certainly, without her eminence as a writer, and her eminence as the particular kind of writer she was, she would not have occupied the personal position she held among contemporaries; but she would not have held it by being a writer alone—in the latter case it would only be the cessation of work which would here give cause for lament. By attempting to enumerate the qualities and conditions which contributed, one may give at first a false impression of 'accidental advantages' concurring to reinforce the imaginative genius and the sense of style which cannot be contested, to turn her into the symbol, almost myth, which she became for those who did not know her, and the social centre which she was for those who did. Some of these advantages may have helped to smooth the path to fame—though when a literary reputation is once established, people quickly forget how long it was in growing—but that fame itself is solidly enough built upon the writings. And these qualities of personal charm and distinction, of kindness and wit, of curiosity about human beings, and the particular advantage of a kind of hereditary position in English letters (with the incidental benefits which that position bestowed) do not, when enumerated, tell the whole story: they combined to form a whole which is more than the sum of the parts.

I am well aware that the literary-social importance which Virginia Woolf enjoyed, had its nucleus in a society which those people whose ideas about it were vague—vague even in connection with the topography of London—were wont, not always disinterestedly perhaps, to deride. The sufficient answer *ad hoc*—though not the final answer—would probably be that it was the only one there was: and as I believe that without Virginia Woolf at the centre of it, it would have remained formless or marginal, to call attention to its interest to the sociologist is not irrelevant to my subject. Any group will appear more uniform, and probably more intolerant and exclusive from the outside than it really is; and here, certainly, no subscription of orthodoxy was imposed. Had it, indeed, been a matter of limited membership and exclusive doctrine, it would not have attracted the exasperated attention of those who objected to it on these supposed grounds. It is no part of my purpose here either to defend, criticize or appraise *élites*; I only mention the matter in order to make the point that Virginia Woolf was the centre, not merely of an esoteric group, but of the literary life of London. Her position was due to a concurrence of qualities and circumstances which never happened before, and which I do not think will ever happen again. It maintained the dignified and admirable tradition of Victorian upper middle-class culture—a situation in which the artist was neither the servant of the exalted patron, the parasite of the plutocrat, nor the entertainer of the mob—a situation in which the producer and the consumer of art were on an equal footing, and that neither the highest nor the lowest. With the death of Virginia Woolf, a whole pattern of culture is broken: she may be, from one point of view, only the symbol of it; but she would not be the symbol if she had not been, more than anyone in her time, the maintainer of it. Her work will remain; something of her personality will be recorded: but how can her position in the life of her own time be understood by those to whom her time will be so remote that they will not even know how far they fail to understand it? As for us—*l'on sait ce que l'on perd. On ne sait jamais ce que l'on rattrapera.*

127. Hugh Walpole, in *New Statesman and Nation*

14 June 1941, 602–3

Hugh Walpole (1884–1941), Novelist. Became a friend of Virginia Woolf in the 1920s and acknowledged her influence on his later work. His article was preceded by the following note: 'This article by the late Sir Hugh Walpole, must be one of the last things he wrote before his death. We are very glad to print it, not only for the portrait it gives of Virginia Woolf, but for the delightful self-revelation of its author visiting Bloomsbury.' In his biography, Rupert Hart-Davis described the effect of Virginia Woolf's death on Walpole in the following way:

> April was a cruel month. It opened with the shattering news of Virginia Woolf's suicide. She had occupied a very special place in Hugh's life, and though the war had accustomed everyone to the expectation of sudden death, this blow seemed unbearably wanton and unnecessary. Hugh broadcast about his dead friend and wrote at least two articles about her, but her death haunted him, and his grief for her certainly hastened his own end *Hugh Walpole* (1952), 440.

I read *Jacob's Room* for the first time in a Turkish Bath in Marseilles. I didn't open it until I had reached my warm, dry cubicle and been rolled and rolled securely inside sheets and blankets by the fat one-eyed attendant who was afterward murdered for raping the young daughter of the bath's patron.

All this may seem irrelevant now. It did not seem so then, for I was lazy and comfortable after my bath and not at all inclined for reading. Everything was then relevant. I looked up lazily at the one-eyed attendant and said: 'I feel in my bones you will be murdered one day.'

'Very likely, monsieur,' he agreed, smiling.

It is my only successful prophesy. I must have slumbered, but later I awoke and began *Jacob's Room*. When I came to Jacob and the sheep's skull on the seashore I sat up, my wrappings falling from me, and I knew that I had found one of the books of my life. The books of *my* life are supposed by my detractors to be too many. They are not really so, but they are very varied and include *Vathek*, *Alice in Wonderland*, *Clarissa*, *The Prelude*, *Bleak House*, *Death's Jest Book*, *The Woodlanders*, and *Siren Land*. They have no reason—my likings for these particular works. They may be good or bad. *Jacob's Room* is one of them. *Orlando* is another.

No other of Virginia Woolf's works are in this personal collection of mine, although I think *Mrs Dalloway* her best novel, and *The Waves* her most beautiful poem. This reminiscence, however, is not to be about her books, but about herself. I mention my reading of *Jacob's Room* only because it was my true introduction to her. I had read *The Voyage Out* and some small things. Before the 1914 War I had been startled by reading that Mr. Clive Bell said that there were three living English novelists who really mattered, and only three. One of them was Virginia Woolf. At that time—1913 I think it was—this saying was a dark one. I did not think then, I do not think now, that Clive Bell, a delightful writer and an enchanting companion, knew or cared much about the art of novel-writing. Nevertheless, his words had an oracular sound. Who then was Virginia Woolf? I read *The Voyage Out*. I was not greatly impressed by it. It appeared to me stuffy, laboured and derivative.

So it was that *Jacob's Room* enchanted me all the more by its surprise. I thought it marvellous that Jacob, who scarcely speaks from the first to the last, should be so intimate to me, and so endearing. It was this book, I suppose, that made me unjust to Maugham's *Of Human Bondage*, read by me at this time. How melodramatic and cheap did it seem and still does seem beside *Jacob's Room*! When later than this I saw Virginia Woolf I was terrified. Literary ladies from Rhoda Broughton through Katherine Mansfield and Rebecca West to Gertrude Stein have worn, from time to time, the robes of priestesses engaged in throwing fragrant incense on to their own altars. Katherine Mansfield's *Letters*, brilliant and touching, seem to me exactly to do this.

Virginia Woolf had at that first meeting for me the air of a priestess, but of a priestess who was at the same time for me strangely home-familiar. I mean that in her beautiful deep, slow voice, her delicate hostess care of one at the tea-table, her courtesies and dignities, she resembled many of my relations in my own youth—aunts and cousins; she was, in fact, a lady.

I don't know whether it is snobbery that comes in here, but I do know that I had been growing tired, for a long time past, of meeting so occasionally the beautiful courteous manners of my childhood. I had so often been told that they were stuffy, hypocritical and especially restricting to females.

It was pleasant to discover that Virginia, who, more than any other woman writer of her time, was modernist in her passionate championship of women, could not help but be courteous in the Victorian tradition even had she wished to. And she did not so wish.

As to throwing incense on her own altar, that was not at all the thing at this first tea-party. Virginia Woolf was ironic about her own work and delicately humorous about others'. I had discovered before this that Bloomsbury was not the mutual admiration society the outside world supposed it. Nowhere in Fleet Street had I watched so gay and ribald a treatment of Helen Schlegel's absurd baby from *Howards End* as in Bloomsbury, nor was Aldous Huxley's companionate *Encyclopaedia* considered entirely serious in Tavistock Square.

At that first tea-time in that little room with the Duncan Grant murals, the muffins and the two conscious, watching, over-hearing teapots I tasted the best honey of my life. And always, afterwards, up to a year ago, that honey was there.

Nevertheless, I was frightened. I was frightened, as it has been all my life my nature to be frightened, by people who think before they speak. I don't mean, of course, that that is a thing I never do, but words rush from me more swiftly than they should. Now Virginia saw folly more quickly than it flies and always she slew it without a second's compunction. Not fools, I hasten to say, but folly. Of fools she could often be exceedingly tender and she enjoyed them sometimes as friends.

My own fears increased with my own sense that I was not nearly such a fool as I seemed to be, and then there came a day when she attacked me fiercely for my printed praise of a certain novel. This was a mystical story concerned with death and poetry. Virginia attacked it on the ground of the insincerity of the author, whom she did not know. It was humbug; he did not mean a word that he said.

Now, I happened to know the author, and I was certain that whatever else he might be, he was sincere. I told her some facts about him and suddenly her interest in the curious psychology of that author overcame all her dislike of his book. All she wanted was the truth and I gave her as much as I could of it. From that day I was never afraid of her again. I saw that if with her at least I was not a humbug, I need have no fear. I saw that her eagerness to know the truth was inexhaustible. In this she exactly resembled Henry James, whose curiosity about this strange confusion called life was without end. Virginia took your stories from you in two ways. Either she was gay and creative, would snatch something from you, make something charming, fantastic, beautiful from it, and then hand it back to you pretending it was all your own. Or, more serious, she would investigate and investigate, delving further and further—and then when you had given her everything you could, then would come that little pause, as it used to come in the old days with James, and that unspoken question: 'Well—is that all? Can't we find anything else? Surely you know that we haven't discovered the *real* pattern in the carpet?'

Nevertheless, I told her more than I ever told any other human being, more than I shall ever tell any human being again.

Then it was that I discovered that beneath the mocking humour, the sometimes stern enquiry, the sharp wonder, the restless investigation, there was a kindliness of heart and tenderness of feeling rich with an intense personal charity.

I remember my surprise at finding that she realised, better than any save my closest friend, the suffering that a truly fearful attack of arthritis caused me. We are, most of us, bored with the pains and agonies of our friends. At any rate, we cannot listen to tales of woe for very long. She did not say a great deal nor invite many details, but I loved her from that time.

I suppose then that all of us who were her friends feel a kind of bewilderment. Always when some friend leaves us in physical death, we realise with a new sharpness that *that* particular human being was unique. The uniqueness, while the friend was still here, was veiled. At any time we might see the friend again, write or receive a letter, have a message. The uniqueness composed of such various qualities had been sometimes annoying or boring or exacerbating. But now—how one longs for him to open the door, stand, smiling, in the doorway!

And if that is true of other friends, how poignantly is it true of Virginia Woolf! How, as I am writing this, I long to be able to go up the narrow stairs again to see that little book-bursting room, to greet the two intelligent teapots and hear that deep, lovely voice explaining to some other friend a foible, an absurdity of her own, of mine, of a stranger in the street.

Her loss is something from which I shall now never escape.

BETWEEN THE ACTS

17 July 1941

128. David Cecil, review, *Spectator*

18 July 1941, 64

Lord David Cecil (b. 1902). Professor of English at Oxford University 1948–70. He first met Virginia Woolf in the early 1920s.

It is with curiosity as well as delight that we have learnt to approach a new book by this great writer. For Mrs Woolf never repeated herself. The different phases of her work represent a logical process of development. Like other serious authors, she was concerned to convey what she felt to be the essential truth about life. But, sternly faithful to her own extremely individual outlook, she did not find that any of the systems, moral and philosophic, by which mankind has tried to impose an order on experience, corresponded with her view of reality. She therefore went back to the beginning and sought to record the actual process of living, to paint the unordered sequence of impressions which floated across her consciousness. Her picture had its pattern, however. For to her contemplative eye two aspects of existence loomed out as predominantly significant, and round them everything else fell into order and proportion. The first was life's beauty. Her sensibility to this was both strong and varied. In the most diverse aspects of experience, from a pageant to a picnic, an English slum to an Italian garden, she could detect any element that gave aesthetic pleasure. The very intensity of her response to it made her also aware that beauty is fleeting. The second dominating feature in her picture of life is its mutability. It is not only that the hair grows white, the daffodil withers. Under the inexorable finger of time man's thoughts and affections also dissolve into oblivion. Earthly existence, which seems so solid, reveals itself to her searching gaze to be as unsubstantial as a fleece of cloud.

This vision of life forms the subject of all her important works until *To the Lighthouse*. Whether she speaks of a single life or a family's, it is to the same refrain: 'Life is exquisite and life is ephemeral.' The mingled ecstasy and sadness implicit in such a view give these earlier books a unique poignancy. But her intelligence was too profound to be content with it. For it leaves existence a bewildering paradox. How can we feel such ecstasy of the spirit if there is no spiritual significance in the universe? Her later books brood on the problem. In *The Waves* she simply poses it. She brings her characters to the verge of death, and then 'What comes next?' she asks. *The Years* goes a step farther and hints very tentatively at the possible existence of some eternal spiritual principle transcending mortality. *Between the Acts* is a fresh comment on the same problem. Its theme, a day at a country house during which an historical pageant is performed, recalls both *Mrs Dalloway* and *Orlando*. The day is envisaged both as a moment in the lives of the characters and also, by means of the device of the pageant, as a moment in English history. In either aspect it seems to express a further stage in her effort to reconcile life's permanent significance with its apparent mutability. The gist of her thought is something like Wordsworth's when bidding farewell to the River Duddon. There is an eternal principle behind life; but it is of its nature to manifest itself in change. The waters of the river flow by, but it is always the same river. Miss La Trobe, the author of the pageant, who seems to symbolise the artist in relation to reality, despairs for a moment at the short life of her work. But soon her mind begins to conceive a new drama. This eternal rebirth is the expression of the vitality of the spirit of the universe.

However, it must be confessed that Mrs Woolf does not make her meaning altogether clear. And it is further darkened by the fact that her picture is drawn in two conventions, which do not blend. The setting of the story is realistic; most of the characters speak as real people speak. But in order to achieve the expressive intensity of poetry she shifts now and again into the non-realistic convention of *The Waves*. One character, Isabel, talks to herself in a sort of loose verse. This confusion of convention leaves the reader confused. Perhaps had she lived to revise the book, Mrs Woolf would have brought it into clear pattern and harmony. As it is, it must be counted as in part a failure.

But Mrs Woolf's failures are more precious than most writers' successes. The predominant impression left by *Between the Acts* is of the extraordinary distinction of her talent. Her scope may be narrower than that of many fellow-authors; but, unlike theirs, it is of the very first quality. What she says no one has said before, and she says it perfectly. This gives her work, almost alone among contemporary literature, the authority and permanence of classic art. It is with gratitude and reverence we bid her farewell as she goes to join the company of Emily Bronte and Jane Austen.

129. From an unsigned review, *Times Literary Supplement*

19 July 1941, 346

That mark on the wall, the small round mark just above the mantelpiece—is it a nail, a rose-leaf, a crack in the wood? One could get up and look, but even then could one be sure? Meanwhile images of uncertainty multiply and dissolve in a twilight privacy of mind. To what remote reaches of fancy, what precarious heights of speculation—the Greeks, Shakespeare, the human past, the laws of Nature—a mark on a wall may take us! Such was Virginia Woolf's habit of association. Like all her devices of style, it sprang from a peculiar constancy of vision. Other novelists of an equal constancy have sought, as she did, to communicate the incommunicable, but in so doing they have rarely been content with the evidence of the senses alone. For that is ordinarily a way of poetry, not of prose. It happened to be Virginia Woolf's way. Hers was the poet's or the mystic's apprehension of the unity of the visible universe, in which every perception of sense brought with it the intuition of truth. For her the hard, separate facts of existence were on the surface only; beneath, the tide of sensation flowed in unceasing mystery. Above all else, it was what she saw, the visual images she conjured from the here and now of experience, that held mystery for her. In a garden a woman plucks a flower, remembers a face, drops her flower ('What single, separate leaf could she press? None.'), and goes on:

'Where do I wander?' she mused. 'Down what draughty tunnels? Where the eyeless wind blows? And there grows nothing for the eye. No rose. To issue where? In some harvestless dim field where no evening lets fall her mantle; nor sun rises. All's equal there. Unblowing, ungrowing are the roses there. Change is not; nor the mutable and lovable; nor greetings nor partings; nor furtive finding and feelings, where hand seeks hand and eye shelters from the eye.'

After The Waves

The passage comes from *Between the Acts*, Virginia Woolf's last novel, a rarefied touching and imperfect book. One had wondered in some sadness of mind what it would be like. What would or could she have chosen to do? It was not merely that Virginia Woolf was a gay and daring experimentalist, who had tried one fastidious form or style of prose narrative after another and in the end had stepped almost beyond the bounds of communication. The doubt was rather whether she could resume from the point where she had left off in *The Waves*. In the piercing consummated vision of that strange and lovely book sensibility is stretched taut and is naked to the nerve; thought has been purged away, the veil of illusion lifted, the whole of life is in the image of an unfolding leaf, the pattern on a plate, the memory of a crimson tassel with gold threads. *The Years*, which came after, was much praised, but it was only the shadow of earlier books, a pale and mechanical copy. Imagination, after the ordeal of sense and spirit of *The Waves*, seemed drained and indeed vulnerable; from the striving for order and discipline came what seemed almost a pastiche of Virginia Woolf. It was with an eager warmth of hope and curiosity that one looked forward to her next book.

Between the Acts is not among Virginia Woolf's best work, though it has spells of loveliness and flashes of poetry that in style are hers alone. It is written round the performance of a village pageant, with the personal interest focused upon a small group of spectators, and fragments of the pageant are rendered in verse of studied simplicity. Her exquisite sensibilities, caught for a moment in individual cadences of language, do not fail of their effect; a butterfly's flight, a leaning birch tree, a weathered old stone barn yield their pleasure at sight. And there is a description of a lily pond that holds something of enchantment:

[Quotes pp. 54–5 'There had always been lilies' to 'off they flashed.']

There is less, however, of this evocation of tangible beauty than in almost any of her novels. Still like a swallow skimming the grass she now seems absorbed in the rhythm of her flight. It is an unvaried rhythm. Waves of light and shadow move up and down, a blade of grass is tipped with fire from the sun, but there are few chance discoveries to stay flight; the wonder of creation is in movement not in the arrested moment of discovery. It is a singular reversal of Virginia Woolf's habitual imaginative practice, though the conclusion of the matter is unaltered. On the one side of experience is perpetuity, continuity, timeless and changeless order; on the other the bright evanescent bubble of human mutability.

This, as always in Virginia Woolf's work, is the antinomy which she resolved in part by a certain austerity of personal emotion. Her aloofness, no doubt, owed something to the classic mould of her thought, something to the cultivation of mind and the graces of manner on which she evidently set so much store, something also to what she may have considered the obligations of breeding, but at the same time it must surely have been a defensive necessity. Only once, in the firmest and perhaps the loveliest of her books, *To the Lighthouse*, did she seem able to surmount necessity. In this last work, as in all the others, the impersonal quality of her emotion is very pronounced, all the more pronounced indeed because the human material of her narrative is here reduced to fragile and unsubstantial shape. Nowhere does Virginia Woolf explore the depths of character in this novel. Isa and Giles Oliver, Lucy Swithin, old Bartholomew Oliver, Mrs Manresa, Mrs Sands the cook—they are figures in a private pageant between the acts of a local pageant of English history. In both instances the pageantry all but ignores the accidents of personality.

[Plot summary omitted]

. . . One characteristic quality of Virginia Woolf's way of thought has made itself strongly felt. Her social sympathies were narrowly, almost ostentatiously, restricted. She knew her own kind, it seems, and no other, and only as an act of indulgence did her imaginative curiosity extend further. It was not so much her emphasis on 'class', her division of mankind in the country, whatever the towns of England might be like, into 'the gentry and the servants', her discovery that Mrs Manresa could ogle the butler Candish 'as if he were a real man, not a stuffed man'—it was not so much this that betrayed the novelist in her as the eclecticism of taste and manners derived from it. The great gulf, as she saw it, was between the cultivated and the uncultivated. Since hers was a cultivation that excluded much else she shrank instinctively from forms of goodness and beauty other than those she had absorbed into her private vision. The limitation is obvious in *Between the Acts.*

Under-Current

Nevertheless, it is a rare and sometimes haunting book, with a deceptively light under-current of sorrow. Something left over from the high, pure song and poignant harmonies of *The Waves* can be heard in the muted accompaniment to her single and brief motive, repeated with only the slightest of variations, of the transitory finite. To it is added a new note. The pageant takes place on an afternoon in June 1939. Beyond the words and the miming looms an enveloping dark shape. At the end—and here, presumably, if rational implication were needed, is the rational implication of it all—the producer's voice, blaring and anonymous through a megaphone, breaks the rhythm and forgets the rhyme, while a mopping and mowing chorus armed with mirrors of every description hold them up to the audience. 'Orts, scraps and fragments that we are', the blaring voice affirms—'look at ourselves, ladies and gentlemen!' But Miss La Trobe, who may have been Russian and was certainly not quite a lady, knew well enough that she was the slave of her audience. Reluctantly, it may be, Virginia Woolf knew that too, and in this shimmering, tenuous and inconclusive last novel of hers she may have had to submit what was most constant and most secret in her vision to the claims of intelligibility.

130. Frank Swinnerton, review, *Observer*

20 July 1941, 3

If a novelist has lived actively and seen and suffered the physical cruelties of man, the whole fabric of his work will be toughened. If, on the contrary, withdrawn from rough and tumble, he has suffered in mind and spirit only, the fabric, delicate indeed, and sometimes extremely beautiful, will seem bloodless. Few novelists, having dared adventure in youth, have then reflected subtly and profoundly upon human affairs. One of those to do so was Joseph Conrad. Mrs Virginia Woolf, like Henry James, was condemned by temperament as well as by circumstance to great labour of ingenuity because she had almost no practical experience of life. She was like somebody bedridden in a house in the country, hearing and explaining every sound, speculating as to meanings and possibilities, dreaming a little, occasionally quite piercingly uncovering a mood or attitude, but incapable of more than subtle guesswork about her own species.

She had compensations, of course. She could write beautifully, and she could suggest with much more than common skill the interweavings of mood and memory. She 'caught' likenesses with whimsical sympathy. And although her intellect was not powerful it had grace and distinction. These qualities are apparent in *Between the Acts* as they were in *Orlando*, with which this last book has certain affinities. Again she is concerned, as in *Orlando*, with the passage of time and the repetitions of character; and by the use of a pageant play which summarises old moral and social attitudes and their equivalents in successive periods of time she shows the unchanging nature of men and women. She goes farther: she asks whether it is to remain changeless, and how unity and understanding are ever to be achieved within the limits of human consciousness. It is a curious and interesting theme, decorated with ingenuities and subtleties and beauties; and it remains abstract only because the author, with all her gifts, could never test intuition by any but literary and conversational contacts with reality.

131. Edwin Muir, review, *Listener*

24 July 1941, 139

The appearance of Virginia Woolf's last novel makes one realise with renewed force, almost objectively, what a loss her death is to English literature. *Between the Acts*, though comparatively short, is both one of her most ambitious and most perfect novels. It reminds one indirectly of several of its predecessors, *Mrs Dalloway*, *Orlando*, and *The Waves*, in particular, for in it she weaves into one pattern the themes with which she dealt separately in them.

The means by which she achieves this result are quite simple; she describes a summer day, and stages in it a pageant of English history, thus packing ages of change, separation and vicissitude into a few hours. In all her novels she is preoccupied by the fact of separation, and therefore by memory, which gives us our keenest apprehension of separation—the separation from ourselves; confronting us across a gulf with what we were and what we are. Beyond this recognition she had a sense, sometimes faint, sometimes vivid, of a union of some kind behind the separation, a union among the living, and between the present and the past, the living and the dead. This recognition, a mystical moment, appeared only when the present became quite motionless, no longer a floating bridge between the past and the future, but pure present from end to end, a simultaneous intensification and expansion of the instant of living. She was concerned with it not merely as a mystery but as a fact of experience; the novels which mark her progress as an artist, *Jacob's Room*, *Mrs Dalloway*, *To the Lighthouse*, *The Waves*, deal more and more essentially with the finest, the most elusive and profound kind of experience, trying to catch it in the flying moment, its perpetual vanishing place. The perpetual moment is infinitely rich, infinitely worth preserving, but is gone at once. Separation is self-evident; the union of all things, past and present, can be seized only by a rare act of the imagination. The sense of separation in *The Waves* is almost unbearable. In this last novel it is expressed even more strongly, but along with it an evocation of the moment of realisation, when all things know that, in spite of themselves and Time, they are bound together.

In its treatment of these two aspects of life *Between the Acts* surpasses all Virginia Woolf's other novels, and is perhaps the most complete expression of her world of imagination. Memory has inevitably a large place in it; memory which, as in her other novels, opens like a gulf beneath the ordinary surface of life, displaying a strange and disconcerting landscape. The memory is not confined to the actual lives of the people who remember; but goes far back. Old Mrs Swithin, early in the summer morning, recollects older things:

[Quotes p. 13 'She had been waked' to 'we descend.']

The rhododendron forests of Piccadilly recur throughout the book, along with images of the dead perpetuating their memory through time: 'the old families who had all intermarried, and lay in their deaths intertwisted, like the ivy roots, beneath the churchyard wall'. Parallel to the dead, forming a strand in the complete pattern, are the herds of domestic animals and their keepers, who might easily have lived among the past generations, and belong to them as much as to the living. Bond, the cowman 'contemplated the young people hanging roses from one rafter to another. He thought very little of anybody, simples or gentry. Leaning, silent, sardonic, against the door he was like a withered willow, bent over a stream, all its leaves shed, and in his eyes the whimsical flow of the waters.' This exquisite image suggests the timeless life of the farm servant, and prepares us for the chorus of peasants who serve as a static background to the various scenes in the pageant. Finally there is the audience, made up of the neighbouring gentry, who live as much in the present as anyone can live, that is, never quite there.

The changing past, the unchanging or more slowly changing life of the herds and the peasants, and the present itself—the sum total of past change and the involuntary cause of change to come: these make up the strands of the pattern. The audience, the contemporary characters, are at odds with one another, despondently or complacently lost, except for old Mrs Swithin with her faith in a reality beyond the reality of the moment. The pageant unrolls before them, a Chaucerian scene, an Elizabethan scene, a Restoration scene, a Victorian scene. Finally comes the Present Day, representing 'Civilisation (the wall) in ruins; rebuilt (witness man with hod) by human efforts; witness also woman handing bricks'. The audience applaud this flattering idea of themselves; but then the players appear holding up all sorts of mirrors 'hand glasses, tin cans, scraps of scullery glass, harness room glass, and heavily embossed silver mirrors'. The members of the audience are caught and split to pieces in this chaos of mirrors; they do not know where to look; they want to run away. A voice out of a bush addresses a long denunciation to them, ending: 'Look at ourselves, ladies and gentlemen! Then at the wall; and ask how's this wall, the great wall, which we call, perhaps miscall, civilisation, to be built by (here the mirrors flicked and flashed) orts, scraps and fragments like ourselves.' But after this castigation the voice asks them to attend; a record of music is played on the gramophone, and the orts, scraps and fragments are for a moment resolved into a unity. It is as if the pageant had flared up into a different reality; as if experience had suffered a violent displacement, nightmarelike at first, and then pleasurable beyond expression. The scene is an extraordinary piece of imagination, though whether quite successful is doubtful. The nightmare part is very fine, and in its bare directness unlike anything else by its author; the resolution of the nightmare is not so effective as it should be, is slightly unconvincing, more because of the way in which it is said than because of what it says. Perhaps if Mrs Woolf had lived to make the final revision of the book this might have been avoided; perhaps all that was needed was a slight alteration in the wording which only she could have made. But as it stands this scene embodies more intensely than any other scene in her novels the essential quality of her imagination.

Apart from *The Years*, a reversion to her early style, her prose has shown an increasing economy ever since she wrote *Mrs Dalloway*. She has never written better prose than the prose in this last book, with its flashing, almost imperious curtness, its exact colouring, and its rapid, unhesitating movement. One is tempted to go on quoting from it impression after impression perfectly rendered. The characters stand out with unusual solidity and clearness in the exquisitely radiant atmosphere which fills this as almost all her books; a light unlike any other light. What we remember chiefly in her other novels is that strange light; but from this one we shall remember with equal distinctness the characters and the working out of the situation, the symbolic form in which a woman of genius saw the human state.

132. Hudson Strode, from a review, *New York Times*

5 October 1941, Section 6, 1, 30

Hudson Strode (b. 1893). Travel writer and Professor of English at the University of Alabama.

As in most of her novels, the cream of *Between the Acts* lies between the lines—in the haunting overtones. And the best of the show—the part one really cares about—happens between the acts and immediately before the pageant begins and just after it is over. So the play is not really the thing at all. It is merely the focal point, the hub of the wheel, the peg on which to hang the bright ribbons and dark cords of the author's supersensitive perceptions and illuminated knowledge. It is in her imagery, in her felicitous gift for metaphor, for cadence, for exciting association, in her 'powers of absorption, and distillation' that her special genius lies. She culls exotic flowers in the half-light of her private mysticism along with common earthgrown varieties and distills them into new essences. Her most interesting characters move in an *ambiente* of intuition. With half a glance they regard their fellow-mortals and know their hidden failures. They care less for the tangible, the wrought stone, than for fleeting thought or quick desire.

In ten novels Mrs. Woolf lifted veil after veil to reveal what she perceived as the secret meaning of life. When one finishes a book of hers it is not characters he remembers but their spiritual emanations, which are in reality manifestations or facets of Virginia Woolf's super-vision. Her peculiar interest was not in surfaces but in mysterious motivations and subterfuges that do not meet the eye. And no other English novelist has ever written more dazzling passages of poetry undefiled than Virginia Woolf. Like the great poets—Shakespeare, Donne, Shelley, Blake—Mrs. Woolf could say the unsayable, and it is there in her books for those who have ears attuned to unheard melodies, even if they can never recommunicate it in any language except Mrs. Woolf's own precisely.

At once a woman of profound erudition and intuitive intelligence, she is also the most poignantly sensitive of English novelists. Yet there was a leaven of zest and humour in her make-up, and her wit was akin to that slyly malicious kind that ran in the veins of Prince Hamlet. Steeped in the classical tradition, she was an audacious experimentalist. She looked upon existence as a maze of paradoxes, but she was continually uplifted and renewed by the transient beauty of the world. One passage from *Between the Acts* seems to epitomize the attitude of mind, the prose style, the whole art of Virginia Woolf:

> Here came the sun, an illimitable rapture of joy, embracing every flower, every leaf. Then in compassion it withdrew, covering its face, as if it forebore to look on human suffering.

133. Malcolm Cowley, review, *New Republic* (New York)

6 October 1941, 440

Malcolm Cowley (b. 1898). Associate Editor of the *New Republic* 1929–44.

American travellers in England before this war often felt that they were strolling—no, were being wheeled in comfortable chairs—past the neat showcases of a museum. These trains that always ran on time were obviously toy trains, built and kept in order by some retired millionaire. These fields were covered with excelsior dyed green; no grass was ever so free from weeds. These earthen dykes that surrounded the fields—and kept them from being worked by machinery—were preserved as a relic of Saxon times; and the wild flowers that grew on the dykes were planted there by the same pious hands that had thatched the cottages and painted a soft mist over the horizon. Even the people sometimes looked like wax figures dressed in authentic costumes and labelled Mine Host or Farmer Hobbs or The Costermonger. And the general supervision of this country was by a political subcommittee of the Society for the Preservation of British Antiquities; one pictured them as kindly men who met on the steps of the British Museum with their umbrellas raised to protect them from the gentle rain. The oldest of them would say, 'We must break no glass,' and the next-to-oldest, 'We must shatter no illusions,' while even the pigeons would be cooing, 'Peace in our time.'

This England under glass, this England where people of breeding were sometimes not quite sure whether they were themselves or their family portraits, is the subject of Virginia Woolf's last novel. The local scene is Pointz Hall, outside an English village; the time is a summer's day in 1939. The plot—well, *Between the Acts* has no plot, strictly speaking, but the action is concerned with a pageant given for the benefit of the local church. This pageant deals with the history of England from the earliest times. It is brilliantly written, and while it lasts it holds the audience together, after a fashion. When it ends, the spectators and the actors disperse to their homes, their daily papers and their daily quarrels; for each of them, 'the curtain rises.' A summer day has passed and much has been revealed, but nothing has been changed.

It has often been pointed out that Mrs Woolf's method has little to do with that of the ordinary novel. There is no conflict in her books, no sense of drama or dialectic; there is no progress through difficulties toward marriage or a deathbed. There is not even a story, in the usual sense of the word. Mrs Woolf in her heart did not believe in stories; she thought of herself as living in a world where nothing ever happened; or at least nothing that mattered, nothing that was real. The reality was outside the world, in the human heart. And her literary method, based on this philosophy, was not to deal explicitly with a situation, but rather to present the shadows it cast in the individual consciousness. When the last shadows had moved across the screen, and when the attentive reader had caught a glimpse of something motionless behind them—'this peace, this rest, this eternity'—Mrs Woolf had nothing more to say. Her story had ended without having begun.

This method—as I think William Troy was the first to observe—is that of lyric poetry rather than fiction. And *Between the Acts* is the most lyrical of all her books, not only in feeling but also in style. The historical pageant is written chiefly in verse; the characters in their private meditations are always breaking into verse; and even the narrative passages have an emotional intensity and a disciplined freedom in the use of words that one does not associate with prose. Moreover, Mrs Woolf uses almost as many symbols as Yeats does in his later work. The first scene in the book is a meeting to discuss a new cesspool for the village—nobody could overlook her meaning here—and the pageant is being held to buy a new lighting system for the church. It is enacted by the villagers themselves, as if to indicate the continuity of English life; Queen Elizabeth after all must have looked like Mrs Clark the tobacconist. The village idiot wanders across the scene, playing no one but himself. In the last tableau, entitled 'The Present Time—Ourselves', the characters bring mirrors on the stage and hold them up to the audience, while a voice howls from a megaphone that they are nothing but 'scraps, orts and fragments.'

The coming war is scarcely mentioned. Once a dozen airplanes fly overhead in military formation; twice the heroine finds herself thinking—she doesn't know why—about a newspaper story she had just read of a girl raped by soldiers. Yet the spirit of war broods over the novel, and one feels at every moment that bombs will soon be crashing through the museum cases. Factories will rise on the site of the wrecked cottages; the green lawns will be an airfield; the 'scraps, orts and fragments' will be swept away.

Virginia Woolf herself would soon become a war casualty, though not in the simple manner that was suggested by the first accounts of her suicide. A phrase in the coroner's report led to an exchange of letters in the *Sunday Times*; a bishop's wife was superior, and Leonard Woolf wrote a frank and dignified answer. It seems that Mrs Woolf had suffered a mental breakdown during the First World War and, after her recovery, had been haunted by the fear of relapsing into madness. This fear was especially vivid during the period of tension that always followed the completion of a novel. In other words, it was the mental strain of writing *Between the Acts* and not the physical strain of living under bombardment that caused her death. But the book itself is her comment on the war, or rather her elegy for the society the war was destroying, and so we are back at our starting point. When the bombs crashed through the glass that covered England, she was one of the people—and they were not the weaklings or the cowards—who were too finely organized for life in the wind and the rain.

Her books, too, are not written for this new age. If one rereads several of them in succession, as I did recently, one is more likely to be impressed by their narrow range of characters and emotions than by their cool wit and their warm imagination. The outside world has made itself real to us as it never was to the people in her novels. But it would be wrong to treat the judgment of our moment in time as if it were that of history. The days will come again when people have leisure to appreciate her picture of the inner world and her sense of the living past. The spirit if not the body of Georgian England survives in her novels.

134. Louis Kronenberger, review, *Nation* (New York)

11 October 1941, 344–5

Long before she died, Virginia Woolf had, I think, said all it was in her to say as a novelist. If this last of her novels is also by all odds her weakest, it yet represents only another step in her steady creative decline. It is of course true that the book had not been finally revised, and even more worth remembering that it must have been written by an ill and tragically overwrought woman; but for all that, the heart of the trouble lies elsewhere. For from the time of *Orlando* onward Virginia Woolf had relaxed her interests, had slipped more and more out of life, farther and farther away from the main stream of literature, indulging that side of her which, no matter how exquisite it was, contributed to her breakdown as a novelist without raising her high enough as a poet. *Orlando* and *The Waves* and in spots *The Years* have special qualities enough, but no substantial ones. Virginia Woolf had begun by bringing to the novel something more rewarding than the patterned 'realism' with which it was clogged. *Mrs Dalloway* and *To the Lighthouse* are high-bred and delicate books, but not too high-bred and delicate to have their own sharp kind of reality. But with her later novels Mrs Woolf, rejecting realism, threw the baby out with the bath water and rejected reality as well. The separate image got in the way of the central vision; the poet of words and moods and almost naked sensibilities recoiled from flesh and blood; psychological truth was discarded for philosophic symbols. The sense of time, for example —something which dominates most great creative writing—laid hold of Virginia Woolf so strongly as to obliterate almost everything else. But she did not cope with it as a Tolstoy did, or even a Proust: she felt it *too* poetically, as something not dramatic but elegiac, not full of mystery but only full of pathos; and she ended by sentimentalizing it horribly.

In all this, however, there was more than the triumph of the poet over the novelist, or the dreamer over the observer; more disastrously, there was the intrusion of something even more thin-blooded, something purely literary. From having been nourished by culture, Virginia Woolf was at last emaciated by it. Culture joined to brilliant perceptions made her a delightful critic, but creatively it displaced an interest in life itself. She came to be preoccupied by words and phrases, by literary tags and echoes and the bright harness of tradition and the byplay of the cultivated—one might almost say the over-cultivated—mind. Her work, even though it remained imaginative, was no longer spring-fed.

By the time Mrs Woolf wrote *Between the Acts* culture had quite won out. We feel at times that she fought against having it win, that embers of fine creative feeling still feebly glowed; but there was no helping it. The book, unless one obtusely chooses to see it as a deliberate *jeu d'esprit*, is merely from start to finish an evasion of the problems it raises. It introduces us to people, some of them with frustrated and fractured lives, and, instead of exploring them, makes us sit with them while they watch a pageant. The pageant reels off solemn travesties of Elizabethan, Restoration, and Victorian drama, which are given in full; and the pasteboard dramas completely overshadow the flesh-and-blood ones. Even an ironic intention of showing that the real people are as dead and done for as the stage puppets cannot justify Mrs Woolf's dabbling in human beings while expending great space and effort on her Sir Spaniel Lilylivers and mid-Victorian Eleanors. The book ends with two of the real people about to confront each other: it should, of course, have begun there.

In smaller ways, too, one feels how slack the book has gone; even its imagery becomes, at times, a fault or a foolishness. 'She had been waked by the birds. How they sang! attacking the dawn like so many choir boys attacking an iced cake.' Here Mrs Woolf, having long ago abandoned the real for the poetic, has come to abandon the poetic for the weakly fanciful. Had she lived, no doubt she would have pruned *Between the Acts* of such infelicities, and tightened it, and perhaps cut a little deeper into her characters. But the book would not have been substantially any different. The retreat from life had gone too far, the very immersion of self in a pool of pictures and phrases had become too deep, the talent which had once been shining and concentrated as a piece of gold had been broken up into a coppery heap of small change. If through it all there remained a touch of high distinction, it may remind us how Virginia Woolf in her prime, writing *Mrs Dalloway* and *To the Lighthouse* and the two *Common Readers*, was one of the few splendid literary figures of our age.

135. B. G. Brooks, review article, *Nineteenth Century*

December 1941, 334–40

Virginia Woolf was characteristic of her age, at least in its best aspects. Behind the superficially Wellsian, or even Tono-Bungayish, exterior of the early nineteen-hundreds, there was coming into being a body of sincere, questing, mocking, intelligent and integrated workers in all spheres of artistic endeavour. Against the apparent trend of their time, as they would have been against the apparent trend of any time, they bore within themselves the seeds of the new age. The War of 1914–18 and its successors were to throw the world of ordinary folk, not several generations back culturally, and artistically, for that would imply a folk culture of sorts, but simply on to the bare and burnt surface of the mental slag heap. For two succeeding decades these few men and women were to stand almost alone, enshrining what was left of the fragile perfections of their period.

With Proust, Yeats and Joyce among her fellow dead, and Miss Gertrude Stein and Mr T. S. Eliot among the yet living, Virginia

Woolf devoted herself to a disinterested research into the fundamentals of her art, much as the painters and musicians, her contemporaries, did of theirs. She, too, kept her immediate 'material', sensual or conceptual, constantly in mind, and shut out all that vague mass of cheap idealism and subjective emotionalism which masqueraded under the loose name of philosophy. Nevertheless she differed from most in that the satisfaction of her audience in the wider sense, that of the novelist, remained her steady aim throughout. And though she was probably about the hardest thing it would have to tackle, she did in fact, and partly from the very limitations of her subject-matter, manage to build up some sort of causeway across which to approach the average intelligence of her day.

This search for fundamentals early established itself in her case through contact with post-impressionist propaganda. As one reads *Roger Fry*, one can see how the ideas which the then revolutionary art critic was evolving from the classics, and which he was finding in a state of vigorous renewal in the despised French group whom he introduced to England in 1907, were flung on to the fertile soil of her mind. 'Why,' he demanded, 'was there no English novelist who took his art seriously? Why were they all engrossed in childish problems of photographic representation?' And we find him praising a writer (Marguerite Audoux in *Marie Clare*) who had 'contrived to express the emotions of a peasant at the sight of a wolf without using a single adjective'. Later we are told that 'Writers lacked conscience; they lacked objectivity, they did not treat words as painters treat paint.' 'Novelists should be more sparing of violent action—it increases the element of mere chance which one knows the author can turn either way he likes—whereas if you remain within the ordinary course of civilised life the situation, whatever it is, develops with some appearance at least of logical inevitability.' And he says significantly of Balzac, that he 'made a kind of texture . . . out of the purely external conditions of life'. The general aesthetic theory behind Virginia Woolf's novels can be summed up in his statement about the function of content. 'It is merely directive of form. . . . All the essential aesthetic quality has to do with pure form.' Twice she records what were presumably kindly warnings, once against 'poetisation', and once against forcing the overtones. The story of Virginia Woolf is largely the story of her struggles to solve on her own terms the problems here presented.

It is surprising how much, not only of her own development, but of subsequent drift of the English novel, is to be found in her very early work, *The Voyage Out*. The book is far too packed, too heavily written, and the content of a type that offered no scope for her particular technical experiments. There is much dramatic incident. The dying of the heroine at the moment when the author has completed her analysis under crisis and has frankly nothing further to say of her for the time being is even theatrically melodramatic. There is a very successful sociological study of the woman of the period seeking to navigate her ignorant bark with such imaginative charts as Ibsen, Shaw, Emily Brontë and Meredith could offer, and discovering the divergencies between their guidance and what her instincts told her was really profound experience. There are the intellectuals, Hirst and Hewet, unpleasant but fascinating—honest, clever, abrupt and tortured. Strangely convincing in spite of their odd incomprehensibility, they put Mr Wells to shame, and were to offer models to Mr Aldous Huxley. There is the excursion up the unexplored South American river which, on its emotional side, feels towards D. H. Lawrence, and, on what one may call its novelistic side, to Miss Ann Bridge's *Four Part Setting*. There are, finally, exasperatingly brilliant tricks of construction, as when, after an intensely emotional passage, much as a poet might throw out a confusion of unconventional images, Virginia Woolf pitchforks masses of queer people from the recesses of the hotel to dance in the limelight a grotesque Dickensian ballet. But these things were to be discarded. She, like Hewet, wanted to write 'a novel about silence, the things people don't say'. Like Rachel, she had the sensation that 'one did not know where one was going, or what one wanted . . .; but one thing led to another and by degrees something formed itself out of nothing, and so one reached at last this calm . . . and things formed themselves into a pattern . . . and in that pattern lay satisfaction and meaning.' And this search for the pattern was her life's work, while the reader, in novel after novel, 'was content to sit silently watching the pattern build itself up, looking at what he hardly saw'.

It is even possible to trace elements from which individual novels developed. For instance, when one of her characters 'considered the rusty inkstand, the pen, the ash-tray, and the old French neswpaper' and found that 'these small and worthless objects seemed to her to represent human lives', she is of course thinking in terms of the famous *Natures Mortes* of Cézanne, or Braque, or Picasso. But she is also seeing life as Virginia Woolf saw it when she wrote *Jacob's Room*, about which the strangest thing is that it is actually the 'room' which matters. The central figure, like the Percival of *The Waves*, is shown in blank.

We never enter his mind. We never feel from him any special call of interest. But his 'room', the space around him, is packed with things of all sorts, physical and psychological entities. It is the closeness of the packing that makes the empty volume of space so clear cut and so significantly shaped that we are prepared to concede that we have known Jacob Fleming[1] sufficiently to regret his death. In this novel Virginia Woolf uses one of those strange unifying devices which serve to bring out the inner pattern of her material. With Mrs Dalloway, it is the pocket-knife which Peter Walsh is constantly fingering in his pocket, or the recurring sound of Big Ben which, in a more mechanical sense, more completely dominates the movement of *The Years*. With *Between the Acts* it is the chimes of talk which follow unchanged from the opening phrase about the weather, or an obsessing image like that of the wasps in the peach, which, established by one character as a sense impression, recurs in the unconscious symbolism of another with tenfold force. The most obviously patterned of the novels is *The Waves*, whose sections are divided by elaborate prose poems which associate the movements and rhythms of the sea at different times of the day with the changes in the lives of the characters. *Jacob's Room* uses the psychological convention of allowing one person, say in England, to echo the words of another, say in Athens. The words then form a bridge across which, in this early work, they swing backwards and forwards, at times with a bewildering gymnastic which was not to be re-created later. In *Mrs Dalloway*, and still more in *To the Lighthouse*, this device recurs, but in the latter more particularly, the contacts of the characters provide credible psychological links which compel a more ready acceptance.

The style that pervades each novel depends very much on the special technical problems which she happened to be handling, and though I suppose there are countless passages which an admirer could identify immediately, it seems only fair to say that she has a far wider range of 'brushwork' than any of her contemporaries. How conscious her efforts were may be judged from many an indication in *The Common Reader*, especially her discussion of the use of prose in *The Countess of Pembroke's Arcadia*. Simple play of sound appears from the first pages of *The Voyage Out*. 'The ship was making her way steadily through small waves which slapped her, and then fizzled like effervescing water, leaving a little border of bubbles and foam on either side.' One can well imagine how she amused herself recording brief

[1] But not sufficiently well to know his name, perhaps, which is Flanders.

notes of that sort and using them at all points of her career. *Jacob's Room* and *Mrs Dalloway* are full of them, short, picturesque and deliberately poetical, a sophisticated poetry as of South Kensington, which made one feel at the time of their publication that the author was a minor and unintentional Proust. The 'gong' piece in *To the Lighthouse* shows the further use of rhythm and echo, and might be contrasted, to illustrate her growing power, with the similar passage in *The Voyage Out*, which is mere description.[1] Here is the more mature one, made to read aloud as most of her work starting from *Mrs Dalloway* is, if it is to be given its full effect. After Mrs Ramsay's fear that the Boeuf en Daube might overboil:

> the great clangour of the gong announced solemnly, authoritatively, that all those scattered about, in attics, in bedrooms, on little perches of their own, reading, writing, putting the last smooth to their hair, or fastening dresses, must leave all that, and the little odds and ends on their washing-tables and dressing-tables, and the novels on the bed-tables, and the diaries which were so private, and assemble in the dining-room for dinner.

Into this poetic use of words, however, other elements enter. The great discovery of *Jacob's Room* was that the novelist could in fact completely efface herself, and simply present her material through the sensations and reactions of her characters. The convention whereby she could use her own language and attribute to her puppets, uncondemned, something of her own sensitivity to impressions, persisted. But it was obvious that free association of ideas must become more and more her basis if she pursued this path. Actually she did use it, but quite simply, in *Mrs Dalloway*. Blocks of writing that vary from ten to thirty pages reveal, in a form rather closer to the soliloquy of the traditional novel than the psychologist would admit of, the flow of conciousness through the being of Clarissa, Peter, Richard or Septimus Smith. The occasional quality as of Addison or Lamb which isolated passages assume from the nature of the mind from which they emanate—the sketch of Hugh Wakefield,[2] with its delicately mannered satire is an instance—led some readers to feel, wrongly, that Virginia Woolf was not a novelist, but an essayist who wrote novels. These massive blocks are interspersed with quick movements involving staccato jerks, which extend among the minor characters. The effect on the style is to give a mock conversational and colloquial tone, not to the actual words

[1] p. 135.
[2] Whitbread.

themselves, a point in which she differed markedly from Joyce, but to the rhythm and lilt of the sentences. What is notable in some of these books is that the people themselves are frequently most ordinary. Their recorded talk is banal. The whole value is in the art, as Roger Fry wished. And here, Virginia Woolf shows something of the skill of Henry James, who managed, in such a novel as *In the Cage*, to hang on to a gossamer thread of completely pointless small talk the most marvellous and exciting reactions and emotions.

To the Lighthouse adds further complexities of both style and subject-matter. Here one has the feeling that there is some attempt to rival the modernist musicians. Like Debussy, or Ravel, or Stravinsky, she takes some trivial theme of the sophisticated present, and gives it a mock splendour by parading it in the pomp and ceremony of Victorian or Edwardian event, all the time with an undercurrent of irony, and yet retaining a delightful sense of the fragile poetry of the whole, from the very contact of the human element. Such a moment is the dinner given in honour of William Bankes with the superb entry of the Boeuf en Daube, the contrasting and flickering pettiness of the talk about the French and their vegetables, the magical episode of the lighting of the candles, and that quiet dignified exit of Mrs Ramsay, which is also to be, only she does not know it, her exit from life. We can trace the literary sources of all this in the admiration for De Quincey expressed in *The Common Reader*: 'The emotion is never stated; it is suggested and brought slowly by repeated images before us until it stays, in all its complexity, complete.'

By comparison, this is by far the most complex of her novels. Apart from these stylistic studies, the prose poems which fill the middle section, *Time Passes*—and like those of Mallarmé, grotesque, fantastic or romantic, pervaded with a delicate mingling of irony and melancholy—there are at least three conflicting themes. First we have the mystery of the reality of Mrs Ramsay of which one becomes, oddly enough, more aware when she is dead than during her life, then the psychological study of the son James, whose lighthouse 'fixation', after distorting his youth, disappears at the moment of fulfilment, and finally the very profoundly wrought experience of Lily Briscoe, the painter, in which, as in other portraits of creative artists, one can detect the personal echo. The complexity of these themes, and the fact that she gives her characters in this novel such a wide awareness of the world and the emotions evolving around them, mean that the sentences tend to become very long. Their chatty rhythms are strained to the uttermost, with interjected phrases of memory, description or observation, and are liable at any moment to swing out into a semi-paragraph of Ruskinian splendour, before recoiling and closing up into the 'tone of good talk' with which they had started.

Behind Virginia Woolf's methods lies a very definite philosophical outlook. This is characteristically modern in that it is empirical, it imposes itself from her artistic experiences, and is not the result of *a priori* thinking. Here we have the difference between her work and Proust's. Both live and feel that they live at the moment of the aesthetic experience, the moment when something in the flux of things suddenly shifts into position, and puts the whole of being into focus, before it uncoils and winds on its way. In both there is an element of waiting for this moment, a sort of passivity. So, in *To the Lighthouse*:

> To be silent; to be alone. All the being and doing, expansive, glittering, vocal, evaporated; and one shrunk, with a sense of solemnity, to being oneself, a wedge-shaped core of darkness, something invisible to others. Although she continued to knit, and sat upright, it was thus that she felt herself; and this self having shed its attachments was free for the strangest adventures.

The same conception is set with a finer sense of dramatic contrast in the symbolism of the two pictures in *Between the Acts*.

> In real life they had never met, the long lady and the man holding his horse by the rein. The lady was a picture; the man was an ancestor. He had a name. . . . He was a talk producer, that ancestor. But the lady was a picture. In her yellow robe, leaning with a pillar to support her, a silver arrow in her hand, and a feather in her hair, she led the eye up, down, from the curve to the straight, through glades of greenery and shades of silver, dun and rose into silence. The room was empty. Empty, empty, empty; silent, silent, silent. The room was a shell, singing of what was before time was; a vase stood in the heart of the house, alabaster, smooth, cold, holding the still distilled essence of emptiness, silence.

But there is no attempt, as with Proust, to impose on, or draw out from, this experience the patterns of the traditional thought of her race, perhaps because her race had none, in the sense that the French have. One feels behind Proust the formal clashings of Classical Tragedy, the fiercely logical construction which welds into a grandiose unity the fantastic grotesqueries of Balzac, the overriding principles established by the penetrating moral comment of La Rochefoucauld. Here, the pattern is more evanescent: the author is—Lily Briscoe, whose brush descended, flickering, on the white canvas. 'And so pausing and flickering she attained a dancing rhythmical movement, as if the pauses were one part of the rhythm and the strokes another, and all were related.' This alternation of 'pauses and strokes' which pervades nearly all the novels was challenged once only, in *The Waves*, where Virginia Woolf seems to be trying to work with strokes only. Here the purely narrative part of the story moves from mouth to mouth of the characters as it progresses, so that one has to accept a convention of complete awareness on their part at every stage, and complete power of artistic expression synchronising with that awareness. One realises how difficult it is to do for the novel what Shakespeare does for the drama. In fact, to use a phrase from *The Voyage Out*, each of the characters 'made some sentence' and then passed on. The realistic meandering associational style developed to its most flexible in *To the Lighthouse* is dropped. The people here, even when children, speak as immortal spirits might, expressing adultly even their child reactions, where, of course, the convention is most bewildering. The style has become hard, metallic, unfeeling. One is reminded of Rhoda's comment:

> With intermittent shocks, sudden as the springs of a tiger, life emerges heaving its dark crest from the sea. It is to this we are attached, it is to this we are bound, as bodies to wild horses. And yet we have invented devices for filling up the crevices and disguising these fissures.

Virginia Woolf, in this strangest and most difficult of all her books, has cut out all the fillings, and behind the staccato utterances of the widely varied characters, types not hitherto included in her work, one can detect that passion for establishing the essential pattern which will make life tangible. In this case, it is pointed by the comment of the literary man, Bernard, who considers his friends much as the imagined novelists do in Mr Huxley's *Point Counter-Point* and M. André Gide's *Faux-Monnayeurs*. Thus, like them, she maintains by this artifice the modern convention that the novelist must eliminate herself, yet builds herself into the novel.

It is possible to think of the latest and last of her novels as a falling away from her individual outlook, a concession to the wider public. I do not feel that this is the case. *Between the Acts* purports to be the story of a day in a country house within whose grounds a local pageant is being performed. The mere selection of the topic has the genius of Chaucer behind it. It is simple, it is true to period, and it enables the author to bring together an unusual range of personages and interests in a perfectly natural way, and to free them from the restraints of convention sufficiently to give her creative power full play. I have indicated the fundamental philosophical idea. The play, which with dramatic accuracy is a modern attempt along the lines of *The Rock*, reveals the past as felt by the post-war poet and intellectual (there is an astounding surrealist scene where the actors show the modern world to itself through broken mirrors), but the performance is mellowed by the naively beautiful and sublimely unconscious folk spirit in which the village worthies interpret it. The style is very simple, a recoil from the elaborate colloquialism-cum-preciosity of the middle period, and the formal isolation of the sentences in *The Waves*. But it is easily comprehensible, and as delicate and effective as anything she ever used. The truth is that her literary intentions had been sufficiently established for the public, her own public, to appreciate her fuller meanings on relatively slight indications. Her earlier books had established her peculiar sensibility as part of the life of the modern intelligence. She therefore was able in this book to attack with a classical and deft simplicity the more general reader. The 'overtones', at least, no longer swamp the main tune. There is some truth with the critic who said that she perhaps wanted to write one understandable book before she ended. But the whole truth needs to imply that the book was a triumph, not a concession: and that behind the ease and lightness of touch of which all must be aware, there is the same brilliance in exploration, the same intellectual integrity, as in the others, together with an added breadth of character interest, and a queer implication from the title and the conclusion that all life as the novel normally presents it is only a waiting space between the acts of our real life, which is lived in solitude. And on this note Virginia Woolf died.

Select Bibliography

BEEBE, M., 'Criticism of Virginia Woolf: A Selected Checklist', *Modern Fiction Studies*, Lafayette, February 1956, 36–45.
(A supplement to this appeared in the same periodical, vol. 18, no. 3, Autumn 1972).

CORNEY, C. P., compiled the section on Virginia Woolf in *The New Cambridge Bibliography of English Literature*, ed. I. R. Williamson, Cambridge University Press, 1972.

GUIGUET, JEAN, *Virginia Woolf and her Works*, trans. Jean Stewart, London, 1966 contains an extensive bibliography.

HAFLEY, JAMES, *The Glass Roof: Virginia Woolf as Novelist*, Berkeley, California, 1954, includes a fairly comprehensive bibliography. Lists some reviews and foreign material.

TORIEN, B. J., *A Bibliography of Virginia Woolf*, 1882–1941, Cape Town, 1943. The earliest checklist of Virginia Woolf criticism. Gives abstracts from articles and reviews.

Index

I JOURNALS AND PERIODICALS

II SIGNIFICANT COMMENTS ON INDIVIDUAL WORKS

III CRITICS AND COMMENTATORS

IV GENERAL INDEX

DATE DUE

JUN 21 1994	
JAN 31 2001	
MAY 28 2002	
DEC 09 2002	
JAN 31 2003	
OCT 13 2004	
NOV 17 2004	

THE CRITICAL HERITAGE SERIES

GENERAL EDITOR: B. C. SOUTHAM

Volumes published and forthcoming

MATTHEW ARNOLD: THE POETRY	Carl Dawson
JANE AUSTEN	B. C. Southam
THE BRONTËS	Miriam Allott
BROWNING	Boyd Litzinger and Donald Smalley
ROBERT BURNS	Donald A. Low
BYRON	Andrew Rutherford
THOMAS CARLYLE	Jules Paul Seigel
CLARE	Mark Storey
CLOUGH	Michael Thorpe
COLERIDGE	J. R. de J. Jackson
CONRAD	Norman Sherry
FENIMORE COOPER	George Dekker and John P. McWilliams
CRABBE	Arthur Pollard
STEPHEN CRANE	Richard M. Weatherford
DEFOE	Pat Rogers
DICKENS	Philip Collins
DRYDEN	James and Helen Kinsley
GEORGE ELIOT	David Carroll
HENRY FIELDING	Ronald Paulson and Thomas Lockwood
FORD MADOX FORD	Frank MacShane
E. M. FORSTER	Philip Gardner
GISSING	Pierre Coustillas and Colin Partridge
GOLDSMITH	G. S. Rousseau
THOMAS HARDY	R. G. Cox
HAWTHORNE	J. Donald Crowley
IBSEN	Michael Egan
HENRY JAMES	Roger Gard

Continued